THE 43rd WESSEX DIVISION AT WAR 1944–1945

The C.-in-C., Lieut.-General Horrocks, and Major-General Thomas in Cleve area, 26th February, 1945

THE 43rd WESSEX DIVISION
AT WAR 1944–1945

Compiled by

MAJOR-GENERAL H. ESSAME

The Naval & Military Press Ltd

Published by

The Naval & Military Press Ltd
Unit 5 Riverside, Brambleside
Bellbrook Industrial Estate
Uckfield, East Sussex
TN22 1QQ England

Tel: +44 (0)1825 749494

www.naval-military-press.com
www.nmarchive.com

CONTENTS

LIST OF ILLUSTRATIONS

LIST OF SKETCH MAPS

WRITER'S PREFACE

I SET out to write the story of the 43rd (Wessex) Division primarily for the benefit of those who fought with it during the campaign in North-west Europe. Now that I have finished, I realize that I have, in addition, almost inadvertently evolved a character-study of its Commander. The truth is that the influence of his original mind and dynamic drive was so great that any account of the Division's battles would lack colour and life if he were treated merely as a highly efficient military calculating-machine. I hope I have given no offence. After all, who am I to judge?

I am greatly indebted to the War Office for the facilities lavishly and promptly placed at my disposal by the Officer in Charge of Records, Droitwich; and, for the loan of invaluable material and maps, to the Commandant of the Staff College, Camberley; to Headquarters B.A.O.R; to the Director, Imperial War Museum; to the Canadian Army Liaison Establishment; and to General Sir Miles Dempsey. This book also owes much to the labours of the historians of 30 Corps, 15 (S.) Division, 8 Armoured Brigade, 4/7 Dragoon Guards, 13/18 Hussars, 94 Field Regiment, the Divisional Engineers, the Somerset Light Infantry, Worcestershire Regiment, Duke of Cornwall's Light Infantry, Dorset Regiment, Middlesex Regiment, the Wiltshire Regiment and the 43 Reconnaissance Regiment. In particular, my thanks are due to Colonel Mervyn Crawford, Colonel D. E. B. Talbot, Lieut.-Colonel I. L. Reeves, Major Caines and Major K. J. White-head for allowing me to consult their private diaries and to Brigadiers C. G. Lipscomb, G. Taylor, H. A. Borradaile and M. C. A. Henniker, Lieut.-Colonels the Viscount Tryon, M. Concannon, W. G. Roberts and M. Trethowan, Majors R. G. Levett, D. B. Wilson, W. J. Chalmers, J. N. Denison, E. F. J. Barker and Captain D. I. M. Robbins for their constant help and encouragement in what has not been an easy task.

HONITON, DEVON.
20th August, 1951.

H. ESSAME,
Major-General (Retired)

CHAPTER I

PRELUDE IN KENT

THE choice of a divisional sign is a task not to be lightly undertaken. It should not, for instance, be based on the whim of its commander of the moment. The general who selected his own initials raised an awkward problem for his successor. Above all, it must not lend itself to ribald comment on the part of the troops, as in the case of the division which adopted the harp. Sardonic comments concerning the likely permanent occupation of the troops in the near future as a result of their association with the division were not slow in coming. If possible, it should call to mind the region from which the division comes and the spirit which has animated its past triumphs in war. The choice of the wyvern in 1935 as the sign of the 43rd (Wessex) Division must therefore be considered particularly fortunate and appropriate.

In both the Eastern and Northern mythologies the dragon is the bringer of death and the serpent the symbol of guile. When the West Saxons landed in the West Country in the fifth century, they bore dragons painted on their shields and carved on the heads of their long ships. Sometime in the Dark Ages, realizing that in the grim business of war the will to destroy must be combined with cunning, they blended the snake with the dragon and the wyvern was born. Thus the winged dragon, with two feet like those of an eagle and a serpentlike barbed tail, became the emblem of the Wessex kings. Alfred the Great certainly carried it on his battle standard in his many campaigns in Wessex and Kent in alliance with the Celts of Wales and Cornwall. Harold raised it at Hastings, for it twice appears in the Bayeux Tapestry. Ever since it has been the badge of the fighting men of Wessex, in whose coats of arms it appears time and time again.

The wyvern thus links the division with the age-old traditions of the Anglo-Saxon kingdom of Wessex and at the same time gives it a symbol which typifies the essentially pagan spirit of the art of war. It recalls deeply buried memories of the old warrior gods, Odin and Thor.

Major-General G. I. Thomas's long tenure of command of the Division gives this book a peculiar unity. It is not only the narration of a chain of events but also inevitably an account of the application to the conduct of war of one man's ideas, formed as the result of profound thought and prolonged experiment over a long and most exacting period before June 1944, and put into practice in the face of the finest divisions of the German Army in almost continuous battle for nearly twelve months. By the time the Division took the field in June 1944, he and all under his command had so completely identified themselves with each other as to make reference to his predecessors almost irrelevant. Indeed it is doubtful whether any other divisional commander of the period impressed his own personality and ideas of those under his command, or indeed on those above him, with greater or more incisive effect.

Memories are short. To understand the problems which faced Major-General Thomas when he took over command of the Division on 2nd March, 1942, from Major General C. W. Allfrey, promoted to command the 5 Corps District, the military atmosphere of the period between Dunkirk and Alamein must be recalled. The overwhelming superiority of the German army in numbers, equipment and battlefield technique was evident to the whole world. Dunkirk, despite skilful counter-propaganda, had been a disaster of the first magnitude. The reverses in North Africa and the Mediterranean lowered the prestige of the Army, at least so far as the other services were concerned. Finally came the greatest defeat in the history of the British Army—the surrender of 60,000 men at Singapore. Both equipment and manpower were short. The former could be remedied; only, however, with the utmost ingenuity and national sacrifice could the Army's need for men be met. Before the war could be ended, the German Army had to be beaten in the field. It was evident that only an army commanded at all levels by leaders of the highest quality and trained with the utmost rigour could possibly hope to survive, let alone defeat the enemy in battle. Field-Marshal Lord Alanbrooke, the C.I.G.S., and General Sir Bernard Paget, the Commander-in-Chief Home Forces, therefore rightly insisted on the elimination from active commands of all officers whose battle-worthiness was in the slightest doubt and introduced the rigorous and realist training which alone offered any prospect of success. Efficiency for battle therefore over-rode all other considerations. Few realize now by what a narrow margin the war was won. The B.L.A. when it finally invaded France represented the best trained and equipped army which ever left these shores. That this was so is to the everlasting credit of those who commanded and trained it during the darkest years of the war.

Before the war the training of the Army had not, for reasons which it is unnecessary to elaborate here, been conducted on realistic lines. With certain exceptions the element of physical hardship as an essential component of all training had been omitted. Modern war is fought in all climates and at all seasons of the year. It is therefore vital that all ranks should be conditioned to accept privation and hardship as part of the essential make-up of war. The first commander in England to insist on the introduction of prolonged exposure to the elements in his training—or at least the first adequately to publicize the need—was Field-Marshal Montgomery himself. His exercises with 5 Corps in the winter of 1940–41, when he kept his troops out in the open, with snow lying on the ground, for ten days, set the tone of the subsequent training for the remainder of the Army in Great Britain for several years. As soon as the threat of invasion receded, the division followed suit. Few can have trained on more austere lines. For this purpose war-time Kent was admirably suited, and it was here from 1940 to D-Day, with a few brief excursions outside on large-scale exercises, that the Division trained. More than any other county, owing to its close proximity to France, the constant air raids and its general shabbiness, it reflected the atmosphere of war. It is also undoubtedly the coldest part of the British Isles. The Division's main training area was at Stone Street, north of Folkestone. All the colder winds from Central Europe seem to converge here. It is a tangle of squalid woods and muddy lanes embodying all the nastiest elements of Nature at her worst. A midwinter night spent in the open here is calculated to leave no man in doubt as to the reasons why the Scandinavian conception of eternal punishment was, unlike the Hebrew, linked with extreme cold and not excessive heat. In real war some shelter from the elements can usually be found. This was not the case in Stone Street. Even the Reichswald had, in fact, more amenities. The philosopher who asserted that eternity is beyond human conception never trained with the 43 Division, otherwise he would have been less dogmatic. The beaches at Lydd, the South Downs, and the areas around Hythe were slightly less inhospitable. Here for three winters the Division grew to accept hardship as the natural order of things. By a lucky chance, also, the enclosed country around Stone Street strikingly resembled the Normandy *bocage*. Without realizing the fact, therefore, the Division, in contrast to those accustomed only to the limitless open spaces of the Western Desert, became particularly well attuned to the conditions it had to face from the very moment it landed in France.

The Divisional Battle School, formed in 1942 under Major E. L. Luce and afterwards established at the Golf Course at Sandwich under Lieut.-Colonel B. A. Coad and later Lieut.-Colonel J. W. Atherton, served as a laboratory for the development of new techniques. Through it passed all the company and platoon commanders and section leaders of the Division to spread the approved doctrine. In Brigadiers G. H. L. Mole and F. Y. C. Knox, both of the Royal Ulster Rifles, who commanded 129 and 130 Infantry Brigades, the Division possessed two commanders of long experience and outstanding shrewdness and ability to train. The departure of the latter to another Division a few months before D-Day was a severe blow. Imperturbable commanders with his profound knowledge, inexhaustible patience and unshakable determination are rare.

Until the late summer of 1943 there were only these two infantry brigades. As a "mixed division" the 34 Tank Brigade under Brigadier W. S. Clarke constituted the third brigade. This lopsided and cumbrous organization, whilst it had advantages from the point of view of training—which were thoroughly exploited—was rightly abolished. 34 Tank Brigade departed to be replaced in October 1943 by 214 Independent Infantry Brigade under Brigadier H. Essame. This brigade, after service in the Isle of Wight, had received specialized training in combined operations under the Royal Marines at Inverary, and possessed an individuality of its own which it never entirely lost. On its arrival all the training resources and experience of the Division were lavishly and unreservedly placed at its disposal. The Brigade rapidly adapted itself to the atmosphere of the Division with the versatility which might have been expected from a formation whose standards of morale and physical fitness were already high and which had been called upon to fulfil three widely divergent roles in the short space of six months.

The normal grouping of the supporting arms with the infantry brigades is given in appendix C. It is most important that the intimacy of association which it ensured should be thoroughly grasped. Of necessity the accounts of the Division's many battles are built up on the framework of the Commander's plan and the actions of the infantry brigades. When, however, 129 Brigade for instance, is mentioned as having achieved a particularly remarkable success, its affiliated units, 94 Field Regiment, 235 Anti-tank Battery, "A" Company 8 Middlesex, 260 Field Company, its S.P. troop of 360 L.A.A. Battery, and 129 Field Ambulance, equally share the honour. This grouping should never be overlooked. The unity of thought and action which it ensured goes far to explain the Division's almost unbroken record of success.

The infantryman who fought in North-west Europe would be the first to admit that the Royal Artillery were the most uniformly efficient arm. In fact, it can be said without exaggeration that they excelled the gunners of all other armies. The testimony of the Germans on this point is unanimous, and they, of all the participants in the war, should be fully qualified to judge. Brigadier G. W. E. Heath, who trained the Divisional artillery and fought it for the first half of the campaign, became the first Commandant of the School of Artillery after the war. Comment therefore with regard to the character of and standards reached in the training period is almost unnecessary. Apart from the purely technical aspect, two of his achievements must be mentioned. Throughout the fighting the regimental and battery commanders lived with the brigadiers and commanding officers, whilst the F.O.Os were always in continuous touch with the forward companies. All plans, therefore, were evolved on a co-operative basis to such an extent that it is almost impossible to give any individual the entire credit. This unanimity of thought and trust is only attained as the result of long association and training. It is naturally only feasible with good communications. In this respect, under Brigadier Heath's guidance, the artillery sections of the Divisional signals and the regimental signallers of the Royal Artillery rose to an astonishingly high level. Many a vital decision in battle was based on information obtainable only over the R.A. net.

During the protracted training period and the first part of the operations, the Division was equally fortunate in its C.R.E., Lieut.-Colonel H. E. Pike. He possessed not only a complete grasp of the technicalities of his arm but also the unique gift of being able to appreciate in apparently simple terms all the engineer implications of a large-scale operational plan. Under his direction 260, 553 and 204 Field Companies bridged and re-bridged almost every river in Kent. When therefore the time came on the Odon, the Noireau and the Seine, the lessons taught by him, on the Rother, the Medway and the Reading Sewer (aptly named), proved their value. The development of the Division's technique in dealing with minefields owed much to his inspiration and guidance. In particular the long hours and careful supervision given by him and his field company commanders to the training of the infantry pioneer platoons were to prove of inestimable value. In the affiliation of his field companies with the infantry brigades he achieved a particularly happy balance between the necessity for centralized control, where possible, of his limited technical resources and the needs of the infantry brigadiers for constantly available engineer advice and help.

Probably no arm of the service has a more thankless task than the Royal Corps of Signals. When all is going well their achievements are taken as a matter of course. In the accounts of most battles their vital contribution is almost invariably ignored. The vagaries of radio communication give no scope for printable writing. For most commanders the sky alone is the limit to the standard of inter-communication required. It is a platitude, however, that a commander without communications is useless. This constitutes the explanation and justification for the high pressure to which the Divisional signals were subjected during the long months of training. The high standard insisted upon was at last reached and Lieut.-Colonel M. Trethowan enabled to command a unit of his corps in whose technical ability and resource all ranks in the Division had the utmost confidence.

The peculiar role of 8 Middlesex, the Divisional machine-gun battalion, presents the historian with a task of considerable difficulty if justice is to be done. Inevitably the three machine-gun companies

2

trained and operated very closely with the infantry brigades. The reluctance invariably displayed by brigadiers to relinquish control of their services is a measure of the work done by their commanding officer, Lieut.-Colonel Mervyn Crawford, during the training period. He himself and his headquarters from the earliest days acquired a reputation for running the Regulating Headquarters essential for the passage of the Division through defiles, whether rivers, minefields or merely congested areas. In spite of this constant distraction, however, he succeeded in bringing his battalion to a level of efficiency which it retained until the very end of the war. In his 4·2-inch mortar company he had a particularly deadly weapon whose services were always in demand. Before it left England it had reached standards of accuracy and speed comparable, subject to the limitations of the weapon, to those of the Royal Artillery, with whom a friendly rivalry had developed as early as 1943.

The R.E.M.E., R.A.S.C. and R.A.O.C. were from the start infected with the Divisional spirit. Whilst in Kent their weapon training, fieldcraft and physical training followed the same lines as those of the rest of the Division. Like the rest, they learnt how to round up snipers, clear houses, remove mines and protect themselves without outside help. No opportunity to include them in any exercise was ever missed. With regard to their more normal duties, it is doubtful whether any other division was ever given supplies or services with greater alacrity. From the earliest days, Lieut.-Colonel T. Leland, C.R.A.S.C., and Lieut.-Colonel V. A. Lines, C.R.O.A.C., established a reputation for obtaining with the maximum speed and the minimum fuss whatever was essential. Blackout conditions, extremes of weather and the Division's ceaseless exercises, in areas only just practicable for motor transport, placed a burden on the vehicle maintenance and repair resources of R.E.M.E. comparable only with that to which they were later to be subjected across the water. Lieut.-Colonel J. M. Neilson, C.R.E.M.E., and his workshop commanders and craftsmen evolved a flexible system which took the strain of the Division's 3,000 vehicles with apparent ease.

Although the Division trained from start to finish on spartan lines which forbade such peace-time amenities as "elevenses" and special provision for officers' messes, and ensured invariably that exercises were carried through to the end whatever the weather conditions, the exact amount of fatigue and exposure to which the troops were exposed was, in fact, gauged with extreme care. In the A.D.M.S., Colonel K. A. M. Tomory, it possessed an R.A.M.C. Commander with a mind militarily in accord with that of Major-General Thomas. Their association was extremely close and ensured that the hardships to which the troops were exposed were kept within reasonable and carefully judged limits. In fact, the general health standards of the Division continued to rise. As the Field Ambulances themselves shared the rigours of the training and were always on the spot to provide advice and assistance, they won the confidence of all ranks in the Division. Their contribution to the ever-rising morale of the Division was therefore very great. A man fights all the better when he knows that if wounded he will pass into competent and humane hands. Not the least of Colonel Tomory's contributions to the battle-worthiness of the Division was his development and training of the two field dressing stations. These ensured that valuable men suffering from minor sicknesses and wounds were treated within the Division and not lost in the soulless machinery of reinforcement holding units in the rear. Thus Colonel Tomory not only played an outstanding part in the building up of the Division's morale but evolved at the same time the flexible and strong medical organization which was to handle over ten thousand casualties during the campaign and to sustain the Division until the end of the war.

The majority of men cannot face the more sinister side of modern war without spiritual backing. Indeed, commanding officers were to find in Normandy that had it not been for the help of their chaplain the morale of their men would have rapidly declined. The Senior Chaplain, Rev. I. D. Neill, during the training period collected around him a team who rapidly identified themselves with the Division, shared its hardships and triumphs and gained its universal respect. It is impossible for a layman to estimate the full extent of their influence. It was a plant of slow growth, but when it eventually bore fruit the harvest was great indeed.

A modern army manual contains the astonishing statement that "a staff officer must satisfy himself that in the eyes of regimental officers his contribution to the success of operations justifies the privileges which are associated with life on the staff." In the Division, the staff had no privileges. They lived hard and worked for incredibly long hours. So far as they were concerned the efficiency of the Division was the only consideration. They were selected with the utmost care and subjected from the start to very heavy strain. Only the highest standards of staff work would suffice and the needs of the fighting troops were the only consideration. The highly efficient machinery for command built up during the training period was to a great extent the production of the commanders' own experience and drive. The share of Lieut.-Colonel the Lord Tryon, the G.S.O.I. from February 1943 to March 1944, must however be mentioned. It was under his auspices that the organization of the Division in the form in which it actually took the field was brought to perfection. The perversity of events ordained that he should serve as a regimental commander away from the Division during the campaign. His limitless patience, grasp of essentials and ability to handle the most embarrassing personal problems would have been invaluable. Fortunately, the G.2 (Ops.),

Major R. S. Williams-Thomas remained. In the A.Q.M.G., the late Lieut.-Colonel J. B. McCance, the Division possessed a battle administrative staff officer of generous and genial temperament, unusual shrewdness and common sense. Whatever was wanted the need had been foreseen, and it was immediately forthcoming. He had the capacity without apparent effort for finding an immediate solution to the most intricate administrative problems and for creating an atmosphere of cheerful and extremely effective teamwork between his own staff and the services. In its administrative arrangements the Division led the Army at the time, especially in the matter of the organization of the administrative area. This was largely the creation of Lieut.-Colonel McCance's farseeing and supremely practical brain.

Outside critics with less exacting standards were wont to describe the Division as "the most over-exercised in the Army." Subsequent operations in the field were to dispose finally of this comment. It is worth while, however, to recall in some detail the form which these many exercises took. First, there were the "cloth models" in huts and halls in Kent around which battalion, regimental and brigade commanders and the Divisional Commander himself assembled their officers almost as a matter of day-to-day routine. Even the most minor was not complete without the presence of Major-General Thomas himself. Whether the problem under discussion was the occupation of a reverse-slope position, the passage of a minefield or the layout of the Bren guns, he missed nothing. The slightest flaw in reasoning, the least departure from principle, the most successfully concealed ignorance brought immediate and—when deserved—devastating retribution. For many they were an ordeal, physical because they were almost invariably held in unheated huts and lasted many hours, and moral according to the mental capacities of the individual concerned. They were essentially group exercises, for not only did he expect all arms to train and fight together: he insisted that they should think as teams as well. Although quick to detect an error and to demolish a heresy, he was nevertheless always ready to listen to the comments of the younger officers. In fact, his ready sympathy with them and his ability to detect potential capacity to command resulted in the Division going overseas with a magnificent team of junior commanders, imbued with his ideas and aggressive outlook.

He himself primarily conceived war in terms of speed—speed of thought and decision, of rapid issue of orders and of quick and effective communication. Signals exercises at very frequent intervals to practise all headquarters and staffs were therefore incessant. On the air he was formidable. He had a voice which seemed able to blast its way through interference from wireless programmes, Fighter Command operations, other formations' activities, and even the worst splutterings and explosions of the wireless sets of the period.

This, combined with his own absolute mastery of the none too simple radio technique, brought home to everyone the standard he required and eventually, not without travail, resulted in its achievement. His aim was to ensure that all operations should be based on verbal orders alone. In fact, during eleven months' continuous fighting he never once issued a written order. The almost unceasing and at times tedious exercises in Kent therefore achieved their end.

It would be almost pointless to enumerate in detail the hundred and one exercises carried out in Kent. All were at full scale. When a bridge had to be built, the Sappers built it. When a minefield had to be crossed, it contained real mines. When a patrol reported booby-traps in a wood, booby-traps were there and exploded at the touch of the unwary. Each lasted not less than three or four days. All the administrative complications which arise in real war were introduced. When the final objectives had been gained, units did not at once march home, like school-boys after a "field day." The exasperating reorganization period, often worse in actual fact than the battle itself, was seen through right to the end. No bedevilment conceivable in war, if the Director could simulate it, was omitted. Finally came the concluding conferences, staged usually in the cinemas of Kent, at which, with a clarity and forcefulness the memory of which survives even after eight years, the shortcomings of all concerned were revealed. It is not surprising therefore that the Division had by 1943 attained such a facility of movement that it could pass through two major obstacles within twenty-four hours with almost mechanical ease.

The exercises with live ammunition on the South Downs reached the climax of realism. The artillery, 8 Middlesex, and in fact all arms of the Division took part. They constituted the nearest approach to actual war possible in the absence of a real enemy. The infantry learnt how close they could approach the bursting shells; they became inured to the bullets of 8 Middlesex passing over their heads and the fire of their own Brens flanking their advance. Smoke in vast clouds enshrouded the Downs. They acquired the art of dodging the splinters of their own three-inch mortar bombs and came to regard the devastating explosion of the 4·2's nearby as an essential element in any battle. The platoon-troop practice "runs" with 34 Tank Brigade were dramatic in the extreme and, it can now be admitted, dangerous. There were inevitably a few fatal casualties. These, however, were a small price to pay for the experience gained. In war it is the ignorant who pay the heaviest penalty. The knowledge bought on the South Downs ensured success later on : regarded in this light, the risks run in the end saved many lives. The damage done to property was considerable. The people of Brighton suffered much from having their electricity supply cable continually severed by the firing and the occupants of the R.A.F. Station at Trueleigh Hill received an occasional burst of Beza through their ante-room. On the whole they accepted the inconvenience and minor risk with normal British stoicism in time of war. It must be admitted, however, that the Division left its mark on the South Downs. The scars of its shells and bombs are still evident to this day. The archaeologist in two thousand years' time studying weapon development in the mid-twentieth century will unearth ample material deposited by the Division beneath the chalk and clay.

The Division was called upon to carry out many experiments on behalf of the War Office. Whenever a new flare, a new weapon, a new piece of equipment, or a new procedure had to be tried out, the task fell to it. When a new line of thought had to be explored, Major-General Thomas's supremely lively and critical brain was directed in that direction. He certainly invented "quick lift"—the drill by which a battalion group mounted on its tanks and "F" echelon transport made itself in a flash as mobile as a tank regiment. The technique of "Monty's moonlight," that is, the use of searchlights in the forefront of the battle to enable operations by all arms to continue through the hours of darkness, owed much to his inventive brain.

From the point of view of the Division itself, however, it is probably the system developed for the control of the administrative group which must closely affected its daily life during the campaign. If the operations described in this history are to be seen in their true proportion and the efforts of the staff and services are to be given the credit they deserve, the system must be understood. The total vehicle strength was 3,300, which included 600 belonging to R.A.S.C., R.A.O.C. and R.E.M.E. and a further 400 administrative vehicles of the forward arms, that is "B Echelon" vehicles normally controlled by the brigade transport officers. These thousand vehicles had to be located, moved, and defended both against ground and air attack.

The Divisional Administrative Area thus came into being. It was commanded by A.D.O.S., Lieut.-Colonel V. A. Lines, with as his staff officer the versatile and untiring Captain L. S. Dack. It comprised four sectors corresponding to the operational grouping of the Division. The basic composition of each sector was one of the four R.A.S.C. companies, together with the "B" echelon vehicles and the men left out of battle (L.O.B.).

Within the area the services, under the control of their own heads, carried out their normal functions with the exception of R.E.M.E. workshops, which it was not always practicable to site there. From here all the material needs of the Division were sent forward, including the mail, most efficiently handled by the Divisional postal unit, the laundry effectively performed by 306 Mobile Laundry and Bath Unit, and the "Wyvern News Sheet." It was by way of the Administrative Area that reinforcement drafts joined their units, usually with great relief after a chequered and usually frustrating and most uncomfortable passage along the L. of C. By the end of the campaign over 12,000 men had passed through this channel. Daily, the maintenance columns left for the forward area conveying reinforcements, rations and mail on their own regimental transport. On reaching the forward areas the columns dispersed to units, the vehicles returning later for the next day's trip. Ammunition and petrol were not included since ammunition and petrol points were already maintained by the R.A.S.C.

The Administrative Group when unwound into road convoy numbered about eight hundred vehicles, and changed its location on an average once every ten days during the campaign.

All the difficulties the services would have to surmount were foreseen long before the Division finished its training. What is more, they were faced and solved time and time again in the Division's many exercises. It is not surprising therefore that from the time operations started, the successful functioning of the services came to be accepted almost as a matter of course and no Division in any war was ever better maintained. In fact, petrol for seven million miles was supplied to move the 3,300 vehicles. Food sufficient for over three million meals was sent forward. Two million rounds of artillery ammunition were handled. The link with brigades was particularly close. Many a driver and craftsman worked himself to the last stage of exhaustion for the sake of his brigade. The morale and Divisional pride of the services, created during the long training period, reached as high a level as that of any unit.

All the results of the Division's training were embodied in the Standing Orders, which to this day are surprisingly modern in outlook. It was said that they had a drill for every conceivable operation and contingency of war. A formation, however, like a religious sect, must have a doctrine. That of the Division was set out in simple, crystal-clear and precise form. The normal criticism of the exercise of military forethought in this detail is that it is liable to produce rigidity of mind. This may be the case in formations which continue to retain the services of the stupid. So far as the Division was concerned, this was a risk which could not be run. By the spring of 1944 only those leaders remained, no matter at what level, who were mentally and physically capable of adapting to changed conditions the knowledge gained in training. The Division's Standing Orders and doctrine in fact ensured that no one in Normandy was called upon to face a problem which he had not already studied in Kent.

Under another commander it is conceivable that the Division, as a result of the prolonged, tense and arduous period of preparation,

might have become stale.   As in athletics, a military body normally
reaches a climax of efficiency in a training cycle and then faces
a decline.   This stage was never reached.   This is surprising.
214 Brigade of course, the late-comers, were kept so busy until the
last moment learning all the Division had to teach that they never had
a moment to reflect or feel that they might justifiably cease working
at the highest pressure.   The remainder of the Division, who might
well have felt that some relaxation of effort was justified, never for one
moment showed any decline in enthusiasm.   Probably the explanation lies in the fact that its morale was based on such firm foundations
as to be impervious to monotony.   In any case, it was obvious to the
whole world when General Montgomery was appointed to command
21 Army Group, early in January 1944, that the opening of the Second
Front was due in the late spring or early summer.

1944   He appeared in person to inspect the greater part of the Division,
4th   drawn up in a hollow square at Rye on 4th February in the early
Feb.   winter dawn.   All had risen long before daylight.   As he walked
along the ranks, snow began to fall.   Finally, he mounted a jeep and,
calling on the men to break their ranks and gather round, addressed
the troops.   He said that the Eighth Army had been a great army.
Now he knew that he had another quite as good.   Standing in the
slowly falling snow with the troops around him, hanging on to every
word he said, he recalled one of the great missionary bishops of the
Middle Ages calling upon the soldiers to embark upon a crusade.
His bearing with the troops at this time always contained a hint of the
ecclesiastic.   If he had been born in another age he would probably
have been a towering figure of the Church.   As a great political
Cardinal of the Renaissance he would have been thoroughly at
home.

There is a Norman proverb, "Si tu veux etre heureux, vas entre
Caen et Bayeux."   So far as 21 Army Group was concerned, this
errs on the side of overstatement.

1944   The actual site of the landing in Normandy was known in the
21st   Division as early as 21st February, when all the Divisional and
Feb.   Brigade commanders of 12 Corps assembled for a three-day exercise
in an oversize Nissen hut at Broadwater Down, Tunbridge Wells.
On the wall hung a large outline map showing the Normandy coast,
with the objectives of the assault divisions and the lines it was hoped
to reach in the various phases.   Lieut.-General N. M. Ritchie, the
Corps Commander, described the whole conception of "Overlord"
in considerable detail.   12 Corps was destined to be part of the
follow-up element, landing about twelve days after the assault with
the task of breaking out of the bridgehead.   In fact, the Division,
except for a month in 1945, never operated under 12 Corps.   The
two days at Broadwater Down were spent in map-reading exercises
and tactical discussions.   The Brigadiers became absorbed in the

meanderings of the River Orne and its tributaries, the Odon and the Noireau, and saw on the maps how in violet layers of increasing density the country, broken and irregular in parts with steep hills and narrow valleys, rose to its highest level at a point 18 miles south-west of Caen. This was Mount Pincon—a name they now heard for the first time. The atmosphere of the hotels where they lived during the exercise provided a particularly incongruous contrast to the closely guarded secrecy of the Nissen hut. It seemed that all the oldest people in England had been corralled in Tunbridge Wells. Even the waiters and maids were in the eighties. The town was well described at the time as a cemetery with traffic lights. On the second day, at the end of the morning, all were invited to walk out into the grounds to inspect a new type of vehicle—a weasel ! They were to see it again under very different conditions and to bless the inventor.

The tension increased with the unusually early arrival of spring. The Division completed its concentration around Battle, Hastings and Rye. All leave was stopped on 6th April. Field censorship of letters was started. Banking accounts were closed and money drawn instead from field cashiers. The last details of loading and waterproofing were put in hand. Exercises continued. The Division waited in instant readiness to move. There could be no doubt now that D-Day was imminent.

The Prime Minister himself appeared on 13th May. His train drew into Rye Station after lunch. First appeared Field-Marshal Smuts, a most distinguished and arresting figure in a gabardine tropical uniform. He had a word for everyone. Then Mr. Mackenzie King, the Prime Minister of Canada, and Mr. Godfrey Huggins, the Prime Minister of Southern Rhodesia, emerged from the Edwardian dining-car. The Army, Corps, Divisional and Brigade Commanders stood drawn up correctly in line. At last, wearing a curious brown, square bowler-hat, of a type apparently worn about 1898 by foremen carpenters, and with the usual cigar, the greatest man of his age, leaving a haze of cigar smoke behind him in the corridor, stepped out on the platform and immediately called for the station-master. This official was unearthed with some difficulty and thanked for the privilege of using his station. The commanders were then presented and the exuberant and triumphal progress through the divisional area began. Perched up high beside Field-Marshal Smuts in the back of a large open car, the Prime Minister acknowledged the cheers of the troops of the Division on his slow progress through Wittersham, Brede and Battle. A demonstration of flame-throwers filled him with youthful delight. With him as supreme leader, no one could doubt the certainty of overwhelming victory ahead. He radiated the spirit of offensive battle and conviction of overwhelming success. Field-Marshal Smuts whispered to a gunner, "It's coming very soon now, boys."

The battalion and equivalent commanders were to hear General Montgomery once more before D-Day, at the Headquarters of 12 Corps in Tunbridge Wells. None who was present could feel other than supremely confident of certain victory ahead. He stressed that he commanded the finest and best equipped army in the world, supported by 10,000 aircraft, and that once landed nothing could stop it. All left to pass on to their men their own complete trust in his leadership.

On the morrow of D-Day, Major-General Thomas was at last able to reveal to all officers, in the Ritz Cinema at Hastings, the exact nature of the task ahead.

The code word "Mary," sent out from Divisional Headquarters at Tenterden at 6 p.m. on the 12th placed the Division at 6 hours' notice to move. Early next morning it began to pass, unit by unit, into the maw of B.U.C.O., the vast transit organization controlling the move across the Channel. The marching troops headed in lorries for the marshalling areas around Newhaven : the waterproofed guns and vehicles for the London docks. Not without relief that the long and exacting period of preparation now lay behind them, officers and men alike faced whatever might come with sober confidence in the fitness of their Division for battle. For years all had lived, planned and worked for this day alone. Now at last the day had come.

CHAPTER II

THE BATTLE OF THE ODON

(See Sketch Maps 1 and 5)

THE LANDING

It had been originally intended that the Division should complete its landing on 20th June. However, the rate of turn-round of craft from the south coast of England and the slow rate of discharge from ships, coasters and L.S.T. alike over the French beaches, gave cause for anxiety. Then came the storm which blew from 19th to 22nd June across or directly on to the British and United States beaches. Consequently the shipping programme was thrown into confusion and units arrived piecemeal, sometimes ahead of their advanced parties. A great semicircle of ships waiting to be discharged lay off the low coastline in serried ranks.

The infantry, with what they could carry on their backs, embarked at Newhaven and Southampton on L.C.Is. and cross-channel steamers. Space was very cramped. In many cases the troops had to spend over forty-eight hours on the stuffy 'tween decks in an atmosphere which the smell of cooking soup (self-heating or "jet-propelled") did nothing to improve. One company in each battalion embarked with bicycles. These caused considerable embarrassment not only in getting up and down the ships' gangways but also when the time came to disembark in landing craft.

Some units were lucky enough to land under the protection of the Mulberry Harbour at Arromanches and had merely to walk down the long floating piers to the beach. The majority, however, came ashore in L.C.As. on the open beaches near Courseulles. For those who landed at low tide this involved a long wade chest-deep through the shallows. After the storm had subsided on the 22nd, beached coasters and wrecked landing craft lay piled up at high-water mark. The troops passed through the sand dunes and the line of huge concrete pill-boxes past what remained of pleasant seaside villas, out of which peeped a few civilians, to assembly areas taped out in the trampled corn of the fields beyond. The water-front presented a forest of formation signs, notice-boards, traffic directions, arrows—all the many-coloured paraphernalia of Movement Control. Many changed their socks and broached their 24-hour landing ration. All enjoyed using the "Tommy" cookers and were amazed at their efficiency. They then took the dusty road to the Divisional concentration area, a few miles north-east of Bayeux, where, in pleasant fields and orchards, they awaited the arrival of their transport and guns. Overhead they watched great fleets of allied heavy bombers going out, soon to return pursued by millions of shell bursts. From the east came the rumble of heavy artillery fire around Caen. The nights were cold and star-lit.

The remainder of the Division and all M.T., after waiting for several days in the marshalling areas in the East End of London and watching with interest the arrival of the first V.1's, or doodle-bugs, in the area, embarked in British transports and United States "Liberty" ships at the Royal Albert, Royal Victoria, King George V, West India and East India Docks. As loading was completed the ships pushed off and dropped down the estuary as far as Southend. Here the ship's masters, accompanied by the senior officer in each ship, went off to the pier to receive their final sailing orders. Convoys sailed each night, rounded the North Foreland and ran close to Dover Cliffs. In the convoy which sailed on the night of the 18th, one ship was set on fire by guns from Cap Gris Nez and was later beached at Deal. The outbreak of the storm on the 19th made landing impossible and compelled everyone to remain at sea for a further four days. The reserve rations on board in some cases consisted of Compo Pack F only—treacle pudding, Russian salad and tinned salmon. By the time the storm had abated sufficiently to permit landing to be resumed, this diet had begun to pall.

At the easternmost end of the long line of shipping, opposite Ouistrehem, the ship M.T.41, *Derry Cunihy*, with 43 Reconnaissance Regiment on board, rode out the storm. Early on the morning of June 24th, before reveille, a landing craft came alongside with orders to move to another and safer beach to unload. Nearly all were still asleep, the men in the holds or on deck and the officers either in the cabins beneath the bridge or on the boat deck. The ship's engines started up, and with the first throb there was a violent explosion which split the ship in two between the engine room and No. 4 hold. The stern began to sink rapidly and, in a matter of seconds, No. 5 hold was under water.

The sea was soon full of struggling figures and floating debris and patches of oil began to spread. M.T.Bs, landing craft and even rowing-boats appeared very quickly and rescue work began. A large motor gun-boat came alongside, and one by one the wounded were taken aboard.

There was no vestige of panic and very little noise. Wounded men disregarded their hurts and struggled to help less fortunate comrades. There were many deeds of bravery. In the sinking and burning hold, the Padre, Rev. J. E. Gethyn Jones and the Medical officer, Captain J. M. Ellis, worked on regardless of their own safety. Sergeant Law, although wounded, and Trooper F. M. Greener saved many lives.

A few of the survivors were taken direct to the beaches, but the majority were transferred to a large depot ship which had been in peace-time a French luxury liner—the *Cap Tourain*. When the C.O. and Adjutant came to call the roll, besides 150 wounded, 180 men were missing. Those who died of wounds and the bodies of men whose bodies had been recovered were buried at sea.

Landing proceeded over the open beaches. Vehicles and guns were transhipped off Juno beach to tank landing craft or "Rhino" ferries, being swung overside on derricks and dropped with neat precision into the waiting craft. These beached, down came the ramps and vehicles and men charged through the surf. Only now and then did the engine of a truck or a carrier give a sickening spurt and stop dead—the waterproofing had been well done. When this happened, a recovery vehicle would dash forward to winch the casualty ashore. Once on dry land the vehicles, signalled on by Military Police, pushed rapidly ahead through the traffic, dodging bulldozers and recovery vehicles, past the working parties of Pioneers making new tracks, to assembly areas a few hundred yards inland. Here, if they were lucky, they were picked up by their advance parties and, the first stage of de-waterproofing completed, directed on their way to their unit's concentration area. They entered the endless stream of traffic moving at sixty yards interval.

The Provost Company had done its work well. The familiar Wyvern signs and black arrows on a white ground clearly marked the circuitous route to the Division's concentration area north of Bayeux. Here and there the eye caught sight of a brewed-up tank which had come to grief in the original landing. Beside the roads, great dumps of ammunition and rations had come into being—visible evidence of the far-sighted planning of the administrative staffs. Some farm buildings and villages had been completely obliterated. Others were untouched. Near the coast there were notice-boards marked "Danger—Mines." The few local inhabitants to be seen looked on at the dense traffic and the clouds of dust with apparent indifference. The corn was uncut and trampled down.

By sunset on the 24th the concentration of the Division was practically complete. The infantry had once more linked up with their transport, kit packs had been handed out and blanket bundles unrolled. It was a perfect midsummer night, clear and cool. De-waterproofing, thanks to the untiring efforts of the drivers, was well advanced. With a few exceptions, which were adjusted on the following day, the 43 Division, despite the dislocation caused by the storm, was at last ready to advance towards the battle for which it had so long prepared.

Wireless silence had been ordered until 0800 hours on the morrow, June 25th, and all commanders down to lieut.-colonels summoned to a Divisional "O" Group at this hour.

THE GENERAL SITUATION ON 24TH JUNE

If the operations of 43 Division are to be seen in their true perspective, it is essential to grasp General Montgomery's overall plan, which he had explained to the General Officers of the field armies in London on 7th April. This was, once ashore and firmly established, to threaten to break out of the bridgehead on the eastern flank—that is, in the Caen sector. By means of this threat he intended to draw the main enemy reserves into that sector, to fight them there and to keep them there, using the British and Canadian Armies for the purpose. Having got the main enemy reserves committed on the eastern flank, his plan was to break out on the western flank, using for this purpose the American armies under General Bradley, and to pivot the whole front on Caen.

This was his original conception and he never once had cause or reason to alter it.

When the Allies landed on 6th June, Rommel had promptly committed all the armoured reserves he had locally available—that is, 21 Panzer Division, 12 S.S. Division and the Panzer Lehr in a series of fierce but rather disjointed counter-attacks. When these failed, he had changed his tactics and decided to cordon off the bridgehead so as to gain time to stage a really powerful armoured counter-offensive.

General Montgomery, on his part, having gained the initiative, had given him no respite. Putting in one limited offensive after another, he had succeeded in using up Rommel's reinforcements piecemeal as they arrived. On the 24th, however, four further high-quality Panzer divisions had still to come, followed possibly by three other Panzer divisions and several infantry formations.

Despite the delay caused by the storm, he was now ready to strike. The First U.S. Army was therefore ordered to capture Cherbourg and the Second Army to capture Caen, starting on 25th June.

For the past ten days the bridgehead territorially had remained fairly constant. From the right at Caumont it followed approximately the line of the Caen road as far as Fontenay Le Pesnel, thence to Putot en Bessin and Cairon and on to the slender bridgehead east of the River Orne still partly held by 6 Airborne Division. On the right every village in the close *bocage* country was held in the most obstinate manner, and the German mortars, like our artillery, were constantly in action. Fighting for Tilly had been particularly fierce and frequently at close quarters. In the uncomfortable bulge northwest of Caen the enemy had proved equally obstinate.

The Second Army had re-grouped for the coming operation with 30 Corps on the right, 8 Corps in the centre and 1 Corps on the left. Operations were to start on 25th June, when 49 Division was to advance to seize the high ground at Rauray north of Noyers in order to protect the right flank of the thrust to be made by 8 Corps on the following day. This was to be on the front of 3 Canadian Division in the general direction of Bretteville sur Laize with the object of forcing the crossings of the Rivers Odon and Orne and seizing the high ground due south of Caen, thus isolating the city from the south. Later, 1 Corps was to clear up the Caen pocket.

This, then, was the situation to be revealed at the Divisional "O" Group on the morning of 25th June.

THE FIRST "O" GROUP
(See Sketch Map 1)

A hot June sun was shining when the officers attending the "O" Group began to arrive about half-past seven at Divisional Head-quarters at Sommervieu. They parked their cars in a field under the guidance of military police and made their way to a great Norman barn. There were notices everywhere—"To 'O' G.P."; "No Vehicles past this point"; "OPS Room—No OFFICER BELOW THE RANK OF BRIGADIER ALLOWED INSIDE"; "HAVE YOU CALLED AT THE SIGNAL OFFICE?"; "NO MOTOR-CYCLES PAST THIS POINT"; "A MESS ONLY"—and many others. The layout of the headquarters had been practised again and again during training in England and had been worked out in great detail.

Inside the barn four rows of nondescript chairs and camp-stools had been placed facing a long table taken from the farm nearby. Along the far side of the table were six chairs and behind them, propped up against the wall of the barn, stood a large 1/50,000 map of the bridge-head covered with talc. The I.O., Captain G. Matthews, was putting the finishing touches to the blue lines representing our own positions and the enemy layout, so far as it was known, in red. There were many question marks.

On each chair facing the table lay a ticket showing the appointment of the officer for whom it was reserved. The three infantry briga-diers, each with a staff officer on his left and the C.O. of his affiliated artillery regiment on his right, with the addition of the C.R.A., filled the front row. The staff officers immediately became involved in the marking on the talcs of their commander's maps of the tracings handed to them as they entered. The lieut.-colonels commanding the Royal Engineers, Royal Signals, the Machine Gun Battalion (8 Middlesex), the Anti-Tank Regiment, the Light A.A. Regiment and the heads of services made up the second row. In their rear sat the more junior members of the staff and services, including the Senior Chaplain.

Precisely at eight o'clock the Divisional Commander entered fol- 25th lowed by the G.S.O.1, Lieut.-Colonel H. F. Meynell, and the plump June figure of the A.A. & Q.M.G., the late Lieut.-Colonel J. B. McCance.

The General was wearing high oiled boots, light-coloured riding-breeches and a battledress blouse. The red band on his cap was faded. This was to be his dress throughout the campaign, except that in the winter he wore a leather coat. Before leaving England he had announced that officers might dress as they pleased. The results as the campaign progressed were surprising.

All rose to their feet. As soon as the General had taken his seat, the G.S.O.1 placed before him a millboard on which four or five pages of notes had been typed with double spacing, and took his seat beside him. The A.A. & Q.M.G. sat slightly in rear.

Whenever operations permitted, divisional "O" Groups were to take this form throughout the campaign.

The opportunity to strike the enemy, for which the Division had waited for so long, had now arrived. The Divisional Commander revealed that it now formed part of 8 Corps, the spearhead of the operation which had now started with the attack of 49 Division on the Rauray feature on the right. According to the latest reports this was progressing in the face of strong opposition. The attack on the morrow, supported by all the available artillery of the corps, including the Division's three field regiments, was to be continued by 15 (S.) Division on a two-brigade front, 46 Brigade on the right, 44 Brigade on the left. These two brigades, starting from the line of the road from Le Mesnil Patry to Putot en Bessin, were to seize the ridge which runs from Le Haut du Bosq south of Cheux to La Gaule. When this objective had been taken, the 227 Brigade was to pass through and secure the crossings of the Odon some five miles from the start line. The 11 Armoured Division was then to advance in its turn and to exploit to the south-eastward.

The task of the Division was to follow the 15 (S.) Division, taking over each objective as soon as possible after capture so as to enable the advance to be continued. The Commander emphasized the great importance of St. Mauvieu on the left flank.

The commander of 129 Brigade, Brigadier Mole, was therefore ordered to get in touch at once with the commander of 44 Brigade so that relief in St. Mauvieu after it had been captured could be carried out with the minimum delay. Brigadier Essame, 214 Brigade, was similarly told to see the commander of 46 Brigade, so that in due course he could take over reponsibility for Cheux and the high ground to the south of it. As operations developed the Divisional Commander anticipated that all brigadiers would be called upon to clear the flanks and later, when the Odon had been reached, to intervene in the advance beyond.

Brigades were to move immediately to a forward concentration area around Brecy and Rucqueville, about five miles south-east of Bayeux, so as to be ready next morning to take over from 15 (S.) Division as they advanced.

1. A corner of Cheux, 5th July, 1944

2. The road from Cheux to Colleville—vehicles of 179 Field Regiment passing refugees from Verson

In conclusion, the Divisional Commander emphasized his complete confidence in the outcome of the battle. In the face of our command of the air, the enemy, although he might stage a counter-attack, could never hope to mount a counter-offensive. The build-up was rapidly improving, especially in the vital matter of ammunition. Everyone must act as he had been taught to act during training. In some respects it would be just another exercise, but this time there would be a real enemy and no umpires.

Before joining their troops, some of those present at this memorable "O" Group attended Holy Communion conducted by the Senior Chaplain, Rev. Ivan Neill, C.F., nearby.

The brigades were soon on the move. It was very hot. An endless stream of traffic in both directions choked the battered roads. The dust swirled in thick clouds and the air was sickly with the fumes of petrol and hot rubber. Some men passed out with the heat. The fields on either side were full of ripening corn. Peasants, apparently indifferent to the war, were still cutting the hay. For the men of the cycle company in each battalion it proved a particularly trying march. Towards evening, however, the infantry were once more concentrated in bivouac around Brecy. Commanding officers collected their battalions and told them what they knew of the situation and the task which lay ahead. The sky had now clouded over and there were signs of rain.

15 SCOTTISH DIVISION ADVANCE ON 26TH JUNE

The country over which the advance was to take place resembled in many ways the richer parts of Devon. Fields of standing corn alternated with pastures surrounded by high hedges and old dry ditches. Many of the minor roads and tracks were sunken, offering perfect cover to a resolute defender. Viewpoints were few in number and limited in range. The many small villages were strongly built with very narrow passages between the farms and houses and set amidst orchards. Some of the farms and manors were of great age and had massive stone walls and heavy timbers.

Le Mesnil Patry and Norrey en Bessin had been battered into rubble by incessant mortar fire. Ahead, the cornfields sloped downwards towards the Muc stream, then rose gradually upwards towards the ridge of high ground which extended from west to east from the Rauray spur to the "100 ring contour" south of Cheux. From here the ground descended gradually towards the wooded country along the Odon. Towards the east, open cornfields stretched towards Carpiquet Aerodrome. The main roads from Caen to Caumont and Caen to Villers Bocage straddled the battlefield.

In the attack on Rauray, 49 Division and 8 Armoured Brigade later to be so closely associated with 43 Division, struck the tank

3

regiment of 12 S.S. Panzer Division (Hitler Jugend). Bitter fighting ensued and only partial success. By nightfall, Rauray was still in enemy hands. Despite the fact that this exposed their right flank, 15 (S.) Division attacked at 7.30 a.m. on the 26th. It was a miserable morning of low cloud and drizzle. Visibility was so bad that the bombing programme had to be cancelled. Reconnaissance parties of 129 and 214 Brigades followed closely on the heels of the attacking brigades. For many, this was to be their first introduction to the stark realities of war.

26th
June

Supported by a barrage, 46 Brigade on the right advanced through the standing corn. They found themselves opposed by tough young S.S. soldiers in camouflage smocks who stood their ground. Hidden in the corn, they took a heavy toll. Light machine-guns and mortars came to life everywhere, especially from the right flank, where 49 Division's grim battle still raged. A quarter of a mile from the start line, the brigade ran into a minefield, but pushed on. In spite of delays, by 11.30 a.m. Cheux was in their hands. Here the two leading battalions held on under a ceaseless rain of shells and mortar bombs. Early in the afternoon, the reserve battalion passed through and in the face of very heavy opposition got as far as the north edge of the "100 ring contour."

On the left, 44 Brigade also assaulted through thick corn full of snipers and under heavy fire from the direction of Carpiquet. By 10.30 a.m. La Gaule had fallen. On the left, however, bitter and confused fighting went on all day in the burning and reeking wreckage of St. Mauvieu. In the afternoon the enemy counter-attacked from Marcelet with elements of 12 S.S. and 21 Panzer Divisions. These were beaten off, but casualties were severe.

All day 227 Brigade had been moving up slowly towards Cheux. It was not till 6 p.m. that they were able to start their advance southwards down the two roads leading past the church. In the ruins an appalling traffic jam had developed. The narrow streets were flooded and in the ruins many snipers still held their ground. Many tanks and trucks were burning. At the Haut du Bosq end truck after truck went up in flames. Several houses were on fire. As a result battalions became separated from their transport. The H.L.I. on the right almost immediately ran into dug-in tanks in the gathering darkness, and therefore consolidated just south of Cheux. On the left, the 2 Gordons succeeded in advancing about a mile south of Cheux on the Colleville road. Night came with heavy rain. It was decided accordingly to reorganize and continue the advance at first light.

Meanwhile 129 and 214 Brigades advanced through the darkness to relieve 44 and 46 Brigades in St. Mauvieu and Cheux. The tracks were deep in mud and choked with transport, which, especially at the crossing of the Muc, churned the mud to buttery slime. It was on this march that the cycles were finally abandoned. The 4 Wilts, moving into St. Mauvieu in pouring rain about midnight, found fighting still in progress. The village had been full of civilians, most of whom had been killed by shells or flame. Our tanks, closed down tightly, were still firing. Not until the dawn was the relief complete. The 5 Wilts had taken over La Gaule from the Royal Scots by 3 a.m. To attempt to take over Cheux until first light, in the general confusion and darkness, would merely have added to the frightful congestion and mounting casualties within the village, already crowded almost to suffocation with the greater part of two infantry brigades and two regiments of tanks.

214 Brigade therefore waited for the dawn on the fringe of Cheux.

THE D.C.L.I. AT CHEUX

On the right the struggle for the Rauray spur on the 26th had ended 27th with 8 Armoured Brigade on the outskirts of the village. Fighting June of a sanguinary character was to continue throughout the 27th. Again and again the Germans counter-attacked here, only to be beaten back with grim determination by 49 Division and 8 Armoured Brigade.

With the dawn, the great mass of tanks, carriers and trucks congealed amidst the debris of the main street in Cheux once more began to heave forward. Eventually the 2 H.L.I. extricated themselves from the confusion and pushed on towards their start line south of Le Haut du Bosq. Before they could reach it, however, they once more ran into the enemy's dug-in tanks. Close-quarter fighting with infantry and armour ensued and continued all day.

Meanwhile in the early morning sunlight 5 D.C.L.I., their 6-pdr. guns still somewhere in the great traffic jam in the main street, entered the Le Haut du Bosq end of the village, having moved across the fields, now crowded with 25-pdr. guns being dug in. Owing to some misunderstanding the 9 Cameronians, who had captured this part of the village at a heavy price on the previous day, withdrew with their 6-pdr. anti-tank guns before the D.C.L.I. could replace them. One company found the locality allotted to it still in possession of the enemy. The battalion started to dig in amongst the orchards. A lively hunt for snipers began. The young S.S. troops were detestable young beasts, but, like good infantry, they stood and fought it out when overrun.

Suddenly, without any warning, six large tanks rumbled down the sunken road from the south and passed through the right company of the battalion almost unnoticed. The leading tank on turning a corner met head on the troop of 17-pdr. anti-tank guns moving in to support the D.C.L.I. In a flash, it had knocked out all four guns.

At the same moment the other five tanks turned into the minute orchard occupied by the headquarters of Major John Fry, commanding "D" Company, and halted literally on top of the slits. He rose to the occasion and his men with him. This was their first taste of action, but they knew what to do. Disdaining cover, he called upon them to fall upon the tanks.

Captain H. Jobson, the second-in-command of the company, joined in the battle. On his orders, Sergeant Hicks and Corporal Ronan opened up with their Piat on the rear of the tanks. He then brought forward the three Piat teams from the three platoons of the company in the surrounding orchards. The stalking of the six Panthers began. Two German motor-cyclists suddenly burst in, to be shot at ten yards' range by the two officers. Edging forward, the tanks now opened up on the two 6-pdr. guns, knocking them out and wounding all the crews. The carriers and trucks of battalion headquarters, 50 yards ahead in the road, were their next prey. Trucks and carriers burst into flames.

Hearing the din in the village, the commanding officer, Lieut.-Colonel J. W. Atherton, came forward. Despite the confusion with great gallantry he succeeded in getting one 6-pdr. gun in action. He was acting as loader when a shot from one of the Panthers' 88's killed him and the crew instantly.

Two stretcher-bearers carrying a wounded man on a stretcher approached the company headquarters. The tanks opened fire on them. One tank then deliberately ran over the man lying on the stretcher.

Enraged at this disgusting act, the four Piat teams now closed in on the tanks from the rear. Hit three times, one turned tail and fled. Sergeant Hicks knocked out another by killing all the crew. In the mêlée two more Panthers turned a corner where Private Blackwell's Piat party was waiting for them. A shot at close range disposed of one; the other overturned in attempting to escape. Another fell to a 6-pdr. and burst into flames. Deprived of the protection of their tanks, the crews were now an easy prey.

In less than half an hour in their first action, the D.C.L.I., magnificently led, at a cost of 20 killed and wounded, had knocked out five Panther tanks manned by S.S. troops. The news flashed from wireless set to wireless set. The D.C.L.I. and 43 Division, to use a favourite expression of Field-Marshal Montgomery, had stepped off on the right foot.

THE SCOTTISH CORRIDOR

Whilst this battle raged in the western end of the village the 1 Worcestershire Regiment took over from the sadly depleted Glasgow Highlanders east of the battered church in the centre of Cheux. The 5 Wiltshire Regiment was now firmly established in

La Gaule; 4 Wiltshire carried on with the mopping up of the straggling village of St. Mauvieu on the far bank of the Muc and took over the village of Marcelet and the wood south-east of St. Mauvieu; 4 Somerset Light Infantry, with a counter-attack role, on Cheux, dug in near La Gaule. All these positions were in full view of the enemy at Carpiquet Aerodrome. Consequently, mortar and Nebelwerfer fire rained on them throughout the day. Slits were dug with an enthusiasm unknown in training exercises. One bomb falling on the outskirts of Cheux wiped out the complete "O" Group of a company of the Worcestershire Regiment, killing amongst others Major P. J. Riddle, a most outstanding young company commander, who, had he lived, would have gone far. All day the bombardment continued, especially on the bottleneck of Cheux. Lieut.-Colonel G. Pethick, 179 Field Regiment, was amongst the wounded on this day.

Meanwhile, 227 Brigade, despite the fact that one of its battalions, 2 H.L.I., was firmly pinned south of Le Haut du Bosq, forged ahead with the 2 Argylls. Soon they were in Colleville fighting their way from house to house. Regardless of their open flanks, they reached the twin villages of Mondrainville and Tourville, which stand on the highway which runs across the front as straight as a die from Caen to Villers Bocage. Sweeping all opposition before them, they stormed on down the road to Tourmauville. By 5 p.m. they had seized the bridge across the River Odon. By 7 p.m. the whole battalion stood firm on the far bank. Tanks of 29 Armoured Brigade, close on their heels, crashed over the bridge in the direction of that hill of ill-omen, Pt. 112. Despite the fact that Grainville on the right flank still obstinately resisted, the 15 Scottish Division had driven a long, narrow wedge through the heart of the enemy position —the "Scottish Corridor" had been born.

As the Seaforth moved forward in the early afternoon, 7 Somerset moved into their positions in the high standing corn, on Hill 100 south of Cheux, and dug into the stony ground. That night and all next day their fighting patrols probed deeply into Mouen.

To the east, Carpiquet Aerodrome lay in full view. Ahead, beyond the cornfields, the tops of the trees around the enclosures of Colleville and Mouen could be seen. On Hill 100, Brigadier Heath, the C.R.A. in his Ark, watched the shooting of the Divisional artillery, now all in action. Movement over the crest brought a shot from an 88 or a flurry of Nebelwerfer bombs. Occasionally a glimpse of enemy tanks on the north edge of Mouen caught the eye. On the left, the wide expanse of Carpiquet Aerodrome seemed uncannily quiet. It was, in fact, held in great strength by dug-in tanks and infantry in concrete defences, as the Canadians were later to find to their cost. It is amazing to relate that a fighting patrol of 4 Wilts under Captain D. I. M. Robbins, with Captain T. Greenshields as

F.O.O., actually penetrated the aerodrome on the following day unchallenged and then went on to reconnoitre the southern edge, where it drew fire from the houses and hangars.

28th June   The 28th proved to be a day of fierce and confused fighting along the narrow corridor. Beyond the Odon, 11 Armoured Division fought a battle from dawn to dusk around Esquay and Pt. 112. The battle continued until nightfall, when they were withdrawn into the bridgehead. In the mid afternoon 2 Argylls captured the Gavrus bridge intact. 15 (S.) Division at last broke down the fierce resistance at Grainville and pushed on to Le Valtru. On the eastern axis, a struggle now developed with enemy tanks and armour for Colleville.

Towards evening 2 H.L.I., having been relieved at Le Haut du Bosq, were moved to the left flank and ordered to clear the area beyond Colleville to Mouen.

After a day of hard and confused fighting, the Scottish Corridor was still a bare 2,500 yards wide and completely open to attack from either flank. It was served, south of Cheux, by one road only, the battered track through Colleville. This was under enemy observation in many places. On either flank, enemy formations were gathering like wasps. Elements of four fresh Panzer divisions had been identified. Major-General Macmillan, the Commander of 15 Scottish Division, appreciated that on the morrow a strong enemy counter-attack would develop from the south-west directed against the bottleneck at Cheux. Events were to prove him right.

The time had now come for 43 Division to assume responsibility for the flank east of the road from Colleville to Tourville and Baron on the Odon. As a first step, 214 Brigade were therefore ordered at 2000 hours to capture Mouen.

MOUEN

29th June   When the Commander of 214 Brigade received this order, nothing was known of the progress of the attack of 2 H.L.I. from the axis north of Colleville through the fields and orchards towards the western outskirts of the village. Two and a half hours of daylight, at most, remained. All day tank and infantry fighting had raged round Colleville. Lieutenant E. F. Larret, a Canadian officer attached to 7 Somerset Light Infantry, had led no less than three patrols into Mouen and found it packed with tanks and infantry. The second time, he had had to fight his way out. Nevertheless he had gone in a third time and confirmed that in the evening the enemy still held the village in force. No easy task therefore lay ahead.

In the hope of being able to exploit the success of the H.L.I. by passing through them and carrying Mouen by a night assault, Brigadier Essame moved 1 Worcestershire Regiment to an assembly

area in the fields south of Cheux. Accompanied by the C.O.,
Lieut.-Colonel A. R. Harrison, and Major Alexander, his battery
commander, he then went forward to reconnoitre, turned off the axis
just north of Colleville and followed in the wake of the H.L.I.
Amongst the high hedges and meadows the party found the battalion
grimly fighting its way forward inch by inch and at heavy cost.
Eventually they penetrated as far as the western outskirts of the
village, where in the fading light they saw that the H.L.I. had finally
come to a standstill in the face of tanks and infantry with Spandaus.
Snipers had come to life behind them. A bullet hit Major Alexander's jeep.

Back amongst the tightly packed traffic on the axis, the brigadier
decided that a night advance through the H.L.I. with the enemy still
holding out in the narrow fields and orchards could only end in
confusion and that an assault at first light from the north over the
open fields would be more effective.

The Brigade "O" Group assembled at 3 a.m. by the light of a
pressure lamp in a 160-lb. tent near La Gaule. The 1 Worcestershire Regiment were to seize Mouen by an attack over the open
cornfields on the extreme east flank of the corridor and to exploit as
far as the main road to Caen. No tanks were available, but Major Sir
John Backhouse, who had taken Lieut.-Colonel Pethick's place in
command of 179 Field Regiment, in addition to the whole Divisional
artillery had secured the support of two medium regiments.

Accordingly at 8 o'clock the Worcestershire Regiment, deployed
on a two-company front, R.S.M. Hurd well to the fore brandishing
a shovel and calling on the troops to close with the enemy, advanced
behind the barrage. In it Major Backhouse had mixed smoke with
the H.E., to which C Company and a platoon of 4·2 mortars of
8 Middlesex and the 3-in. mortars of 7 Somerset added their fire.
Through the cornfields, a line of concrete electricity pylons led
straight to the objective. Crossing the shattered railway line, the
battalion forced its way into the small fields, gardens and orchards of
Mouen. The fire of the mediums had caught some of the enemy's
tanks in the sunken road on the fringe of the village. The Worcesters
fell on the survivors with their Piats. Deceived by the smoke as to
the direction of the attack, the enemy put down his defensive fire
not on the Worcesters but on the right flank, the direction from
which it had been intended to assault the previous night.

By eleven o'clock, thanks to the brilliant leadership of the company
and platoon commanders, notably Major A. J. Gutch, who although
wounded in the neck remained with his men until they had consolidated, the battalion had reached the main road. The sun came
out from behind the clouds. Mouen had finally fallen. Amongst
the wreckage of heavy mortars, tanks and abandoned equipment, the
remnants of the Germans, who for the most part fought it out to the

end, were rounded up. So tenaciously did they fight that the last of the survivors was not finally eliminated for several days.

Thus to the 1 Worcestershire Regiment fell the honours of 43 Division's first formal battle of the campaign. It had been a neat and orthodox operation, supported with supreme effectiveness by the Divisional artillery and executed with determination, courage and professional skill by infantry facing, almost without exception for the first time, the ordeal of fighting at close quarters with a brave and skilful enemy.

THE ODON BRIDGEHEAD

29th
June

It was now the turn of 129 Brigade to intervene. Relieved of responsibility for St. Mauvieu by the 2 Guards Brigade, it now advanced in the late morning with a squadron of the Greys under command, with the task of clearing the woods and orchards astride the River Odon between Tourville and Baron on the corps' left flank. Deployed on a two-battalion front, 5 Wiltshire on the right and 4 Somerset Light Infantry on the left, it advanced over the railway and past Colleville under heavy mortar fire until the ribbon of houses along the main road to Caen was reached. Here the battalions paused to reorganize and then thrust forward into the thick woods ahead. They reached the Odon and found it to be little more than a stream, but sufficient to hold up their carriers and anti-tank guns. On the right the Pioneers of 5 Wiltshire built a crossing of brushwood and earth. On the left 4 Somerset Light Infantry found that the stream ran through a deep gorge and except for a narrow strip of grass on either side was steep-sided, rocky and heavily wooded. This was to earn the name of "Death Valley" in the days ahead.

Having forded the Odon, 5 Wiltshire advanced up the slope into Baron and dug in around the village under ceaseless mortar fire. Lieut.-Colonel N. C. E. Kenrick, the commanding officer, was wounded. 4 Somerset Light Infantry entrenched along the road to Fontaine Etoupefour also under heavy fire. It was not till nightfall that their 6-pdrs. were able to reach them by crossing on the front of 5 Wiltshire and moving down the road which led through the forward localities. In the half-light enemy infantry crept through the corn, only to be wiped out by the defensive fire of the Divisional artillery. The reserve battalion, 4 Wilts, dug in on the rocky spur in the woods east of Tourville.

On the right, 159 Brigade and 11 Armoured Division prolonged the bridgehead.

Ahead, around Hill 112, Evrecy and Esquay, tanks of 11 Armoured Division and 4 Armoured Brigade fought a bitterly contested and decisive battle. The Argylls in Gavrus beat off attack after attack until nightfall.

By the early afternoon a serious threat to the west flank of the salient had developed. The expected counter-attack came in from the south-west, one prong astride the river and the other in the general direction of the main road from Noyers to Caen. Gavrus was cut off. The northern thrust turned northwards towards Grainville and Le Haut du Bosq. In Mondrainville and the streets of Le Valtru 15 Scottish Division fought the enemy hand to hand. Tourville and Mondrainville were in flames. In Grainville the situation was critical. Until the late evening the battle ebbed and flowed amidst the ruins.

In the open cornfields between Grainville and Cheux squadrons of tanks and batteries of self-propelled guns swirled round amidst the dust. 32 Guards Brigade moved into Cheux. Night fell with the whole west flank under heavy artillery and mortar fire and at close grips with the enemy. It began to rain.

The situation had radically changed. 1 and 2 S.S. Panzer Divisions had appeared in the Gavrus area. Prisoners had also been taken from 9 S.S. Panzer Division, the first arrival from the eastern front. Thus there were now no fewer than seven Panzer divisions, two-thirds of the enemy armour in France, on the twenty-mile front between Caumont and Caen. Clearly, therefore, all hope of an immediate break-through to Bretteville sur Laize had gone. It was time temporarily for the 8 Corps to revert to a defensive role.

Accordingly, Lieut.-General Sir Richard O'Connor, the Corps Commander, issued orders to take effect that night for 11 Armoured Division to withdraw behind the Odon into Corps reserve and for 43 Division and 159 Brigade to take over the bridgehead. Major-General Thomas therefore now ordered 214 Brigade to advance to the eastern outskirts of Mouen and hold the flank facing Caen and Carpiquet. At the same time, 130 Brigade were to move up into divisional reserve at Cheux and La Gaule.

CLIMAX OF THE ODON BATTLE

With the decision to withdraw the armour north of the Odon, the 30th congestion on the only axis, the narrow cross-country track through June Colleville, now reached its climax. The intermittent rain had in many places reduced it to a quagmire. From the early hours of the 30th June, traffic in both directions, double-banked, stood nose to tail. Had the enemy been capable of seizing local command of the air over the battlefield for even half an hour, the carnage would have been appalling. As it was, heavy and continuous mortar and artillery fire rained down on the track and the houses and orchards of Tourville, Mondrainville and Mouen. Around the bottleneck by the church in Tourville buildings were in flames. The woods along the Odon and the main road remained under concentrated bombardment all day. Casualties began to pile up. Much of the fire came from a Werfer regiment to the south of Pt. 112.

Late on the night of the 29th, a very heavy Nebelwerfer concentration caught 7 Somerset Light Infantry in the process of relief by the Welsh Guards south of Cheux. There were eighteen casualties in the battalion headquarters alone. The commanding officer and second-in-command of the Welsh Guards were killed outright. Although badly shaken by the blast, Lieut.-Colonel R. G. P. Besley led his battalion through the darkness across the open ground below Carpiquet Aerodrome into Mouen. After a night of frustration and confusion, the battalion deployed astride the main road at the east end of the village. In the dark two companies became involved in the congestion in Tourville and were not traced till daylight. Ahead, the dead straight road leading towards the chimneys of Caen lay in full view. Patrols and snipers were pushed into Verson and the battalion dug in. On their left, 1 Worcestershire Regiment prolonged the flank facing the runways and concrete defences of Carpiquet Aerodrome. 5 D.C.L.I. during the morning moved up from Le Haut du Bosq into reserve in Colleville.

With the coming of daylight, 4 Somerset Light Infantry and the 5 Wiltshire Regiment, amidst the damp woods and around Baron, strengthened their defences. 260 Field Company, under Major W. A. Vinycomb, had followed closely on the advance of 129 Brigade on the previous afternoon. By dawn, under intense mortar fire, they had constructed a crossing over the Odon with logs and stones from a nearby quarry. This was to be a black day for them. The slate below the grass in the Odon valley proved to be so hard that they could not dig for shelter. The second-in-command was killed; three officers were wounded; vehicles blew up; the bulldozer tipped over into the water. A surveyor's plan, found by chance, disclosed an overgrown metalled track running through the wood. Regardless of their heavy casualties, the Sappers pushed ahead with what was to be 129 Brigade's only supply route. The first Riegel mines came to light and were disarmed. In Baron the fire grew more and more intense as the day wore on. Single enemy tanks supported by infantry probed the front.

Apart from its great weight, the enemy bombardment was well directed. Mouen and the axis were under direct observation from the high ground south of the river and from Carpiquet Aerodrome. In addition, enemy observers still lurked in the labyrinth of trees and walled gardens and orchards of the houses along the Caen road. Major-General Thomas and the two brigadiers were driven to take shelter, at a rendezvous overlooking the river, by a number of well directed salvoes. The conference proceeded whilst his A.D.C., Lieutenant P. F. Spencer Moore, searched the houses nearby for the concealed observer.

Well hidden platforms had been constructed in the trees. For several days the Worcesters continued to search out and exterminate the occupants. A well directed concentration of 88's caught the Headquarters of 214 Brigade in the middle of an "O" Group and riddled the big command vehicle with fragments, which wounded Captain C. R. Dale, the G.S.O.3, as he sat at the set. Throughout both brigades "O" Groups proceeded in the never-ceasing din of exploding mortar bombs and shells. A continuous stream of wounded poured into the field ambulances, themselves exposed to the all-enveloping fire.

Meanwhile, 94, 112 and 179 Field Regiments hit back, firing battery, regimental and even Corps targets all day. The 4·2's of 8 Middlesex came into action side by side with the infantry. The 3-in. mortars of the forward battalions opened up. Even captured mortars were pressed into service.

In the early afternoon a critical situation developed on the front of 159 Brigade on the immediate right of 129 Brigade. The bombardment of Baron reached a crescendo. Gavrus, caught in a most accurate and intense artillery and mortar concentration, was lost. Elsewhere on this day the front held firm.

It had been the object of General Montgomery to draw the enemy's reserves into the Caen sector, to fight them there and to keep them there. With seven divisions at least on the front of the 8 Corps, he had succeeded. Three Panzer divisions, 1, 9 and 10, were at grips with 43 Division alone. Two, if not three, Panzer divisions now stood poised ready to strike a concentrated blow at the thin west flank of the narrow salient. Five miles south-west of the Division on the Caen road lay the network of roads radiating from Villers Bocage, which the enemy could not bypass and through which all his supply echelons must come. At 9 p.m. that evening on General Montgomery's orders 250 Lancasters dropped 1,253 tons of bombs on to this bottleneck, including a percentage with delayed action up to 36 hours. They completely obliterated the town and with it any hopes the enemy may have had of turning the tide.

The forward brigades of the division, now rapidly becoming inured to the incessant fire, although forced temporarily on the defensive, turned grimly to the task of hitting back so as to give the enemy no rest and to pin him to the ground.

CHAPTER III

"HILL 112"

1st–7th July ALTHOUGH the advance had been temporarily suspended on the divisional front and our positions lay in full view of enemy observers on the commanding ridge south of the Odon and from Carpiquet Aerodrome, who subjected them to incessant and effective mortar and artillery fire, the gunners and infantry hit back. On the 2nd July the Divisional artillery broke up four counter-attacks on the front of 129 Brigade. They were amongst the first to develop the elaborate counter-mortar organization which progressed rapidly and effectively as the campaign went on. Officers with "4-pen recorders" arrived in the forward area. Gradually, as retaliation became more and more effective, Nebelwerfer fire became more spasmodic. In this vigorous offensive action, the 4·2-in. mortars of 8 Middlesex played a prominent part. Artillery ammunition had to be expended with economy. Mortar ammunition, however, was plentiful. All day and all night 8 Middlesex subjected the enemy to constant fire, denying him rest and forcing him to remain below ground. In front of 214 Brigade on the left lay a wide no-man's-land. As the 3-in. mortars of the battalions were out of range of the enemy, sallies by this brigade became a nightly occurrence. Covered by a rifle company, the mortars of the brigade moved out to positions reconnoitred in daylight, put down in a few minutes an enormous weight of shell and then withdrew with all speed. When the inevitable retaliation came, it fell on empty ground.

Patrolling never ceased by day or night. On the right, patrols of 129 Brigade soon established the fact that the enemy continued to hold Hill 112 in great strength and pin-pointed his positions. A fighting patrol of 4 Somerset Light Infantry under Lieutenant Pinkham penetrated the enemy's position and captured a valuable prisoner. During the following days battalions managed to edge forward three to four hundred yards closer to the enemy. 4 Wiltshire patrols found the enclosures of Les Dauns and Château de Fontaine to be strongly held. They were accordingly attacked by Typhoons.

The unoccupied area of Verson on the main road to Caen offered 214 Brigade wider scope. Throughout the hours of daylight snipers of 7 Somerset Light Infantry turned the tables on the enemy. On 2nd July Major S. C. W. Young led a company patrol with a section of carriers, mortars and anti-tank guns into the long, straggling village. Under a protective screen of anti-tank guns and carriers, they searched the village and bombarded snipers in the church with Piats. One platoon actually closed with the enemy's main position at the far end of the village and was only extricated after a smoke-screen had been put down. Information having been obtained of great value both to the Division and 3 Canadian Division on the left, Major Young then withdrew his force with conspicuous skill. Further patrols from this battalion on succeeding days continued to probe the enemy's positions around Jumeau and Carpiquet Aerodrome. Reconnaissance by Lieutenants Tharp, Jones and Mercier—incidentally all Canadian officers—obtained information of the greatest value, expecially with regard to Tiger tanks dug in at the aerodrome. Clashes with enemy patrols in Verson became a daily event. In one of these Lieutenant Mercier was seriously wounded, to the great regret of the battalion, who had found in this young Canadian a patrol leader of genius. The carrier platoon of 4 Wiltshire Regiment under Lieutenant Smith, another Canadian officer, also took part in these skirmishes and encountered Tiger tanks in the tile-strewn streets of Verson. In order to get into closer contact with the enemy Lieut.-Colonel G. C. P. Lance, now in command of the 7 Somerset Light Infantry, Lieut.-Colonel R. G. P. Besley having been wounded, moved the battalion into Haut de Verson.

Although the constant patrolling in the eerie streets of Verson placed a heavy strain on the battalion, they found material compensations denied to the troops in the constantly mortared and gloomy woods on the Odon. Currants, raspberries, new potatoes, green peas, geese, chickens and eggs provided welcome variety to a "compo" diet. In spite of the battle, the hens continued to lay. Opinions differed as to the quality of the cider found in the farmhouses. Fresh milk was plentiful. Many of the cows still survived the constant mortaring and actually came up to the slits in Mouen and Verson to be milked.

Pathetic groups of refugees filtered through from Caen to be welcomed and helped on their way with the kindness characteristic of the West-Countryman. They were indeed fortunate to be safely out of Caen, soon to be exposed to the full blast of Bomber Command. They were usually either very old or very young, their meagre possessions strapped to their backs in blanket rolls or on to wheelbarrows. Their gratitude was touching.

Patrols had found that the little village of Fontaine Etoupefour, south of the Odon on the road to Maltot, was unoccupied. 3 Canadian Division had been ordered to capture Carpiquet Aerodrome on 4th July. To conform with this advance, Lieut.-Colonel R. W.

James, the young commanding officer of 5 D.C.L.I., when darkness fell on 3rd July, led his battalion along the railway into Verson. It was a nightmare march. The rails had been torn up; shell-holes pitted the track; telegraph poles littered the line and worst of all there was wire everywhere like tangled knitting wool. Fontaine Etoupefour was at last reached. The battalion dug in and remained so effectively concealed throughout the day that several enemy patrols walked straight into their arms.

The Canadian attack gained only partial success. The village of Carpiquet was occupied and held against counter-attack, but the airfield to the south, with its concrete defences and dug-in tanks, remained in enemy hands. It was decided, therefore, that 5 D.C.L.I.'s position was, for the moment, unduly exposed. The battalion therefore returned to the stench and flies of Colleville on the night of the 4th.

In front of Fontaine Etoupefour in the direct line of the advance now being planned lay the enclosure of Les Dauns. It was therefore essential to test the strength of the defences and to get an identification. Major D. P. Teichman's company of 4 Wiltshire Regiment was therefore ordered to attack it and bring back a prisoner. The company moved forward into the village in daylight on the 7th. It was a perfect summer's evening. Overhead, squadron after squadron of Lancasters in perfect formation, heedless of the dense curtain of flak shells, dropped their bombs and, great clouds of smoke bellowing beneath them, turned for home. The fires they lit burned right through the night. When darkness had fallen, Major Teichman and his company crawled for three hundred and fifty yards through the corn, then rushed the enclosure and got to grips with the enemy. Having killed ten and taken a prisoner, Major Teichman gave the order to withdraw. He himself stayed behind in an attempt to rescue a wounded man and was killed. This grievous loss marred the success of an operation brilliantly planned and executed with the greatest gallantry and skill.

Meanwhile, planning and reconnaissance for the next bound forward had been in progress since the 2nd July. The stage was now set for the next phase.

THE FALL OF CAEN

If the operations of July are to be seen in their true perspective, it is vital continually to keep in mind General Montgomery's overall plan. In brief, this was to contain the enemy strength and wear it down by sustained offensive action so that the First United States Army could launch the breakout under the best possible conditions. Although Cherbourg had fallen, the water obstacles and *bocage* country on the west flank, combined with the bad weather which

restricted air support, slowed down the American advance. There
were disquieting signs of enemy withdrawals west of the Orne.
2 S.S. Panzer Division had reappeared in a counter-attack against
the Americans. Congestion in the bridgehead was rapidly reaching
saturation point and the lack of airfields handicapped the R.A.F.
So far Von Rundstedt had kept his Fifteenth Army intact beyond the
Seine. The state of affairs was too good to last. At any moment
he might realize his mistake and send a stream of infantry reinforcements to fight on the decisive front in Normandy. Speed therefore
was the overriding factor.

Accordingly, 1 Corps with three divisions and two armoured
brigades assaulted Caen from the north and north-west. The attack
was preceded by the first operation ever to be launched by Bomber
Command in immediate support of the Army. At 9.50 p.m. on
7th July some 460 heavy bombers in two waves dropped 2,350 tons
of high explosive in forty minutes on a strip 4,000 yards wide and
1,500 yards deep in full view of the whole division. As the Lancasters came over, the enemy on the immediate front was forgotten.
Troops climbed out of their slits and cheered wildly. The effect
on moral was electric. The ground attack followed at first light.
Good progress was made despite the complete obliteration of the
roads, and by the evening of the 9th the whole of Caen, except the
Faubourg de Vaucelles, east of the Orne, had fallen.

Late on the 8th, 214 Brigade moved 7 Somerset Light Infantry
into Verson and 5 D.C.L.I. into Fontaine Etoupefour in the face of
heavy and continuous shell-fire which caused some loss. On
the 9th, the Canadian attack on the airfield of Carpiquet lay in full
view of their observers in the houses and from the church spire of
Fontaine Etoupefour—first, the spurting, dusty smoky barrage as it
crept across the green open space; next the Canadian infantry, small
black dots moving steadily forward. They were reminded of a carefully rehearsed tattoo, the only difference being that, when the first
attack failed, no drums rolled, no searchlights flashed, nor did the
men lying so still get up and walk away.

With Caen at last in our hands it now fell to 43 Division to continue
the offensive.

THE BATTLEFIELD
(See Sketch Map 2)

The triangle between the Orne and Odon rivers immediately
south-west of Caen was now to provide the setting of the Division's
first major battle. The move forward of 214 Brigade on the 8th
linking up with 129 Brigade had secured the wooded valley of the
Orne from Baron to Verson, and the ribbon of houses and orchards
to the immediate south, although continuously under mortar and

shell-fire, at least provided some concealment.   Four tank crossings
had been constructed by the Divisional engineers south of Mouen.
Only one satisfactory crossing for wheeled traffic over the river, the
humped-backed bridge south of Verson, was available when the
battle started, and through this bottleneck, often under heavy bombardment, all traffic had to pass until the Engineers had developed
alternatives to the east and west.   From this bridge the road wound
uphill into the age-old, winding main street of Fontaine Etoupefour.
Here stone-built cottages and great solid Norman barns clustered
around the church and the small village green.

At the outset of the battle, headquarters 214 Brigade established
itself in the farm beside the church.   For ease of access to the battlefield and observation from the church tower, whilst it existed, the
site was well chosen.   On all other grounds, including the never-
ceasing shelling to which the village was subjected, it had little to
commend it.   Three civilians alone remained, M. Geant, a tall and
most distinguished-looking old man, his wife, and the schoolmaster.
M. Geant had the Croix de Guerre and the recollection, many times
expressed, of his wounds at Verdun.   He was involved in a bitter
quarrel with the schoolmaster, and daily throughout the battle
brought his grievances to the brigadier for arbitration.   Accusation
followed accusation.   It mattered not that the village hourly was
disintegrating to rubble.   A matter of principle and the personal
reputation of M. Geant were involved.   The problem was only
finally solved by the forcible removal of the schoolmaster to Bayeux.
M. Geant remained to uphold alone, contemptuous of the bombardment, the honour of France and of an old soldier, "decoré de la croix
de guerre, cinq blessures."

Immediately south of Fontaine Etoupefour for about 2,000 yards
completely open cornfields rose very gradually up to the ridge, which
follows generally the line of the road from Pt. 112 to Eterville.
Point 112 itself is a slight rise on the top of the plateau with very
gentle slopes.   It completely commands both the valleys of the Odon
and the Orne.   It is, however, itself most conspicuous.   Close by it
on the reverse slope is a small copse, later to earn the name of
"Cornwall" wood.   Where the track from Baron crosses the main
road from Evrecy stood a crucifix, the Croix de Filandrières, and
north of it an orchard surrounded by a tree-lined hedge.   Waist-high
corn, red with poppies, stretched north-eastwards past the ruins of
Château de Fontaine to the southern fringe of the large straggling
village, much overgrown with trees and orchards, of Eterville.   A
1,000 yards to the south, also surrounded by orchards, lay the
village of Maltot in a valley close to the Orne.

Until the hangars at the south-west corner of the aerodrome at
Carpiquet were captured, the whole area lay in full enemy view.
The Canadian advance on the 9th put an end to observation from the

3. Infantry of the Division advancing on Hill 112, 10th July, 1944

4. German prisoners, all of whom had won the Iron Cross in Russia and been wounded three times, captured at Maltot 23rd July, 1944

north.   The enemy, however, still held the high ground immediately
east of the Orne.   From here his F.O.Os., both artillery and mortar,
still retained perfect observation of all movement on and over the
slopes of Hill 112 and the ridge above Maltot.

The Division was therefore about to assault a position of great
strength which gave every advantage to the defender.   Until the
high ground east of the Orne was captured the enemy could
manœuvre his Tigers and Panthers unseen south of the ridge and
observe our every movement south of the enclosures between
Fontaine Etoupefour and Baron.

"JUPITER"

This title had been given to the plan now to be put into execution.
Owing to the comparatively slow progress towards Caen it had
already been twice postponed.   In general terms, the intention was
to secure the high ground between the rivers Odon and Orne between
Pt. 112 and Maltot and exploit as far as the Orne at Feugerolles.
31 Armoured Brigade, 4 Armoured Brigade and 46 Brigade of
15 Scottish Division were placed at Major-General Thomas's disposal for the operation.   In addition to the Divisional artillery, the
guns of 11 Armoured and 15 Scottish Divisions and two Agras were
to support the attack.

As a first step 129 Brigade on the right and 130 Brigade on the left
were to capture Pt. 112 and the road leading from it to Château de
Fontaine.   129 Brigade was then to form a secure south-west
flank to the break-through to be carried out by 130 Brigade, which
was to carry forward the weight of the attack by capturing first the
village of Eterville and then Maltot and the high ground to the
south-west.   Finally, 4 Armoured Brigade and 214 Brigade in
carriers were to pass through as far as the Orne and, if the bridges
were found intact, to cross and exploit success.   In order to be able
to intervene in this final stage with the minimum delay, the Commander of 214 Brigade placed his tactical headquarters by the church
in Fontaine Etoupefour.   To 46 Brigade was given the task of left
flank protection of the attack by occupying Verson, and Eterville
when captured, and later of clearing the apex of the triangle formed
by the two rivers.

The artillery plan involved a 3,500-yard barrage, that is, a gun
every 35 yards.   This overlapped the flanks by five hundred yards.
Very heavy 4·2-inch and 3-inch mortar concentrations, provided by
8 Middlesex and all the infantry battalions in the Division, further
augmented the fire.   Support in strength by Typhoons on the roads
leading towards the battlefield had been promised.

Apart from the capture of Hill 112, the major role in the attack
was thus assigned to 130 Brigade.   Circumstances until now had, of

4

necessity, kept this brigade in reserve. They had therefore been denied the advantages of gradual initiation into the realities of battle enjoyed by the other two brigades. Their introduction was now to be both bloody and abrupt.

In the early hours of July 10th they moved into a concentration area at Mouen before advancing to their forming-up places in the fields immediately south of Fontaine Etoupefour.

HILL 112, CHÂTEAU DE FONTAINE, ETERVILLE AND MALTOT

10th July   To the accompaniment of the swish of the shells of our preliminary bombardment over their heads, the two brigades deployed in the fields along the road from Fontaine Etoupefour to Baron. 129 Brigade formed up with 5 Wiltshire on the right, 4 Somerset Light Infantry in the centre and 4 Wiltshire on the left. 130 Brigade prolonged the line to the east with 5 Dorset. Our bombardment had failed to silence the enemy batteries, who subjected the start line to vicious and concentrated fire. In the first light of dawn at 5 a.m. the three battalions, each with a squadron of tanks of 31 Tank Brigade in support, advanced through the waist-high corn. Ahead fell the closely timed artillery barrage. The tanks sprayed a continuous stream of Besa tracer. Resistance at first seemed very light.

This first appearance of easy victory, however, proved deceptive. The corn, red with poppies, concealed many carefully dug positions in which the fanatical S.S. troops held out to the last, fighting on when overrun. On the slopes of Hill 112 many close-quarter battles of the utmost ferocity developed in the corn. The three battalions of 129 Brigade reached the road from Evrecy to Eterville only to find themselves committed to infighting throughout their depth. As the forward companies started to clear their final objectives, the reserve companies fought section and individual battles in the corn. Even when wounded, the S.S. troops refused to give in. Casualties on both sides were extremely heavy. Many enemy dead lay piled up in their slits. The bitter battle continued as the sultry day wore on.

On the left 5 Dorsetshire Regiment, under Lieut.-Colonel B. A. Coad, kept level with 4 Wiltshire. The ruins of Les Dauns were soon taken. They forged ahead and by 6.15 a.m. the remains of Château de Fontaine and the farm near by had been captured. Here also snipers fought it out to the end amongst the farm buildings, hayricks, high hedges and trees.

Brigadier N. D. Leslie, the Commander of 130 Brigade, now launched 4 Dorsetshire Regiment from the outskirts of Fontaine Etoupefour against Eterville. Advancing under an artillery barrage on a two-company front with a squadron of tanks on the left flank, the troops went forward with great dash and entered the long, straggling village. Casualties at first were light. About seventy prisoners were taken and the battalion started to consolidate. A grim struggle for the far side of the village then developed. A Tiger tank was knocked out. Enemy mortar and shell fire rained on the village. The only approach for vehicles was by a sunken lane which became blocked by several of the regiment's carriers, all of which were soon in flames. Casualties streamed into the regimental aid post, which soon overflowed with wounded who could not be evacuated because no ambulance could reach the village. Two company commanders, Majors Gaye and Symonds, were wounded.

The time had now come for 7 Royal Hampshire to capture Maltot. This battalion, supported by one company of 5 Dorset and one squadron of 44 R.T.R. now advanced in the gap between Eterville and Château de Fontaine. It was 8.15 a.m. With the barrage moving ahead they reached the crest and, passing over, moved down towards the orchards and houses of Maltot in the hollow. At this stage there seems to have been some loss of direction and control. The barrage moved on leaving the infantry exposed. Intense fire from mortars and 88's came down on the advancing companies. However, the battalion entered the village and reported that it was in their hands. In actual fact, they had merely superimposed themselves on top of a very strong enemy defended locality. Many Tiger tanks lay concealed in the orchards and dug in on the outskirts. The company of 5 Dorset struggled to overcome a particularly vicious strongpoint which revealed itself as several dug-in Tiger tanks, and although it cleared the southern end of the village eventually, failed with heavy loss. Amongst the houses and orchards companies fought independent actions against the tanks. The wireless truck with the battalion headquarters received a direct hit. Communication with brigade headquarters was cut off. As the morning wore on, the situation went from bad to worse—how badly was not realized at brigade headquarters for some considerable time.

Meanwhile, Brigadier Leslie, in accordance with his original plan, had ordered 9 Cameronians to take over Eterville from 4 Dorset so that the latter could concentrate in readiness to move forward again. Despite the fact that the Cameronians started to move forward at 8 a.m., owing to the intense and persistent shelling and the fighting still going on inside the village, the handing over inevitably went slowly, and it was not until midday that the relief was complete.

By the early afternoon the critical situation of the 7 Royal Hampshire was at last realized. Brigadier Leslie therefore ordered 4 Dorset to advance on Maltot and restore the situation. The battalion moved forward with two companies deployed but with no artillery support. Lieut.-Colonel H. E. Cowie, the commanding officer, arrived at the headquarters of 7 Royal Hampshires on the outskirts of the village just behind his leading companies. Here he found that Lieut.-Colonel D. W. G. Ray had been wounded and was being evacuated. He died on his way back to England. The medical officer, Lieutenant R. R. Waddell, a Scottish International athlete, had been killed whilst treating him. Too late, Lieut.-Colonel Cowie learnt that what remained of the 7 Royal Hampshire was now being withdrawn. Meanwhile, his two leading companies, expecting to take over from the Hampshires in the village, advanced straight into the enemy position and were surrounded. The troop of S.P. guns with the battalion was quickly knocked out. Enemy tanks worked round to the rear of the remainder of the battalion, which lay out in the fields exposed to fire from every direction. The position had become desperate.

For this battle 130 Brigade had been given an additional battalion, 7 Somerset Light Infantry, on loan from 214 Brigade. During the morning this battalion had forced its way through the congested bottleneck of Fontaine Etoupefour and dug in beside 5 Dorset at Château de Fontaine. Here Lieut.-Colonel B. A. Coad had quickly grasped the seriousness of the situation in Maltot and organized the defence of the reverse slope. Later in the afternoon, 214 Brigade moved 1 Worcestershire into the cornfields to the west of the Château, where they dug in, linking up with 4 Wiltshire on the right. The early gains of the day's fighting were therefore in firm hands.

Ahead in Maltot, the battle now reached a climax. The position was hopeless. Lieut.-Colonel Cowie was therefore given permission to withdraw what remained of his battalion. Five company commanders having been lost, there was some disorganization. As the day declined, the survivors collected in the area of 5 Dorset and 7 Somerset around Château de Fontaine. Devastating mortar and shell fire now descended on this position. Lieut.-Colonel Lance, the commanding officer of 7 Somerset, and his battery commander, Major Mapp, were killed by a shell from a Nebelwerfer. Both were outstanding officers of great ability and courage. Lieut.-Colonel Lance had gained the D.S.O. in North Africa and had he lived would certainly have risen to high rank. During his brief period of command he had already become the idol of his men.

From Eterville to Château de Fontaine, the infantry and 17-pdrs. of 59 Anti-Tank Regiment stood firm. Thanks to the courage and initiative of Lieut.-Colonel B. A. Coad, Major Newton and Lieutenant Wetherbee of 5 Dorset and Majors Young and Chalmers of 7 Somerset, what was rapidly developing into a very ugly situation remained under control. Four or five Tigers were knocked out. The Divisional artillery put down a storm of defensive fire and the counter-attack when it came was beaten off with heavy enemy loss.

It is now time to return to the battle on the front of 129 Brigade on the slopes of Hill 112.

Throughout the morning, the confused fighting with the tanks, S.P. guns and infantry of 10 S.S. Panzer Division had ebbed and flowed.

On the extreme right flank, 5 Wiltshire had gained its objectives on our side of the hill. To C Company, however, had fallen a most difficult task. They had been ordered to advance to the crest and then fall back to positions prepared for them on the reverse slope. Despite mortar, shell and small-arms fire, they gained the top and got astride the road from Esquay to Caen, only to be pinned down by intense fire from dug-in Tiger tanks and machine-guns from the direction of Esquay. Ammunition began to run short. Company Sergeant Major Smith, breasting the top of the hill in his carrier with fresh supplies, was suddenly confronted by a tank shooting its way along the road towards the prostrate company. He seized the Piat from the carrier and running forward through the tall corn, fired from the hip and knocked out the tank. On the right the carrier platoon closed with the enemy. Only with great difficulty and loss was the company finally extricated.

Turning now to the left flank of the brigade, 4 Wiltshire had fought their way through the corn as far as the wood and gained their final objective. D Company, under Major R. G. Coleman, advanced a further three hundred yards into the enemy main position and became involved in a fierce battle with infantry with Spandaus sited in enfilade. Casualties began to mount. Major Coleman having been wounded, Captain R. A. Lowe eventually succeeded in withdrawing the company to the reverse slope. Digging in, clearing up the remnants of enemy resistance within the position, and retrieving their casualties crawling through the corn, the battalion consolidated the hard-won position. That no counter-attack developed on a large scale on this battalion's front was primarily due to the outstanding courage of Major J. Duke and Captain Greenshields of 224 Field Battery, who, regardless of the close-quarter fighting going on around them, brought down most effective fire on the enemy's main position, which now lay in full view. Major Duke was wounded. However, Captains Greenshield and Fletcher held on and continued to give the infantry the prompt and accurate support of the guns.

It was in the centre, however, on the front of 4 Somerset Light Infantry that the fiercest struggle had developed. Throughout the morning every weapon was in action—rifles, grenades, phosphorus bombs, light machine-guns and tanks. The 3-inch mortars fired 5,000 rounds. Two counter-attacks by infantry and armour were beaten off. Four Tigers were knocked out.

When he had secured the line of the main road, it had been the intention of Lieut.-Colonel C. G. Lipscomb, the commanding officer, to pass through and clear the plateau down to the 100-metre contour line. As the day wore on, however, it became increasingly clear that the battalion owing to its heavy casualties now lacked the strength to carry the attack beyond the crest. No less than twelve officers, including three company commanders, had been lost. In the face of the enemy's great strength and fanatical opposition around Esquay and on the southern slopes of the hill, the battalion had fought itself to a standstill.

In fact, 4 Somerset had overcome a very strong company, or probably two companies, entrenched on the top of the slope and skilfully concealed. These in turn had been covered by a screen of snipers and bazooka teams lying low in weapon slits in the corn. They had only come to life after the leading elements of the attack had passed over them and an opportune target presented itself in the form of a tank, an officer or N.C.O. At least another two companies with a mortar position in a wooded ravine held the reverse slope. A covered line of approach by a sunken track led down to Esquay.

Hill 112 constituted the very core of the enemy's defence. Amongst the Germans it was said that "He who holds Hill 112, holds Normandy." Accordingly on 4 Somerset and the other two battalions of 129 Brigade now fell the full blast of the counterstroke at the crisis of the battle in the afternoon. They stood firm and, as events proved, saved the Division from disaster.

It will be recollected that the role of 129 Brigade had been to capture Hill 112 and thus form a secure south-west flank for the attack of 130 Brigade. By the early afternoon, with the enemy still established on the hill, the position of 7 Royal Hampshire, thrust a thousand yards ahead in Maltot and isolated on all sides, had become desperate, even though the worst was not yet known. 4 Dorset were now moving forward to their assistance. However, without complete possession of Hill 112, the prospects of retaining hold of Maltot in the face of the enemy's bitter resistance were small indeed. Disquieting reports of the rapid deterioration of the situation on this flank now began to reach Major-General Thomas, who throughout the day had moved between the tactical headquarters of the two attacking brigades. By about 3 p.m. it was clear to him that only a completely fresh attack on Hill 112 could stabilize the battle. Two of the three battalions of 214 Brigade had already been committed at Château de Fontaine. There remained therefore only one battalion available which might still turn the tide. This was 5 D.C.L.I., now snatching what rest it could on the outskirts of Fontaine Etoupefour.

Neither Major-General Thomas nor the commanders of 129 and 214 Brigades, who were with him when he made this decision, were under any illusions as to the necessity for the grim task now to be given to the D.C.L.I. Neither had their commanding officer.

Lieut.-Colonel R. W. James had only been in command for the past fourteen days. Although only twenty-six years of age, he had already made the battalion very much his own. Now his superb leadership and personal example were to inspire in his officers and men courage and tenacity never surpassed throughout the long campaign.

Reconnaissance right up to the main road, regardless of enemy fire and snipers, went forward with precision. Time, as always, was short. Nevertheless, the plan for marrying the tanks with the rifle companies and the arrangements for covering fire to be given by the artillery, mortars and machine-guns were completed. Soon after 7 p.m. Lieut.-Colonel James issued his final orders in the forward positions of 4 Somerset Light Infantry.

After a heavy bombardment to soften up the defences ahead, the battalion advanced at 8.30 p.m. with two companies abreast and two following. The tanks were to follow the two assault companies. Actually, they were late in arriving and supported the two rear companies. About eight hundred yards ahead, over open ground with very little cover, lay the objective. On the right the attack went well. On the left, however, B Company, the left forward company, were caught in the open by heavy machine-gun fire. Major Vawdrey, the company commander, was killed. However, Major Roberts, commanding A Company, which was immediately following, promptly put in a brisk attack, clearing out the machine-guns and killing the crews, thus enabling what was left of B Company to get forward.

Soon the whole battalion had reached the objective. Lieutenant Carmolli, a Canadian officer, dashed ahead and pursued the defeated enemy right into the valley beyond, only eventually to be killed with most of his men. In the fast-fading light, Lieut.-Colonel James decided to consolidate on a line running halfway through the wood. Touch had been lost with C Company on the right and was not regained until late in the night. The 6-pdrs. and the troop of 17-pdrs. came up. Mortar and shell fire now rained on the position, to be followed by a strong counter-attack with tanks and infantry, which withered away in the teeth of the battalion's heavy and accurate fire. The mortar bombardment continued. Digging proved hard going owing to roots in the ground.

Darkness brought no respite. About midnight the enemy put in a particularly vicious attack with tanks and infantry. With the tanks working round the edges of the wood and the infantry trying to get round the flanks, the battle went on throughout the night. Inspired by the magnificent personal courage, endurance and irrepressible spirit of Lieut.-Colonel James, the D.C.L.I. fought on. One tank penetrated to within fifteen yards of the command post.

With the dawn a squadron of the Scots Grey arrived. Lieut.-Colonel James asked the squadron commander to push through and clear the enemy from the rear end of the wood. They succeeded, 11th July but at heavy cost. Five of their Sherman tanks were blown up in ten minutes. Every 88 and mortar the enemy had now opened up. The squadron commander therefore rightly decided that it would be better if he pulled back just over the crest in close support of the battalion rather than remain in their midst. Below the hill and beyond the wood, enemy forming up to attack were now wiped out with superb efficiency by the Divisional artillery.

The D.C.L.I., however, were falling thick and fast. It could only be a question of time now before they would be overrun by sheer weight of numbers. Lieut.-Colonel James with the remnants of his battalion fought on. When last seen, he was directing the fire of the artillery from up a tree. A machine-gun burst caught him in the neck and he fell dead and almost beheaded. With his death the position collapsed, but not for long. On orders from Lieut.-Colonel C. G. Lipscomb, whom Brigadier Mole had now placed in control of the situation on the hill, Majors Roberts and Fry formed the survivors into four platoons and reoccupied the wood. The end was not far off. After a short respite, the enemy's final overwhelming attack came in. The wood was swept by an intense storm of mortar bombs and shells. Tanks and self-propelled guns raked the wood with heavy machine-gun fire and solid shot. The battalion's anti-tank guns were silent, as most of the crews were dead or wounded. Most of the officers and N.C.Os. had fallen. Only about twenty men survived in each company. Major Roberts was now wounded, leaving Major Fry alone. The breaking-point had been reached. Since the battle started at least ten counter-attacks had been driven off. Finally Major Fry decided that the position was untenable and withdrew the survivors under cover of smoke. It had been a magnificent struggle fought against overwhelming odds.

A year later Major Roberts was able to interrogate two men of 10 S.S. Panzer Division who had actually taken part in the battle. It seems that the enemy defences consisted of a strong outpost line just forward of the main road, with the main position just on the reverse slope. Of the nine or ten tanks which attacked, only two got back undamaged. 21 Regiment (lorried infantry) and 22 Regiment (armour) were all committed. Their casualties were so appalling that when they were finally withdrawn they were reduced to five or six effective men in each company. The 9 S.S. Panzer Division, which had also arrived on the afternoon of the 10th, appears to have sustained losses on a comparable scale.

Thus, fought up to and beyond the limit of human endurance, ended the fiercest and most costly single battalion action of the campaign. It is indeed fitting that the Divisional Memorial should now stand on Hill 112 on the very spot where Lieut.-Colonel James and so many of the officers and men of the D.C.L.I., the Somerset

Light Infantry, the Wiltshire and Middlesex Regiments, the Royal Artillery and the Royal Armoured Corps gave their lives.

Similar intense enemy pressure by infantry and tanks had continued throughout the night on the remainder of the Divisional front. Here, however, the infantry had secure flanks and had had longer time to dig in. Night had fallen on the left flank on a tense and uncertain situation. Soon after dark the enemy penetrated Eterville, where hand-to-hand fighting with the Cameronians went on all night and continued till 8 a.m., when he finally withdrew leaving over a hundred dead. On the front of the 5 Dorset and 7 Somerset Light Infantry, a heavy counter-attack with tanks and infantry developed soon after dawn, only to be beaten back with huge loss by our artillery, anti-tank and mortar fire. All day Tiger tanks, lying back beyond the crest, probed the forward defences in the open cornfields. The least movement brought down intense automatic fire. The mortaring went on without respite. It must be admitted that the German armour was less vulnerable than our own. If any of our Churchills appeared on the skyline, they were invariably hit and brewed up. The crest of the hill was littered with evidence to this effect. Meanwhile, the constant stream of casualties continued to flow. It was only too clear that we had been forced on to the defensive.

In the early morning, therefore, 214 Brigade extended its front 11th from Château de Fontaine to the eastern slopes of Hill 112, the July 1 Worcestershire Regiment relieving the 4 Wiltshire. 130 Brigade being temporarily non-effective, this battalion now became the Divisional reserve in Fontaine Etoupefour with a counter-attack role in conjunction with 7 R.T.R.

Much of the credit for the successful defence of the Divisional front on this and on the following days must be given to the overwhelmingly efficient support given to the infantry by the guns and to the daring and skill of the battery commanders and F.O.Os., who regardless of risk kept the enemy's every move under observed fire.

In these conditions, comparable only in the writer's experience to the bombardment at Passchendaele, the Division was to remain in action for a further fourteen days. Officers, N.C.Os., runners and snipers, whose business it was to move around the slits, suffered particularly heavily. There were countless acts of unrecorded heroism. In particular, the regimental medical officers and chaplains set an outstanding example. The story of the Rev. I. J. Richards, C.F., is typical. Unperturbed and approachable he was always to be seen visiting the companies. It must have been a great strain to him, for he knew the men intimately and many of the casualties were his friends. He had many burials to perform and many graves to dig He never flinched from this distressing duty. Often he dug the grave himself when he was unable to get help. On one occasion whilst he was working in his cemetery, a shower of mortar bombs fell, scattering the crosses. Without any fuss, he carried on. He never spared himself danger or strain in his task of comforting or encouraging the wounded or frightened. The Rev. Prebble also, who when wounded threw himself from his stretcher to cover those who were carrying him during a particularly fierce bombardment, will not be forgotten.

Thus at heavy cost the Division became rapidly inured to battle. The S.S. troops of both 9 and 10 Panzer Divisions continued to fight with the utmost ferocity and without mercy. From now onwards they and their less ruthless comrades of the Wehrmacht were to pay the penalty on an ever-increasing scale.

"GREENLINE" AND "GOODWOOD"

On the night of 12th July extensive re-grouping took place in the Second Army. The Division now passed to 12 Corps under command of Lieut.-General Sir Neil Ritchie. 8 Corps was thus released to plan an armoured thrust on an ambitious scale from Caen south-eastwards towards Falaise. To 12 Corps was now given the task of attacking immediately south-west of Hill 112 from the Odon bridge-head down the ridge towards Evrecy, with a view to subsequent advance towards Aunay sur Odon or Thury Harcourt as the situation might indicate. It was thus hoped to draw as much of the enemy armour as possible to the west of the Orne away from our major armoured offensive now developing.

15th July The brunt of the fighting was first to fall on 15 (S.) Division, who, attacking on the immediate right on the night of the 15th, had by daylight on the 16th taken Esquay and established their forward troops on a line extending westwards towards Bougy. Movement light was used for the first time in this battle and proved an outstanding 16th July success. Counter-attacks were beaten off with the tenacity characteristic of this division. On the following night, 53 (W.) Division continued the attack towards Evrecy. This time the movement light failed owing to thick ground mist and Evrecy remained in enemy possession. A further attack on the night of 17th July was also unsuccessful. The brutal fact had to be faced that so long as the enemy's machine-guns, perfectly sited on the reverse slopes of Hill 112, could continue to rake the flank of the attack, further progress was impossible. The division's unremitting attempts to silence them by fire alone proved abortive. The position thus remained the same as at the end of the opening phase and on this line the enemy's counter-attacks were held. The success or failure of this battle is not to be measured in terms of ground won or lost, but rather in the fact that it retained three Panzer divisions west of the Orne, leaving only one Panzer division out of the line in the woods north of Falaise. 18th July

The stage was now set for the thrust by 8 Corps, consisting of Guards Armoured, 7 and 11 Armoured Divisions, the object of which was to strengthen our hold on the Caen pivot and enlarge the bridgehead over the River Orne by seizing and holding the high ground and airfield sites to the south-east. In addition, it was hoped to destroy a large proportion of the enemy's armour.

The attack went in after a heavy preliminary bombardment. Considerable progress was made, though at heavy cost. One hundred and fifty of our tanks were destroyed. Operations continued on the 19th and on the 20th, slowed down by heavy rain, which turned the battlefield into a sea of mud.

By the evening of the 20th the new line ran from St. André sur Orne to Bourgebus, Cagny and Troarn. On this line, the Canadian Corps relieved the armour. Although to some extent disappointing, the results were by no means small. 8 Corps had advanced 18,000 yards to the south, cleared the southern suburbs of Caen and secured sufficient elbow-room to mount the operations which finally drove the enemy out of the Caen–Falaise plain. 2,000 prisoners were captured. Finally, it drew the maximum amount of enemy armour on itself away from the vital west flank, where preparations for the final decisive blow were now well advanced. 20th July

The new situation offered 43 Division the opportunity to resume the advance for which it had been waiting and avenge the reverse on the left flank on the 10th. With the high ground and observation on the far side of the Orne east and south-east of Maltot secure in Canadian hands, preparations and reconnaissance for the capture of Maltot could be pushed forward with speed and a reasonable prospect of success. This was to be the task of 129 Brigade, which had been relieved on Hill 112 on the 18th by 214 Brigade and withdrawn into reserve.

THE WILTSHIRE REGIMENT AT MALTOT

The operation now about to be launched will always rank high amongst the many battle honours of the Wiltshire Regiment. To 4 and 5 Battalions and 7 Royal Tank Regiment the task was now given of recapturing Maltot and the wooded country between this village and the Orne.

On the 19th, 129 Brigade moved over to the east flank of the division and concentrated in the orchards and houses south of Bretteville sur Odon. Nearby was a stud farm, and the sight of the wounded horses, innocent victims of the fighting, was pathetic in the extreme. Despite the torrential rain, morale was high. The troops, who included a large number of young soldiers of nineteen 19th July

years of age brought forward to replace the casualties of the past fortnight, faced the coming battle with confidence.   On the far side of
the Orne, the Canadians meanwhile doggedly fought their way forward throughout the 20th and 21st July.   Full advantage was taken
of this respite to plan the attack in the greatest detail.   Most useful
air photographs were provided and studied by platoons.   A squadron
of Churchill tanks of 7 Royal Tank Regiment had concentrated with
each of the two assaulting battalions, and together the infantry and
the armour, on sand models, maps and where possible in view of the
ground, worked out in detail the part each was to play.   Lieut.-
Colonels Pearson and Luce and their officers, including those of the
artillery and tanks supporting the operation, reconnoitred forward
with the greatest boldness.

The attack was to be carried out on the right by 5 Wiltshire
Regiment with the village of Maltot as its objective.   4 Wiltshire
on the left were to capture the spur and woods to the east of the
village.   4 Somerset Light Infantry constituted the reserve.   The
Divisional artillery, augmented by two Agra's and 8 Middlesex,
provided a closely knit programme of smoke and timed concentrations.

22nd   Ahead the open rolling cornfields fell away steeply towards the
July   water meadows and thick hedges beside the Orne.   At 5.30 p.m.
on the 22nd, the two battalions, each on a two-company front, moved
forward from the start line astride the road from Caen to Maltot.
The sun was shining.   As they surged forward, widely deployed
but steadily moving on, they made an impressive sight, tanks
and infantry side by side.   The men's faces were daubed with
green camouflage cream and their helmets thickly garnished with
foliage and wheat.   Enemy retaliation was prompt and heavy.
Shells and mortar bombs were soon falling amongst the advancing
troops.

It has been said of this battle that it was a set piece in which all the
precepts of the training manuals were fulfilled.   Be that as it may,
the fact remains that it was one in which the individual soldier
throughout proved his superiority over the enemy.

On the right, 5 Wiltshire soon reached the outskirts of Maltot and
closed with the enemy entrenched in the orchards.   The troops
blasted their way ahead with grenades and, aided by the tanks, after
a prolonged struggle overcame the enemy.   Major F. S. Rimmington
was wounded.   Ahead, on the slopes of Hill 112, seven dug-in Tiger
tanks now came to life.   In the teeth of their fire, the troops consolidated under Captain F. I. C. Herridge.   He too was wounded.
Meanwhile, Captain Lincoln with B Company had burst into the
village.   Close-quarter fighting now ensued amongst the houses and
orchards.   The Germans, although they fought bravely, were no
match for the Wiltshiremen with the bayonet and were overwhelmed.

Captain Lincoln consolidated on the far side of the village. The reserve companies now came up. When darkness fell Maltot, despite the hail of mortar bombs and shells, was firmly in our hands never to be lost again.

On the left 4 Wiltshire met equally bitter resistance. In the woods by the Orne, their left forward company soon found itself involved in a grim struggle. A series of section and platoon battles developed in which fighting spirit and skill of the highest order were shown by all ranks, notably Lieutenant Pope. Eventually, the enemy were overwhelmed and Major Jeans was able to lead his company to its final objective. On their right in the waist-high corn the tank squadron commander, Major R. Joscelyn, on foot, saw that A Company was in difficulties. He brought up his tanks and enabled the infantry once more to spring forward and gain their final objective.

Major T. R. M. Ottowell, commanding B Company, now made for the spur east of the village, only to find his advance checked by heavy and concentrated fire from a château, within which it soon became apparent that the enemy had rallied for a last stand. After a struggle, he by-passed it and reached his objective. Whilst digging-in was going on, a German medical orderly emerged from the château bearing a white flag and requested permission to evacuate a large number of wounded under a flag of truce. This was refused, unless the whole garrison surrendered. Instead, No. 18 Platoon assaulted the château. Led by Lieutenant J. H. Rutherford and Sergeant F. A. Eyer and supported by point-blank fire from the tanks, the platoon penetrated the hall, but failed to get up the stairs. Desperate fighting ensued in the pitch darkness, in which Lieutenant Rutherford was wounded. Not until dawn did the garrison of the château finally surrender.

As night fell, a procession of over three hundred prisoners of the Wehrmacht streamed back. Lieut.-Colonels Pearson and Luce, both of whom had been throughout in the forefront of the battle, were able to report complete success. Despite the intense shelling and mortaring to which they were now subjected and the deadly accurate fire from the dug-in tanks overlooking the village, the two battalions held on to their hard-won gains.

When the dawn came, Maltot presented an appalling spectacle: 23rd the streets and fields were still strewn with the dead of the Dorsets July and Hampshires who had fallen on July 10th, and lay in heaps around slit trenches with hardly more than the turf removed; the houses were shattered; the roads cratered and full of debris; everywhere the sickly smell of death and destruction hung heavily over the ruins. During the day further Germans came to light. Eventually the total rose to over four hundred belonging to a Wehrmacht division which had only recently come into the line.

The victory at Maltot of the Wiltshire Regiment and the 7 Royal Tank Regiment, coming as it did at the end of a month's fighting of severity seldom ever exceeded anywhere throughout the campaign, provided a fitting climax to the operations of the Division on the Orne.

Great events were now pending. The clear-sightedness and inflexible will of the Commander-in-Chief and the tenacity of his troops were now at last to reap their reward.

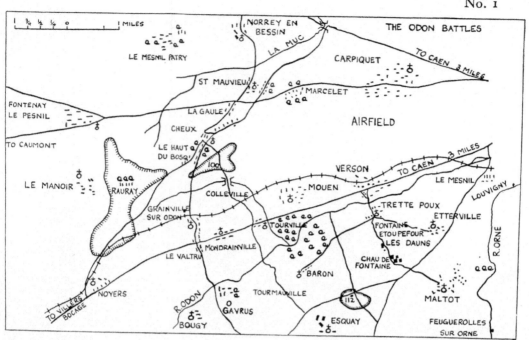

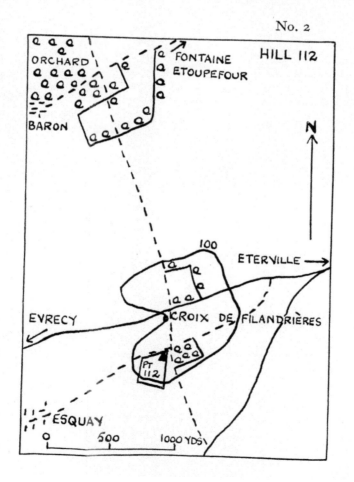

CHAPTER IV

THE ADVANCE TO MONT PINCON

(See Sketch Maps 3, 4 and 5)

BRIEF RESPITE

IT was without regret that the Division handed over the battle-scarred slopes of Hill 112 and the stinking ruins of Maltot to 53 (Welsh) Division on the 25th July and the night of the 25th/26th. All arms had shared to some degree the danger and foul conditions. No part of the area had been free from shell-fire and the atmosphere of unrelieved strain. The Division had fought and held its own in battle with the toughest troops of the German army, whose morale as yet remained unshaken. It had learnt therefore to welcome future opposition when light with enthusiasm and when severe how to overcome it with efficiency and without illusions.

As Major-General Thomas, standing on the track through the yellow corn of the fields north of Mouen, watched the infantry marching back to the rest area around Duoy Ste. Marguerite, four miles south-east of Bayeux, he could reflect with satisfaction that the long hours of training and meticulous preparation in Kent had already met with their reward. A period of a week or ten days in reserve now apparently lay ahead. Losses amongst the most important leaders, such as lieut.-colonels and company commanders, had indeed been grievous. For instance, 7 Royal Hampshire had lost two commanding officers, Lieut.-Colonels D. W. G. Ray and J. R. C. Mallock; 7 Somerset Light Infantry had had two commanding officers killed, Lieut.-Colonels Lance and Bruford, and one wounded; Lieut.-Colonels Atherton and James of 5 D.C.L.I. had been killed; and 179 Field Regiment had lost Lieut.-Colonel Pethick wounded and Lieut.-Colonel Blacker killed. Casualties amongst company commanders had been equally heavy; however, many, thanks to their own high sense of loyalty and enthusiasm and the unremitting efforts of the commander and his staff, were soon to return. All felt it their first duty to come back to the Division at the earliest possible moment after their wounds had healed.

The rest area had been so rapidly overrun on D-Day that much of the corn stood undamaged and ripening in the fields. The Norman countryside had an English air. The churches, village greens and big solid farms had their counterparts across the Channel in the West Country. Even the dour Norman peasants seemed familiar. It was pleasant to bivouac in the shade of the apple-trees away from the din of the battlefield and the all-pervading dust and traffic of the bridgehead, or to visit the mobile bath unit established by the R.A.O.C. on the River Seulles and enjoy the luxury of a bath and clean underwear. There was little to buy except Camembert cheeses, many of which found their way, until the postal authorities rebelled, into the home-going mail. One even is reputed to have travelled as far as a lance-corporal in the A.T.S. at Cairo and to have been delivered somewhat the worse for wear. Bayeux, choked with the apparently necessary but glamourless military population which makes up the tail of an army, offered few attractions. The mobile cinema gave continuous performances of "Four Jills in a Jeep." Wherein the charm of this particular film lay has never been discovered. Nevertheless many members of the Division were to see it at least four times during the coming months. The comments of soldiers brought out of battle, given a bath and a change of underwear, shown this particular film, given cigarettes and a packet of sweets, and then pushed back into battle again with all speed, would be out of place in a history such as this. The performances of George Formby and his wife Beryl came into a different category. These two artistes had been the first to arrive in the bridgehead, and all ranks will remember with gratitude their sparkling performances at this time under very trying conditions in the open and within range of the enemy's guns.

For the administrative staffs, the services and the quartermasters and transport officers, this brief respite provided the opportunity to re-equip their units. So untiring and successful were their efforts that when unexpected orders to move reached units during the night of 28th/29th July, the Division was able to march in an entirely new direction on the following day reinforced to full strength and once more ready for battle. At a corps conference at 10 p.m. on the 28th, Major-General Thomas had in fact been ordered to break out on an entirely new front at first light on 30th, that is in thirty-six hours' time.

29th July   Whilst the Division had been resting and getting ready for action once again, General Montgomery had reached a decision and issued orders which were to result in the complete destruction of the German army and the rapid pursuit of the remnants from the whole of France.

THE LAUNCHING OF THE BREAKOUT
(See Sketch Map 3)

The First U.S. Army thrust due south from St. Lo had started on 25th July and by 27th July was making excellent progress.

East of Noyers, astride the River Orne, there were no less than six Panzer and S.S. divisions. At the western end of the British front, however, opposite Caumont there was no German armour. The situation here thus appeared favourable for delivering a very heavy blow in a southerly direction so as to get behind the German forces, which had been swung back to face west by the American break-through, and knock them completely off their balance.

On 27th July, therefore, General Montgomery ordered Second Army to re-group and strike south from Caumont on the 30th in the general direction of Mont Pincon, and thus smash the hinge of the main German defences.

To this end, 8 and 30 Corps concentrated on the 28th and 29th in the area of Caumont. On the right 8 Corps was to wheel by way of Le Beny Bocage to occupy the area Vire–Tinchebray–Condé. On the left, 30 Corps was to wheel south-eastwards up to the line Villers Bocage–Aunay sur Odon.

During the night of the 28th July orders were sent out from Divisional headquarters for an "O" Group at 8 a.m. the following morning. When this assembled, Major-General Thomas revealed that the Division had now joined 30 Corps, which included in ad-dition 7 Armoured Division, 50 (N.) Infantry Division, 56 Infantry Brigade, and 8 Armoured Brigade. The battle was to open with an assault at first light on the morrow on the front of three divisions, the 15th (S.) on the right, the 43rd in centre and the 50th on the left.

The Division's first task was to punch a hole in the enemy position at Bricquessard and north of Cahagnes. It was then to advance via the important cross-roads at St. Pierre du Fresne to seize the high ground south and south-west of Jurques. At the same time it had been given the duty of protecting the east flank of the Corps by seizing and holding the Robin feature. Finally, it was to swing east and capture the high ground at Ondefontaine as a base for further deep reconnaissance in an easterly and south-easterly direction. A glance at sketch map 3, on which the Division's tasks are marked in simple form, will save tiresome reference to the map and give some idea of the magnitude of the operation.

As a first step, 130 Brigade, augmented by 4 Somerset Light Infantry, was to pierce the enemy's defences between Bricquessard and Caumont. 214 Brigade was then to pass through and advance four miles to St. Pierre du Fresne. Finally 129 Brigade was to continue the advance.

This was an historic moment in the history of the Division, for now, for the first time, it had been joined by the 8 Armoured Brigade under Brigadier G. E. Prior-Palmer. Thus began a partnership which was to be renewed many times before the war ended. Their signs, the "Fox's Mask" and the "Wyvern," were to go forward side by side over many a battlefield up to and beyond the Rhine. The three regiments, 4/7 Dragoon Guards, the 13/18 Hussars and the Sher-wood Rangers, already had behind them a long and brilliant record

5

of gallantry and success both in this and previous wars. This they were now about to augment. Their light-hearted courage and dash were to win immediately the complete confidence of the whole Division. For the fighting ahead their Sherman tanks were not the ideal fighting vehicle. However, so high was the morale of the brigade that if they had been mounted on Fordson tractors, their troop leaders would have closed with the enemy just the same.

Whilst orders were being given out, the infantry, moving on by-roads, were already on the march. It was a lovely day with sunshine, clouds and high wind. On either side stretched unspoiled orchards and high hedges. The Division was at last entering the real *bocage* country. 130 Brigade was able to relieve the 46 Brigade in the line at Livry undisturbed by the enemy. The remainder of the Division moved into bivouac north-east of Caumont.

The majority of the commanders left Divisional headquarters immediately to reconnoitre the new sector. Compared with the country around Caen, the change of scene was striking. On the right, Caumont stood on a high ridge running east and west. Below this lay a wide no-man's-land. Ahead, shimmering in the heat, stretched close and intricate country. 326 German Infantry Division, holding a nine-mile front with two of its three infantry regiments fully committed, showed no disposition to reveal itself. In the valley below an occasional gleam from the little brook of Bricquessard running across the front, caught the eye. Only one road could be seen—the main road from Caumont to Cahagnes as it wound its way into the valley.

The line had been static since the middle of June. Various British and American divisions had laid minefields on an extensive scale, apparently indescriminately. Corps H.Q. at any rate were unable to produce a trace, and the lack of this vital information was to prove a severe handicap to the Division in the opening phase of the battle.

The fields were small, fenced by banks and stout hedges often with a line of tall, close-growing trees in addition. The country was intersected with narrow, sunken lanes, some as deep as twenty feet, which linked together the many small villages and farms. These lanes were too narrow for our vehicles and a very serious obstacle to cross-country movement. In addition they provided the enemy with ready-made trenches.

Viewpoints were many, but owing to the enclosed nature of the country, detailed observation of ground ahead was severely limited. Only too frequently it was possible to see as far as the next hedgerow and no farther.

In the intricate nature of the country ahead lies the explanation of the innumerable engagements of varying sizes in which the Division was now to be involved. Great difficulty was to be experienced in locating and forming an exact estimate of the opposition encountered. Deployment off the roads was to prove slow and difficult. Troops in rear were to find themselves engaged in battles with obstinate pockets of resistance which had completely escaped the notice of those ahead.

The timings to which all divisions were at first expected to adhere would, no doubt, have been feasible in the Western Desert. In the *bocage* they proved to be optimistic to the point of fatuity. Fortunately, 43 Division had trained in the thickets and sunken lanes of Stone Street in Kent. For this reason it was to find itself well prepared to deal with problems which were neither entirely novel nor incapable of solution by flexible minds.

BRICQUESSARD

The battle opened at 0800 hours with an unpropitious start. On the left, 4 Somerset Light Infantry, advancing through the closely wooded country astride the narrow country lane leading to the village of Bricquessard, soon ran into trouble. The tanks quickly discovered that the road was mined, and the two leading companies, who were soon suffering numerous casualties from Schuh mines scattered in the fields, pushed ahead with difficulty in the face of heavy machine-gun fire. Providentially one of our bombers, flying at a very low altitude, dropped several bombs on their objective, the northern edge of the village. Majors Mallalieu and Braithwaite, the company commanders of C and D Companies, were quick to take advantage of this unexpected support and get forward. Major Braithwaite, despite a serious wound in his foot from a Schuh mine, gallantly remained long enough in command to see his company on the objective. Meanwhile Sergeant Hayman and a party of Pioneers lifted some fifty Teller mines under small-arms fire and enabled the tanks of the Sherwood Rangers to get through.

It was now mid-day. B Company, under Major Thomas, now passed through and seized the bridge across the stream. In a salient thrust forward 1,000 yards in close country the battalion remained for the rest of the day and the following night. Its commanding officer, Lieut.-Colonel Lipscomb, had fulfilled his contract in the face of costly and exasperating difficulties.

The 5 Dorset, attacking on the right, ran into trouble from the start. The left company soon found itself halted on the main road by heavy shelling and machine-gun fire. In the centre a little progress was made. On the right, the leading troops were soon entangled in a dense minefield some three hundred yards from the start line and pinned to the ground. By midday it had become apparent that owing to the very close nature of the country, the clearing would have to be done at night.

30th July

This delay was made all the more galling by the fact that 15 Scottish Division, attacking on the immediate right due south from Caumont, had made a spectacular advance nearly six miles deep and by nightfall had reached St. Martin des Besaces and Pt. 309, or Quarry Hill, at the western end of the Bois du Homme.

Later in the evening Brigadier Leslie therefore moved 7 Royal Hampshire under Lieut.-Colonel D. E. B. Talbot round the right flank of the Dorsets towards the spur immediately north of Cahagnes.

On the east flank 50 Division struggled with obstinate resistance. Darkness slowed down further the tedious task of mine clearance and mopping up. The Divisional engineers had however cleared the main road as far as the Cahagnes feature by the early morning. As dawn broke, the enemy supported by intense mortar fire counter-attacked 7 Royal Hampshire and got to close quarters, only to be beaten off with heavy loss. Lance Corporal Bryant's action typifies the fierce character of the struggle and the fighting spirit of the battalion. In the mêlée, the enemy flung a stick grenade into the slit trench held by his section. Lance Corporal Bryant promptly flung it back and thus saved not only the lives of his men but also killed and wounded a group of the enemy with their own grenade. By the afternoon the smoking ruins of the village had passed into our

31st hands. So far over 180 prisoners had been taken. The enemy had
July put up a determined resistance. Over a hundred dead lay in the well concealed and strongly fortified defences in front of Cahagnes.

ST. PIERRE DU FRESNE AND THE BOIS DU HOMME

For over twenty-four hours 214 Brigade, grouped with 4/7 Dragoon Guards, 12 K.R.R.C., 333 Anti-tank Battery, and two Corps towed anti-tank batteries, had been waiting to advance in the orchards east of Caumont. The time had now come to exploit the "quick left" technique which had so frequently been practised. The prolonged bombardment and dense traffic had raised a cloud of fine dust which, mingling with the smoke put down by the Divisional artillery on the left flank, enveloped the battlefield in a thick fog through which the declining sun shone deep red. The guns and 8 Middlesex now opened up on to the open flank of the division at Amaye sur Seulles, which still resisted all 50 Division's efforts to break in. At 5.30 p.m. the brigade, led by 1 Worcestershire riding on the tanks of B Squadron of 4/7 Dragoon Guards, headed for Caumont and swung left down the main road to Cahagnes. A minor battle with infantry still holding out here caused a little delay, but the smoking ruins of the village were soon reached and passed. A quarter of a mile beyond, A Company, the leading company under Captain Marshall, struck a party of the enemy holding out in some farm buildings. These they hotly engaged. Night was coming on,

5. The Chaplains of the Division with the Chaplain General, 28th July, 1944. Within the next ten days, three Chaplains, with jackets on in the back row, were killed

6. Troops of 7 Royal Hampshire Regiment in a German slit trench at Cahagnes, 31st July, 1944

7. Troops of 1 Worcestershire Regiment searching for snipers south of Cahagnes

8. The 5 Wiltshire Regiment advancing to the Bois du Homme

and if the advance of 7 Somerset Light Infantry, who were following, was not to be held up, time was vital.   B Company of the Worcestershire's, under Major Grubb, therefore swung round the right flank and advanced to its objective about a mile south of Cahagnes.   Before the light finally faded the battalion had curled up into a tight locality and pushed out patrols, which almost immediately met strong resistance from the left flank.   Late in the night the 12 K.R.R.C. when moved out to guard this flank were to experience considerable trouble.   1 Worcestershire, whose captures included two infantry guns, rapidly consolidated.

Meanwhile, 7 Somerset Light Infantry had reached Cahagnes, dismounted and moved forward on foot through the Worcestershires, taking the road towards their objective, the village of St. Pierre du Fresne two miles ahead.   It was now total night, but well lit by a half-moon.   Every building and orchard had to be searched.   An enemy half-track vehicle drove straight into their midst, only to be set on fire by a Piat bomb fired by Private Jones.   Major J. K. Whitehead, the leading company commander, pushed on boldly and at length reached the small village of St. Pierre du Fresne.   This comprised a small stone church and some immensely strong farm buildings.   These he immediately consolidated.   In the dark, the 1st sounds of enemy tank movement nearby could be heard.   Soon after Aug. dawn one of his patrols, reconnoitring towards the stream several hundred yards ahead, reported a Tiger tank about 300 yards away. This he decided to stalk.   Suddenly in the lifting mist he saw several hundreds of enemy infantry coming towards him down the far hillside only 150 yards away.   Leaving Lieutenant Pizzey to deal with the tank, he called down the fire of all three regiments of the Divisional artillery, who at once responded with telling effect.   However, two tanks, both of them monster Ferdinand S.P. guns supported by crawling infantry, had managed to get up along a sunken road very close to his forward platoons.   Private Jones stalked one of them from behind and put four Piat bombs into its rear from close range. Close-quarter fighting with the enemy's infantry, who were bravely and resolutely led, now ensued in which the whole company, including the headquarters, joined.   The first tank, covered by the second, was now right in the middle of the company, firing viciously. Suddenly the crew abandoned it, leaving it still grinding forward in gear.   The other tank, blinded by phosphorus grenades bouncing on its roof, withdrew.   The battle was over and not too soon, for the company had exhausted their whole stock of grenades and smoke bombs.   In this brisk battle over twenty of the enemy were killed and forty taken prisoner.   A Company lost four killed and seven wounded.   Whilst it was going on, Private Catt, Major Whitehead's batman, had calmly continued to cook his officer's breakfast.   Never was a meal better earned or more thankfully enjoyed.

The main attack appears to have been made from two directions as the left rear company of the battalion also beat off a determined attack at this time. Altogether about three companies and seven enemy tanks were involved. Some of the prisoners came from 21 Panzer Division, the first of the enemy's armoured divisions to arrive from the Caen area. It was soon to be followed by the other two Panzer divisions who had fought so obstinately around Hill 112, the 9th and 10th.

In actual fact, 214 Brigade had superimposed itself on the rear elements of the enemy's defences. The wasp, though crushed, could still sting. A large enemy locality south of Cahagnes was not finally cleared up until systematically attacked by the D.C.L.I. twenty-four hours later. Later in the morning of the 1st August, Colonel Taistler, the German regimental commander, with his adjutant and 58 other ranks, justifiably decided that his three battalions having been completely wiped out, further resistance was futile. He therefore surrendered to 1 Worcestershire Regiment. He was correctly received and despatched with his batman and kit to the rear. It may be said that in the experience of the Division, the Regular officers and men of the Wehrmacht obediently did their duty according to their lights and never sank to the level of the S.S. divisions. Had their ranks not been diluted by Ukrainians and other races, considered presumably for geographical reasons to be Europeans, their resistance would have been even more difficult to overcome.

With 214 Brigade now holding a firm base with a strong anti-tank screen disposed against possible counter-attack from the south-east, it now fell to 129 Brigade to continue the advance to the Bois du Homme. Lieut.-Colonel J. H. C. Pearson had arrived ahead of his battalion at St. Pierre du Fresne during the counter-attack. As soon as 7 Somerset Light Infantry had beaten it off, he led forward 5 Wiltshire due south towards the thickly wooded hill of the Bois du Homme on which stood his objective, Pt. 361. Their first capture was a German Red Cross vehicle loaded with bread and loot. Next they clashed with a scout car of 9 S.S. Panzer Division and then a Ferdinand, which B Company knocked out with a Piat. Another was disposed of in the village of Le Parquet. The battalion now deployed for the assault on the hill. A number of tracks led up through the wooded slopes. As they neared the top the trees thinned out, and the leading companies were soon on top and digging in. At this moment three Ferdinand tanks and an armoured car drove straight in amongst them. One became bogged and was immediately destroyed. The remaining two smashed their way through C Company, shooting at the men in the narrow slit trenches. Of these, the first ditched itself and was soon put out of action. The remaining tank swung back and after running over some of

A Company's men was knocked out by a S.P. gun which was just emerging into the clearing below the escarpment. 4 Wiltshire moved up on the right flank and took some prisoners.

All night long the work of preparing the position against further counter-attack went on. Anti-tank guns had to be manhandled all the way up the hill, a climb of well over 200 feet. Forty men were required for each gun. To make matters worse a thunderstorm accompanied by torrential rain burst during the night. Trenches became full of water; the tracks up the hill, already almost impassable by reason of fallen trees and branches, became a sea of mud.

Further advance on this brigade front therefore offered no prospect of success.

On the right of the Division, 11 Armoured Division had made good progress and by nightfall established itself on the high ground east of Le Beny Bocage five miles to the south. 9 and 10 S.S. Panzer Divisions were now arriving fast on the heels of 21 Panzer Division. It might therefore be expected that resistance would stiffen. This proved to be the case. On the left four miles to the north-east, the enemy still held out in Amaye sur Seulles, but there were signs of weakening despite the fact that 7 Armoured Division's attempts to break out in the direction of Aunay in the afternoon had come to naught.

L'OISONNIERE, JURQUES AND LE MESNIL AUZOUF

(*See Sketch Map* 5)

129 Brigade being committed on the right to all the difficulties of mountain warfare on the slopes of Pt. 361, an advance in the direction of Jurques and Ondefontaine alone offered any prospect of rapid progress. 130 Brigade, therefore, in spite of the fact that Phase 3 of the operation as originally planned had not been completed by the capture of Pt. 301 and Le Mesnil Auzouf, was ordered to continue to advance in the direction of Ondefontaine. 2nd Aug.

Starting at 2 a.m. with 4 Dorset leading, Jurques was entered soon after first light. The village was in ruins, the roads cratered and blocked with debris and under shell-fire. In fact, the enemy were holding the commanding ridge about three quarters of a mile to the south in strength and had excellent observation over the road which the brigade now took to La Bigne and l'Oisonniere. It proved therefore a day of comparatively slow progress in the face of heavy mortar and machine-gun fire. However, La Bigne was captured during the afternoon. Patrols now reported that the dense wood which lies between these villages and Ondefontaine was strongly held. The brigade commander therefore decided to pass through 5 Dorset the following morning.

7 Royal Hampshire, who had taken over Jurques during the morning, spent a particularly unpleasant day under heavy shell-fire from 88's to their immediate front. The Tiger tanks were clearly visible on the high ground which dominated the road running uphill due south from the village. All efforts to advance south met obstinate resistance. Typhoons directed against them had no success. Night fell with an obscure situation south of Jurques. A night advance by C and D Companies under Majors L. S. Nayler and J. L. Braithwaite with the object of seizing the Pt. 321 feature and clearing it to the main road, struck heavy machine-gun and tank opposition and was forced to halt short of its objective. Wireless contact was lost. At dawn A Company, under Major C. G. T. Viner, made two attempts to work round the right flank only to be repulsed by heavy fire. The fact had to be faced that the Division was once more up against determined and well-organized opposition on ground which gave every advantage to the enemy.

3rd Aug. Before dawn 5 Dorset, which had concentrated north of La Bigne overnight, endeavoured to resume the advance through the thick woods on the road to Ondefontaine. They soon found themselves faced with fierce resistance from well concealed machine-guns and tanks, and the attack had to be cancelled.

Meanwhile, during the night 214 Brigade, with 5 D.C.L.I. leading, had come forward with orders to clear away the opposition facing 7 Royal Hampshire on the ridge ahead, and exploit in the general direction of Mont Pincon. The operations now to take place bear that peculiar atmosphere of light-heartedness and gallantry which throughout the campaign characterized this remarkable battalion. The commanding officer, Lieut.-Colonel George Taylor, had arrived in Jurques the previous evening. All efforts on his part to ascertain the exact situation in front of the village having proved abortive, he decided to clear the air himself. Captain G. L. Holland and the carrier platoon were therefore ordered to go forward independently ahead of the battalion in the dark, and in the role of advanced guard mobile troops secure the high ground at Pt. 301 and contain the enemy until such time as the rest of the battalion could arrive.

By midnight the platoon had reached Jurques, and making its way with difficulty by the light of the moon through the rubble and craters, at length found the road leading due south. Once clear of the town, the platoon was able to go forward with the proper spacing between carriers. As the leading carrier reached the bridge over the stream at the foot of the hill a Spandau opened up from the hill ahead. The platoon now started its long uphill climb. It was a very long, steep hill with a slight bend to the left about halfway up. Here the platoon halted to listen. All seemed quiet in front. They had been ordered to seize the ridge; so on they went. It was now just after midnight. The leading carrier reached the crest of the hill. Suddenly the enemy opened up. Two or three Spandaus blazed straight down the road; several Tiger tanks started their engines; an 88 fired; flares went up. The leading carrier backed and started for cover, only to be knocked out by a second shot from the 88. By now the second and third carriers had managed to slew round and also make for cover. Unfortunately the second carrier was grenaded from the steep banks on the left of the road and knocked out, the driver and gunner being wounded.

Meanwhile the section behind had quickly dismounted and returned the enemy's fire with their Brens. This enabled Captain Holland to withdraw the platoon to a defensive position half way up the hill. This he held until relieved by C Company at dawn. At the cost of three men wounded and two carriers he had confirmed that the enemy held the ridge in strength with a combined force of infantry and Tiger tanks. Never was an obscure situation more dramatically clarified.

The rest of the battalion and B Squadron 4/7 Dragoon Guards under Major Jenkins, after a difficult night march, reached Jurques as dawn broke. Ahead in the thick mist could be heard the staccato bark of tank heavy machine-guns and the answering beat of C Company and the carrier platoon's Brens. Brigadier Essame, the brigade commander, now arrived in Jurques. He was anxious to reap full advantage from the mist and to capture the ridge ahead with all speed, not only in the interests of his own brigade but also to help 130 Brigade's attack now going in on his left. He therefore ordered Lieut.-Colonel Taylor to clear the high ground with the minimum delay.

Accordingly, at 8.15 a.m., supported by the whole Divisional artillery and the battalion's mortars, 5 D.C.L.I. went forward and at first swept everything before them. Captain Ruck-Keene, the commander of C Company, using fire and movement skilfully, worked round the right flank, thus missing the enemy's heavy defensive fire. Breasting the top of the hill, they soon found themselves amongst the enemy's infantry. Suddenly, cleverly concealed tanks started to fire on them. A struggle with Piat's now developed in which Lieutenant F. W. Durden showed conspicuous courage. Major John Fry of D Company now arrived and continued the fight against the tanks amongst the trees on the left of the road.

B Squadron of the 4/7 Dragoon Guards tried to deploy, but found that the country on either side of the road was covered with rocks and ravines. They therefore advanced straight up the road until the leading tank was knocked out by a German tank, which was waiting for them on the crest. Eventually, although they were unable to get on themselves, they managed to get the infantry on to the objective and to knock out a Panther.

The enemy's mortar fire now increased to a fantastic intensity. Not for the first time, the battalion found itself involved in a hand-to-hand battle with Tiger tanks manned by desperate men, with incidentally all the advantages of concealment on the densely wooded hill to the left of the road. The battle continued as the day wore on. The fire of 25-pdrs. was tried, but proved ineffective. An attempt to use medium artillery caused some disorganization. By the afternoon it had become apparent that further progress on the front of the D.C.L.I. was unlikely to take place on this day.

The D.C.L.I. had fought and continued to fight a gallant battle. Lieut.-Colonel Taylor had every reason to be proud of his command. In fact, the battalion was opposed by eight to ten tanks, mixed Tigers and Panthers of 10 S.S. Division, which had come up from the Esquay area. The battle is remarkable rather for the magnificent spirit in which it was conducted than for any minor tactical lessons to be gained. It should be regarded as an advanced guard action, designed to clear the air. This it certainly did most effectively.

The brigade commander in Jurques therefore decided to outflank the position by moving 1 Worcestershire through the tangled and thickly wooded country on the right flank. Reconnaissance had disclosed that it was penetrable only by men on foot. Although five hours of daylight still remained, it was not until after dark that Major Grubb and B Company, skilfully working round the flank of the fighting, finally gained the crest. The rest of the battalion followed and by dawn were established on the hill top, after a baffling night advance through the forest. Not till several hours later were their jeeps and carriers able to find a way round the steep slopes. When the mist cleared the open country ahead lay in full view. A Company advanced in time to see the enemy rapidly falling back on Mont Pincon. A patrol led by Regimental Sergeant Major Hurd entered Bremoy in the valley below before the enemy had withdrawn, and sped them on their way.

The first news, however, of the dramatic change in the situation came from a patrol of 5 D.C.L.I. On the previous afternoon, Lieut.-Colonel Taylor, baffled in his attempts to smash through astride the road, had turned his attention to the tangled mass of gullies and ferns on his right flank. One of his patrols, consisting of Sergeant Long and Privates Chipman and Nichols, crawled ahead in bright sunlight through the ferns and, dodging the enemy, eventually reached a house in the rear of their position. Climbing into the attic, they started to snipe the German mortar men about two hundred yards away. Three were killed and the rest dispersed. As night was falling Sergeant Long decided to go back and fetch a wireless set. Leaving his two companions in the attic, he made his way to battalion headquarters, collected a 38 set and, once more working his way through the enemy position, regained the house. When dawn broke, the patrol proceeded at leisure to pick off the bewildered Germans from the rear one by one. It is amazing that they were not spotted. Eventually the German rear party with three of their wounded departed in a truck at full speed down the hill. All this had been reported on the 38 set, which was working perfectly, and very quickly A Company arrived on top of the hill, close on the enemy's heels. Other patrols working round the left flank had got into contact with a brave Frenchman, M. Solier, in whose company Lieutenant Stock, the signals officer, was despatched in the direction of Le Mesnil Auzouf to find out what he could. Lieutenant Stock's subsequent adventures behind the German lines were to prove both dramatic and amusing.

4th Aug.

214 Brigade quickly seized the opportunity to advance. The D.C.L.I. were promptly ordered to make good the Ondefontaine road a thousand yards ahead and 7 Somerset directed to advance through 1 Worcestershire on Le Mesnil Auzouf and Montamy.

Throughout the previous day the Reconnaissance Regiment in Jurques, under constant fire from 88's, had awaited its first chance to intervene in the campaign. The opportunity had at last arrived. B Squadron, under Major Carter, now moved out of Jurques up the steep hill. Suddenly a patrol of Typhoons, seeing the armoured cars and the infantry intermingled saw fit to intervene. Delivered twenty-four hours earlier, the attack would have been appreciated. Fortunately only two of the D.C.L.I. were wounded and the assault troop's half-tracks narrowly missed.

Nos. 5 and 7 Troops, after passing the crest, turned left along the road which leads through thickly wooded country to Ondefontaine. The village proved to be still occupied by the enemy in strength. These were engaged by machine-gun fire. A German Mark IV tank rumbled up and then a Volkswagen full of Germans. Suddenly two Panther tanks appeared. A brisk battle now developed in which the carrier platoon of 5 D.C.L.I., apparently anxious not to be left out of any fighting still available in the neighbourhood, also intervened. Clearly, the enemy had no intention as yet of abandoning Ondefontaine.

No. 6 Troop of this squadron meanwhile had passed through Le Mesnil Auzouf and got forward as far as La Tautainerie, where it encountered C Squadron. Moving late in the afternoon, this squadron had driven through the Bois du Homme on the right flank and eventually reached Le Mesnil Auzouf. It had then gone on to Montcharivel and La Tautainerie and Vory. Here in the gathering dusk it caught up with the enemy. Small-arms fire broke out on all sides, including the rear. Heavy mortaring opened up. Houses burst into flames. At Montcharivel 15 Scottish Division had also gained contact with the enemy. Fighting here continued throughout the night. Thus, boldly handled, the Reconnaissance Regiment in its first battle had gained information vital to the success of Major-General Thomas's plan for the morrow.

On the left of the front, 5 Dorset in the early morning mist had also made progress. Major Mead of C Company showed conspicuous courage, on this day destroying two machine-guns. This advance finally unhinged the enemy's position at Ondefontaine, which fell to 4 Dorset after further fighting in the afternoon.

With 214 Brigade established around Le Mesnil Auzouf and the Reconnaissance Regiment in touch with the enemy in front, the Division now at last faced east. Less than four miles ahead lay their goal—Mont Pincon.

MONT PINCON

(See Sketch Map 4)

The general situation on the Allied front was now exceedingly favourable. The Americans after their breakout at Avranches had by the evening of 4th August penetrated deep into Brittany. Their advance was now beginning to turn east on the extreme right flank of the Second Army at Vire. On the left a slow withdrawal had set in. From a strictly military point of view the logical step for the enemy would have been to bring his whole line back to the Orne as a preliminary to an orderly withdrawal to the Seine. To achieve this it was vital to him to hold firm on the line running south-west from Mont Pincon to Vire. This necessity explains his desperate resistance during the next few days. Hitler had not yet decided to intervene and local control of operations still remained in the experienced, if uninspired, hands of professional soldiers.

On the left flank of the Division, 7 Armoured Division's attempts to break through to Aunay had made slow progress. On the right, 11 and Guards Armoured Divisions had struck strong opposition between Estry and Vire. 15 Scottish Division on the immediate right was to find further advance by no means easy.

4th Aug. In the comparative quiet of the crest of the Bois du Homme, Brigadier Mole of 129 Brigade and his staff had found time to plan the advance on Mont Pincon, which the operations of 214 Brigade and the Reconnaissance Regiment during the morning of 4th August had now brought within striking distance. Accordingly in the afternoon this brigade, grouped with 13/18 Hussars under Lieut.-Colonel V. A. B. Dunkerly, took the lead. This was to be the first time this brigade had been able to exploit the Division's "quick-left" technique. With 4 Wiltshire on the right axis and 5 Wiltshire on the left, followed by 4 Somerset Light Infantry, the infantry went forward. Closely packed on top of the Sherman tanks and their own already overloaded carriers, jeeps and trucks, the columns made their way through dense clouds of dust towards the objective, and by nightfall after an advance of 14 miles had reached the mined and burning vehicles of the Reconnaissance Regiment near Montcharivel. For the leading troops this method of moving proved exhausting. At any moment an enemy tank or sniper might emerge from the thickset hedges and narrow lanes in the dense clouds of white dust churned up by the tanks. However, it had the overriding advantage of speed at a time when every moment was vital.

The advance was resumed at a slower rate in the mist of the early dawn. On the right 4 Wiltshire moved forward on foot towards the stream which runs at the foot of the western slopes of Mont Pincon and made for the bridge at St. Jean le Blanc. They found this to be blown and that the banks were mined. On Lieut.-Colonel Luce's orders, Major Robbins led his company across the stream and up the steep and wooded slope ahead. Almost immediately he found himself at close grips with a well concealed and determined enemy. A desperate battle under a burning sun now broke out and lasted all day. The Pioneer Platoon meanwhile, under heavy mortar and Nebelwerfer fire, constructed a crossing over which a troop of tanks was able to pass later in the day to aid the hard-pressed company. 5th Aug

A Company meanwhile had advanced on the village of St. Jean le Blanc, only to find themselves opposed by well entrenched infantry supported by tanks, who fought to a finish amongst the orchards and cornfields. By the early evening, although the whole battalion had crossed the stream, it had become clear that the village was strongly held. The object of the Division was to capture Mont Pincon, not St. Jean le Blanc. Major-General Thomas therefore decided that further advance in this direction offered no advantages, and ordered the battalion to disengage. It was accordingly withdrawn after dark into reserve at Danvou for use on the left flank on the following day. Here, 5 Wiltshire had also closed with the enemy's main defences in the face of equally desperate resistance.

This battalion had advanced by the main road which leads from Le Mesnil Auzouf to Le Plessis Grimault at the foot of the mountain. A Company, which was leading, secured the cross-roads near Duval with little difficulty. Lieut.-Colonel Pearson then passed D Company through with orders to seize the bridge across the stream about eight hundred yards ahead. Major R. M. C. Thomas, the company commander, deployed north of the road and advanced towards a small square wood about a quarter of a mile from the bridge. The two leading platoons successfully reached the wood, passed through and crossed the stream. The rear platoon, however, quickly found itself pinned to the ground in a cornfield on the right by machine-gun fire from the other side of the stream. Here the supporting tanks of 13/18 Hussars came to the rescue and the whole company was soon established about a quarter of a mile forward of the vital bridge which they had by-passed. In actual fact they had succeeded in infiltrating right into the enemy main position ; but the enemy had not fallen back. Indeed, when night fell the company found itself completely surrounded. Meanwhile two direct assaults on the bridge by C Company under Major E. R. B. Field had failed with heavy loss. Lieut.-Colonel Pearson therefore had to face the fact that further advance that day was out of the question. D Company was extricated with great difficulty during the night and the battalion concentrated west of the stream, under continuous mortar and artillery fire, with the intention of resuming the attack on the morrow.

The day's fighting had revealed that the enemy was holding in great strength an exceptionally well sited and concealed defensive position. Thanks to the courage and capacity with which both battalions of the Wiltshire Regiment had forced themselves forward and compelled the enemy to disclose his defences, Brigadier Mole was able by the evening of 5th August to appreciate the formidable character of the resistance now to be overcome.

Mont Pincon rises to a height of over 1,200 feet and completely dominates the whole landscape from Vire to the Odon. From its slopes German observation was uninterrupted and the enemy were able to bring down deadly artillery and mortar fire on any movement.

The crest is a plateau covered with heather and bracken interspersed with a few birch-trees. The higher slopes are well wooded and very steep on the southern and south-western sides. Small fields, divided by thick hedges, stretch down the lower slopes towards the stream at the foot, which is in full view from the top. La Variniere and Le Quesnee are typical *bocage* villages, strongly built of stone, surrounded by orchards and intersected by a labyrinth of sunken lanes and stout walls. The enemy's prolonged resistance here and the evil reputation which the cross-roads at La Variniere were to gain, even after Mont Pincon had fallen, will therefore be readily understood.

How little the strength of the enemy's position and his determination to hold it were appreciated at the time is shown by the Corps orders issued at 1 p.m. on the 5th to cover the operations for the following day. These instructed the Division to complete the capture of Mont Pincon by 10.00 hours on 6th August and then to advance nine miles due south on Condé sur Noireau with 7 Armoured Division, at that moment only just entering Aunay, on its left flank. Under this plan 8 Armoured Brigade and 214 Brigade were to lead the advance. Later this scheme had to be abandoned and a less ambitious course taken, but it is interesting to speculate as to what might have been the result had it been put into practice. If the vigour of the opposition encountered on Mont Pincon is any guide, it would probably have proved both bloody and difficult. The incident is only mentioned to illustrate one of the many stresses to which Major-General Thomas and Brigadier Mole were subjected in the planning and execution of one of the most complex and bitterly contested operations of the campaign.

Brigadier Mole now decided to attack with 5 Wiltshire on the right following the line of the road through the La Variniere cross-roads to the south-west end of the mountain, and 4 Somerset Light Infantry on the left on the axis of the road from La Toque to La Rogeurie and on to Pt. 365 and the road on the high ground on the eastern edge of the hill. Planning went on throughout the night followed by reconnaissance under heavy fire on the following morning. Despite "O" Groups and preparations interrupted by the enemy's incessant bombardment, the attack finally went in at half-past two in the afternoon. 4 Wiltshire, the brigade reserve, moved up towards La Toque along a narrow and sunken lane behind 4 Somerset. 6th Aug.

It was a swelteringly hot day and the Somerset Light Infantry went forward in their shirt-sleeves. Ahead the great long hill, with its gorse and scrub, towered above the thick trees and cornfields which fringed the stream. This the Somersets crossed, but about a hundred yards further on the two leading companies found themselves brought to a standstill by machine-gun fire from both flanks as well as from the front. The thick cover of the hedges, with their double banks, made it easy for the enemy to move about choosing his firing position at will without at any time having to show himself. It was impossible to locate a single automatic weapon, although a dozen or more had opened up at varying ranges. The valley was alive with flying bullets and heavy mortar fire directed on to the roads. Major Thomas, commanding B Company, was killed whilst gallantly leading an attack with a handful of men in La Roguerie. Smoke and movement to the flanks by the reserve companies were tried without success.

The 5 Wiltshire, reduced to two rifle companies by their losses of the previous day, at once found themselves faced with very heavy mortar and shell fire. Machine-guns opened up from the orchards. The most intense fire was encountered by the men on the right as they made their way through an orchard towards the stream. Every weapon the enemy could muster was turned against them. Some dashed forward and took cover behind a high bank; others sought shelter in the bed of the stream.

Meanwhile, Lieut.-Colonel J. H. C. Pearson, with his advanced headquarters, moved along the road. With him in his Bren carrier was his Intelligence Officer, Lieutenant C. D. E. Keeling. Immediately behind came the wireless Scout Car—the link with brigade headquarters, and in this was travelling the Adjutant, Captain

T. H. Peace, and the Signals Officer, Captain J. S. McMath.   It was then that Lieut.-Colonel Pearson, realizing that his men were pinned down, got out of his carrier and strode away down the road, swinging his walking-stick and with a red rose showing defiantly in his hat. He reached the bridge and there, seeing his men taking cover in the stream, urged them on.   Inspired by his example, they were quick to obey, but as they once more pushed forward, the colonel fell, shot through the heart by a German sniper.   Corporal Mackrell seized a Bren gun and brought the body of the sniper, who was in a tree, tumbling to the ground.

The bitter advance went slowly on, only again to be held up by intense fire.   Major J. F. Milne, trying to set an example, got too far ahead of his men and was taken prisoner, but later escaped.

The Adjutant, Captain T. H. Peace, now took over command of what remained of the battalion.   Going forward with the only surviving company commander, Major E. R. B. Field, he inspired the men to fresh efforts.   A Squadron of 13/18 Hussars had now succeeded in crossing the stream.   With their support and a fresh artillery concentration on the cross-roads at La Variniere, the survivors made one final supreme effort.   As the battle raged amongst the houses, the enemy started to surrender.   Over a hundred prisoners were taken between the bridge and La Variniere.   The vital cross-roads were at last gained.   Captain Peace, however, was still undaunted.   He prepared to attack the final objective, Mont Pincon itself, but at this moment was badly wounded.

At this stage Brigadier Mole decided to pass through 4 Wiltshire to capture the hill and ordered the 5th to hold the cross-roads.   The wisdom of this decision became apparent later, when the enemy made repeated attempts to recapture it.

The 4 Wiltshire, however, were over two miles away on the left flank.   Lieut.-Colonel V. A. B. Dunkerley, commanding 13/18 Hussars, was not prepared to wait.   It was now 6 p.m.   He therefore ordered A Squadron to send an armoured patrol to the top of the hill. Captain N. N. M. Denny, with Lieutenants Elliott and Jennison's troops, therefore made for the crest.   One tank overturned in a quarry; another had its track blown off.   Under cover of a smoke-screen, Lieutenant Jennison's tank shot ahead, closely followed by Lieutenant Elliott's and the remainder of the patrol.   By half-past six 13/18 Hussars had seven tanks in an all-round defensive position on the summit.   At 8 p.m. the Colonel arrived, followed by the remainder of the squadron.

Over on the left flank of the brigade, Lieut.-Colonel Lipscomb could see their tanks on the top of the hill.   A troop of tanks having arrived to support him, he quickly made a new plan and resumed the advance.   One tank succeeded with great difficulty in negotiating the minefield, hedge and stream and getting into a position from which it could blast the hillside. This action by one tank proved the turning-point of the battle. The whole battalion, although almost exhausted, now made a supreme effort and gained the crest of the hill. Here around Pt. 365 they dug in. By this time a thick fog had descended. Through it B Squadron of 13/18 Hussars now arrived, led by their squadron-leader on foot, with a compass.

Meanwhile Lieut.-Colonel Luce of 4 Wiltshire was also on the move. He had been ordered to occupy the mountain "any way he liked." Sound instinct led him towards La Variniere, where he found the remnants of 5 Wiltshire still grimly holding out in the face of continued counter-attacks from Le Quesnee. Ironically, it fell to Major Lequesne of 94 Field Regiment to bring them to a halt at the home of his ancestors. It was now about 9 p.m. With B Company leading, the battalion headed for the hill. Lieut.-Colonel Luce led the vehicles by a slightly more southerly route. Enemy resistance was slight, but the sheer physical effort of climbing the hill proved almost too much for the exhausted troops. First to reach the top was Lieut.-Colonel Luce himself. The time was now ten-fifteen. He went back and led his men into the dense fog on the crest, where they started to dig into the stony ground. That night in the fog, in bitter cold, the tanks and the two infantry battalions shared Mont Pincon with the Germans, but it was not until dawn that proper contact was made and the enemy finally eliminated, largely as a result of the efforts of B Squadron of 13/18 Hussars.

During the day, 130 Brigade on the north flank had made substantial progress. With 7 Royal Hampshire under Major D. B. Rooke in the lead it had by the evening got to close grips with at least three companies of the enemy in La Pugorie and had forced the crossing of the stream. When night closed down, their leading troops had reached the foot of the mountain. There is no doubt that this diversionary move served to distract the attention of the enemy and contributed to the startling success of 129 Brigade. The situation now called for fresh troops.

At an "O" Group held at midnight at the headquarters of 214 Brigade, Major-General Thomas therefore ordered this brigade to move forward with all speed and clear the Mont Pincon feature as far as the main road from Aunay. 7 Armoured Division, after many setbacks, was at last moving from this direction. In order to enable it to thrust due south on Condé sur Noireau the capture of the road centre at Le Plessis Grimault had now become urgent. This additional task was therefore given to the brigade. With the same object of helping the armour to break out, 130 Brigade was directed to continue its advance in the direction of Roucamps on the main road.

The commanding officers of 1 Worcestershire and 7 Somerset Light Infantry, Lieut.-Colonels Osborne Smith and Nicholl, at once set off in the dark with their reconnaissance groups for Mont Pincon,

6

leaving their seconds-in-command to bring their battalions forward.
Around the cross-roads of La Variniere the fighting still continued.

It is greatly to the credit of these two commanding officers that
they were able finally to join Lieut.-Colonels Luce and Lipscomb in
the heavy mist on Mont Pincon soon after first light.   According to
prisoners captured that day a strong enemy counter-attack at this
time went astray in the fog.   7 Somerset were quick to take advantage
of the cover and by the middle of the morning had relieved the
4 Somerset on the crest.   1 Worcestershire followed and by eleven-
thirty had taken over from 4 Wiltshire at the western end of the
mountain.

The burning sun now dispersed the mist and every gun and mortar
the enemy could muster opened up.   Around La Variniere cross-
roads the shelling by 88's became particularly intense, continuous and
accurate.   The two battalions lost no time in digging in and 129
Brigade withdrew into reserve.   No rest was ever better earned.

In the afternoon, Brigadier Essame and Lieut.-Colonel Taylor of
5 D.C.L.I., after a dramatic passage through La Variniere, arrived on
the hill and crawled forward to a large hole in front of the Worcestershire position.   The view ahead was excellent, but only the roofs of
the houses of the objective, Le Plessis Grimault, could be seen.   The
southern slopes of Mont Pincon, covered in scrub and with a few
trees, gave a good line of approach.   It was therefore decided that
there should be no repetition of the bludgeon type of attack, as
executed at Jurques, but that a real effort should be made to surprise
the enemy.   The plan decided on was a noisy feint attack down the
road which approached Le Plessis Grimault from the west; meanwhile, the bulk of the battalion was to move silently along the lower
slopes of Mont Pincon, then execute a right wheel and attack Le
Plessis Grimault from the north.   To make room for the D.C.L.I.
and also to stabilize the ugly situation at the foot of the mountain,
1 Worcestershire, except for one company, were ordered to side-step
to the cross-roads at La Variniere.   Their move down the hill at the
same time as the D.C.L.I. were moving up, especially when combined with the feint by 13/18 Hussars from the west and another
blow from the north, go far to explain the enemy's obvious bewilderment during this attack.

At 9.30 p.m. as the light was fading the guns of the Divisional
artillery and two medium regiments, supplemented by the battalion's
3-inch mortars, opened up.   Behind this barrage of smoke, dust and
steel, B Squadron of 4/7 Dragoons, under Major S. Jenkins, and
Lieutenant Welch's platoon of C Company advanced on the village
from the direction of La Variniere.   The enemy was quick to react
with his mortars.   Against the armour of the tanks these had no
effect and the infantry platoon was so dispersed that only two men
were wounded.   Soon the tanks were close enough to fire their Besa

7th
Aug.

machine-guns into the western fringe of the village. It was now dark. Suddenly there was a deafening explosion as an enemy ammunition store exploded in a fury of gold and red flame. This magnificent bonfire acted as a screen to the attacking troops. Light signals went up. The tracer bullets pouring into the village ricochetted across the sky.

Meanwhile A Company of the D.C.L.I. under Major Parker, after a forced march of four miles, had quickly moved down the mountain to the northern end of the village. Here they lay for forty minutes close to the edge of the barrage.

Le Plessis Grimault sprawls for about half a mile on either side of the main road running due south from Aunay to Condé. It is the junction point of no less than seven roads.

At ten minutes past ten Major Parker's company advanced into the village, with No. 8 Platoon and company headquarters following the line of the main road and Nos. 7 and 9 Platoons on either flank with the task of driving the enemy towards the centre to be disposed of by the centre platoon. The bulk of the fighting, in fact, was to fall to this platoon. Almost at once the leading section fell on an enemy post, killed two men and took three prisoners. A second post was quickly disposed of. Raking the houses with Bren fire and No. 36 grenades and flinging in No. 77 grenades to smoke the enemy out, the company pushed on. Houses, set alight by the phosphorus of the grenades, burst into flames in their wake.

Suddenly in the darkness Major Parker and his men heard the sound of tanks ahead around the cross-roads. Moving forward, he could just distinguish the outline of two Tiger tanks, another tracked vehicle and a lorry surrounded by Germans. He shouted for the Piat, only to find that it had been knocked out by artillery fire. He therefore ordered his men to fire rapid at the cross-roads with their rifles, Brens and 2-inch mortars. With amazing luck, the first 2-inch mortar bomb hit the lorry, which proved to be an ammunition truck replenishing the Tiger tanks. In a flash the lorry and one Tiger burst into flames, spewing incandescent ammunition like a huge incendiary bomb. The other Tiger tank at once decamped and the crew of the half-track abandoned their vehicle. Major Parker and No. 8 Platoon promptly charged through the flames at the cross-roads and overwhelmed another enemy post beyond. Fighting its way through the village, the company at length reached the German headquarters. Here close-quarter fighting began in earnest, but smoked out of the house by No. 77 grenades, the Germans decided they had had enough. With a company headquarters and a platoon, 36 men in all, Major Parker took the surrender of 94 prisoners. His other two platoons now joined him, to be followed soon after by Lieut.-Colonel Taylor and D Company. The rest of the battalion followed hot upon their heels and quickly consolidated

in the village.   By 11 p.m. the last Germans in Le Plessis Grimault
had been finally rounded up or shot.   A counter-attack soon after
dawn by tanks and S.P. guns was easily beaten off.   An unlucky shot,
however, from an 88 gun hit Major Parker in the jaw and shoulder.

With the coming of daylight, the D.C.L.I. realized the extent of
their astounding success.   Thirty-one of the enemy lay dead; 125
prisoners had been taken.   A Royal Tiger tank—incidentally the
first destroyed in Normandy—two Nebelwerfers, one half-track, one
staff car and a great deal of miscellaneous equipment had been
captured.   All this had been achieved at the cost of one man killed,
five wounded and one missing.

To this brilliant episode the inspiration of the commanding officer,
the Light Infantry spirit of the troops, and above all the gallant and
resourceful leadership of Major Parker all contributed.   Le Plessis
Grimault will always stand high amongst the battle honours of the
D.C.L.I.

8th   In the early morning the noise of tanks was heard coming down the
Aug. road from the north.   It was 7 Armoured Division at last.   To the
astonishment of the D.C.L.I., the long column of tanks was to remain stationary all day in the village.   Why this was so it is not the
function of this history to explain, for responsibility for continuing
the advance to Condé had now, for the time being, passed temporarily
out of the hands of 43 Division.

The capture of Mont Pincon will go down to history as a very great
feat of arms achieved at the maximum possible speed over an enemy
into the minds of whose forward troops the thought of defeat had not
yet entered, and fighting under conditions which gave every advantage to the defence.   All ranks of all units of the service within the
Division and 8 Armoured Brigade share the honour.   It is fitting,
however, in conclusion to pay especial tribute to the three main
fighting arms in their traditional order—to the Cavalry represented
by 8 Armoured Brigade, who had brought a new spirit into the
Division's battles and whose tanks were the first to gain the crest; to
the Royal Artillery, whose devastating, accurate and unfailing support
time and time again saved the day; and finally to the endurance,
courage and fighting skill of the infantry.   Above all shines the
great sacrifice of Lieut.-Colonel Pearson and the pitifully few
survivors of 5 Wiltshire Regiment, who at the crisis of the battle
finally carried the cross-roads at La Variniere and turned the tide.

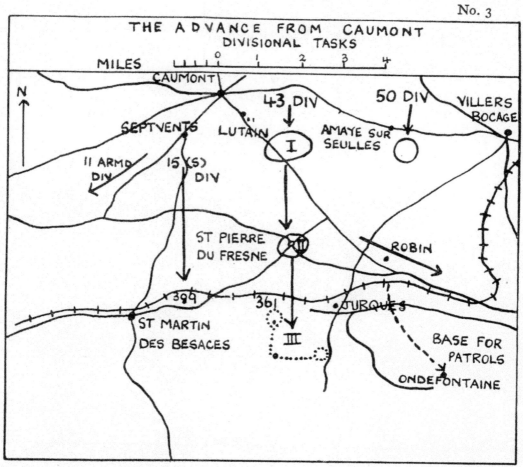

THE ADVANCE FROM CAUMONT
DIVISIONAL TASKS

MILES 0 1 2 3 4

N

CAUMONT

43 DIV   50 DIV   VILLERS BOCAGE

SEPTVENTS   LUTAIN   AMAYE SUR SEULLES

II ARMD DIV   15 (S) DIV

I

ST PIERRE DU FRESNE   II   ROBIN

399   361   TURQUES

ST MARTIN DES BESACES   III   BASE FOR PATROLS

ONDEFONTAINE

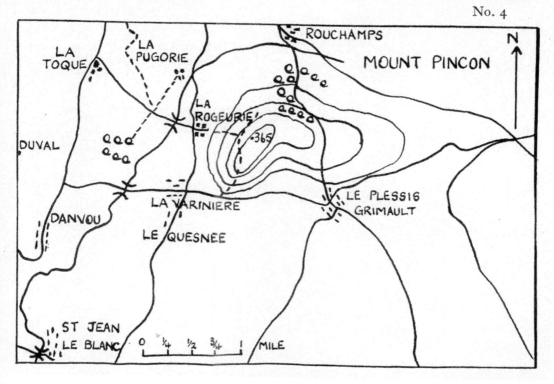

N

LA TOQUE   LA PUGORIE   ROUCHAMPS   MOUNT PINCON

LA ROGEURIE

DUVAL   .365

LA VARINIERE   LE PLESSIS GRIMAULT

DANVOU

LE QUESNEE

ST JEAN LE BLANC   0 ¼ ½ ¾ 1 MILE

CHAPTER V

THE ADVANCE TO THE NOIREAU

(*See Sketch Map 5*)

On the morning of the 8th August an officer of the 7 Somerset Light Infantry was standing on the top of Mont Pincon watching the tanks of 7 Armoured Division crawling slowly forward round the foot of the hill into Le Plessis Grimault. He heard a voice behind him say, "Have you seen the Corps Commander?" "The Corps Commander?" he replied, without looking round. "Good God, you don't expect to find him this far forward, do you?" He then turned to find, to his embarrassment, that he was talking to a major-general.

But the Corps Commander was on Mont Pincon, in fact he had just passed Private Pursey of the anti-tank platoon who saw only a tall officer striding along the ridge, and, failing to notice the General's badges or his red cap band, called out "Any 'gen,' sir?"

Lieut.-General B. G. Horrocks, who had led the 30 Corps from El Alamein to Tunis, had now recovered sufficiently from the wounds he had sustained in North Africa to come back and resume command of his old corps. From this moment a tremendous feeling of confidence began to spread amongst the troops. The effect of standing on dominating ground, of seeing our columns moving up around the lower slopes, the great news from the American right flank and the infectious enthusiasm of the Corps Commander all contributed. The troops began to sense that the Germans were no longer fighting on ground of their own choosing.

General Horrocks walked amongst them and on a company commander's map told them of the dramatic change in the general situation and of his plans for the next few days. From now onwards, driving his jeep, he was to be a familiar figure in the forward areas. On the following day he addressed 129 Brigade and congratulated them on the capture of Mont Pincon. His vivid and amusing description of General George Patton motoring through Brittany stirred the imagination of the troops.

In actual fact at this very moment the battle in Normandy had reached its crisis. No less a person than Hitler himself had decided to intervene. Refusing to believe the situation as presented to him and disregarding the advice of his generals, he had personally ordered that the Panzer divisions should be disengaged, formed up outside Mortain facing west and launched into an attack on the 7th August

73

towards the sea at Avranches. The weather was ideal for air operations and the tremendous power of the Allied air forces was brought to bear against the enemy columns. On the ground, the American counter-measures were swift and efficient and the result of the battle was never for a moment in doubt.

This desperate German move explains the tenacious resistance still to be overcome on the Corps front during the next week. With the bulk of his armour now committed on the extreme west flank, the enemy could not afford to yield an inch of ground, and the whole of the 30 Corps were to find his line, based on village strong-points, each with tanks or self-propelled guns in support, by no means easy to overwhelm.

Responsibility for continuing the main thrust towards Condé and the Noireau had now passed to 7 Armoured and 50 Divisions on the left flank. Meanwhile, what remained of the enemy's defences immediately south and south-west of Mont Pincon had to be reduced.

LE QUESNEE AND LES HAMEAUX

8th Aug.   La Variniere cross-roads had now acquired an evil reputation only comparable with that of Hell Fire Corner on the Menin Road at Ypres in the first war. It was still cut off from Le Plessis Grimault by enemy holding out immediately south of the road. Vicious mortar and machine-gun fire from here and the villages of Le Quesnee and Crepigny, only three hundred yards short of the cross-roads, continued throughout the day. The operations of 1 Worcestershire, to whom the task of cleaning up this surviving opposition had been given, were now to disclose the great strength of the enemy's defences in this area and, incidentally, to explain the heavy losses and outstanding heroism of 5 Wiltshire in the battle on the afternoon of the 6th.

Lieut.-Colonel Osborne Smith first turned his attention to the pocket between La Variniere and Le Plessis Grimault. The strength of this surviving opposition was first revealed by No. 1 Platoon of 204 Field Company under Lieutenant Abbott, who moving to open the route through to 5 D.C.L.I. in Le Plessis Grimault suddenly found themselves caught in heavy machine-gun fire from both sides of the road. They deployed to attack, but found the fire of their five Brens swamped by a dozen Spandaus. Major Evill, the company commander, withdrew the platoon, section by section, to the vehicles. The party then shot its way through to Le Plessis Grimault, followed by the Field Park Company armoured bulldozer, off which the bullets rattled in all directions. Here, skilfully concealed in orchards, bushy hedgerows and sunken lanes, the enemy continued to fight skilfully and stubbornly. Spandaus hidden in enfilade positions and enemy artillery observers took their toll, and after severe losses the attacking company of the Worcestershire had to be withdrawn. They had, however, forced the enemy to show his hand.

The removal of this opposition had become most urgent, for 50 Division were resuming the thrust on Condé due south from Le Plessis Grimault on the afternoon of the 9th. To protect their right flank, 7 Somerset Light Infantry had been ordered to attack and capture Les Hameaux, Hameau au Roi and Le Saussay—three hamlets forming a triangle of which Les Hameaux was the apex about a mile south of Mont Pincon. 9th
Aug.

Until 1 Worcestershire had cleared the start line, this operation could not be mounted. Those with experience in these circumstances will readily imagine the nature of the pressure applied from the rear on Lieut.-Colonel Osborne Smith at this time.

B Company, under Major A. A. Grubb, supported by C Squadron of 4/7 Dragoon Guards and a heavy artillery bombardment, now undertook the task. A hot battle ensued, and it was not until this company had been reinforced that the position was finally carried, and even then not cheaply. Captain Newman, Lieutenants Everitt and Henry were all severely wounded and a number of other ranks killed and wounded also. About eighty prisoners were taken. Many of the enemy appeared to be under the impression that they would be shot out of hand if they were captured. Some fell on their knees and prayed, weeping for mercy, when they saw the slit trenches at battalion headquarters, which they thought were open graves. The victory was saddened by the death of Major T. M. Bell of 4/7 Dragoon Guards, who was killed whilst making a dismounted reconnaissance of the final objective.

7 Somerset Light Infantry, under Lieut.-Colonel J. W. Nichol, were now able to move forward from their assembly area at the western end of the mountain and to advance to their start line, four hundred yards south of the road.

On the right, D Company was directed on Le Haussay and, on the left, A Company on Les Hameaux. C and B Companies were to follow up at a distance of six hundred yards and mop up. Each forward company was allotted a troop of tanks and an assault section of pioneers. The carrier platoon had the task of protecting the right flank.

The attack started at 12.30 p.m., after many delays and alterations in the fire programme and under heavy bombardment from enemy mortars and 88's. The supporting tanks soon got into difficulties, for the thick hedges, interspersed with sizable trees, were tank obstacles and the tracks were heavily mined. The Pioneers started to clear a safe lane up the axis. Major Young, commanding D Company, however, pushed boldly ahead and by 3.30 p.m. had advanced twelve hundred yards and captured Les Hameaux and Le Haussay.

A Company, under Major Baker, found itself faced with hedgerow fighting all the way. It was a question of short bounds of fire and movement across the luxuriant meadows and sharp assaults against the enemy machine-guns dug into the strong hedges. They too gained their objective. On the right, Captain Baden with the carrier platoon fought his way through.

C Company now forged ahead to capture Hameau au Roi. Their commander, Captain U. S. Bailey, was wounded. Major Young therefore came forward to help the only surviving officer, Lieutenant Wreford. Large numbers of prisoners now began to surrender.

Nine hundred yards ahead lay the battalion's final bound, Le Saussay. B Company, organized in two parties each slightly below platoon strength, burst through the tangle of hedgerows, farms and enemy strong-points. Second Lieutenant E. A. Murcott led his party through our own artillery barrage on to his objective and caught the enemy cowering in slit trenches, dug-outs and farms. By 6.30 p.m. all objectives were securely held. Two hundred and forty-two prisoners had been taken. The price, however, had not been light, for the battalion had suffered 79 casualties, of which seven were officers. These included Lieutenant E. F. Larret, a "Canloan" officer who had gained for himself the highest regard of the Regiment for his brilliant leadership and personal qualities. It is recalled that, although severely wounded, he apologized to his commanding officer for the necessity which compelled him to withdraw from the battle.

As night fell and his patrols pushed ahead, Lieut.-Colonel Nichol had every reason to be proud of his conduct of a difficult battle and the fighting qualities of all ranks of his battalion. The tough opposition encountered by the 50 Division on the immediate left makes their success all the more remarkable.

Having cleared the Somerset's start line, Lieut.-Colonel Osborne Smith of the Worcestershire was now able to devote his attention to the ulcer of Le Quesnee by La Variniere. The place was strewn with dead cattle, bloated and stinking, and in the orchard before the village stood a burnt-out German S.P. gun with the charred and decaying bodies of the crews still inside. All around chickens, ducks and geese roamed, tame and unconcerned. Close-quarter fighting between A Company under Major Watson and an exceptionally truculent German garrison continued until a late hour, and it was not until first light on the 10th that this strong-point was finally taken. It proved to be a maze of cunningly concealed earthworks, sited under piles of brushwood, cornstacks and concealed banks. It was little wonder that A Company had had to pay so heavy a price.

10th Aug. Soon after dawn on the 10th it had become evident that a slow withdrawal had started on the Divisional front. A carrier patrol of

7 Somerset reported the village of Lenault unoccupied. A Company promptly moved in.

On the left 1 Worcestershire captured Crepigny on the outskirts of Le Quesnee and advanced a thousand yards to the south.

The Reconnaissance Regiment, who had been holding a position just south-west of St. Jean le Blanc, now seized their opportunity. Nos. 9 and 11 Troops, under Lieutenants Moreland and Teden, proceeded to seize the two bridges in the village. Lifting the mines on the far bank under heavy mortar fire, they penetrated the village, which was still strongly held, and with the Besas of their armoured cars engaged in a sharp battle. A Squadron, under Major Scott-Plummer, now arrived. Seeing the opposition ahead, he decided to probe in a southerly direction. No. 2 Troop, under Lieutenant Schofield, followed by the assault troop under Lieutenant James, continued the advance in this direction, clashed with a German S.P. gun and captured some prisoners. It soon became clear, however, that further progress in this direction was likely to prove slow and costly. Lieut.-Colonel Lane Fox therefore decided to switch this squadron to the east flank.

Moving via Le Plessis Grimault, No. 2 Troop under Lieutenant Howe accordingly moved forward to Lenault. Here they found themselves in the middle of a battle between 50 Division and the enemy. A stray shot from a mortar bomb set alight the camouflage net on Lieutenant Howe's car. This was hurriedly extinguished and the advance continued. Taking no notice of disorganized German infantry, they pressed on to St. Pierre la Vieille. On the far side they finally came upon the enemy digging in tanks. After this most successful day, the squadron withdrew into harbour at dusk.

By the following morning all the high ground dominating the Druance stream had been secured by 214 Brigade. 11th Aug.

OPERATIONS SOUTH-EAST OF MONT PINCON
10th–13th August

By the 11th August, provided relentless pressure was applied by the whole of the British and United States Armies at all points, the certainty of annihilating victory lay within General Montgomery's grasp. In a personal message to every man of his armies he called upon everyone "to make a tremendous effort to 'write off' this powerful German force; it has caused us no small trouble during the last two months; let us finish with it once and for all, and so hasten the end of the war. In these hot August days, amid the dust of the battlefield, it is not always easy to keep up the pressure. But these are momentous days and complete victory lies ahead, and is certain— so long as we do not relax. Let us therefore continue the battle with renewed and even greater energy; and we must remember to give the honour and praise where it is due."

The time had now passed when detailed reconnaissance and meticulous preparation had been the secret of success. The noose was round the enemy's neck. It remained to pull it tight. The Commander-in-Chief made it clear—abundantly clear—that all units must now thrust forward regardless of their flanks and pockets left behind. Speed overrode every other consideration.

The regrouping for the final knock-out blow involved the withdrawal of 7 Armoured Division from the Corps left flank east of Mont Pincon. On the night of 9th–10th August, 129 Brigade replaced it in the area of the villages of La Lande and La Mogisière, with the task of protecting the left flank and supporting the thrust of 50 Division southwards from Cauville on to St. Pierre la Vieille and the high ground beyond.

Between Mont Pincon and Condé a series of spurs runs eastwards towards the Orne. The battle now resolved itself into a desperate struggle on the part of the enemy to hold up our advance on these lines in a vain attempt to gain time for the remainder of his forces to escape to the east. His organization was by now disintegrating. Battle groups named after some particular commander rather than formal military units now began to appear. Their crude direction signs marked their lines of withdrawal as our troops advanced. Desperate bodies of men, by-passed by our leading troops, continued to resist for several days behind our lines.

On the 10th August, 129 Brigade conformed with the advance of the main thrust of 50 Division, entered Cauville and pushed forward in the face of light opposition to about one mile south-east of the village. St. Pierre la Vieille, however, still barred the way. It was 11th not until midday on the 11th that 50 Division finally forced their Aug. way into this village. In the afternoon an attempt to capture the high ground on the far side came to naught with heavy loss. That night B Company of 5 Wiltshire with strong artillery support attacked the village of La Vardière and at once encountered vigorous opposition. As the attack went in again at dawn, the enemy retaliated strongly with mortar fire, which wounded, amongst others, the Company Commander, Major E. Ingles. However, a considerable number of prisoners were taken and this pocket eliminated. South of St. Pierre la Vieille the enemy, supported by armour, continued to resist on the 12th.

12th   This southerly advance had left the mountainous and wooded Aug. country around Mont Gaultier and Culey le Patry still uncleared. On the afternoon of the 12th, 7 Somerset Light Infantry and 5 D.C.L.I. were therefore moved over to this flank and ordered to remove all traces of the enemy down to the Orne. The task of dealing with Mont Gaultier fell to 7 Somerset Light Infantry. In the late afternoon B Company, under Major Harvey, clashed with enemy in the hedgerows and found themselves virtually in the middle of an enemy defensive position and under fire from three sides, with little or no cover. One machine-gun in particular was firing at point-blank range only fifteen or twenty yards away. Major Harvey himself dashed forward and flung a grenade, which, however, rebounded off the parapet of the position. Whereupon he kicked it, causing it to roll right into the trench, where it exploded, killing the occupants.

Major Young now intervened with D Company, and under his fine leadership the opposition was finally overcome as darkness fell.

The enemy's mortars caused some casualties, including Captain B. Pearse, and killed Lieutenant D. F. Bean, the commander of the Pioneer Platoon, who after clearing the roads of mines under fire had intervened in the battle with his platoon and driven off the enemy. Caught in a mortar concentration, with heroic self-sacrifice he shielded a wounded man with his own body and sustained wounds from which he subsequently died.

Meanwhile 5 D.C.L.I. had advanced on the left flank with a view to clearing the spur running down from La Trulandière village near Culey le Patry towards the Orne. C Company, under Captain Ruck-Keene, gained contact with the enemy about a company strong during the afternoon. H Hour was fixed for 8 p.m. At this time Major John Fry with D Company made a skilful flanking movement by a covered approach round the left flank. In spite of opposition from machine-guns which were extremely difficult to locate, he finally drove the enemy from their positions and across the Orne, leaving ten dead and twenty prisoners. Lieutenant R. Prowse's leadership in this action was outstanding.

Lieut.-General Horrocks, in face of the looser situation, now issued the orders which were finally to drive the enemy beyond the Noireau and envelop his west flank. 11 Armoured Division had been placed under his command from first light on the 14th. He therefore decided that this division, with 11 Hussars under its command and followed by the 50 Division in lorries, should press forward on the right flank to the road which runs due south from Condé to Flers and then advance on the whole Corps front. To 43 Division he gave the task of forcing the crossings of the Noireau east of Condé and advancing to the area of Athis, two miles beyond. No orders ever issued by General Horrocks were more crystal clear with regard to the general conception or more emphatically expressed in the matter of the vital need for speed. 19th Aug.

The onus of continuing the advance due south thus passed to 43 Division. 4 Wiltshire, under Major J. E. L. Corbyn, moving forward in the evening from Cauville, found 2 Devonshire re-organizing after their final successful attack on the commanding ridge

a mile south-east of St. Pierre la Vieille. Their objective was the
next ridge, a mile beyond. Only an hour of daylight remained.
Major Corbyn at his "O" Group found himself faced with a confusing situation, which the enemy temporarily solved for him by
counter-attacking 2 Devonshire with armour. Shells and bullets
flew in all directions. Any advance that evening was clearly
impossible. The night was spent in extreme discomfort and
uncertainty. Long after dark 4 Somerset Light Infantry finally
succeeded in taking over the village of La Villete nearby. It stank
of dead cattle, burning houses and rotten food.

13th
Aug.
Dawn came with heavy mist. The country ahead was close and
undulating. The map conveyed little information of any value.
Nothing was known of the enemy. To give definite objectives to
companies was quite out of the question. Major Corbyn therefore
decided to advance deployed. C Company led and after going forward about a thousand yards captured some buildings and about
twenty prisoners. A Company now moved through. Pressing
ahead amongst woods and fields, this company lost touch with its
supporting tanks. Suddenly Major A. D. Parsons, the company
commander, found himself on top of a precipitous crest which was
apparently his objective. In the valley below a large crowd of
Germans round a tank met his eyes. These he engaged with medium
fire, but owing to the inaccuracy of the maps our shells came down
on the top of his own company. Meanwhile B Company had made
good the high ground six hundred yards to the east against slight
opposition, only to be promptly and efficiently subjected to an attack
by our own Typhoons. The enemy now opened up with fire from
self-propelled guns at close range, with considerable effect. Amongst
others, Lieutenant C. J. Mills and Company Sergeant Major Webb,
who had given eighteen years service to the Regiment, were killed.
Finally, at 5 p.m., with the greater part of the ridge in their hands and
after a most confusing day, the battalion called a halt. Small groups
of the enemy still hung out all round and in rear of them in the thick
woods. That night the company quartermaster sergeants with the
food had to fight their way through.

Major-General Thomas had hoped to pass through 130 Brigade to
the Noireau on this day, and with this end in view had moved the
brigade embussed at first light from Mont Pincon to assembly areas
near St. Pierre la Vieille. Here in an atmosphere of frustration,
which confusing reports of the progress of 4 Wiltshire and of the
enemy still holding out north of Proussy did nothing to relieve, they
remained inert all day. It did not take Lieutenant-Colonel Coad
long, however, when he took over command in the afternoon to get
the necessary reconnaissance under way and to evolve a plan which
on the morrow was to smash the last traces of enemy resistance north
of the Noireau.

130 BRIGADE ADVANCE TO THE NORTH BANK OF THE NOIREAU

With the fall of darkness on the evening of the 13th, the situation 14th Aug. ahead still remained vague in the extreme. A general withdrawal behind the Noireau appeared imminent. The enemy's machinery of command, however, was rapidly disintegrating and if orders actually were sent out to fall back, they certainly never reached the forward units. A fighting patrol of B Company of 5 Dorset, sent during the night to find out the exact position of the enemy, reached some farm buildings north of Proussy. These they found to be held in strength. Major W. A. Venour, who had temporarily taken over command in place of Lieut.-Colonel Coad, was thus able to put in a well co-ordinated attack at 7.30 a.m. With the full support of the Divisional artillery and A, C and D Companies of 8 Middlesex, under Major Kaines, B Company assaulted the farm buildings and within half an hour had put up their success signal. C and D Companies, under Major G. R. Pack and Major G. R. Hartwell, now surged forward behind a rolling barrage towards the village of Proussy. This proved to be a long, straggling village in which the enemy continued to resist. However, A Company under Major H. C. Allen pushed ahead to the final objective at the southern end. Prisoners began to stream back towards the rear. In all, over 160 gave themselves up.

In the face of the vigorous action of 5 Dorset they had clearly had enough. Major Mead was quick to seize the hamlet of Les Haies half a mile ahead. In spite of heavy mortaring, the place was quickly consolidated with the assistance of D Company of 1 Worcestershire, who for this operation had been placed under the command of 130 Brigade.

Lieut.-Colonel Coad now directed 7 Royal Hampshire supported by B Squadon of the Sherwood Rangers on to the large and straggling village of St. Denis de Mere, which dominates the north-eastern approaches to Condé and through which pass all the roads from the north leading to the road and railway crossings near Cahan, which constituted his final objective for the day. It was here that Major-General Thomas had planned to cross the river, and the need to get the Royal Engineers reconnaissance parties forward before nightfall had become urgent. 7 Royal Hampshire therefore quickly deployed and after a well-controlled advance entered the village, captured 74 prisoners of 752 Grenadier Regiment and a S.P. gun and thus cleared the way for 4 Dorset.

Between St. Denis de Mere and the crossings at Cahan runs a long plateau which dominates the north bank of the river. It is flat on top and intersected with a network of parallel roads running east and west. Many small farms surrounded by orchards fringe these roads. In this area, concealed from view and difficult to locate, considerable numbers of the enemy still held out. The objective given to 4 Dorset was Pt. 201, which dominates the Cahan crossings on the north bank. It is, however, flanked by a mass of small farms and cottages with all the characteristics of the *bocage* villages which the Division now knew so well. That this battalion achieved this long and difficult advance of a mile and half by the evening is a notable achievement. Large parties of the enemy were inevitably bypassed and continued to hold out for a further twenty-four hours. Nevertheless by nightfall the battalion had reached its objective and pushed patrols towards the crossings. Cleverly laid mines and continued sniping made this a most difficult advance.

Lieutenant Olley of 204 Field Company with the Royal Engineer Reconnaissance party had followed close on the heels of 4 Dorset. Eventually, leaving them to deal with the enemy, he pushed through towards the crossings, to find that both the road and railway bridges had been destroyed. He managed, however, to measure the gaps over the demolished bridges and to return with a report which left the C.R.E., Lieut.-Colonel Pike, in no doubt as to the formidable character of the task which lay ahead and the extent to which the enemy's widespread sowing of mines was likely to hamper operations.

C Squadron of the Reconnaissance Regiment, attempting to get through Proussy and out to the east flank at St. Marc d'Ouilly in the late evening, managed to make progress for about a mile, but were overtaken by darkness. Further to the north at Clécy on the Orne, where the enemy still held out, a patrol under Lieutenant Baker had fought a most effective minor battle.

Since daybreak 130 Brigade had advanced over seven miles through difficult country, hampered at every step by resistance which was exceedingly difficult to locate and bedevilled by mines in whichever direction they moved. Three thousand civilian refugees from the railway tunnel north of Cahan now added to their problems. Contact with the French Resistance here had been close since the 12th, when Captain H. J. Gauthier (Canadian)* had passed through the enemy lines and met their leaders. Altogether the brigade had made remarkable progress, captured over 300 prisoners and large quantities of abandoned equipment.

THE CROSSING OF THE NOIREAU

15th
Aug.   The valley of the Noireau east of Condé bears a strong resemblance to the upper waters of the River Exe in Devon. The high ground on either bank is wooded and exceedingly steep on the southern side. East of the plateau secured by 130 Brigade by nightfall on the 14th, the railway running due south from Thury Harcourt enters a narrow

* Royal 22e Regiment Canadien Français.

ravine and after crossing the Noireau joins the main line from Falaise to Condé south of the stream. The road leading to the crossing is a rough, narrow, winding track. Twelve hundred yards to the east stands a mill, near the village of Cahan. It was between this railway bridge and the mill that Major-General Thomas had decided to force the crossing. The river itself is about twenty yards wide and about three feet deep—no obstacle to infantry, but impassable to vehicles. A good road to Condé runs parallel to the south bank, from which thickly wooded hills rise abruptly to the Berjou Massif. The map gives a poor impression of the formidable character of this feature. Winding obliquely across the precipitous hillside, from near the railway station four hundred yards west of the railway bridge, runs a track leading to the village of Berjou on the crest. From Berjou the high ground extends two miles to the south-east to Pt. 237. This was the objective now to be given to 214 Brigade.

Patrols of 4 Dorset during the night of the 14th forced their way down to the river bank and soon established the fact that the area was thickly strewn with mines. Continuing their operations on the morning of the 15th, they cleared up the remains of enemy resistance on the north bank near the crossing site and later established a company group on the high ground east of the ravine. 15th Aug.

With the coming of daylight on the 15th, C Squadron of the Reconnaissance Regiment moved out on the left flank towards St. Marc d'Ouilly, which lies in the angle formed by the junction of the Noireau and the Orne. Here they engaged the enemy, who were still holding the village in strength. A foot patrol from this squadron also reconnoitred the Noireau. No. 9 Troop reconnoitring towards Condé and No. 10 Troop towards Pont Erembourg found their progress delayed by mines and by enemy still vigorously resisting in this direction. A particularly bold patrol led by Captain J. W. Baden of 7 Somerset Light Infantry worked their way forward in the hot sunshine to the mill, from the top windows of which Germans digging in machine-guns on the far bank were clearly visible. Removing their boots and steel helmets, they paddled the stretch of stream in which they were interested, apparently in full view of the enemy. Lieut.-Colonel Nichol meanwhile reconnoitred a crossing from behind farm buildings nearby, somewhat hampered by a crowd of enthusiastic French peasants. Lieut.-Colonel Osborne Smith was able to plan his advance from the river bank by the broken railway bridge. All parties reported mines strewn everywhere, often only poorly disguised under a covering of dust. These subsequently were to cause many casualties not only to the troops but to the unfortunate French civilians. A little boy was blown up and an unfortunate woman lost her three children in this way during the day.

The plan for the attack included most intense and elaborate fire

support by 8 Middlesex under Lieut.-Colonel M. Crawford. Starting half an hour before the infantry were due to cross the start line
of the river, the medium machine-guns of two companies drenched
the attacking battalions' objectives with concentrated fire continuing
for one hour, whilst the 4·2-inch mortar company blasted the ridge
with H.E. and smoke. This, combined with concentrations by the
Divisional artillery, which set alight the wooded slope ahead and
drove the enemy under cover, enabled the infantry to wade through
the stream at 6 p.m. with the certainty of success.

On the right, A Company of 1 Worcestershire stepped into the
water near the blown railway bridge and waded across. A shower
of mortar bombs fell amongst them, causing several casualties.
One or two small groups of Germans, waving white material, surrendered. The company pushed on to the main road and reached
the junction with the track leading up the hill to Berjou. Here
Teller mines were encountered and left to be dealt with by the
Pioneer Platoon. Followed by the rest of the battalion, the company
crept warily up the track, sweating and cursing at the steep gradient.
On either side of them the woods were burning. Up and up they
went until at last they reached an open field on the reverse slope in
front of the village of Berjou. Two white 2-inch mortar flares fired
to indicate success informed their brigade headquarters that they
were on the ridge. Two other companies of the battalion moved up
on the left and the position was quickly consolidated. Bursts of
Spandau fire now opened up—too late, however, to shake their hold
on the hill.

The covering fire given to 7 Somerset Light Infantry on the left
was even heavier. Supported by their own mortars and the concentrated fire of the carrier platoon, in addition to that of the
Divisional artillery and 8 Middlesex, D Company, under Major
S. C. W. Young, carried the mill in the face of lively small arms and
mortar fire and established a small bridgehead on the south bank.
C Company, under Major D. M. B. Durie, although caught in
Spandau and mortar fire from the far bank, fought their way forward
across the railway towards a commanding bluff and beyond it to their
objective, a high stretch of rocky ground studded with thick gorse.
A Company followed and consolidated on the right. B Company
made a separate crossing on the left. The battalion dug in under
harassing fire on a perimeter which covered a thousand yards.
Next day they were further to appreciate the immense support
given to them by the tremendous volume of fire put down by 8
Middlesex. Several hundred German dead were counted in the area,
the majority of whom had been caught in the fire of the medium
machine-guns.

It had been intended that 5 D.C.L.I. should advance at 8 p.m. by
the crossing near the mill behind 7 Somerset. Their objective was

Pt. 237 and a "potato-shaped" contour on the eastern end of Berjou ridge, three thousand yards south of the river. In the ravine around the crossings the congestion had by this hour reached its climax. As the time approached, with only two and a half hours of daylight left, Lieut.-Colonel Taylor heard on the wireless that the Worcesters had gained the top of the ridge. There was no news of the Somersets. Without more ado he therefore led his battalion over the right-hand crossing and up the hill by the track towards Berjou. He reached the right-hand company of the Worcesters on the ridge just as the light was failing. From the constant ripple of Spandaus ahead, it was clear that the enemy in some force lay about a hundred yards away. Night of unprecedented blackness now descended. Further search for trigonometrical points and potato-shaped contours was therefore no longer a practical proposition until the dawn. Lieut.-Colonel Taylor accordingly announced his intention of digging in his battalion in a tight triangle in front of the right and centre companies of the Worcesters. This he proceeded to do. The resulting congestion on the top of the ridge can be well imagined. Thus by nightfall the brigade had two battalions outside Berjou and one on the high ground commanding Cahan. They were, however, without their vehicles and anti-tank weapons. Fourteen hours were to elapse before these could reach them.

Meanwhile, 204 Field Company, with a waterproofed bulldozer, three tipper lorries of flexboards, four landing-stage units and two boat units, had got to work on the crossings. In spite of the heavy shell-fire No. 1 Platoon, thanks to the cool leadership of Sergeant Hicks, had cleared the approaches of mines and built a tank ford and a trestle bridge, which was named "Genesis," near the broken railway crossing. Downstream where the Somersets had crossed, Lieutenant Harding with No. 2 Platoon found two streams, not one. However, they set to, cleared the mines and made two Class 9 trestle bridges.

553 Field Company had been given the task of building the Division's first Bailey bridge across the site of the demolished bridge. Lieutenant Blow, after a difficult reconnaissance in the heavily mined area, decided that the Bailey set held by 207 Field Park Company, with careful setting out, would suffice. The advanced party picked their way through the mines and found a harbour area for the equipment. They started to set out the bridge in the darkness, when to their consternation they found the road width on the bridge abutments too small to take the baseplates. A move back for a considerable distance became imperative before the road widened sufficiently. This meant that a 120-ft., not 80-ft., bridge would have to be constructed. It was not until daylight that work could be started. All night Lieutenant Martin's platoon bravely struggled to lift the booby-trapped mines on the site. To blow them up on

7

the spot by pulling was out of the question on account of the congestion in the area.   For the next two days the Sappers were to struggle unceasingly to clear the multitude of mines which the enemy had strewn in the valley.   204 Field Company lost a complete section.   To Lieutenant Martin and Sapper Murphy belongs the credit for the first discovery of the devilish TMIZ 43 igniter.   This rendered the mine, once armed, incapable of neutralization, and this discovery led to a complete change in the recovery drill throughout the army, thus probably saving hundreds of lives.

On returning from the site, the reconnaissance car of Lieut.-Colonel Pike, the C.R.E., overturned in the darkness, causing him severe internal injuries.   Despite his violent protests, the A.D.M.S., Colonel Tomory, insisted on his being evacuated.   His departure was a great loss to the Division, for he possessed a grasp of the engineer aspects of the larger tactical problems attained by few of his rank, and his mature judgment would have been invaluable on the Seine, the Waal and the Rhine.

Throughout the night, under shell fire, the work on the crossings continued.   With the tanks of the Sherwood Rangers, the 17-pdrs. and the transport of the three attacking battalions all converging on the narrow track leading down to the river, the congestion reached its climax in the hours before the dawn.   Occasionally a vehicle would strike a mine in the verge of the road and blow up.   A large truck blew up at the crossing site and 214 Scammel, which went to the rescue, itself touched down on a mine.   It is not surprising that in the darkness progress was slow.   Only the united will and courage of all ranks at the crossings kept the traffic moving.

16th Aug.   Only when daylight came was it possible to obtain a clear picture of the situation and to see the dramatic events of the night in their true proportion.   At first the normal uncanny lull which in war usually comes with the dawn, reigned over the Noireau.   At this time friend and foe alike are prone to pause and adjust themselves, after a night of doubt and confusion, to another day of fighting.   It was so now.   Tank and carrier crews in the long column straddling the river brought out their Primus stoves and brewed up tea.   Men who had lost their units asked their way.   Casualties moved to the rear.

On the crest of the hill before Berjou the D.C.L.I. and the Worcesters had spent a cold night, drenched by a thunder-storm about 2 a.m.   Neither their tanks nor anti-tank guns had arrived, but Major Brewis, R.A., the battery commander with the D.C.L.I., had managed to get his big artillery wireless set up the hill, thus maintaining touch with the guns and Brigade Headquarters.   The early-morning quiet did not last for long.   Soon mortar bombs began to fall in black vivid crashes on the two battalions.   B Company of the D.C.L.I. attacked under cover of a small screen and destroyed two machine-gun posts, but was held up later by withering fire of Spandaus. An enemy counter-attack now developed on the left-hand company of the Worcesters, in which Major Matthews, the company commander, was wounded. A further attack now came in round the D.C.L.I. right flank and succeeded in bringing the track down to the valley under heavy fire, thus cutting off communication with the rear. Casualties in both battalions began to mount.

Meanwhile, the column of tanks of the Sherwood Rangers, interspersed with the armoured car and Bren carriers of A Squadron of the Reconnaissance Regiment under Major Scott-Plummer, whose arrival, though welcome, was somewhat premature, stood nose to tail on the main road to Condé with their head at the group of cottages by the junction with the track leading obliquely up the hill to Berjou. Mortar bombs and heavy shells were exploding around the crossings and on the roads. From the woods on the hillside came the crackle of rifle bullets and the clatter of machine-gun fire. For a brief moment the enemy, well handled and fighting with courage, had gained the initiative. He was not to retain it for long. The Brigadier, who had arrived with Lieut.-Colonel Christopherson, commanding the Sherwood Rangers, ordered the tanks to join the two battalions. Without more ado they thundered up the road, followed by A Company of the D.C.L.I., who fought their way through, dealing with small parties of enemy riflemen on the way. Thanks to the dogged efforts and initiative of Captain Gorman, the Adjutant of the D.C.L.I. and Captain N. V. Jones and Captain A. M. Ford of the Worcesters, a hot meal was got through to the troops. This was their first meal since the previous afternoon.

Lieut.-Colonel Osborne Smith and 1 Worcestershire now turned to the task of destroying the enemy in Berjou. D Company on the right and B Company on the left formed up along a hedgerow on the right of their position with A Company, a hundred yards in rear, followed by C Company, to whom had been given the task of mopping up. The tanks of the Sherwood Rangers moved to hull down positions on the crest. Supported by a tremendous weight of artillery and mortar fire, they swept up the slope in perfect formation, to see the village on the flat tableland four hundred yards ahead. Before them the shells poured down; from behind came the full blast of the Sherwood Rangers. Excitement ran high. This was too much for the enemy. The few who stayed to fight were wiped out. For the most part they fled as the companies stormed the village.

Equally devastating support by the Sherwood Rangers enabled A Company of the D.C.L.I. to push forward to the crest of the ridge a thousand yards to the east. The platoons of Lieutenants B. M. Williams and J. Olding particularly distinguished themselves, and a considerable number of the enemy were killed or captured.

Whilst this fighting was going on around Berjou, Major Scott-Plummer, with A Squadron of the Reconnaissance Regiment, decided to try and work round the west flank. No. 1 Troop, moving down the valley road towards Condé, almost at once found itself under heavy mortar fire and sniping. The first enemy sighted were in trenches, but facing the wrong way. These were engaged with machine-gun fire and then mortared for fifteen minutes. Going forward to observe the effect, Lieutenant Clibbery's car was suddenly struck by a bazooka bomb from the woods. Baling out, he and his gunner were at once attacked with hand grenades. Corporal Hall, the gunner, was killed, but Lieutenant Clibbery, although wounded, managed to escape. When Berjou fell, the roads were found to be so extensively mined that further progress proved impossible that day.

On the left, 7 Somerset Light Infantry, supported by tanks of the Sherwood Rangers, were ready to continue the advance through the group of villages a mile south of the Noireau. In a series of small battles, C and D Companies drove the enemy relentlessly back. He was now beginning to lose heart and to abandon his equipment. Considerable numbers of prisoners were taken. By nightfall the battalion had gained contact with the D.C.L.I. two miles south of the river. The enemy had gone, leaving behind masses of mines, which were to continue to cause casualties for some days.

Further west, at St. Marc d'Ouilly, 11 Troop of the Reconnaissance Regiment fought a running fight all day with the enemy and took a number of prisoners.

17th Aug.   As night closed in the noise of mortar- and shell-fire died down. Soon only a solitary 88 and a long-range gun remained in action on the front. After 1 a.m. all was silent. For the first time for many weeks the Division was out of contact with the enemy.

One of the last of his shells killed Regimental Sergeant Major Hurd of the Worcestershire Regiment. A little time before he had been seen, his face beaming with pleasure, bringing in thirty German prisoners at the double.

This redoubtable old Warrant Officer—he was over fifty—had concealed his age so as to be able to accompany his battalion. Disdaining cover and always amongst the first to seek out and kill the enemy, he embodied in his person the highest traditions of the

In this operation, 214 Brigade were greatly helped by the French Resistance Force under M. Raymond Pierre (as Raymond 1929 of the Maquis), who penetrated deep behind the enemy lines at great personal risk and supplied accurate and detailed information. His force, also in co-operation with Captain J. H. Gauthier, Royal 22e Regiment Canadien Français, supplied guides with intimate knowledge of the local roads and tracks and the location of the enemy mines. Amongst these MM. Rene Lassu, Julien Lassu, Jacques Leboucher, Paul Leboucher and Raymond Mellion notably gained the esteem of all ranks of the brigade.

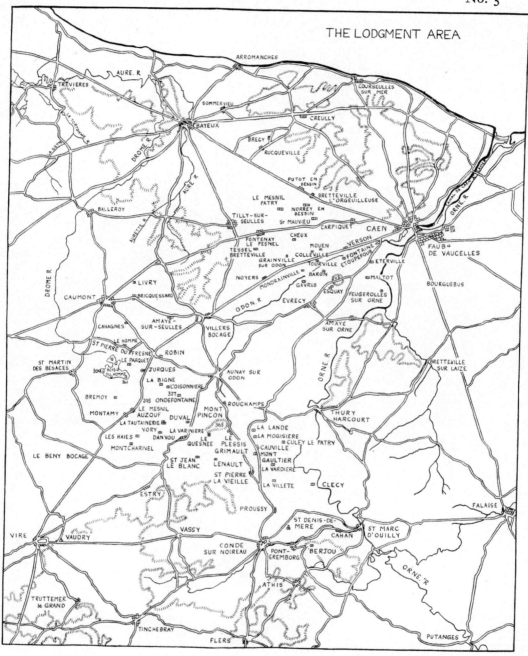

THE LODGMENT AREA

Regular Infantry of the Line. It is grimly appropriate that he should have fallen in the hour of victory on the Berjou Ridge.

LAST DAYS IN NORMANDY

The enemy having abandoned the struggle on the Divisional front, 129 Brigade, preceded by the Reconnaissance Regiment, were able to advance early next day hampered only by mines. 5 Wiltshire reached St. Honorine la Chardonne by midday without opposition, to the sound of church bells and the cheers of enthusiastic crowds. 4 Somerset found a similar welcome in La Fertie. The cars of the Reconnaissance Regiment were decked with flowers. *17th Aug.*

Lieut.-General Horrocks now decided to conclude the final round up with 50 and 11 Armoured Divisions. Orders were accordingly sent out for the Division to concentrate south of the Noireau and complete the clearance of mines. These still continued to cause casualties, including Lieut.-Colonel O. W. R. Dent, commanding 110 Light A.A. Regiment, who was killed whilst driving his jeep at the crossings of the Noireau.

The British, Canadian and American Armies now rapidly closed in around the remnants of the German Seventh Army, trapped in the triangle around Trun, Chambois and Argentan. The Allied air forces, the guns, the armour and the infantry all took an enormous toll. By the 21st August, General Montgomery in a personal message to all troops was able to announce "definite, complete and decisive victory."

Statistics of the vast quantity of vehicles and equipment destroyed convey little to the imagination. 130 Brigade, moved to the Chambois area on 22nd August, were to see the carnage in all its final horror. On either side of the 12-mile stretch of road through the Foret de Gouffren, from Argentan to Chambois, lay the wreckage of innumerable burnt-out tanks, S.P. guns, trucks, half-tracks and wagons. Paper from destroyed office trucks littered the fields. Horse-drawn batteries and their drivers lay dead amongst the bloated bodies of stinking cattle. Flies rose in their millions. French peasants and their children moved unconcerned amongst the corpses of German troops which lined the road for many miles. *22nd Aug.*

In the words of the Commander in Chief, here lay the evidence that the victory had been "definite, decisive and complete."

CHAPTER VI

THE CROSSING OF THE SEINE

(See Sketch Maps 6 and 7)

GENERAL SITUATION

22nd
Aug.
OPERATIONS were now developing with lightning speed. In the hope of saving the remains of the Seventh and Fifth German armies from being again surrounded, 2 S.S. Panzer Corps, according to a captured order dated 22nd August, endeavoured to stage a withdrawal in four bounds to the Seine. These hopes were thwarted by the direction of XV U.S. Corps on the crossing at Mantes Grassicourt and the XIX U.S. Corps straight across the British front on to Elbeuf south-west of Rouen. At the same time the First Canadian Army were ordered to block the east side of the pocket and the Second Army to drive through it to the Seine.

Bridging equipment for the crossing had begun to arrive early in August. The Royal Engineers had studied in England the technique of crossing wide rivers with considerable care. Formations of Engineers had been specially trained in assault and bridging operations, while special equipment, such as storm boats, had been developed. By 18th August two bridging columns had been formed. These each consisted of 366 task vehicles and carried sufficient storm boats, close-support rafts, and Bailey, pontoon and folding boat equipment for a corps assault on a one-divisional front, together with track material and hard-core preloaded on tippers for the bridge approaches. One of these columns was now allotted to 30 Corps.

By the evening of 22nd August the majority of 43 Division, after its brief rest along the Noireau, had just moved up into the rear area of 30 Corps behind Ecouches. 130 Brigade was in the Chambois area and 214 Brigade was due to arrive at Gacé on the morrow. For the moment the Division's task of picketing the left flank of the Corps axis against any offensive action by the last of the remnants of the enemy in the Falaise gap presented no serious military problem. In fact, the enthusiastic welcome of the liberated population, the complete absence of battle noises and the presence of both Army and Corps Headquarters in the neighbourhood gave it an air of unreality.

In the evening Major-General G. I. Thomas reported at Headquarters, 30 Corps.

THE PROBLEM

This was the task verbally given to Major-General Thomas—
"To force the crossing of the Seine at Vernon on or about 25th
August—to cover the construction of a Class 9 and a Class 40 bridge
—to form a bridgehead of sufficient depth to allow the passage
through of the remainder of the Corps (i.e. two armoured divisions,
one armoured brigade and one infantry division)—to ensure the
protection of the left flank of the Corps axis between the rivers Eure
and Seine."

To Major-General Thomas belongs the credit for the plan now
evolved. His also was the drive behind it and his were the troops
whose valour carried it through. It is therefore profitable to
consider the situation at the time when on that evening he retired to
his caravan with his maps and air photographs, to emerge at 9 p.m.
with the essentials of the plan which in three days was to secure, in
the face of opposition, a bridgehead 90 miles away over a major river
more than 600 feet wide and to ensure within six days the passage
across of the armour of 30 Corps.

At this time, in its drive north along the west bank of the Seine,
the U.S. XIX Corps had reached a line running approximately east
and west through Evreux. Their patrols were believed to be in
Vernon, but little was known concerning the enemy in that area.
An opposed crossing of the Seine against at least a strong enemy
screen was to be expected.

The route to Vernon by way of Argentan, Breteuil and Pacy cut
right across the American lines of communication. This complication materially influenced the plan. Prolonged negotiations on an
army level eventually secured use of the road east of Breteuil between
8 a.m. and 12 noon and 2 p.m. and 6 p.m. on 25th August and between 1 a.m. and 6 a.m. on the 26th. These restrictions forced the
Division to move in three main groups of about 2,000 vehicles each.
The exact composition, particularly of the leading group, had therefore to be a compromise between what was essential for the task and
what could be included in the overall total. The wide distribution
of the Division made it necessary for the first group to halt for the
night of 24th/25th August at Breteuil, whilst the remaining groups
could go straight through.

At the nine o'clock conference on the 22nd, Major-General
Thomas announced that 129 Brigade with the addition of the 1
Worcestershire from 214 Brigade would form the basis of the
Assault Group. The leading battalion, assisted by a squadron of the
Reconnaissance Regiment and a squadron of 15/19 Hussars, was to
occupy Vernon. The brigade was then to assault on a two battalion
front in storm boats and Dukws. The bridgehead would first
comprise a close perimeter, which would later be extended to deprive

the enemy of observation of the river and cover the construction of a Class 9 F.B.E. bridge. All the Divisional engineers were included in this group and all the equipment for the assault crossing and the F.B.E. bridge.

The second group was to consist of 214 Brigade Group, which included Seventh Army Troops R.E. and the bridge equipment for the Class 40 bridge. The third group comprised the remainder of the division.

On this basis planning went forward at high pressure throughout the night and all the following day.

The Dukws and storm boats had to come all the way from Arromanches; the heavy bridge and other technical R.E. vehicles from far to the rear. By the evening of the 23rd, the bivouac areas among the orchards near Ecouches presented an incongruous sight. Eight days' rations had to be collected and extra ammunition, including a high proportion of smoke, loaded on to the vehicles.

The success of the operation clearly depended on surprise. If on arrival on the river bank time were spent on the long and detailed reconnaissance prescribed by all the text-books, the delay would give the enemy time to strengthen his defences at the crossing. The only course therefore was to plan the operation in detail before the Division left Ecouches and make whatever adjustments seemed necessary on arrival.

The absence of information with regard to the bridge over the Eure at Pacy raised a further complication. In the table showing the composition of the three groups sent out at 1.30 a.m. on the 23rd there appears the item: "One set Bailey for Pacy—14 vehicles" in the Assault Group—as events turned out an instance of foresight well rewarded.

To assist Major-General Thomas, Brigadier Mole and the Sappers in the planning, Army Headquarters were able to provide 1/50,000 and 1/25,000 maps, one large-scale vertical air photograph and a mass of technical engineer information and general topographical data.

The Scine at Vernon is between 600 and 650 feet wide and flows with quite a strong current. It is spanned by two bridges. The stone road bridge had been destroyed in 1940, but some of the piers still survived, and on these the Germans had built a metal bridge. It crosses the river from the centre of Vernon to Vernonnet. The railway bridge crosses the river 800 yards downstream.

In this reach of the river there are many islands. Above the road bridge there is a single island, upstream of which lies a shallow covered with weeds. This sunken island was to figure prominently in the actual operations. Between the two bridges, there are two islands in midstream. The railway bridge crosses the first of three large islands which are close to the eastern bank and extend for about

9. Royal Tiger Tank knocked out by 5 D.C.L.I. at Le Plessis Grimault, 7th August, 1944

10. Transport of 43 Reconnaisance Regiment crossing the newly bridged river Eure at Pacy sur Eure, 25th August, 1944

11. Infantry of the Division in Vernon making for the boats, 25th August, 1944

12. Infantry of the Division crossing the Seine—evening, 25th August, 1944

13. The bombed bridge over the Seine forced by the Worcesters early on
26th August, 1944

14. 553 Field Company R.E. working on the pontoon bridge. Note the smoke
screen maintained by the Divisional artillery

a mile downstream. The banks of the river are steep and consist of earth covered with grass.

Vernon, a charming and well laid-out provincial town of about 10,000 inhabitants and a summer resort of the more sophisticated inhabitants of Paris, extends for about three miles on either side of the road bridge. Along the riverside is a road with an avenue of trees and the tow-path. To the west wooded slopes studded with neat villas rise rapidly to the plateau.

Opposite Vernon, on a narrow strip of flat ground, lies the suburb of Vernonnet. Immediately behind it the ground rises rapidly in an escarpment which completely dominates the river and both banks. This escarpment is divided into three conspicuous spurs by the two re-entrants through which pass the roads to Gasny and Gisors. The Foret de Vernon extends for five miles from the outskirts of Vernonnet and is intersected by many tracks and rides, by means of which the enemy could move his reserves and deploy for action completely unobserved.

In view of the overwhelming necessity for speed, the selection of bridge sites other than at Vernon was out of the question. Only here were the essential road approaches available for the mass of material necessary. The railway bridge was known to have been destroyed, but according to an air photograph the road bridge had one long girder blown out of position. It was hoped that this bridge might be passable for infantry and there was a chance that a certain amount of ramping might make it possible for tanks. The R.E. initially selected the site of the Class 40 bridge as downstream of the road bridge, with the Class 9 bridge 150 yards upstream. In the end, the Class 40 had to be built upstream.

The situation on the north flank was vague in the extreme. One battalion of the assault brigade had therefore to be kept in hand. Thus only three battalions were available for the actual assault. This meant that the initial bridgehead had to be close to the proposed bridge sites. To land the infantry close to the exits of the railway and road bridges at Vernonnet would involve them immediately in all the complications and delays of fighting in a built-up area. Upstream the far bank was open and, apart from the unknown hazards of the submerged island which might impede the passage of the assault craft, appeared suitable. This site was therefore selected for the landing of the right assault battalion.

For the landing of the left assault battalion, the two large islands fringing the east bank were clearly separated from the main stream. Of these, the left-hand island was obviously cut off from the mainland by an appreciable backwater. The other island, which carried the railway line by means of a bridge to the mainland, appeared to offer possibilities. It was difficult to be certain whether the cut under this bridge was wet or dry. However, the representative of the

Army Photographic Interpretation Section (A.P.I.S.) considered that this cut was probably shingly and dry, with perhaps a water trickle in the middle. To land further downstream would have pushed the assaulting battalion too far out. It was therefore decided, subject to local confirmation, to land it on the island traversed by the railway track.

Little difficulty was anticipated in launching Dukws, and it was initially decided to cross in them, using the storm boats only as a reserve and for ferrying 6-pdrs. and jeeps. Finally, it was proposed to provide one Class 9 raft on each battalion front to get the carriers over. Class 40 rafts were not considered, as it was thought that they would be difficult to handle in the current.

Provided all went well, there appeared to be a reasonable prospect that the Class 40 bridge would be ready by the evening of August 26th or early on the 27th.

When the column of the Assault Group started to move forward at 6 a.m. on August 24th, the plan was complete. It had been evolved in the short space of 30 hours. Instances are rare of more vigorous direction in planning by a commander or of more effective response by his subordinates and staff.

THE ADVANCE TO THE SEINE

24th Aug.
Early on the 24th the long column of the Assault Group set out for Breteuil. First came the Reconnaissance Regiment and a mass of reconnaissance parties—infantry, sappers, machine-gunners and gunners—followed by 4 Wiltshire Battalion Group, destined for the control of Vernon. Next came C Squadron of the Reconnaissance Regiment and the 15/19 Hussars, whose task was to be the protection of the north flank; then the two assaulting battalions, 5 Wiltshire and 4 Somerset Light Infantry, the follow-up battalion the 1 Worcestershire, all in Dukws; the headquarters of 129 Brigade and Major-General Thomas's tactical headquarters, and finally the whole of the Divisional engineers with all their equipment. The route lay through the ruins of Argentan and then out into the undamaged country beyond to Laigle and Breteuil. Cheering and waving crowds sped them on their way, throwing roses to the troops and demanding "Cigarettes for Papa." Officers moved up and down the column on every available motor-cycle and pushed aside all vehicles not belonging to the Division. Here and there, wrecked 88's and abandoned enemy transport littered the roads. In the afternoon the staging area west of Breteuil was reached and the column curled off the road in pouring rain.

No. 9 Troop of the Reconnaissance Regiment under Lieutenant Teden, accompanied by Lieutenant Cresswell of the Divisional engineers, had been sent on ahead to find out the situation at the crossing of the River Eure at Pacy.

One mile west of the river, at the little village of St. Acquilin de Pacy, they found the road cratered and a block of burnt out vehicles. Worse still, the bridge at Pacy had been destroyed. On the east side of the town the railway bridge had also been demolished. Major-General Thomas was early on the spot in his Ark to meet the only available representative of the U.S. Forces—a solitary but supremely competent military policeman.

260 Field Company soon arrived to deal with the craters and suffered some casualties in dealing with the road block, which was found to be booby trapped. 553 Field Company's bridge reconnaissance party, moving on foot into Pacy, found there on the opposite bank a number of American engineers under a sergeant preparing to build a timber trestle bridge. An international agreement was quickly reached whereby the British built a Bailey bridge over the Eure and the Americans made a diversion round the damaged bridge over the railway by bulldozing a by-pass through the station and over the railway line. As 553 Field Company was required for the Class 9 bridge over the Seine, 11 Field Company undertook the construction of the Bailey under the protection of the Reconnaissance Regiment. The work went on throughout the night.

B and C Squadrons of this regiment and the reconnaissance parties of the Assault Group who had left Breteuil at daybreak were allowed to pass over immediately. In spite of the need to construct a further thirty feet of bridge to take the load off the badly cracked second span of the old bridge, the road was opened at 10.15 a.m. *25th Aug.*

The wild race for Vernon now began. All normal considerations of speed and density were abandoned. Drivers were told, "Interval, as close as you can get. Speed—flat out." Heavily laden jeeps and carriers, Cromwell tanks and overloaded Dukws, three-ton lorries and the rest surged forward though the dust and heat towards the Seine. No less than 1,600 vehicles passed the American check point in four hours. In the time allotted the complete Assault Group was through the Pacy defile.

It must be recognized that only the complete dominance of the Allied air forces made possible this high-speed, congested burst forward. Whilst it was going on, the Luftwaffe suffered its worst defeat since the start of the campaign. Some 330 enemy aircraft were destroyed. Of these, 130 were shot down over France.

ARRIVAL IN VERNON

It was noon when 4 Wiltshire Regiment, preceded by B Squadron of the Reconnaissance Regiment, wound down the steep and winding road into Vernon, to be faced by a situation without parallel. A few troops of an American reconnaissance unit had arrived there several days previously and the Germans had withdrawn to the far bank.

The Resistance Movement had at once seized the barracks near the river and barricaded themselves inside. Most of the local population had acquired arms of some sort and now promenaded the streets in a state of wild excitement, accepting cigarettes and offering advice and fruit with Gallic exuberance. Masses of spectators, sometimes in the role of guides, threatened to disclose to the enemy the presence of British troops, whose arrival it was essential to conceal. The whole town was overlooked by the cliffs on the north bank of the river. German troops were plainly visible sunning themselves on the cliffs on the far bank.

Every now and then an American mortar team engaged them by direct fire from the streets amid a crowd of excited spectators, Below the cliffs in the suburbs of Vernonnet six German posts could be seen without the use of binoculars. Many Frenchmen came forward and said they had personally crossed the river. The mayor arrived and invited Lieut.-Colonel Luce and his officers to a civic banquet.

The other commanding officers of the Brigade now appeared on the scene. Reconnaissance under these bizarre conditions went forward with considerable difficulty, led by the Maquis. Lieut.-Colonel Luce and others crept forward through yards, back gardens and alleys into the lounge of the Hôtel de France on the waterfront, from the uncurtained windows of which an excellent view could be obtained of the far bank. The experience of other reconnoitring parties was equally fantastic. The strictest orders had been issued with regard to secrecy, including provision for the wearing of American steel helmets during reconnaissance. In their role of traffic police 4 Wiltshire found their hands more than fully occupied. However, the rifle companies were soon in their pre-arranged positions and started to dig in, hiding their vehicles amidst trees and buildings as well as they could. It is astonishing that no inkling of what was afoot reached the Germans across the river, especially when the French police came and hoisted the Union Jack, the Stars and Stripes and the Tricolour on a tower which the mortar platoon were using as an observation post. C Squadron of the 15/19 Hussars remained under cover at the top of the hill.

Meanwhile C Squadron of the Reconnaissance Regiment had moved far out to the left flank without interference and was established in observation posts from near Les Andelys on the Seine to Louviers on the Eure. United States reconnaissance units were already in the area, as were a large number of straggling and cowed Germans and several enemy tanks abandoned for want of petrol. The 15/19 Hussars also had no difficulty in occupying the stop line, about five miles north of the road from Pacy to Vernon. Anxiety with regard to the north flank being thus removed, 4 Wiltshire could now be released on the morrow for operations across the river.

By 4 p.m. the last of the vehicles of the Assault Group had drawn into the harbour area in the western outskirts of the Foret de Bizy and the villages of La Heuniere and St. Vincent des Bois. Major-General Thomas and Brigadier Mole had established their tactical headquarters together, and by the time the final co-ordinating "O" Group assembled were in a position to adjust the plan for the crossing in the light of the mass of conflicting information obtained from the French Forces of the Interior (F.F.I) and the local inhabitants. Vernonnet appeared to be held by about 250 Germans, and Giverny, two miles upstream, to be garrisoned by an equal number. The main German reserve was said to be located at Beauvais, some 35 miles to the northeast. This information tallied well with the latest intelligence forecast that the area was held by the German 49 Division, which had not been engaged in Normandy. In view of the wide front allotted to it, these dispositions appeared reasonable. The local population were emphatic that the cut between the railway-bridge island and the mainland was dry. They were equally certain that the submerged island in the right sector would not hinder the free passage of boats. The F.F.I. also pointed out with accuracy the exact positions of certain machine-guns in houses, some 20-mm. Flak guns and some manned slit trenches. The Germans themselves, in spite of the excitement in Vernon, still blissfully remained unaware of the Division's arrival.

Unfortunately time had not permitted the reconnaissance of the infantry and the sappers to be co-ordinated. Lieut.-Colonel Evill, the C.R.E., reported that adequate launching sites for the Dukws were hard to find. It was therefore agreed that storm boats should be used as much as possible for the assaulting battalions and that Dukw's would be used later when the ramps were complete. This decision was to have unfortunate results, as the infantry had had little practise in the use of these rather awkward craft. Otherwise the outline plan was confirmed and H hour fixed at 7 p.m.

94 Field Regiment, which together with 121 Medium Regiment provided the only artillery support for the assault, were now in action behind the town. A Company of 8 Middlesex established all three machine-gun platoons in buildings and gardens overlooking the river. D Company (4·2-inch mortars) took up four platoon areas in positions previously chosen from the air photographs and deployed three observation posts to control the fire. Two troops of C Squadron, 15/19 Hussars, moved forward to positions in some gardens about 60 yards from the river, from which they could support the assault by observed fire. In brief, the fire plan involved fifteen minutes' preliminary bombardment, followed by ten minutes during which a smoke-screen was to be created. The infantry were then to cross and the smoke screen was to be maintained for the remaining hours of daylight.

The commanding officers of 5 Wiltshire and 4 Somerset Light Infantry had barely time to issue their orders and see their men fed before they moved off. 5 Wiltshire advanced down the main road and, passing the Château de Bizy, until recently the headquarters of a German Army Group, entered the town by the boulevard now known as the Avenue Maréchal Montgomery. 4 Somerset took the straight tree-lined road, the Avenue des Capuchins, leading towards the railway bridge. The streets were crowded with men and laughing girls in summer frocks. Children ran beside the columns trying to get a ride. Suddenly the guns opened up, and in a flash the streets were empty. The battle had begun. It was 6.45 p.m.

In a moment the opposite hillside was carpeted with mushroom-like puffs of smoke, with the high explosive of the guns and mortars intermingled with the tracer and machine-gun bullets of 8 Middlesex and the tanks.

THE ASSAULT ON THE RIGHT

When the bombardment opened 5 Wiltshire had assembled in an orchard and some houses surrounded by a high stone wall about a hundred yards back from the river-bank.

Immediately opposite on the far side of the river flat fields led to a road and railway running side by side at the foot of a precipitous hill covered with bracken and gorse. This escarpment stretched for over a mile to the right along the river, and on the left dipped down into Vernonnet. It was honeycombed with tunnels and bristled with well hidden machine-gun posts.

Eight storm boats manned by 15 (Kent) G.H.Q. Troops Engineers had been provided for the crossing. B Company, whose task it was to carry them down to the river, had never seen this type of craft before. They proved to be exceedingly heavy and required a whole platoon to carry them. However, the first two carrying No. 8 Platoon of A Company under Lieutenant Selby, slipped into the water at 7 p.m. All went well until with only 30 yards to go both boats grounded on the submerged island. By ill luck the wind at this moment dispersed the smoke-screen on the far bank. Both boats were immediately raked with murderous machine-gun fire. Lieutenant Selby's boat capsized into deeper water. There were no survivors. In the other boat, Sergeant Mackrell shouted to his men to swim for it and plunged into the water. On reaching the far bank, he found he was alone. He therefore swam back to the boat and with the help of the one survivor of the crew managed to swim it back under the lee of the nearby island and thence back to the shore. Meanwhile most of the other boats attempting to cross had been sunk before reaching half-way.

By the end of an hour only one of the eight boats survived. In this the officer in charge of the Royal Engineers—dressed only in a duffle-coat and a pair of socks, for he had already been in the water several times—regardless of the machine-gun fire, managed to make several trips by taking a wide detour upstream of the submerged island. In this way about 60 per cent. of A Company got across. Lieutenant Drake and his party on landing made for their objective, a house on the road about 200 yards from the bank. Here they joined No. 7 Platoon. Major J. F. Milne, the company commander, now arrived after his second attempt to cross and dug his men in around the house. As darkness fell the enemy counter-attacked along the line of the roadway and the road from the south east. The first two attacks were beaten off with heavy fire. Finally in pitch darkness the enemy put in a stronger attack. The defenders fought valiantly until their ammunition was exhausted and they were overwhelmed. Their courage, however, was not in vain, for they held out long enough to enable the rest of the battalion to get across the river and establish itself firmly on the east bank.

Meanwhile, the disaster to the storm boats had created a crisis on the Vernon side of the river. Lieut.-Colonel Roberts decided to use Dukws. It was now dark. Of the four immediately available, three at once grounded and were useless. In the fourth Dukw, one platoon of C Company now crossed and made for its rendezvous on the far bank. This solitary Dukw then ferried over the whole of the rest of the battalion in repeated trips. It was now past midnight. A bulldozer had by this time been brought into use and just before midnight completed a runway down to the water for the Dukws, more of which could now be got into the water.

Lieut.-Colonel Roberts and his advanced headquarters arrived on the far bank in the midst of the confusion of the counter-attack in which A Company were finally overwhelmed. In the darkness it was impossible to tell who was friend or foe. However, by about 2 a.m. he had managed to fill the gap on the right flank with a platoon of B Company, and by first light the whole of this company was firmly established on the right flank.

By 3 a.m. in spite of its chequered crossing, C Company, largely owing to the efforts of Company Sergeant Major N. L. Haines, had been collected on the bank with not a single man missing. Lieutenant Holly, the only officer, led it forward up the steep escarpment ahead and in spite of falling earth and stones and an iron fence halfway up, reached the objective. With this company on the top of the hill, B Company on the right flank and D Company on the left, the position was secure by dawn. By 5 a.m. D Company had extended its flank to the southern edge of Vernonnet.

THE ASSAULT ON THE LEFT

In the firm belief that the watercourse between the railway-bridge island and the mainland was dry, A Company, the assault company of the 4 Somerset Light Infantry under Major Acock, embarked in the storm boats of 15 (Kent) G.H.Q. Troops Engineers at 7.10 p.m. and within half an hour had established themselves without difficulty in their initial bridgehead. C Company, under Major Mallalieu, followed quickly and attempted to advance inland. It was then discovered that the cut under the railway was sixty feet wide, with steep muddy banks, deep water and an immeasurable depth of very soft mud. A few men of A Company tried to get across the debris of the destroyed railway bridge, only to be pinned down by fire. One or two, however, did succeed in reaching the gardens and allotments on the far side.

It had been intended that 1 Worcestershire should cross on the right behind the 5 Wiltshire and take over the centre of the bridgehead on the high ground immediately above Vernonnet. With this end in view, the battalion had moved into the streets of Vernon, where it waited in its vehicles. As night was falling and news of the misadventures of the two assaulting battalions began to filter through, Headquarters 129 Brigade ordered Lieut.-Colonel Osborne Smith to attempt to cross by the road bridge. A Company debussed and moved forward to the foot of the bridge, to be greeted by a shower of mortar bombs from the far bank. The leading platoon under Sergeant Jennings clambered on to the broken bridge and moved warily across. On approaching the far end he touched off a booby trap of egg grenades. A hail of Spandau fire at once swept the bridge. Although severely wounded Sergeant Jennings managed to withdraw his men with the loss of only one man killed. Attempts to silence the machine-guns by 6-pdr. fire assisted by 2-inch mortar fire proved abortive. Lieut.-Colonel Osborne Smith was just about to order the company to burst through regardless of loss when Brigadier Mole decided to use the 5 Wiltshire to clear the opposition from the far bank. A Company therefore withdrew to the nearby houses and made use of the opportunity to have a hot dinner.

At midnight, therefore, Major-General Thomas and Brigadier Mole at the headquarters of 129 Brigade faced a grim prospect—the 5 Wiltshire meeting fierce resistance on the right, a deadlock on the broken road bridge and two companies of the 4 Somerset marooned on an island on the left. Brigadier Mole on the radio therefore ordered Lieut.-Colonel Lipscomb to re-embark his battalion and land again upstream nearer the bridge. At the same time, it was decided that the Worcesters should make a second attempt to force their way across the bridge at first light.

THE BRIDGING STARTS

Realizing that his two leading companies were in a cul-de-sac, Lieut.-Colonel Lipscomb had already decided to land B Company in Dukws 500 yards upstream on the mainland near the road bridge. 260 Field Company bulldozers had by now completed a Dukw ramp. B Company accordingly started to embark. The leading Dukw entered the water successfully, but the second sank at the foot of the ramp, putting it out of action. Meanwhile the leading Dukw grounded on a mudbank in mid-stream and eventually had to be towed off by one of the storm boats. The rest of the company, therefore, were transferred to storm boats and crossed without difficulty. Once landed, they cleared the ground between the river and the village.

Lieut.-Colonel Evill had given the task of constructing the Class 9 bridge "David" to 553 and 204 Field Companies under Major K. Nealon, and bulldozing on the bridge approaches had started at 8 p.m. Each time the engine started a shower of mortar bombs descended. At 10.15 p.m., although the situation on the front of the 5 Wiltshire was most obscure, and in fact barely one company had crossed the river, Brigadier Mole gave permission to start work. Fortunately, the raft-building site was sheltered from the far bank by an island and Lieut.-Colonel Evill decided to carry on with the raft building there, hoping that the enemy would be cleared from the far bank by dawn.

In the darkness, with Spandau and 20-mm. A.A. gunfire and mortar bombs falling around them, the Sappers assembled the thirty-four rafts required—two had vanished. The two Spandaus continued to fire down the centre line of the proposed bridge. Orders were therefore given to moor all the rafts under the lee of the island until the enemy could be cleared from the far bank. When day broke, however, it became impossible to move on the near bank owing to enemy fire and the remaining rafts had to be left moored where they had been built.

A patrol of A Company of 1 Worcestershire now made a second attempt to cross the bridge. To their astonishment they found that the enemy had departed from the far end. Evidently the Spandau teams, whilst prepared to hold out under cover of darkness in their exposed position at the head of the bridge, had no stomach to face the concentrated fire of the guns when day came, or the threat to their rear by 4 Somerset. Under cover of artillery smoke the remainder of A Company quickly followed, with the rest of the battalion hot on their heels in single file, and entered Vernonnet. 26th Aug.

Thus soon after dawn on the 26th, the Division had the majority of three battalions across the river. Vernonnet, however, was not completely clear. Moreover, the enemy still held the three wooded

8

spurs dominating the bridging site and the crossings. The Sappers therefore faced the bleak prospect of constructing in broad daylight a floating bridge in the face of observed enemy rifle, machine-gun and artillery fire.

OPERATIONS OF 26TH AUGUST

Now, with our intentions plainly revealed and his machine-guns still commanding the bridging site and crossings, was the enemy's opportunity. A strong counter-attack in the early hours of daylight, with the three battalions strung out on the far bank, without their anti-tank guns and still in the process of reorganization after the confused operations of the night, might have been decisive. Realizing this threat to the full, Major-General Thomas quickly imparted fresh vigour to the operations. Clearly, the enemy had to be cleared with all speed from the spurs on the far bank. There was no need to impress this on 129 Brigade. Major-General Thomas discovered, however, that the close-support rafts which had been built during the night by 553 Field Company had not been used owing to the confusion on the far bank. Ferrying on the right accordingly started, and three carriers and three 6-pdr. anti-tank guns were got across. On the left, however, all attempts to use the rafts were foiled. Until the infantry had extinguished the opposition on the far bank, the construction of the bridge was bound to be slow and costly.

214 Brigade Group had arrived in the concentration area west of the Foret de Bizy on the previous evening in time for the remainder of the Divisional artillery to come into action before midnight. 130 Brigade Group, moving via Conches, had begun to enter the assembly area.

Luckily the north flank gave no cause for anxiety. The 15/19 Hussars with C Squadron of the Reconnaissance Regiment, despatched early on an offensive sweep between the Seine and Eure, reported little opposition as far north as Louviers. In order to confuse the issue and create the impression that a further crossing was imminent in the north, Captain Anslow of the D.C.L.I. with one 25-pdr., one 3-inch mortar and a carrier section was sent to simulate a crossing opposite Gaillon ten miles down stream—a congenial task. In addition, Brigadier Heath, the C.R.A., ordered ostentatious registration of targets up and down the river. These attempts at deception may partly explain the enemy's curious reluctance to counter-attack in strength throughout the day.

With the coming of daylight the 5 Wiltshire turned their attention to the machine-guns in the face of the cliff which were interrupting work on the bridge and which quickly brought it to a standstill. About 10 a.m. a patrol of B Company under Sergeant Clarke destroyed one of these in a cleverly concealed position. Later a second patrol of this company located another which the dismounted carrier platoon at last removed. By the early afternoon this battalion had consolidated on either side of the re-entrant running east from Vernonnet and taken over 100 prisoners.

On the 4 Somerset front, D Company under Major Garner disembarked just before first light and started to clear up the maze of houses and gardens at the northern end of Vernonnet. Eventually they succeeded in turning the spur from the rear and establishing themselves up the Gisors valley, destroying four 22-mm. guns dug into the side of the road and commanding the crossing. Vernonnet was found to be full of enemy dead. Thirty prisoners, including two officers, were taken. The other two companies were re-embarked in the storm boats and were ferried into the bridgehead. By the early afternoon the battalion was finally dug in along the spur 1,200 yards north of the village.

The whole of 1 Worcestershire completed the crossing of the damaged bridge by 8 a.m. and on a three-company front advanced to capture the high ground immediately to the north-east. The two left-hand companies reached their objectives with comparative ease, dealing with two Spandaus and taking a few prisoners. B Company on the right, however, had considerable difficulty with a concealed machine-gun sited in the thick country on the Gasny road.

Brigadier Mole now decided to use 4 Wiltshire to clear the area to the south of Vernonnet between the escarpment and the river. The 4 Wiltshire therefore crossed by the damaged bridge during the morning and, deployed on a three-company front, in the hottest part of the day made their way through the tangled and precipitous country to the south. Many deep caves were found and scattered parties of the enemy mopped up, including, surprising to relate, one engaged in playing a game of cards. D Company encountered several self-propelled guns. The advance went forward steadily throughout the afternoon and evening and by last light the spur about 1,700 yards south-east of Vernonnet had been reached.

The technicalities of bridge and raft construction in the face of enemy resistance which, as the sun got hotter, confronted Major-General Thomas and the large number of senior Sapper officers now upon the scene might well form the subject of a treatise of value to future generations of higher commanders and engineers. Such a study should throw light not only on the engineering and tactical aspects of the problem, but also on the reaction of many men of high intelligence to the stress of war. Space, however, does not permit, nor is it desirable to develop this theme here.

The opening of the sluice gates upstream by the Germans, thus raising the level of the river by over 3 feet, added to the complexity of the problem. This not only influenced the siting of the main bridges but necessitated the switching of the site for the tank rafts from above the bridge to their final site below it.

At the bridge site the smoke got thinner and thinner and finally vanished.   The advance of the Worcestershire Regiment in Vernon-net by 9 a.m. began to have its effect and the Sappers resumed work once more.

Taking advantage of this brief respite, the sappers of 553 and 204 Field Companies soon finished the rear trestle and approach and started to move in the rafts to form the bridge.   At the sight of this the German machine-gunners in their emplacements on the escarpment opened up.   The rafts in midstream were easy targets.   In a short time only a third of the crew of each raft remained alive or unwounded.   Inspired by the example of Sergeant Hicks the Sappers struggled on.   Although shot up in midstream, he manœuvred his raft into the bridge, sent back all but two of his crew and then, with bullets zipping all around him, fixed the connectors.   Corporal Sutton, although his raft was repeatedly hit by fire, remained defiantly erect.   By midday only half of the bridge had been completed.   Every movement on the bank brought down a hail of fire. So intense did this become when the bridge was about three-quarters constructed that the rapidly increasing casualties and the damage to the material compelled Lieut.-Colonel Evill to order work to be temporarily stopped.

Major-General Thomas and Brigadier Mole had now arrived upon the scene.   Clearly, until the action of the Worcestershire Regiment and the 4 Wiltshire had removed the opposition ahead, further progress with the bridge was impossible.

Major-General Thomas had by now reached three decisions which were to have a considerable effect on the course of the battle.   Firstly, he ordered two armoured cars of the Reconnaissance Regiment to be put across in the close-support rafts to reinforce the infantry.   They were to prove invaluable on the morrow.   Secondly, on being informed that at least another twenty-four hours must elapse before the Class 40 bridge, which alone could take tanks, could be completed, he decided that a Class 40 raft should be constructed at once so that the infantry on the far bank should have at least the support of a limited number of the tanks of 4/7 Dragoon Guards.   This decision, the wisdom of which was unquestionable, raised many engineer difficulties, and additional Sappers of 588 Field Company had to be ordered up from Conches.   In the meantime, 207 Field Park Company started on this task, although it was realized that they would take much longer to do it than the highly trained G.H.Q. Troops engineers.   A suitable site for it was found about a mile downstream.   This however was not covered by the bridgehead. Major-General Thomas therefore ordered 214 Brigade to cross the river and to extend the left flank as far as Pressagny l'Orgueilleux.

It had been intended to put this battalion across downstream in its Dukws and with this end in view it was now waiting in the streets of Vernon.   Early in the morning Captain Spencer and the scout platoon had been despatched across the broken road bridge with a wireless set, to report the situation on the far bank and if possible to get to the edge of the forest south of Panilleuse. At 3.45 p.m. their wireless opened up. Apparently they had reached some cross-tracks in the centre of the forest without opposition. On receiving this information the brigadier at once ordered the D.C.L.I. to cross the broken road bridge and make for Pressagny l'Orgueilleux to cover the left flank of the bridgehead and the Class 40 raft site, and 7 Somerset Light Infantry to follow and seize the spur 1,000 yards north of Vernonnet. The marching troops accordingly started to struggle across the fallen sections of the road bridge, mended and repaired in places with ladders and planks. As they crossed, enemy fire suddenly ceased and the Sappers hurriedly finished the Class 9 bridge. On arrival in Vernonnet, the French population emerged and pressed wine and cider upon the advancing troops. The column, however, steadily moved forward. With B Company as a right flank guard, it pressed on along the road on the east bank. No opposition was met. On reaching the edge of the forest, a few hundred yards south of Pressagny, Lieut.-Colonel Taylor decided not to enter the village, as it was felt that the welcome from the French might cause the men to relax their vigilance. B Company therefore took up a defensive position on the left of the main road, with A Company on the edge of the forest and D Company holding some cross tracks about 500 yards further back. Battalion headquarters moved into a château on the banks of the river. 7 Somerset Light Infantry followed the D.C.L.I. and marched to its objective without opposition. By nightfall it had taken up a tight all-round defensive position on the wooded spur in front of the 4th Battalion of their regiment.

The sites selected for the Class 40 raft, a thousand yards downstream, were thus reasonably secure.

Meanwhile the Class 9 bridge had at last been finished, at 5.30 p.m. Immediately the badly needed transport of the two brigades started to flow across. At long last "David," the first British bridge across the Seine, was complete.

In this short space of time, with two brigades across the river, the Class 9 bridge successfully completed and the infantry transport crossing over it at a steady rate, the situation had thus dramatically improved. The Class 40 raft had been started and the prospects of being able to use some of the tanks of the 4/7 Dragoon Guards on the east bank in the morning appeared bright. Work had begun on the Class 40 bridge. The bridge sites were still under fire. Nevertheless, Major-General Thomas could now face with equanimity any counter-attack the enemy might be able to mount on the morrow, and ordered both forward brigades to advance as soon as possible after first light to the edge of the wooded area on a semi-circle about three miles from Vernonnet.

OPERATIONS OF 27TH AUGUST

The enemy's reaction during the first twenty-four hours of the crossing had presented a most un-German mixture of casualness and spasmodic ferocity. It is, however, possible from the mass of information extracted from prisoners and captured documents to throw light on this unusual behaviour. The 49 Division, which had not been engaged in the Normandy fighting, had arrived on the Seine about six days previously. It was a normal Wehrmacht division, but it had been weakened by being continually compelled to find drafts for the fighting in Normandy. The ranks had been filled by foreigners and immature Hitler Youth. Most probably the latter and the surviving N.C.Os. were responsible for the resistance on the 26th. The former certainly looked forward to an early opportunity to desert.

At his headquarters in Beauvais, General-Lieutenant Macholtz, the divisional commander, must undoubtedly have been looking anxiously over his shoulder. Paris had fallen on the 25th and the 12th U.S. Army Group sweep south-east of the capital threatened his communications. His colleague on his left, commanding 18 G.A.F. Division and faced by the United States crossing at Mantes Gassicourt, was in no position to reassure him as to the safety of his southern flank. Probably the news of the serious nature of the crossing at Vernonnet may well have been withheld from him until about midday on the 26th. British commanders have had similar experiences.

During the afternoon a strong armed enemy reconnaissance of M.E.110's had flown over the crossing and can have left him in no doubt that he was faced with a major thrust across the Seine at Vernon. If prisoners' statements are to be relied upon, General Macholtz ordered the counter-attack to be made on the evening of the 26th. The orders, however, seem to have arrived too late to be carried out on that day.

He was apparently holding the front opposite 43 Division with the Battle Group Meyer, composed of both 148 and 150 Regiments. In the course of the fighting on the 26th units seem to have become inextricably mixed.

His reserve consisted of the remainder of the division, organized as the Battle Group Schrader. According to a captured order, this was subdivided into two further groups. To the first, consisting of four companies formed from miscellaneous units of the Division and reinforced with three Tiger tanks, was given the task of advancing from Tilly on Vernonnet and seizing the spur immediately to the east commanding the site of the Class 40 bridge. The other group constituted the reserve, but as a first step was to capture Bois Jerome St. Ouen. It appears to have consisted of approximately two companies.

15. While light traffic is using the pontoon bridge the Divisional engineers prepare a Bailey bridge, 27th August, 1944

16. The nearly completed Bailey bridge and the pontoon bridge, 27th August, 1944

17. The Nijmegen Road bridge, 21st September, 1944

18. The Nijmegen Railway bridge after destruction by the German frogmen. Dukws and ferries being used to cross the Waal, 30th September, 1944

Had these orders been put into force at any time up to the afternoon of the 26th their effect might have been very serious. When Macholtz or his staff finally galvanized the Battle Groups Meyer and Schrader into action, the blow came far too late.

The first to feel the enemy's recoil were 5 D.C.L.I. in their all-round defensive position south of Pressagny l'Orgueilleux. At dawn B Company, holding a defensive position about 500 yards south-east of the village, was overrun by a strong attack, which, bursting through the gap, surrounded A Company. Major Parker, the company commander, seeing that he was heavily outnumbered, therefore took the drastic step of calling down the fire of the artillery on to his own position. Response was quick and decisive and the enemy dispersed. A further attack on D Company east of the road followed, to be likewise beaten off with the loss of one section. For a time to the brigade commander, who was issuing orders for the advance by 7 Somerset Light Infantry and 1 Worcestershire in Vernonnet, the situation looked ugly. Anxious for the security of the rafting site covered by the D.C.L.I., on which his reinforcement by the tanks of 4/7 Dragoon Guards depended, he therefore diverted several armoured cars to the D.C.L.I. and sent the first troops of tanks when landed soon after 8 a.m. to this flank.

Having dealt with this unexpected complication at Pressagny he ordered 1 Worcestershire, now complete with all its vehicles, to advance on Tilly by the Gisors road, and 7 Somerset Light Infantry to move on its left through the thick forest to its northern edge south of Panilleuse. The advance began at 8.10 a.m.

The Gisors road winds up a steep re-entrant, steep-sided on the right and falling way on the left. Trees and thick undergrowth came right down to the road, making it impossible to see for more than fifteen yards on either side. After advancing four hundred yards, the leading platoon was held up by a machine-gun. This was dealt with. A few hundred yards further on the sound of the tracks of a Tiger tank was heard. The company deployed and the 6-pdr. section came into action on the road. The Tiger slowly nosed round a corner, and the leading anti-tank gun with only the offside of the hull and part of the turret visible immediately engaged it at a range of 300 yards, securing three direct hits. As the crew baled out the gun fired two rounds of H.E. and the tank caught fire. By this time it was 11 a.m.

Meanwhile 7 Somerset Light Infantry, advancing through the forest on the left flank, had also met opposition. A company sent out to guard the south-east flank, out of supporting distance from the remainder of the battalion, had been surprised by the enemy and surrounded.

In fact, both these two battalions had struck the Battle Group Schrader, which advancing with four companies forward and three

Tiger tanks down the road, and handled with the skill of the German when fighting in woods, now developed a confused battle which was to cost the Worcestershire Regiment over sixty casualties. Fighting went on all day, with the close-packed column of carriers, jeeps and anti-tank guns continually under fire. However, with the arrival of two tanks of the 4/7 Dragoon Guards the situation both on the front of this battalion and that of 7 Somerset was stablilized. 5 D.C.L.I. moved into Pressagny and beat off an attempt by the enemy to infiltrate round the right flank.

On the right sector of the Divisional front, 129 Brigade started to advance at the same time. 4 Somerset Light Infantry, guided by two members of the Maquis, plunged into the dense forest with the object of capturing Bois Jerome St. Ouen. The leading company, D Company, lost direction and clashed with infantry and two dug-in tanks. At the same time the second company, B Company, ran into enemy occupying the château 500 yards west of the village of Bois Jerome and captured it by midday, only to be ejected by a sharp counter-attack supported by light armoured vehicles early in the afternoon. At the same time the enemy endeavoured to surround A and C Companies, moving at the rear of the battalion. In the midst of this vague and sporadic fighting in the woods, the reconnaissance parties of the Divisional artillery became involved in a clash with a German 88-mm. gun at close range, and Major Sir John Backhouse of 179 Field Regiment was killed. He had played a distinguished part in the Normandy fighting and his premature death deprived the Divisional artillery of one of its finest officers. Finally, three armoured cars of 43 Reconnaissance Regiment arrived and the château was re-taken with their assistance. Lieut.-Colonel Lipscomb then dealt with the enemy in his rear, using C Company for the purpose. Early in the evening the arrival of a troop of tanks enabled A Company to attack and capture Bois Jerome by 8.30 p.m.

5 Wiltshire, advancing by the Gasny road at about 8 a.m., was held up by a 37-mm. A.A. gun. This was rapidly disposed of and the battalion continued its advance to its objective. 4 Wiltshire continued to clear the high ground along the river bank to the south-east and extended its positions to the outskirts of Giverny.

Throughout the morning an enemy gun firing from the south on the Class 9 bridge "David" and the Class 40 "Goliath" caused considerable inconvenience. A direct hit on "David" completely destroyed two floating buoys and sank the boats, which then remained suspended from the damaged road bearers. Altogether the bridge was closed to traffic for 1¾ hours. Another shell killed or wounded twenty Sappers working on "Goliath," but work was soon resumed. Air-bursts over the bridges and Vernonnet caused further casualties, luckily not including Major-General Thomas, who narrowly escaped whilst crossing.

This fire, however, did little to delay the passage of 130 Brigade across the river. Work on the Class 40 bridge "Goliath" went ahead steadily throughout the afternoon. At 5.15 p.m. the first vehicle, a bulldozer, crossed the bridge. At 7.30 p.m., only 28 hours after the order to start work had been given, the remainder of the tanks of 4/7 Dragoon Guards and 15/19 Hussars started to cross the river. Traffic continued all night and all next day.

By last light the bridgehead was secure. Major-General Thomas could now order the Division, with 129 Brigade on the right, 130 Brigade in the centre and 214 Brigade on the left, to advance to the final bridgehead, on an approximate radius of 8,000 yards from Vernonnet, on the morrow with complete certainty of success.

THE ARMOUR GOES THROUGH

(See Sketch Map 7)

The stage was now set for the final advance and all went well. On the right 4 Wiltshire carried the village of Giverny and the high ground to the east, and the village of Le Pressoir. 5 Wiltshire, in a formal attack at 10.30 a.m., swept on towards La Chapelle, wiping out an enemy position well camouflaged amidst the corn stooks. The supporting squadron of 15/19 Hussars passed through the village and seized Pt. 142 beyond it. By noon, 4 Somerset Light Infantry had cleared Haricourt.

28th Aug.

4 Dorset, advancing on the left of the Gisors road, was firmly established on the north-east edge of the wood by 1 p.m. On the right, 7 Royal Hampshire forged ahead in the face of scattered but still persistent resistance in the woods to reach Tilly by 2.30 p.m. The attack by 5 Dorset through the woods went slowly but steadily forward. By 5.30 p.m. the battalion had reached La Queue and, one and a half hours later, the whole village was cleared. Patrols pushing ahead into Heubecourt found the enemy had gone.

On the extreme left 5 D.C.L.I., relieved in Pressagny by 1 Worcestershire, now staged a formal attack on Panilleuse. Supported by tanks of the Sherwood Rangers, they drove the enemy out of some farm buildings half-way between the woods and the village. The enemy fled. On their right 7 Somerset Light Infantry reached the spur between Pressagny and Panilleuse. No. 7 Troop of the Reconnaissance Regiment under Lieutenant Baker pursued the enemy right into Notre Dame de Lisle and killed or captured no less than fifty Germans.

The battle was finished. Major-General Thomas and his Division, with a bridgehead four and a half miles deep, had fulfilled their contract to the letter and on time. Control of the bridges passed to 30 Corps in the afternoon and the tanks of 11 Armoured Division began to rumble across. On the morrow the Corps, with

8 Armoured Brigade on the right and 29 Armoured Brigade on the left, was to sweep forward to Amiens and beyond.

So long as the art of war is studied, the Division's crossing of the Seine will serve as a model.   Admittedly the element of luck played a part.   Unlucky commanders, however, as Napoleon remarked, should never be employed in war.   Primarily it is a supreme example of quick planning and ruthlessly efficient execution by a commander who had not only thought out in advance and practised over many years the major operations of war, but who also had selected and trained others who realized instinctively what was in his mind.

The operation therefore stands unchallenged as the triumph of an exceptionally clear military mind.

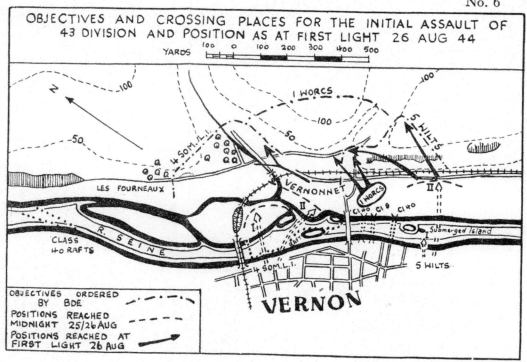

OBJECTIVES AND CROSSING PLACES FOR THE INITIAL ASSAULT OF 43 DIVISION AND POSITION AS AT FIRST LIGHT 26 AUG 44

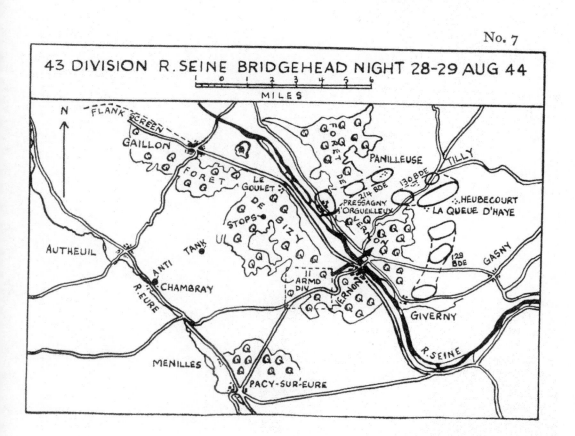

43 DIVISION R. SEINE BRIDGEHEAD NIGHT 28-29 AUG 44

CHAPTER VII

"THE ISLAND"

(*See Sketch Maps* 8, 9 *and* 10)

FROM THE SEINE TO THE ESCAUT

THE Division's brilliant *coup de main* on the Seine had opened the sally-port for the most spectacular and decisive pursuit in the history of the Army. 30 Corps, under Lieut.-General Horrocks, crashing over "Saul" and "Goliath," soon became the spearhead. Clear of the bottleneck—8 Armoured Brigade and Guards Armoured Division on the right, 11 Armoured Division on the left and followed by 50 Division in lorries—the Corps surged forward towards the crossings of the Somme at Amiens, the old battlefields of 1914–18 around Arras, into Belgium and beyond. At last our less heavily armoured but more mobile tanks came into their own. Great risks were taken, both operational and administrative, but ahead lay the glittering prizes of Brussels and the great port of Antwerp. On 3rd September the Guards entered the Belgian capital in triumph and pushed on to Antwerp, where they linked up with 11 Armoured Division on the following day; 250 miles had been covered in six days.

This dramatic advance stretched the Army's administrative resources to the limit. The Division was therefore temporarily grounded and practically all its three-ton lorries taken away to enable the pursuit to be sustained.

The war suddenly became very remote. The inhabitants of the villages on the banks of the river returned to their homes and vied with each other in expressing their gratitude to their liberators. Long-hoarded wine appeared. The shops and cafés in Vernon began to open, though they had little to sell except Citronade, a drink with no future outside France, and books of a morally uplifting character with the added disadvantage of being written in French. Dances were held in the "Salle des Fêtes" and the Life Guards Band was enthusiastically acclaimed wherever it went on its tour of the Divisional area.

For the first time since the landing there was now a little leisure. The storm boats were pressed into service for pleasure trips on the Seine. 5 D.C.L.I. had a boar hunt in the Foret de Vernon (the only boar encountered was accidentally stepped on by one of the beaters whilst fast asleep, but made a most effective getaway). It must also be confessed that fishing with 36 grenades yielded spectacular if unpalatable results. Many visited the enormous caves near Vernonnet, which the Germans had started to convert into a headquarters for Field-Marshal Rommel. Vast numbers of wooden buildings had been built inside and provided with electric light, refrigerators, hot and cold water and indoor sanitation. Immense quantities of equipment had been installed, which the local population were not slow to remove. Visitors to this area in time of peace can in consequence legitimately expect a higher standard of sanitary conveniences than is usual in the rest of France.

Ensa parties appeared. Flanaghan and Allen, Florence Desmond, Kaye Cavendish and Richard Hearne performed in the open to audiences of a brigade at a time. Flanaghan struggled bravely against an appalling cold; Florence Desmond, for once, seemed somewhat at a loss faced by an audience unacquainted with the finer points of metropolitan life; Richard Hearne did well. Kaye Cavendish, however, received an ovation—probably not entirely on account of her artistic merits. When exhausted by encore after encore, she was told by her audience to remain where she was and "just sit."

Despite the fact that Paris lay in the American Area, the Divisional staff managed to arrange for twenty-six men a day of each unit to visit the city. These were among the first British troops to be seen and were given a demonstrative reception. Voluble and astonished crowds gathered round the lorries parked in the Place de la Concorde, where, without any feeling of incongruity, the men proceeded to "brew up" true to the tradition of *sang froid brittanique*. They, in their turn, marvelled at the large number of well-dressed men and women to be seen, the profusion and luxury of the great shops, the girls with wide-flowing skirts on bicycles, and the boulevards and public buildings practically untouched by war.

The first list of decorations gained by the Division covering the fighting up to July 18th arrived. Major-General Thomas held three investitures, one for each brigade. There were the names of fifty-five officers and men included in it. Only twenty-eight of these appeared on parade; the rest were dead or wounded. The price of victory had indeed been heavy.

Despite the dramatic news from all parts of the front coming in hour by hour, all realized that much hard fighting still lay ahead. All units hastened to make up their deficiencies in men and equipment for the next advance. Administrative staffs worked long and late. Large drafts of battle-seasoned reinforcements arrived from 59 Division, which, owing to the shortage of manpower in the Army, had had to be disbanded. These were quickly to be absorbed and though not forgetting the reputation of their old division, to become as much a part of 43 Division as those who had served it from the beginning. Kits were inspected, vehicles and weapons overhauled, platoons, troops, batteries and companies reorganized.

Training began again and the lessons of the recent fighting were applied. The woods and valleys beside the Seine resounded with the noise of Brens and Piats. Battalions, mindful of the many rivers ahead, carried out river-crossing exercises in Dukws. The Divisional artillery re-calibrated its guns on to an island in the Seine —a most necessary proceeding, as the field regiments had each fired well over a quarter of a million rounds since the landing. 8 Middlesex also were not to be outdone and re-calibrated their 4·2-inch mortars.

Germany is a country of many forests. At the crossing of the Noireau and in the Foret de Vernon the enemy had displayed his exceptional skill in fighting in woods. Realizing the problems which lay ahead, Major-General Thomas, on the afternoon that Brussels fell, held a "cloth-model" exercise on wood fighting in a large hall at Tilly. The exercise reached the normal high standards of the 3rd Division. In fact, there were many present who would sooner have Sept. faced the fire of the enemy than the demolition of their unsound arguments by the director of the exercise. All the Divisional "cloth-model" exercises were practical, clear and instructive. Few, however, look back on them as social occasions. Real battles were much less tense; the enemy at least often gave more time to think and did not pounce on every error.

With the war now two hundred and fifty miles away, these halycon days clearly could not last long. First to move were C Squadron of the Reconnaissance Regiment, who set off with the dawn on 6th 6th September to provide protection to Tactical Headquarters of Second Sept. Army near Amiens. On the following day they moved with General Dempsey through Arras and Douai, crossed the Belgian frontier and harboured about fifteen miles from Brussels. Two days later, on the heels of Field-Marshal Montgomery, the squadron passed through Brussels amid crowds of cheering people to Perk, a few miles north of the capital.

On the 8th, 7 Royal Hampshire set off in haste to Brussels to rein- 8th force the garrison. Next to move were the Divisional engineers. Sept. Without waiting for their vehicles on supply duties, they passed 10th Sept. through Gisors and Beauvais, crossed the Somme at Sailly Laurette, entered the zone of the battlefields of the First World War, and, moving by way of Albert and Bapaume, reached Arras.

Next day the column pushed on over Vimy Ridge past the Canadian War Memorial, on to Lille and Roubaix and into Belgium. Down came the tricolour, to be replaced by the red, black and yellow flags pressed upon them by the delighted Belgians. After a night at Alost, they at length reached Brussels, to be welcomed by cheering crowds, who pressed fruit upon them, including luscious black grapes; then on to Louvain into harbour at Winghe St. George. 130 Brigade followed close on their track and on the 11th reached a position eight miles east of the capital.

In the early hours of the 13th verbal instructions from 8 Corps ordered the rest of the Division forward to rejoin 30 Corps and to concentrate with all speed east of Diest by last light on 15th September. Early next day, in bright sunshine, the move began.

By the early afternoon the long column had started to file past the red, yellow and black frontier posts of Belgium. Soon the troops found themselves in a densely populated country of small houses flush with the streets; estaminets; sprawling ribbon development and slipshod villas; but the steam trains were running, the mines were working, the signs of vigorous life were everywhere! The Belgians were hungry, but they were free. In spirit they had never surrendered. The long-hoarded bottles of brandy and Burgundy were dug up from the back gardens and pressed upon the troops. Even the bearded priests came out to cheer and nuns acknowledged the soldiers' greeting. The troops had come back to the great battleground of their ancestors from the days of Marlborough, to show once again that the glory of the Army still shone undimmed.

As the sun set, the columns curled off the road to bivouac for the night. Crowds of children swarmed around the cooks' lorries, with their roaring petrol burners, and clamoured for cigarettes and sweets. It was good to lie on the grass in the midst of an admiring crowd and exchange primitive but well understood comment with the older girls.

The long columns were off again soon after daylight under a cloudless sky. Over the cobblestones of the little Flemish towns they forged ahead. Sparks rose from the tracks of the carriers. The bombardment with apples continued. Skirting Brussels by way of the Forest of Soignies, they at length reached the great main road which leads from the capital to Louvain, Diest and beyond—the immemorial route of the invader. Towards early afternoon little groups of advanced parties met each unit by the roadside and led them to their bivouac areas.

The Division had entered a dead flat country, densely cultivated, interspersed with dykes and thickly populated. In the distance rose the slag heaps of coalfields. Numbered arrows and divisional signs met the eye everywhere. Every side-road was packed with troops and transport. The Second Army was here *en masse*. From the east came the distant rumble of gun-fire. Something was in the wind. Like an enormous cobra, 30 Corps was coiling up for another smashing blow. As the light faded on the 15th, the Division stood concentrated east of Diest ready for action.

"The Corps Commander will address all officers of the Corps down to and including Lieut.-Colonels on forthcoming operations at 1100 hours on 16th. B.M.'s may also attend. The address will take place in the Cinema, Bourg Leopold, opposite the railway station" stated a message sent out from Divisional Headquarters at 6 p.m.

The weather had broken. Night set in with heavy rain.

THE "O" GROUP AT BOURG LEOPOLD

(See Sketch Map 10)

Bourg Leopold is a mean little mining town which seems to have strayed out of its true setting in the industrial area of South Yorkshire. Its shabby streets are paved with the cobblestones; the houses and shops are cheap and makeshift. The cinema, an ugly, nondescript structure, faces the squalid railway station.

By ten-thirty on the morning of 16th September the officers bidden to the Corps "O" Group had begun to assemble outside. To get into the hall each had to produce his identity card to the field security police at the entrance. This was a slow business—in consequence, the waiting crowd rapidly acquired the air of any army assembly at a point-to-point or demonstration on Salisbury Plain in time of peace. The normal conversational currency on these occasions passed. "What are you doing now? I haven't seen you for ages." There was much laughter and exchange of Christian names. Wellington apparently never took the slightest interest in what his officers wore. In fact, the only order he ever issued on the subject of dress was to forbid the wearing of the enemy's uniform. Under Field-Marshal Montgomery the Army had returned to his tradition with enthusiasm. The variety of headgear was striking—berets of many colours seemed the most popular. No one deigned to wear a steel helmet. The Royal Armoured Corps affected brightly coloured slacks or corduroys. The Gunners still clung for the most part to riding breeches or even jodhpurs. Few had retained their ties, but wore in their place scarves of various colours dotted with white spots. Snipers' smocks, parachutists' jackets, jeep coats, all contributed to the amazing variety of costume. Some even were in shirt sleeves. Other Armies found it necessary to plaster their rear areas with notices forbidding irregularities of dress with threats of heavy fines. The Field-Marshal, however, was more interested in the way his officers fought than the way they dressed. Sartorial disciplinarians of the future should therefore remember that at the time when the morale of the British Army was as high as at any time in its history, officers wore the clothing they found most suitable to the conditions under which they had to live and fight, and that even in the rigid framework of an army individual taste can still flourish.

It is possible to divide great commanders into two classes—the Olympian, that is the great strategists and planners, and the soldiers' generals. In the first class fall Ludendorf and Moltke, both alike brilliant and intellectual but humourless and to the ordinary soldier remote. In the second come Suvoroff, Ney, Patton and Rommel. There could be no doubt as to the class to which the Commander of 30 Corps belonged. He could take his place in that dramatic company and claim as added assets perfect manners, a lively sense of humour, good looks and great personal charm. He epitomized every quality the British soldier expects in his leaders in the heat of battle. Men fought well for him because they liked him personally and trusted him, because in a crisis they knew he would be with them, because he possessed in an enhanced degree the fighting qualities within themselves.

By eleven o'clock the cinema was full. In a flash the chatter ceased as Lieut.-General Horrocks entered. As he advanced towards the platform he hailed commanders here and there in the audience: "Hullo, Jo. How's Stonk Hall? I'm not coming to see you again after the way I was treated last time. Do you always live in a barrage?" "Hullo, Von Thoma, how's the Wicked Wyvern?" "Hullo, Errol, what's this I hear about a mobile cocktail bar?" Finally he mounted the platform and took a long pointer handed to him by the staff officer who had just completed the finishing touches to the enormous sketch map on the screen, which is reproduced as sketch map 10. It showed the whole of Holland between the Belgian frontier and the Zuyder Zee.

Across the upper half, like an enormous contorted three-pronged fork, sprawled the great water obstacles of the rivers Maas, Waal and Lower Rhine. South of these lay two transverse canals, the Wilhelmina, north of Eindhoven, and the Zuidwillemsvaart, which runs parallel with the River Maas and links the towns of S'Hertogenbosch and Helmond. The Corps axis, marked as always "Club Route," traversed these obstacles. It showed a sixty-mile thrust forward through Eindhoven, Veghel, Uden and thence to the great bridges of Grave, Nijmegen and Arnhem. North of Arnhem an elipse of red tape stretching to Apeldorn indicated the destination of 43 Division. Further north still, and reaching right up to Nunspeet on the Zuyder Zee, a similar loop was marked "Gds Armd Div." Further loops in violet tape encircled Arnhem, Nijmegen, Grave and the route to the north of Eindhoven. These were the objectives of the Airborne Corps.

"This is a tale you will tell your grandchildren," began the Corps Commander, then, his sense of humour getting the better of him, added as an aside, "and mighty bored they'll be!" Loud laughter greeted this sally. When it had subsided he proceeded with even more than his normal skill and capacity to convince, to give out his orders for the highly complex plan for the operation "Market Garden" now to be launched.

During the latter part of the advance to the Escaut Canal hard fighting had taken place. Although disorganized, rearguards, mainly composed of infantry supported by Tiger tanks and self-propelled guns, had offered stiff resistance. Behind this screen the enemy was attempting to build up defensive positions based on the great rivers which would have to be crossed if the Second Army was to debouch into the North German Plain before the winter set in and cut off the large German forces still in western Holland. Information as to the movements of these forces was unfortunately far from clear. It was known that there had been some movement across the mouth of the Schelde and thence into southern Holland. East of Antwerp it was thought that, apart from 719 Division, the enemy forces were still made up largely of paratroops, German air force units and a contingent of S.S.

In outline, the Second Army plan was to use the three airborne divisions to seize all the crossings over the major water obstacles and hold the road from Eindhoven to the River Maas. This would thus form a carpet over which the main thrust, carried out by 30 Corps, would join up with the airborne forces holding the bridges at Arnhem, Nijmegen and Grave and then seize the area north of the Lower Rhine right up to the Zuyder Zee. On the right, 8 Corps was to move up to protect the east flank of this corridor and on the left 12 Corps had a similar task.

General Horrock's intention, therefore, was to advance at maximum speed and secure the area between Nunspeet on the Zuyder Zee and Arnhem. Guards Armoured Division were therefore ordered to thrust forward to Arnhem, by-pass Apeldorn and dominate the area to the north. If the bridges at Grave, Nijmegen and Arnhem were found to be destroyed they were to fan out to the flanks and do what they could to facilitate bridging operations to be carried out by 43 Division, which was to follow next in order of march.

To 43 Division the Corps Commander assigned the task of securing the high ground running south from Apeldorn to a point of junction with 1 British Airborne Division in the area north of Arnhem. Detachments were to be sent to seize the crossings over the river Issel at Deventer and Zutphen. If the bridges over the three major rivers were found to be destroyed, then 43 Division would carry out such assault crossings and bridging as might be required. 50 (N.) Division was to follow as Corps reserve. For the early stages of the operation 101 U.S. Airborne Division was also under command of the Corps, with the task of capturing the crossings over the canals between Eindhoven and Uden.

The engineer plan was on a vast scale and an enormous engineer dump had been formed at Bourg Leopold. No less than three Army Groups Royal Engineers were placed under command of the Corps for the operation. If all the bridges were demolished, it was estimated that no less than 2,277 vehicles would be required for stores and equipment.

With his normal light-heartedness and supreme self-confidence, the Corps Commander announced that the battle would probably start, weather permitting, the following afternoon.

Thus was the news of this most audacious operation, staged at

9

short notice and at a time when the lines of communication extended 400 miles back to Bayeux, broken to the unit commanders of 30 Corps.   The part played by 1 Airborne Division has been justifiably glamourized in many books and on the screen to such an extent as to obscure the fact that other troops fought equally bravely as well. The action of the airborne divisions formed a very important part, but only a part of a vast and intricate operation, as will now be shown.

The 43 Divisional "O" Group, to which the brigadiers, commanding officers and staffs now went on straight from Bourg Leopold, was conducted by Major-General Thomas with the same confidence, if less theatrical effect, as that of the Corps Commander.   He opened with the statement that the total German force ahead was quite inadequate to offer a prolonged resistance on any line and that armoured reserves of more than squadron size were most unlikely to be met.   He revealed that the Division had 8 Armoured Brigade (less the Sherwood Rangers) 147 Field Regiment, 64 Medium Regiment, a heavy battery and the Royal Netherlands Brigade Group under its command for the operation.   On arrival north of Arnhem, the Reconnaissance Regiment with the 12/60 Rifles and a squadron of 13/18 Hussars were to seize the crossings over the Issel.   130 Infantry Brigade were directed on to the area immediately south of Apeldorn, 214 Brigade were to hold the centre and 129 Brigade to link up with 1 Airborne Division due north of Arnhem.   The Royal Netherlands Brigade were to seize Apeldorn and raise the population against the enemy.   The Division was then to be prepared to face both east and west.   Static defence was forbidden.   Brigadiers were ordered to make dispositions so that the most active offensive steps could be taken against all enemy approaching the position.   Had 1 Airborne Division succeeded in its task of capturing intact the bridges over the Rhine and the high ground immediately north, there is no doubt that operations of a lively, highly mobile and dramatic character would have developed.   Such speculation is, however, academic.

The move up the main axis (Club) and possibly the subsidiary axis (Heart) was to be regulated by an elaborate Corps movement control organization, groups being called forward as the operations developed. With this end in view, the Division was to move to a transit area astride the axis immediately south of Hechtel cross-roads.   The Divisional column consisted of no less than thirteen groups, making a total of nearly five thousand vehicles.   Roughly in order of march, this placed the Reconnaissance Regiment in the lead followed in order by 130 Brigade, 214 Brigade, the Royal Netherlands Brigade and 129 Brigade.   Four days' rations and petrol for 250 miles were to be carried—a most fortunate provision as events turned out.   No time was wasted on public speculation as to the Division's secondary task of being ready to carry out assault crossings of the Maas, the Waal and the Lower Rhine should any or all of the airborne operations fail. When the "O" Group broke up, however, the Brigadiers were called aside and their thoughts directed towards planning on these lines. They were to have ample time during the next few days of frustrated waiting in the sandy transit area south of Hechtel to ponder, with the assistance of air photographs, these operations which were fortunately unnecessary. One plan even contemplated the seizure of barges in Nijmegen, the embarkation of a whole brigade group and a voyage on the Waal and the Lower Rhine to Arnhem. It is sufficient to observe that only first-class troops whose morale was at its highest would have dared to plan on these astounding lines.

In this atmosphere of exuberant optimism the whole Division faced the coming battle.

THE CORRIDOR TO NIJMEGEN

(See Sketch Map 9)

The passage of time enhances rather than diminishes the brilliance of the operations of Guards Armoured Division on the next four days. In effect, they were given the task of attacking on a six-hundred-yard front to a depth of sixty miles astride a single road running through country so flat and marshy that their tanks could not manœuvre. Only the most efficient and battle-hardened troops with superbly high morale could have done what they did. The battle opened on the afternoon of 17th September under the eye of Lieut.-General Horrocks, standing at a point of vantage in a high building near the Escaut Canal. 5 Guards Armoured Brigade, supported by a heavy artillery barrage and a continuous flow of 83 Group rocket-firing aircraft, attacking on either side of the road just ahead of the tanks, burst out of the bridgehead and forced their way across the frontier into Holland. By nightfall the little red-brick town of Valkenswaard was in their hands. The air drops ahead appeared to be proceeding according to plan, but there was no news from Arnhem. Determined counter-attacks at the base of the salient were beaten off. 17th Sept.

Next day the large Dutch town of Eindhoven was found to be strongly held. 5th Guards Brigade swung west with a view to by-passing the town. 32 Guards Infantry Brigade attempted to turn the east flank and encountered fierce resistance. The Grenadier Guards Group therefore returned to the central axis and by the early evening finally overwhelmed the enemy and gained contact in the town with U.S. troops of 101 Airborne Division, who had entered from the north. The bridge at Zon was reputed damaged, but the corridor was apparently clear for the next twenty miles and held open by the strong hands of 101 U.S. Airborne Division. At Nijmegen 82 U.S. Airborne Division had established a firm east flank on the ground overlooking the Reichswald Forest. Fierce fighting was reported in 18th Sept.

the town, but the bridge was still in enemy hands.   Information from 1 Airborne Division was alarmingly scanty : 1 Parachute Brigade appeared to be somewhere to the west of Arnhem ; there was no news of the other Parachute Brigade, but the road bridge seemed to be still in enemy possession.   The weather had turned to rain.

19th Sept.   Advancing at first light, Guards Armoured Division bounded forward thirty-five miles and by nine o'clock made contact with 82 U.S. Airborne Division, at the bridge over the Maas at Grave, which was fortunately intact.   The canal bridge at Neerbosch, three miles south-west of Nijmegen, however, proved to be damaged. After crossing the Maas, the Division therefore swung right to Heuman and then north to Nijmegen.   By the early afternoon 5 Guards Brigade had concentrated three miles south of the town, where 82 Airborne Division with inadequate forces was attempting to capture the bridge and, at the same time, holding off determined counter-attacks from the east.   A quick plan made by Generals Horrocks and Browning to seize the bridge that evening, although it made progress in clearing the town—one detachment actually reaching the Post Office, where the control apparatus was believed to be— proved abortive.

It had now become evident that the situation of 1 Airborne Division at Arnhem was critical and that the need for speed overrode all other considerations.   Owing to bad weather, re-supply had failed. 1 Parachute Battalion was believed to be somewhere near the north end of the Bridge.   The remainder of the Division had consolidated in an ever-decreasing perimeter at Oosterbeek, west of the town.

20th Sept.   The capture of Nijmegen Bridge on the afternoon of the following day constitutes one of the most remarkable exploits in the history of the British and United States Armies.   504 Regimental Combat Team forced its way across the railway bridge, and not to be outdone, 3 Irish Guards in the late afternoon carried the main road bridge. Meanwhile, at Arnhem, contact had been made by wireless with 1 Airborne Division.   Their situation was critical in the extreme. Major-General Urquhart, the divisional commander, stressed the need for the earliest possible relief.   In fact, what was left of the division had been compressed into a tight perimeter at Hartestein, where it fought on, weary, hungry and sadly depleted in numbers, but with its morale unshaken.

From the morning of the 18th, 43 Division, concentrated in order of march on the sandy waste immediately south of Hechtel crossroads, awaited orders to intervene.   Only confused and, in the circumstances, practically unintelligible reports of the fighting ahead filtered through to the troops.   On the 19th the Division was warned to be ready to assist at Nijmegen.   As news of the state of the bridges ahead came through, old plans were discarded and new ones made. The tension of waiting became exasperating.   The complexity of the ever-changing situation and the many fronts on which fighting was taking place made coherent planning impossible. At last, early on the 20th, the order to advance came through and 130 Brigade Group and Major-General Thomas's Tactical Headquarters passed the battered cross-roads at Hechtel and joined the congested stream of traffic on "Club Route," only to remain practically stationary throughout the morning. In fact, tanks and self-propelled guns of 107 Panzer Brigade, attacking from the direction of Helmond on the right flank, had cut the road at Zon, five miles north of Eindhoven. It was not until about midday that 8 Armoured Brigade with 502 Regimental Combat Team succeeded in re-opening the road and traffic once again started to flow north. In the afternoon the Division was given priority on the road, and at last, moving through the vehicles of the seaborne tail of 1 Airborne Division, began to move freely forward. Eight burnt-out tanks of Guards Armoured Division near De Groot Bridge bore witness to the cost of the initial breakout. On either side of the road stretched flat marshy fields with the neat Dutch houses and windmills dotted here and there. Whilst daylight lasted the Dutch, waving orange flags, cheered the troops on. Night found the head of 130 Infantry Brigade Group just south of the great bridge at Grave. Brigadier Walton, as his column in its Dukws had become much spread out, decided to halt for the night. Major-General Thomas had reached the neighbourhood of Malden on the road from Heuman to Nijmegen late in the day and established contact with Lieut.-General Horrocks. At 3 a.m. he ordered Brigadier Walton to take over responsibility at first light for the bridges at Grave and Neerbosch and with the remainder of his brigade to help the Guards to clear Nijmegen. 4 Dorset accordingly took over the defences of the Grave Bridge and despatched a company group to Neerbosch. 5 Dorset and 7 Royal Hampshire, after a hasty breakfast, drove on to the outskirts of Nijmegen and prepared to clear the town. No Germans were found. It was with the greatest difficulty, however, that any progress could be made through the excited inhabitants, who garlanded the troops with flowers and thrust apples into their pockets. By the early afternoon 5 Dorset had established themselves in a tight bridgehead on the north bank of the Waal, covering the road and railway bridges, and 7 Royal Hampshire had taken over responsibility for the south bank.

214 Brigade Group had moved out of the concentration area at Hechtel as the light was beginning to fade on the 20th and joined the slow-moving column on "Club Route." Night found it in the deserted streets of Eindhoven. No traffic police were in sight. The streets were dark and empty. A wrong turning into the yard of the big Philips factory caused delay and it was not until after midnight that traffic began to move freely.

Near Zon burning lorries and exploding ammunition on the road,

21st Sept.

the wreckage of the battle in the afternoon, betrayed the fact that the flanks were open.   The column, however, pressed on unimpeded and by dawn had reached the open stretch of road between Veghel and Uden.   Dutch women and children brought milk and news of German troops and tanks on either side of the road.   With the advantage of a clear road ahead, the column therefore made all speed for the great bridge at Grave.   Here the harbour parties with Major John Denison, the D.A.A.Q.M.G., guided the battalions into a harbour area at Alverna, six miles south-west of the Waal on the road to Nijmegen.   The concentration was complete soon after midday.

Beyond the fact that Guards Armoured Division had been ordered to press on direct on Arnhem by the main road and that the road bridge was reserved for their exclusive use, there was scanty information of the situation north of the Waal.   The road bridge over the canal at Neerbosch had, however, been repaired and the railway bridge, although damaged, was vaguely reputed to be practicable at least for infantry.   Major-General Thomas met Brigadier Essame immediately on his arrival and ordered him to cross the river by the railway bridge, find out how the Guards were progressing and advance in the direction of Arnhem round their west flank.   The meeting was enlivened by a low-flying attack by a FW 190 and a crowd of excited Dutch children.   General Thomas emphasized the necessity for the utmost speed, as the position of the 1 Airborne Division, although still vague, was desperate.   Brigadier Essame therefore directed his brigade on to the railway bridge and having fixed a rendezvous with his commanding officers at the foot of the bridge, drove on ahead.   The passage through Nijmegen, which is a town of considerable size, was by no means easy.   Large crowds blocked the streets in the southern half of the town.   At the main road bridge, now under shell-fire from heavy artillery, a traffic jam caused considerable delay.   The railway bridge, however, was clear. He therefore crossed by it, and soon found Brigadier Norman Gwatkin, of Guards Armoured Division, on the far side, engaged in a lively battle with enemy tanks and infantry of considerable strength astride the Arnhem road.   Attempts to turn both right and left flanks had met with strong resistance.   The country ahead was a maze of orchards.   No view-point could be found.   The enemy, in fact, firmly held the gridiron of roads south and south-west of Elst in considerable strength and the close country gave him every advantage.   His west flank clearly rested on the maze of houses, orchards and trees around Oosterhout.   This, the two brigadiers agreed, must be taken with all speed to enable the advance to be continued. Further progress that day on the front of the Guards appeared improbable.   By the time this decision was reached two hours of daylight remained.   There appeared to be just sufficient time to close with the enemy in front of Oosterhout, find out more exactly by physical contact where and what he was, and thus save time next morning. Unfortunately, however, the leading battalion of 214 Brigade, the 7 Somerset Light Infantry, had been held up by a traffic block in the town. Part of the battalion was directed in error over the road bridge, and night had fallen by the time the battalion commander had regained control. The Brigadier therefore had to content himself with concentrating his brigade on both sides of the Waal in the area of the railway bridge for the night and preparations for the resumption of the advance at dawn. This was a bitter disappointment, but judging from the fierce character of the resistance, it is extremely doubtful whether a hurriedly planned attack, had it been feasible, would have had any better luck than that of the Welsh Guards in the afternoon.

The situation on the Corps front that night was by no means easy. Enemy reinforcements were known to have arrived in the area from Germany, including Divisions Scherbening and Raesler, with a depot division from Bremen. S.S. troops were concentrating north of Arnhem. Guards Armoured Division's operations during the day had disclosed the fact that enemy armour in strength barred the way to the north. 82 U.S. Airborne Division, east of Nijmegen, was only just holding its own. The main artery right back to Eindhoven was most vulnerable. Weather conditions for the R.A.F. had gone from bad to worse. 1 Airborne Division at Arnhem were clearly at their last gasp. Lieut.-General Horrocks therefore ordered an all-out effort for the morrow by 43 Division, on a front of two brigades, 129 on the right, 214 on the left, with the object of securing Arnhem and making contact with 1 Airborne Division. The Division was further ordered to pass through Guards Armoured Division not before 1000 hours.

At the time this order was issued, 129 Brigade was strung out along the axis back to Eindhoven, and did not in fact reach Grave until dawn next day. 214 Brigade, however, in view of its reconnaissance beyond the river in the afternoon, could be ready to attack at first light. Major-General Thomas therefore instructed this brigade to advance left of the main road to Arnhem with all speed on the morrow and gave it the exclusive use of the railway bridge, which although damaged luckily proved to be capable of taking the Sherman tanks of 4/7 Dragoon Guards. He similarly allotted the road bridge to 129 Brigade and ordered it to advance astride the main Arnhem road. At the same time he created a reserve by handing over the Grave bridge to the Royal Netherlands Brigade and arranged for the relief of 130 Brigade in Nijmegen by 69 Brigade of 50 Division, which was expected to arrive on the tail of 129 Brigade. In view of the desperate position of the 1 Airborne Division, he demanded a supreme effort. How well his division responded will now be shown.

OOSTERHOUT AND DRIEL

The country between Nijmegen and Arnhem is a bog which the industry and ingenuity of the Dutch have transformed into a highly developed area of closely cultivated fields and gardens.   It is studded with orchards and neat and attractive modern houses.   The fruit industry, centred around the market at Zetten, is organized on the most up-to-date lines.   Only one good road traverses it, the main concrete road which runs via Elst to Arnhem, and astride which the Guards Armoured Division's advance had been brought to a halt on the 21st.   South-west of Elst is a gridiron of secondary roads connecting this considerable village with Oosterhout and Valburg.

Oosterhout also is a large village completely surrounded by orchards, which effectively conceal not only the houses but also the approaches.   Looking northwards from the 20-foot high embankment, or *Bund*, running parallel to the Waal it is impossible to get a clear view for more than a hundred yards.   In fact, there are no viewpoints whatever in the whole island.   The boggy nature of the soil and the embankments make it impossible for any tank or vehicle to move off the roads.   Every tactical advantage therefore lay with the enemy.   The whole area, in fact, was ideally suited to employment of the tactics of battle-groups of infantry and tanks operating in close country which the enemy had employed with such deadly effect in Normandy.

22nd Sept.   Dawn broke on the 22nd September with a heavy mist hanging over the Waal.   Profiting by it, two troops of the 2 Household Cavalry Regiment succeeded in slipping through by way of the Bund to the Neder Rijn.   The third troop, however, clashed with an enemy tank which knocked out the leading armoured car and incidentally drove Brigadier Essame in his jeep off the Bund.   Closely behind came the Vanguard Company, D Company of 7 Somerset Light Infantry under Major Sidney Young, followed by the remainder of the battalion.   Enemy infantry and a tank now came to life on the southern fringes of the village of Oosterhout and pinned the leading platoon to the ground.   Major Sidney Young in making his reconnaissance was mortally wounded.   Thus passed one of the best and bravest company commanders of a Division even more than usually fortunate in the high standard of officers of his rank.   Held up frontally by a concealed enemy, Lieut.-Colonel H. A. Borrodaile now endeavoured to turn the enemy's east flank.   Here again strong resistance was encountered and only slow progress was possible amidst the dykes and orchards.   A number of prisoners were taken.

Meanwhile, the remainder of the battalion were strung out along the Bund, the transport evenly spaced and unable even to turn round. Solid shot from 88's whistled viciously across the road.

By midday it had become evident to the brigadier that infiltration methods by infantry and tanks alone were unlikely to overcome the opposition. Despite the alarming shortage of artillery ammunition, he therefore ordered an attack supported by the whole Divisional artillery, a medium regiment and a heavy battery, and supplemented by the 4·2-inch mortars of 8 Middlesex. A forty-minute fire plan was evolved. Lieut.-Colonel Borrodaile accordingly attacked at 3.20 p.m., with A and B Companies, each supported by a troop of A Squadron 4/7 Dragoon Guards. Stunned by this determined blow, the enemy surrendered in considerable numbers. Two enemy tanks were knocked out at the entrance to the village; another was captured undamaged along with an 88-mm. gun; over 130 sullen troops from an S.S. division gave themselves up. By 4.30 p.m. the battalion had completed the occupation of the smoking ruins of the village and thus brutally and effectively opened the way.

Meanwhile 5 D.C.L.I. had been moved forward to the shelter of the Bund, where Lieut.-Colonel George Taylor had established his headquarters within fifty yards of those of Lieut.-Colonel Borrodaile. He was thus ready immediately to exploit the success of the 7 Somerset.

Picture, therefore, Lieut.-Colonel Taylor, dressed in a parachutist's smock and wearing a despatch rider's helmet, with his company commanders in a ditch by the Bund. Oosterhout is burning and the country ahead is wreathed in smoke. The ripple of Spandau fire and the spurts of Bren are dying down. Prisoners, many of them wounded, are streaming back, a pitiful sight. It is five o'clock and already the light is fading. B Company of the D.C.L.I. has deployed with orders to clear the western exits of the village. Lieut.-Colonel Taylor has been ordered to thrust forward ten miles to Driel on the banks of the Neder Rijn, get in touch with a Polish gliderborne brigade reputed to be on the south bank, and finally make contact with the 1 Airborne Division and deliver to them two Dukw loads of ammunition and medical supplies. To this end he has organized his force into two columns, one armoured, the other of soft vehicles. There are convincing reports of enemy tanks ahead. The armoured column consists of Lieut.-Colonel Taylor's Command Group, B Squadron, 4/7 Dragoon Guards (Major Richards), D Company (Major Fry), A Company (Major Parker) and a machine-gun platoon of 8 Middlesex. The soft-vehicle column comprises C Company (Major Kitchen) and B Company (Major Hingston). Night is fast approaching. The Airborne Division are known to be in desperate straits.

Faced with this situation, Lieut.-Colonel Taylor gave the order to advance with all speed. With the armour leading, the column roared ahead along the Bund. Slijk Ewijk was soon reached and the column turned north towards Valburg. Here the astonished Dutch went wild with joy as the armour crashed over the cross-roads and

headed for Driel.   As the light faded, the leading tank blew up on a
mine at the entrance to the village.   The journey had been accomplished in less than thirty minutes.   All however was not well
behind.   The despatch rider, dropped at Valburg cross-roads to
direct the soft-vehicle column, reported that he had signalled on a
number of tanks and then realized they had black crosses on them.
As it was now dark Lieut.-Colonel Taylor felt that the rear companies
could be relied upon to deal with opposition of this type on their own
and turned his attention to the problem ahead.   By the light of a
burning building, contact was made with the armoured cars of the
Household Cavalry Regiment who had slipped through in the early
morning mist.   Lieut.-Colonel C. B. Mackenzie, the G.I. of 1 Airborne Division, having swum the river now arrived on the scene.
He reported that their losses had been so heavy that barely sufficient
men remained to man the perimeter, and that they were faced by
enemy in great strength especially in armour, tanks and S.P. guns.
No news had been received from the heroic battalion at the bridge
for thirty six hours.   They had, in fact, been overwhelmed early on
the previous day.   A proposal by Lieut.-Colonel Taylor to advance
on the bridge was nevertheless discussed and reluctantly abandoned.
The headquarters of General Sosobowski, the commander of the
Polish Brigade, was then found.   Arrangements were put in hand
for ferrying the sorely needed supplies across the river.

Meanwhile the situation in rear had taken a dramatic turn.   Major
Parker, who had placed himself at the tail of the armoured column,
suddenly encountered a number of German tanks at the De Hoop
cross-roads between Valburg and Driel.   He therefore drove on with
all speed to join his own company ahead.   His company sergeant-
major, C.S.M. Philp, was following in a carrier, six hundred yards
behind.   He met the two leading tanks head on, and at once opened
fire with his Bren at the head of one of the tank commanders sticking
out of the turret.   Both machine-guns of the tank opened up.
C.S.M. Philp and his two companies therefore jumped for the ditch
and making use of its cover made their way back to the remainder of
the column.   There were five tanks in all and they had come from
the direction of Elst.   Acting on this information, Major Kitchen
made a detour with his company and joined the armoured column at
Driel by 9 p.m.

Major Parker, having reported the situation ahead at battalion
headquarters, now turned back to find his missing men and to deal
with the tanks.   He could hear the noise of their tracks and engines
ahead in the darkness.   Sooner or later he decided they must return
to Elst.   Accordingly he set a trap for them at the De Hoop cross-
roads, which they must pass.   No. 75 mines were strung across
the roads and men with Piats stationed round about.   These
shrewd dispositions met with a swift reward.   Silent in the darkness,

Major Parker and his men waited for their prey. First a despatch rider from Elst literally disintegrated on one of the mines. Next came five Tiger tanks headed by another motor cyclist. He also blew up. Someone in the leading tank fired a Verey light. As the tank reached the mines, Major Parker gave the order to fire. Six Piat bombs hit it. There was a tremendous explosion. The second tank received a similar volley. The third tank now tried to back out, but hit a string of mines which Major Parker's men had pulled behind it. Every time it tried to move, another mine went off. Private Brown therefore decided to finish it off from a range of a few yards. He succeeded. It was his first action and he lost an eye. As he relapsed into unconsciousness he remarked, "I don't care—I knocked the . . . out!" The crews of the two surviving tanks, their nerves no doubt shaken by this reception, now decided to back out in a hurry and toppled over into the ditch. Finally, to make quite certain the tanks gave no further trouble, C.S.M. Philp dropped a grenade into the turret of each. The party then returned to Driel.

On the river bank the attempt to get the Dukws across the river miscarried. A heavy ground mist had come down and in spite of the greatest care, the big, awkward Dukws, with their loads of supplies, ran off the slippery road into the ditch and could not be moved.

Meanwhile the remaining battalion of 214 Brigade, 1 Worcestershire, had moved up in its Dukws and by 10 p.m. had established itself in an all-round defensive position at Valburg cross-roads. In addition, the Reconnaissance Regiment further strengthened the new axis by taking responsibility for the defence of Slijk Ewjik.

On the right of the Divisional front astride the main road to Elst, 129 Brigade, with 4 Wiltshire leading, had crossed the main road bridge late in the morning, and become involved almost immediately in bitter close-quarter fighting amidst the apple orchards and ditches five feet wide. A Company (Major A. D. Parsons) gallantly fought its way forward in the face of violent tank and mortar fire. A series of bitter section battles developed. Mortars had to be manhandled. The tanks of the 13/18 Hussars could not deploy from the road. Lieut.-Colonel E. L. Luce endeavoured to work round the flanks with B and C Companies. Little progress, however, could be made. At last light four tanks of 13/18 Hussars attempted to burst through down the main road, only to be knocked out in a flash. Night fell with the 4 Wiltshire dug in within fifty yards of the enemy, equal in strength and determined to fight to the last. It had been a black day for the regiment. However, the sacrifice had not been in vain, for their unrelenting struggle to fight their way forward had held the enemy to his ground and thus contributed to the sudden and dramatic developments on the left flank of the Divisional front in the last two hours of daylight.

THE NEDER RIJN

22nd
Sept.

In spite of the success on the Divisional front, it had become apparent to the Army Commander on the evening of 22nd September that, in view of the strong and increasing resistance of the enemy, he now lacked the resources to pursue his intention of establishing a firm bridgehead north of Arnhem.   52 (L.) Division, organized on an air portable basis, constituted his only reserve.   It was now learnt that, owing to the continued bad weather and the lack of suitable landing-grounds, it was unlikely to be available for another week. He accordingly abandoned his plan to reach Arnhem as far as the 43 Division was concerned and directed it to make a crossing west of the town on the morrow.

Whilst the Somersets were battering their way into Oosterhout, the situation during the afternoon on the long and practically unprotected single line of communication of the Corps had taken a serious turn.   A German column of approximately 30 tanks and 200 vehicles, from Erp on the east flank, established itself astride the main axis north-east of Veghel, thus isolating the troops in Nijmegen from 101 U.S. Airborne Division to the south and bringing all traffic to a standstill.   32 Guards Infantry Brigade therefore had to be turned back from the Nijmegen area to re-open the road.   The situation was not cleared up until the following afternoon, when traffic once more began to flow after an interruption of 25 hours. Amongst those isolated by this exasperating diversion was the Corps Commander, Lieut.-General Horrocks, who had gone back to meet General Dempsey at Veghel.   He was unable to rejoin his Corps until the following day, when, with an escort of six carriers, he succeeded in evading the Germans and reaching his headquarters near Nijmegen.

During the afternoon of the 22nd, 129 Brigade with 4 and 5 Wiltshire astride the railway from Nijmegen to Elst, like the Guards whom they had replaced, had found progress almost impossible. The tanks of the 13/18 Hussars were unable to move off the roads into the thick orchards.   German artillery fire was heavy and accurate.   214 Brigade, spread out between Oosterhout and Driel, needed time to concentrate before striking its next blow.   130 Brigade, however, stood ready to continue the advance round the open west flank.   Major-General Thomas therefore ordered Brigadier B. B. Walton, the commander of this brigade, to advance at first light on the 23rd along the Bund to Slijk Ewijk and, moving via Valburg, to establish contact with the D.C.L.I. in Driel, thus gaining touch with 1 Airborne Division on the far side of the Neder Rijn. He further ordered 214 Brigade to clear the east flank of the Divisional axis by capturing Elst from the direction of Valburg after 130 Brigade had passed.

The dawn of 23rd September came with cold and driving rain.
Led by 5 Dorset, 130 Brigade was directed by the Regulating Headquarters, established by the 8 Middlesex near the roundabout by the
main road bridge in Nijmegen, on to the Bund and the route taken
by the D.C.L.I. the previous evening.   The 7 Royal Hampshire
group followed 5 Dorset: then came brigade headquarters and
finally 4 Dorset group.   It had under its command the 13/18 Hussars
and included a number of lorries carrying assault boats for the
crossing of the Neder Rijn.   The brigade was mounted in Dukws.
On the narrow embanked roads these unwieldy vehicles were to
prove a serious liability.   The slightest error in driving landed them
irrecoverably in the ditch.   The sharp corners proved particularly
difficult to negotiate.   As the head of the column reached the cross-
roads at Valburg, enemy artillery opened up.   Roofs crashed down,
houses were blasted and several Dukws received direct hits.   Enemy
tanks from the direction of Elst now opened fire and cut Lieut.-
Colonel Coad's battalion, 5 Dorset, in two.   He pushed on, however,
with the front half and by 11.30 a.m. had reached Driel.   The rear
of his column meanwhile proceeded to fight its way through under
cover of smoke from their mortars and fire from their anti-tank guns.
The infantry crawled ahead along the ditches; the vehicles ran the
gauntlet.   All had joined their commanding officer in Driel by evening.   A Company (Major H. C. Allen) was soon established on the
river bank near the broken railway bridge, with D Company (Major
G. R. Hartwell) a thousand yards to the left.   The other two
companies were disposed in an orchard with battalion headquarters
about half a mile from the river.   Contact was established with
5 D.C.L.I. and the Polish Airborne Brigade in Driel.   Overhead,
gallant flights of Dakotas and Stirlings came in at low altitude to drop
coloured parachutes with supplies.   They were greeted by intense
anti-aircraft fire and several were shot down.   Few of their loads
found their mark.   Temporarily at least air superiority had been lost,
for many German aircraft could be seen attacking the Airborne
Division beyond the river.   On the ground it soon became evident
that the enemy had excellent observation.   Shelling and mortaring
became intense as the day wore on.

    It was not until well on in the afternoon that the tail of 130 Brigade
Column bedevilled by the fire of 88's and machine-guns, finally
cleared Valburg cross-roads.   7 Royal Hampshire deployed on the
river bank near Heteren.   4 Dorset, in reserve, took up a position at
Homoet, where Brigadier Walton opened his headquarters.

    Until 130 Brigade, who had priority on the road, had cleared
Valburg cross-roads, it was impossible for 214 Brigade to start their
day's task—the capture of Elst.   The only road available for their
mortars, carriers and anti-tank guns ran through Valburg.   Movement
by any type of vehicle across the soggy fields was quite out of the

question. Some difficulty was experienced in explaining this embarrassing fact to Major-General Thomas on the wireless. He
accordingly arrived at Valburg cross-roads to verify the situation in
person. Here he found the Commander of 214 Brigade and his
commanding officers seated round the bright green billiard table of
the local public house engaged in settling the final details for the
advance on Elst, now at last feasible. A more than usually vicious
concentration of 88's, which smashed all the windows and killed
several men outside, greeted his arrival. In the circumstances his
opinion, expressed with his normal brevity and force, that the rendezvous was ill chosen, must be regarded as fair comment. A second
salvo, equally well directed, brought the conference to an even
speedier conclusion than the normal in this brigade.

The difficulty of staging a brigade battle with another brigade
advancing through your assembly area on the only available road will
be realized. However, the attack started at 5 p.m. supported by the
whole Divisional artillery. On the left, D Company of 1 Worcestershire and tanks of C Squadron of 4/7 Dragoon Guards deployed in
the open country. Small-arms fire greeted them from the farm
buildings ahead. A Panther appeared and was knocked out.
D Company closed with the enemy; C and A Companies now followed. Solid shots twanged over their heads. A second Panther
and a Tiger tank were destroyed. At last the outskirts of Elst were
reached, and it being now dark and house-to-house clearing out of
the question until daylight, Lieut.-Colonel Osborne Smith decided
to call a halt. On the right, 7 Somerset, after an exceedingly difficult move across country by the rifle companies, were eventually able
to link up with their tanks, carriers and anti-tank guns and thrust
forward to the cross-roads south-west of Elst. The attack met
slight opposition only. Lieut.-Colonel H. A. Borradaile therefore
pushed through D Company to secure a road junction south of the
town and astride the main road. This prompt action met with a
startling reward, as the company had placed itself in the gathering
darkness across the communications of the enemy facing 129 Brigade.
Within the next hour two despatch riders, a 20 mm. A.A. gun complete with crew, an artillery officer and a ration truck had been
eliminated. Confused fighting with enemy coming from both
directions continued throughout the night.

During the day 43 Reconnaissance Regiment were quick to exploit
the open flank on the west. Soon after first light A Squadron moved
out of Slijk Ewijk followed by C Squadron along the banks of the
Waal, and turning north took the road to Andelst, Zetten and the
Neder Rijn.

Stray parties of men from German anti-aircraft and searchlight
units found in these pleasant and prosperous villages offered comparatively little resistance. No. 1 Troop under Lieutenant Jackson

reached the Neder Rijn at Randwijk.   B Squadron established itself
in Zetten and cleared the area north of Slijk Ewijk.   Thanks to these
operations and the advance of 214 Brigade towards Elst, the main
axis of the Division through Valburg could therefore be considered as
reasonably secure at last light.

In spite of the enemy's fierce reaction during the day, the fact that
his only line of communication had been cut for twenty-five hours
south of Grave, the bad weather and the consequent chaotic failure
of air supply and the ever-increasing evidence that strong armoured
enemy reinforcements were now concentrating against him, Lieut.-
General Horrocks did not abandon hope.   For the night of 23/24
September he ordered three operations.   Firstly, the Airborne
bridgehead north of the river was to be re-supplied.   Secondly, the
Polish Parachute Brigade at Driel was to be passed into the first Airborne bridgehead, and thirdly, 43 Division was "to enlarge the
bridgehead westward using two battalions."*   This third task, in
the circumstances, was not feasible.   The Neder Rijn is a major
European river with a fast current.   In addition, the enemy held the
banks in strength backed by ample armour.   He had perfect observation over the approaches to the south bank.   There were only
sufficient assault boats for a single-battalion crossing.   In addition,
130 Brigade had only shaken itself free of the bottleneck at Valburg
by the late afternoon and when the light necessary for reconnaissance
was rapidly fading.   Brigadier Walton was therefore ordered to
confine his operations for the night to passing over into the airborne
bridgehead as many Poles as possible and some Dukws with supplies.
The only available assault boats were accordingly handed over by
4 Dorset to General Sosobowski and the Polish Brigade, which had
been at Driel since the 21st.   This decision was to have unfortunate
results on the following night, as will be seen.   This Polish Brigade
was of little more than battalion strength.   There were many delays
in the darkness.   It must be recorded that General Sosobowski's
attitude was the reverse of co-operative.   Enemy shelling and
mortaring added to the confusion and the operation did not start
until a late hour.   The stout-hearted Poles, ferried across in sixteen
assault boats by 204 Field Company and 5 Dorsets, and supported
by every weapon 130 Brigade could bring to bear, persisted
in their efforts despite their heavy losses from the fire of an enemy
fully aware of their intentions.   They were however, unfamiliar with
this type of operation and by dawn only about two hundred had
succeeded in reaching the far bank.   Unfortunately they left the
assault boats on the river bank, where many of them were shot to
pieces during the day.   Within the perimeter, what remained of
1 Airborne Division, subjected to incessant attack, very heavy

* This at any rate seems to have been the impression of some staff
officer (unknown), who recorded it in the War Diary.

mortaring and shelling, short of food and dropping with fatigue, still fought on.

The results of the night's work pleased neither Lieut.-General Horrocks nor Major-General Thomas as they surveyed the country on the banks of the Neder Rijn from the church steeple in Driel early next morning. The time had come to withdraw what was left of the Airborne Division from an operation which from the start had been daring in conception and hazardous in the extreme. That at the decisive moment the Corps Commander lacked adequate forces was no fault of his, the Army Commander's or the Field-Marshal's. It will be recollected that after the crossing of the Seine, the Supreme Command had compromised and given part of the Allied resources to General Patton's thrust and part to Field-Marshal Montgomery's. Had the entire effort been placed in the hands of the Field-Marshal he might have ended the campaign in the autumn of 1944. He himself thought so and he is not given to rash statements.

Lieut.-General Horrocks faced the facts. The position held by the Airborne Division had no military value. It was merely a nebulous area in the wooded hills with very little control over the river bank, which ran dead straight for well over half a mile. The enemy held the high ground overlooking the river and the approaches to it. It would therefore be impossible to bring bridging-lorries down to it in daylight. Even if a bridge were built it would still be under small-arms fire from the opposite bank both above and below the bridge site. He therefore instructed 43 Division to carry out the evacuation.

The final decision was reached at a conference at headquarters, 43 Division, on the morning of the 24th. Both Lieut.-General Horrocks and Major-General Sosobowski, the Polish Brigade Commander, were present. The Airborne Division controlled so small a part of the river bank that it was considered essential to get a firmer grip on the far side in order to enable them to be withdrawn. For this reason, 130 Brigade were ordered to pass over 4 Dorset on the left and to reinforce the Airborne position with a further party of Poles on the night of 24/25th. Lieut.-Colonel E. C. W. Myers, the C.R.E. of the 1 Airborne Division, who had come over to the south bank two nights previously, was to cross with the 4 Dorset and take to Major-General Urquhart the plan for the evacuation, evolved by Major-General Thomas in conjunction with Major-General Pyman, the Chief of Staff of Second Army. Action was to be taken on receipt of the Code word "Berlin." General Sosobowski's attitude at the conference cannot honestly be described as cordial. Having heard the outline of the plan, he said, "I am General Sosobowski, I command the Polish Para Brigade. I do as I like."

Lieut.-General Horrocks and Major-General Thomas exchanged glances. Then Lieut.-General Horrocks said: "You are under my command. You will do as I bloody well tell you." To this forth-right statement, General Sosobowski replied: "All right. I command the Polish Para Brigade and I do as you bloody well say." The conference then continued on more formal lines.

The site selected for the crossing was the ferry at the western end of the perimeter of 1 Airborne Division. It was overlooked by the enemy on the high ground on the far side. Incessant mortar and machine-gun fire made movement in daylight between the houses and orchards of Driel and the river bank impossible. Lieut.-Colonel Tilley and the Company Commanders of 4 Dorset, who had been given the task of carrying out the crossing, managed, however, to get a good view from the top of the church steeple in Driel. A factory about six hundred yards inland was selected as the battalion's objective.

At a brigade "O" Group held at 4.30 p.m. the plan for the operation took its final form. In brief, the assault by 4 Dorset was to be supported by intense fire by the whole Divisional artillery and from 5 Dorset on the right flank and 7 Royal Hampshire on the left, each supplemented by a squadron of 13/18 Hussars and machine-gun and mortar platoons of 8 Middlesex. Simultaneously the Polish Brigade were to cross on the battalion's right in the assault boats remaining with them from the previous night's operations. Zero hour was provisionally fixed for 10 p.m. The urgency of the earliest possible start needed no stress, as it was known that the strength of the current was likely to increase rapidly after midnight. The actual ferrying of the assault boats was entrusted to 204 Field Company, who had moved up to Valburg. The assault boats, however, had still to arrive from the rear. After the battalion had crossed, it was intended to use these boats supplemented by four Dukws to ferry over supplies. This task was entrusted to Major Rooke and B and C companies of 7 Royal Hampshire.

As night closed in, 4 Dorset made their way forward along the slippery and treacherous track to their assembly area at Driel. The weather had turned to a cold drizzle. Soon it was pitch black. Heavy enemy shell and mortar fire hampered the move and the battalion finally reached the village in scattered parties. Reorganization caused delay, but by 10 p.m. Lieut.-Colonel Tilley was ready to take over the twenty assault boats which had been promised and advance the final six hundred yards to the river. No assault boats, however, had arrived.

This is what had happened. In the darkness two lorry loads of boats took the wrong turning at Valburg and drove into the enemy lines at Elst. Two more lorries slithered off the muddy road into the dyke and could not be traced. The remaining lorry load, when it eventually reached the Poles, had no paddles.

Brigadier Walton had established his tactical headquarters in

10

Driel. Time was passing. The Poles were unco-operative. He therefore decided about midnight to suspend their crossing and transfer the assault boats with them to 4 Dorset. Thanks to the energy of Captain Dawes of 5 Dorset, these were eventually collected on carriers and delivered to the battalion, who had now been waiting for three unpleasant hours in their assembly position. At 1 a.m. the battalion picked up its boats and advanced through the orchards to the river bank.

For twenty minutes the Divisional artillery and the battalions on the flanks pounded the far bank. The enemy retaliated with mortars. One boat was set on fire and others holed on the way forward. As the boats of A and B Companies who formed the first flight approached the bank, heavy machine-gun fire opened up. More boats were holed and a number of men were hit. However, A Company under Major Grafton, on the right, and B Company on the left under Major Whittle, entered the water. On the far bank two burning factories lit up the wooded slopes. Everywhere Spandaus spluttered at close range. Some of the boats got out of control and were swept downstream. Others were sunk by enemy fire. However, in spite of the current, four of B Company's boats succeeded in landing about a hundred yards east of the burning factory. Here Major Whittle found himself with Lieutenant Macdermott and about thirty men. Ahead rose a steep bank about a hundred feet high held in strength by the enemy, who rolled grenades down upon them. Weak though he was, Major Whittle at once advanced to the attack. The party gained the crest and drove back the enemy, but at the cost of half their numbers. Here they were joined by Lieut.-Colonel Tilley, Major Roper and about twenty men of C Company, who had crossed in the second flight. Lieut.-Colonel Tilley now tried to gain contact with A Company on the right, but was surrounded and eventually when dawn came forced to surrender after bitter fighting. Major Whittle continued throughout the rest of the night to try to link up with the rest of the battalion, but everywhere clashed with strong and obstinate parties of the enemy. At dawn, therefore, he collected the thirty men of B, C, D and S Companies remaining and dug in behind a bank half-way between the river and the trees. A Company's landing, it eventually transpired, had been even more scattered. Major Grafton, his F.O.O. and a few men did eventually succeed in getting through to the Airborne Division bridgehead. The rest were drowned or overwhelmed. By half-past three about two hundred and fifty men had been embarked. 204 Field Company therefore turned to the task of ferrying stores. About two tons were taken to the far bank. Of six Dukws standing by with supplies, only three were able to enter the water owing to the steepness of the banks. These three, however, stuck on the mud on the far side. Their drivers, Corporal Varney and Driver Chilton of the R.A.S.C., therefore swam back for help. Then dawn and enemy fire put a stop to further operations. It had been a night of heroic struggle against hopeless odds.

Whilst the preparations for this heroic but abortive operation were in train, 214 Brigade, which had been ordered to complete the occupation of Elst, had found itself involved in savage house-to-house fighting in which two company commanders of 1 Worcestershire, Majors Souper and Gibbons, lost their lives. The enemy consisted of Waffen S.S. and they fought to the end. Every house seemed to contain a German with an automatic. Night fell with both sides in close contact in the centre of the town. To the south, 4 and 5 Wiltshire continued the bitter struggle and made some ground.

In the air enemy fighter aircraft in squadron strength appeared and swooped down on the sorely tried Airborne Division. Black bursts of flak darkened the skies over Arnhem and many brave British and American aircrews met their end.

Further back along the main axis the situation now took a serious turn. In the evening an enemy thrust from the west cut the road north of St. Oedenrode. In fact, two German divisions had crossed the Schelde and were now in action along with a strong battle group of paratroops. On the other side of the road three enemy divisions had been identified. Operations on an extensive scale involving 7 Armoured and 101 Airborne Divisions had to be put in hand, and it was not until the morning of the 26th that the road was again opened and supply columns for 30 Corps could again flow through.

In this sombre setting of a severed supply line, of over-extended forces, of artillery ammunition down to a dangerously low level, of loss of command of the air over the battlefield, of rapidly deteriorating weather and disintegrating roads between the rivers, and evidence of rising enemy strength and morale, the decision was taken early on the morning of the 25th to evacuate what remained of the 1 Airborne Division that night. The code word "Berlin" was therefore transmitted to the Airborne Division by the only existing wireless link, that is, from 64 Medium Regiment to the Airborne C.R.A. *25th Sept.*

Major-General Thomas's detailed plan for the evacuation was ready. In addition, he was ordered to finish the reduction of Elst; to hold the east flank from Elst to the south bank of the Neder Rijn; to protect the west flank of the Corps; and to hold one brigade group and an armoured regiment centrally placed in reserve. At the same time, Guards Armoured Division on his right were entrusted with the east flank from the Waal to Elst and instructed to capture Bemmel.

To meet this new situation, Major-General Thomas had already withdrawn 129 Brigade into reserve. During the 25th, 214 Brigade consolidated the east flank and finally completed the clearing of Elst. These operations, hampered by shortage of ammunition, were protracted and bitter. In all, no less than two Tiger tanks and six

Panthers were accounted for by this brigade and the 4/7 Dragoon Guards. A touch of comedy was provided during the afternoon by D Company of the D.C.L.I., who, suspicious of a number of trucks on the railway embankment on their front, engaged them with an anti-tank gun. An appalling explosion resulted which destroyed not only the railway embankment but also all the houses in the vicinity, in which the troops were sheltering from the weather. The trucks in fact contained ammunition which the station-master at Elst had wisely removed from the village.

The extent of the disaster to 4 Dorset was not at first realized at Headquarters 130 Brigade, all communications having broken down with what remained of the battalion. However, they were in touch with Major-General Urquhart. Fortunately Lieut.-Colonel Myers had succeeded during the night in getting through to the Airborne Division's Headquarters with General Thomas's plan for the withdrawal. At 10.30 a.m. General Urquhart signalled that he agreed with the plan and asked for it to be put into force. In brief, 43 Division promised to provide assault boats on the far bank at 10 p.m. that night and to cover the withdrawal with 4 Dorset and a heavy artillery and small-arms fire programme. 130 Brigade was to be responsible for the operation up to and including the near bank. Therefrom evacuation would be a Divisional responsibility. Lieut.-Colonel W. C. A. Henniker, C.R.E. 43 Division, was placed in control of the actual ferrying operations.

To draw the enemy's attention away from the Airborne Division, 129 Brigade staged a feint on the west flank during the late afternoon. This consisted of a motley column of mortar and carrier platoons, a machine-gun platoon, a number of empty Dukws, and pontoon and bridge lorries under the control of 5 Wiltshire. As dusk approached, it moved ostentatiously to the village of Heteren on the banks of the river and opened up for one hour with Bren guns, machine-guns and mortars on to the far bank. This deception undoubtedly gave the impression that the crossing attempted the previous night was being repeated further west and thus contributed to the success of the withdrawal.

Four field companies were entrusted with the ferrying, 260 Field Company and 23 Canadian Field Company at the site opposite the Airborne Division's perimeter and 553 Field Company and 20 Canadian Field Company a mile downstream at the point where 4 Dorset had crossed the previous night. Sixteen assault boats manned by the Divisional engineers were allotted to each site. The Canadians provided twenty-one storm boats at each crossing.

A night of intense blackness descended with heavy rain. It was so dark that men had to walk in front of the vehicles and even they could scarcely be seen by the drivers. Some lorries slipped off the narrow roads into the ditch and had to be over-turned to keep the way clear. A reconnaissance party under Lieutenant Bevan went forward from the assembly area over a high flood bank and two or three ditches and taped out the way to the embarkation point. On the far bank the burning factory cast a light over the dark swirling waters of the river. Sustained and accurate machine-gun fire from the direction of the railway bridge up river clipped the near bank.

At nine o'clock the whole Divisional artillery opened up with overwhelming effect, tracer from the L.A.A. Regiment marking the flanks of the crossings and A and C Companies of 8 Middlesex thickening up the fire. The noise was deafening and awesome as the first parties of Sappers carried the assault boats over the dyke walls and down to the water's edge. The crews dipped their oars and disappeared into the darkness. More boats followed. Punctually at 9.40 p.m. the first reached the far side and waited for the Airborne troops who were due at ten.

Luckily the dark night, the heavy rain and the strong wind concealed the unobtrusive move of the Airborne Division down to the river bank and the waiting boats. They embarked. Soon the first flotilla had brought across about a hundred men and some wounded, and returned to the north bank. Throughout the night the Sappers crossed and re-crossed the river. One boat contained sixteen wounded and room only for three Sappers to ply their oars against the strong current. The glow of the burning factory waxed and waned as the fires were fanned by the strong wind. The Canadian storm boats plied manfully to and fro across the river. Still the work went on. The strong current carried some of the boats downstream. Crews became strained and tired and had to be increased, first to six men and then to eight.

Throughout the night a steady stream of exhausted but unconquered men of the 1 Airborne Division made their way back from the river bank to the reception area organized by Major G. R. Hartwell and D Company of the 5 Dorsets. There they were quickly and effectively passed back to a large barn at Driel lit by the headlights of a jeep, where blankets and rum, tea and hot stew awaited them. Outside in an orchard, Lieut.-Colonel J. McCance, the A.Q.M.G., had ready forty jeeps equipped with stretchers, for only jeeps could master the narrow, slippery roads back from Driel. The barn and its cellars were soon full of wounded. Many of the men had discarded their clothes to swim the river, and the houses had to be ransacked to provide covering for them.

At intervals during the night the enemy subjected the area to intense mortaring, over two hundred bombs falling in the space of half an hour. It was now that the genius for administrative improvisation of Lieut.-Colonel McCance and Colonel K. A. M. Tomory, the A.D.M.S., showed at its brilliant best. Despite the appalling conditions, by dawn over 2,000 men of the Airborne

Division had been swiftly passed to the rear, either in medical charge or to the large red-brick school situated in a quiet tree-lined thoroughfare in Nijmegen which had been organized as a reception centre.

26th
Sept. It had been hoped to evacuate the 4 Dorset after the Airborne Division. Few, however, could be found. As dawn broke the enemy rained down a murderous fire on the boats, manned for the most part from 4 a.m. onwards by the Pioneer Platoon of 5 Dorset; 88 mm. shells began to fall; spurts of spray in the Neder Rijn marked where mortar bombs struck the water. The enemy closed in amongst the reeds on the far bank and set up machine-guns which skimmed the surface with deadly effect. Our guns fired smoke to screen the operation, but to no avail. Major Vinycomb made one last trip in a storm boat to the far bank, loaded it with men, and as the enemy drew near made his way back under heavy fire. A young Canadian officer dashed over with two loads of German life-jackets and left them on the far shore. Hardly an occupant of his boat was alive or unwounded when he at last reached the home bank. Lieut.-Colonel Henniker, the C.R.E., had remained throughout the night imperturbable on the river bank directing the operation. All that could be done had been done. To continue in daylight would merely mean useless sacrifice of life. He accordingly ordered ferrying to cease.

Major Hall of 4 Dorsets crossed during the evacuation with orders for the withdrawal, but his efforts to find the battalion proved unavailing. Major Whittle and about fifteen men found a sound boat for the wounded and swam back during the night. Major Hall again crossed on the night of the 27th and succeeded in bringing back four more men. Altogether the battalion had lost thirteen officers and two hundred men.

Whether the Division could ever have established a firmer lodgment on the north bank of the Neder Rijn will always be a matter of conjecture.

The position of the Airborne Division from their own point of view was desperate from the start. In addition, it offered no facilities for exploitation by anyone else. The difficulties inevitably inherent in operating with Allies when a situation has taken a turn for the worse and the element of bad luck both played their part. No bridgehead could at any stage ever have been permanently sustained. Nevertheless, the decision to pass 4 Dorset across the river as part of the evacuation plan was in every way sound and the individual courage with which it was implemented will always remain a shining example in the history of the Division.

LAST DAYS ON THE ISLAND

26th
Sept. The Corps Commander was particularly anxious that the reasons for the temporary abandonment of the offensive should be understood

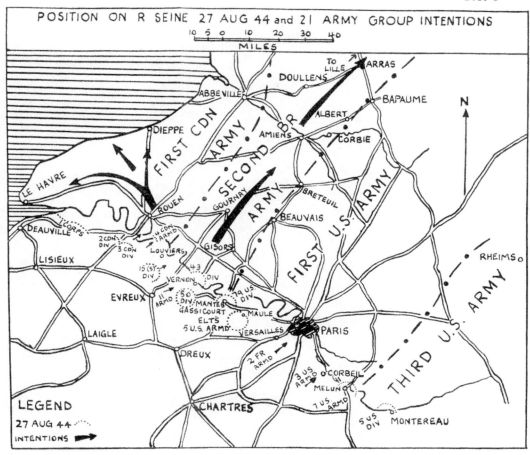

POSITION ON R SEINE 27 AUG 44 and 21 ARMY GROUP INTENTIONS

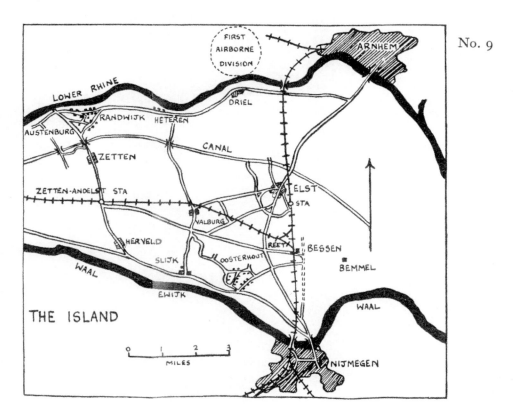

THE ISLAND

by the troops. In a personal message to all commanding officers he stressed that for some weeks 30 Corps had been privileged to lead the advance of the Second Army and that their recent operations had been one of the most daring ever attempted in modern war. "In conjunction with the Airborne Corps, we were asked to penetrate deep into enemy territory, along one road, and to force a passage over three of the most formidable rivers in Europe. We have burst through the enemy's defences and secured a passage over two of these rivers. We now stand poised between the second and third rivers, ready to advance again as soon as our larders have been re-stocked. I want all ranks to realize that the German is putting up a stubborn resistance as we approach his frontier. He is, however, very stretched, and provided we can maintain the offensive as we have done in the past, he is bound to crash in time. Very soon I hope we shall be advancing into Germany and carrying on the war on German soil." At the same time he passed on Field-Marshal Montgomery's congratulations on what had been achieved.

The bridgehead over the Neder Rijn having been abandoned, the Corps soon found itself temporarily forced on to the defensive. Two Panzer divisions, 9 and 116, which had been fighting on the First U.S. Army sector, now arrived, to be reinforced later, south-east of Nijmegen, by 108 Panzer Brigade and part of 1 S.S. Panzer Division. The enemy's purpose was to pinch out the bridgehead across the Waal and to recapture Nijmegen. Signs were not wanting that a strong and capable enemy commander now had charge of the conduct of operations and that he knew how to handle his guns with effect, that is, concentrated.

Owing to the interruption of the main axis the Corps had now to face a serious shortage of artillery ammunition and supplies. Luckily, large quantities of German rations had fallen into our hands. These saved the situation so far as food was concerned, although adverse comment amongst the troops was not lacking on the issue of tinned black pudding for breakfast, tea made of chopped-up leaves and super-hard biscuits filled with carraway seeds. Fortunately, large quantities of Dutch gin, brandy and Velasquez cigars were available as a counterweight.

It was the state of the roads, however, on the island which gave the greatest cause for anxiety. These were merely embankments, sur-faced with brick designed to take light traffic only across the surrounding fens. Now the bad weather and the continued heavy traffic were rapidly completing their disintegration. In the Division's area movement had to be restricted to a minimum and the passage of more than twenty vehicles in one convoy, without per-mission from headquarters, to be forbidden.

In the altered circumstances, Major-General Thomas regrouped the Division. 129 Brigade now took over the east flank from Elst to the Neder Rijn and 214 Brigade withdrew into reserve in the still unspoilt area of neat farmhouses and villas around Andelst. 130 Brigade remained in its exposed positions along the Neder Rijn, subjected to ever-increasing mortar, machine-gun and shell fire.

27th Sept.

Since the 24th, 43 Reconnaissance Regiment had been guarding the west flank of the Division. Lieut.-Colonel F. Lane Fox, who also had at his disposal the 12/60, the motor battalion of 8 Armoured Brigade, had established B Squadron at Dodewaard and C Squadron facing Orpeusden, where they held the enemy at a distance. A Squadron meanwhile, concealed around Randwijk and with posts overlooking the northern bank of the Neder Rijn, sent continual reports of enemy movement on the far bank. It was fascinating to watch the activities of large numbers of Germans only a few hundred yards away, but galling to be forbidden to fire. Major-General Thomas however was anxious to conceal the fact from the enemy that his flank extended so far to the west.

26th/ 27th Sept.

During the 26th Major Scott-Plummer, the squadron commander, had been manning these O.Ps. with men from the armoured car troops. When night came he relieved them with his carrier crews. The front was nearly two miles in length and the three scout troops were up. It was a dark moonless night. Soon after two o'clock in the morning a listening post reported that Germans were digging behind them on our side of the river. Next, Sergeant Taylor of 2 Troop was astonished to see in the gloom six Germans hauling an anti-tank gun into position a few yards away from him. He opened fire at once and cut down the whole party. Twenty Germans now approached the troop position. These were driven off, but confused fighting continued. It became evident that the enemy, taking advantage of the intense darkness, had succeeded in crossing the river in strength. Major Scott-Plummer therefore established his three troops in a position where they could command the orchards flanking the dyke road. At dawn Lieutenant Howe, with Sergeant Carleton and Sergeant Corless, advanced with three armoured cars and opened fire with deadly effect on large numbers of the enemy now visible digging in around the dyke. Sergeant Carleton's 2-inch mortar ranged accurately on the enemy's trenches. A violent battle now developed and bazooka bombs and shells began to drop amongst the vehicles. As Lieutenant Howe gave the order to disengage, a shell exploded under his car, which lurched over the dyke bank on to a party of Germans, and he and his crew were captured. Meanwhile the Squadron, although outnumbered, pinned the enemy to the orchards and prevented them from breaking out. Some of them however, penetrated the houses of Randwijk. The situation had taken an ugly turn.

27th Sept.

Faced with this threat to his west flank, Brigadier Walton, commanding 130 Brigade, now ordered 7 Royal Hampshire, who were still holding their position to the east of Randwijk, to intervene. Violent artillery and mortar fire had broken out on their part of the front. The reserve company (" C ") of this battalion and a troop of 13/18 Hussars therefore advanced to recapture the village of Randwijk. Amongst the houses a violent and confused battle now developed in which heavy losses were sustained. Towards midday it became necessary for them to be withdrawn from the village to reorganize on the eastern edge.

Realizing the seriousness of the situation, Major-General Thomas now placed Brigadier Prior-Palmer, the commander of 8 Armoured Brigade, in charge of the operations. Arriving on the spot, he ordered the company to hold fast on to the eastern edge of the village and disposed A Squadron of the Reconnaissance Regiment and two platoons of the 12/60 so as to prevent any further extension of the enemy's bridgehead. The position was thus temporarily stabilized. It was evident, however, that enemy forces in battalion strength had secured a firm footing on the southern bank of the river and that there were not enough troops on the spot to eject them. Major-General Thomas therefore ordered 214 Brigade, which had now concentrated in the Andelst area, to intervene and drive the enemy back into the river. In fact three or four Wehrmacht companies and a S.S. company had crossed in the darkness in rubber boats, manned by engineers who apparently had been ordered to build a bridge.

7 Somerset Light Infantry accordingly in the early afternoon left their comfortable billets in Herveld, where they had arrived the previous night, and mounted on the tanks of A Squadron 4/7 Dragoon Guards, roared down the road to Zetten and Randwijk. Dismounting on arrival at the canal north of Zetten C Company, under Major D. B. M. Durie, took the road to Rustenburg on the left flank and A Company, under Major L. Roberts, headed for Randwijk and the river bank. The bright autumn sunshine of the morning had now faded, to be followed by black clouds and torrential rain. Ahead for 800 yards stretched completely flat and open marshy fields, in full view of the high ground on the far side of the Neder Rijn. Messerschmitts swooped down on both company columns as they advanced. The fire of 88's made it impossible for the tanks to operate beyond the canal. 179 Field Regiment covered the advance with smoke. On the right, the vanguard of A Company, commanded by a Canadian Officer, Lieutenant W. B. Mottrom, hugged the hedgerows and under heavy fire from 88's at last entered the maze of houses of Randwijk, where lively and confusing fighting now developed. By the time night fell the company had closed with the main enemy position and, thanks to the skill and courage of Captain Ian Bridges, 179 Field Regiment thoroughly and accurately registered the guns. Throughout the night Captain Bridges battered the enemy with incessant shell-fire. At 6.30 a.m., supported

by the whole Divisional artillery and the battalion's 3-inch mortars, the attack went in.   So effective was the artillery support that many of the German slits received direct hits and the company accepted the surrender of prisoners in numbers greater than their own strength.

On the left, C Company, harried by low-flying attacks, worked their way up the wet ditches and by the time the light began to fade had reached a position about five hundred yards south of the river. Here they were subjected to a fantastic bombardment of solid shot, smoke bombs and flares.   Lieut.-Colonel Borradaile now came up and by the light of burning buildings made a plan for a night-attack to clear the orchard ahead and capture the dyke road.   The attack went in and was completely successful.   As dawn broke many demoralized Germans came in to surrender.   Mopping up of the village, in which C company of 7 Royal Hampshire joined, occupied the morning.   Altogether about a hundred and fifty prisoners were taken.   Thus thanks to the initiative and courage of the infantry and the brilliant handling of the guns, the enemy bridgehead south of the Neder Rijn was effectively destroyed.

28th
Sept.

In the face of the rapidly developing counter-offensive, the ground beneath his feet literally reverting to the marsh from which it came, Major-General Thomas assumed the bankrupt legacy of responsibility for the defence of the whole island.   A commander of not dissimilar calibre had obviously taken charge of the battle on the German side and the vigour he now imparted to it compels respect. Before the war, according to the Dutch, the advance from Nijmegen to Arnhem had apparently been a stock question in army promotion examinations.   Any officer who took the direct route invariably failed.   General Thomas was now to prove that the operation conducted in the reverse direction was equally unsound.   He ordered every available weapon to be brought to bear to harass the enemy.   The programme included an elaborate programme for all anti-tank guns co-ordinated by 86 Anti-Tank Regiment.   Lieut.-Colonel Crawford of 8 Middlesex ensured that all machine-guns and mortars were employed to secure the maximum offensive value from these weapons.   General Thomas had now under his command no less than five infantry brigades.   On the extreme right, beyond the Arnhem road, 5 Guards Brigade held the maze of orchards and ditches east of the Arnhem road.   Next, 69 Infantry Brigade, under Brigadier F. Y. C. Knox, stood south-east of Elst.   Brigadier Knox had trained 130 Infantry Brigade for three years and been posted away three months before D-Day.   His return under command of the Division was doubly welcome both on personal and military grounds.   He was ordered to plan the capture of the villages and factories of Haalderen.   Brigadier Mole with 129 Brigade in the featureless and exposed polders around the railway embankment, prolonged the line to the junction with 130 Brigade on the Neder Rijn. 214 Brigade held Randwijk and 43 Reconnaissance Regiment continued to be responsible for the open west flank. 5 D.C.L.I. with a squadron of 13/18 Hussars under command at Oosterhout constituted the "island" reserve.

Five infantry brigades, an armoured brigade and four additional artillery regiments constitute a force seldom given to a major-general. Theoretically a force of this size is beyond the capacity of a divisional commander and his staff to handle. General Thomas, however, undertook the task with a light heart.

Not the least of his many liabilities was responsibility for the two bridges at Nijmegen. It is almost incredible to relate that at no time since their capture had the enemy been more than five hundred yards away from the road bridge; he had perfect observation over it from two factories on the north bank of the Waal. Shelling and low-flying attacks on the bridges had been persistent for several days and traffic had had to run the gauntlet. A low-flying attack early on the 28th caught the army A.A. battery responsible off their guard, put the railway bridge temporarily out of action and hit the road bridge, though not seriously, on the Nijmegen side. Practically General Thomas's first act on taking over the "island" was to establish the Divisional engineers as a "close bridge garrison." Lieut.-Colonel Henniker, the C.R.E., in addition to his own field companies and field park company, was also given two batteries of 73 Anti-tank Regiment and B Company of 8 Middlesex to assist him in this task. These troops moved into position during the 28th. To his astonishment on carrying out his reconnaissance, Lieut.-Colonel Henniker found little between himself and the enemy, who were extremely active only a short distance up-stream. In consequence, he laid out his defences primarily to meet ground attack. The possibility that the enemy might arrive by water was realised by no one. When night came, enemy aircraft viciously bombed the town and guns opened up on to the area south of the bridge. Many houses were struck and fires broke out. Under the bridge, the Waal, dirty brown and in shadow, flowed on. Anyone swimming down it in the darkness would be quite invisible.

In the early hours of the morning, German "frogmen" entered the river from the east. They were sailors, who had been trained in Venice in long-distance swimming under water with special equipment. They wore tight-fitting rubber suits and breathing masks, their feet had large flappers attached to them, the only weapon that they carried was a sheath knife. They were complete even to waterproof wrist-watches.

They swam down the Waal in the darkness towing two large torpedo-like explosive charges which were destined to be fastened to the road bridge and the railway bridge. These were so designed that

28th Sept.

29th Sept.

when they were placed in a vertical position the time mechanism came into action and, after allowing the swimmers time to get clear, they exploded.

The frogmen had no difficulty in swimming under the wire boom which had been placed across the river, but the current gave them some trouble when they reached the bridges and they found they could not fasten the charges in a vertical position. The charge fastened to the road bridge failed, although part of it exploded and caused some damage. The attack on the railway bridge, already in dubious condition, was more successful. A complete span collapsed in the middle and subsided into the river beyond repair.

The swimmers, with every reason to be satisfied with the success of their venture, now moved down with the current, intending to land in the German positions around Ochten. They landed too early, however, and walked straight into the arms of 10 Troop of 43 Reconnaissance Regiment. Our men opened fire on them with Brens, one of the enemy surrendered at once, whilst the others took to the water and swam towards the far bank of the river, only to be rounded up by Dutch Resistance troops. Five more were captured by B Squadron further along the dyke bank. They were certainly brave men and were, perhaps, a little unfortunate in misjudging the distance to Ochten and their own troops.

No record survives of General Thomas's comments when, on arriving at the Waal in the early morning, he saw the evidence of this remarkable exploit and had to be transported to the far bank in a Dutch tug. Needless to relate, the next night found searchlights illuminating the river. A Dukw with headlight blazing patrolled the waters between the two bridges. Anti-tank gunners dug in on the bank and waited hopefully for anything that might come down the river. The enemy now displayed a sense of humour usually regarded as foreign to his nature, and entertained himself by floating haystacks and large logs down the stream. In the dark these were taken for more frogmen or even one-man submarines. Anti-tank shells and bullets ricochetting off the water made life for everyone in the vicinity extremely uncomfortable for many nights to come. Drivers of lorries breathed many a sigh of relief after finally crossing the surviving bridge.

1st
Oct.   The expected enemy counterstroke intended to recapture Nijmegen and to drive us out of the island finally came in on the morning of 1st October. Carried out by fresh troops, including considerable armour, and supported by artillery fire of an intensity not experienced since the days of Normandy, the attack descended on the whole Corps front from Wyler east of Nijmegen to the Neder Rijn. Some ground was lost south of the Waal. For two days 5 Guards Brigade and 69 Infantry Brigade fought a bitterly contested and costly battle in the orchards and fields south of Elst, but held

their ground. Within 43 Division, the brunt of this savage defensive battle fell upon 129 Brigade between Elst and the Neder Rijn. Elst was held by 4 Somerset Light Infantry, who beat off all attacks in a forty-eight-hour battle. The fact that they took over eighty prisoners gives some idea of the fierceness of the fighting and the tenacity of the battalion. No less than a hundred and fifty casualties were sustained, but not an inch of ground was given.

On their left along the railway embankment, 5 Wiltshire fought one of the bitterest battalion defensive battles of the campaign. The scene of the fiercest fighting was a level crossing roughly midway between Elst and the river. Here a branch road led off to the main route to Arnhem, from which direction armoured attack seemed most probable. Astride this crossing, therefore, Lieut.-Colonel Roberts had placed D Company under command of Major Wheatley. About 300 yards in rear B Company under Major E. R. Norris occupied a group of farm buildings. A and C Companies guarded the left flank. Captain David Hadow, the F.O.O. of 94 Field Regiment, occupied a building beside the railway line.

At 10 a.m. a tremendous concentration of shell-fire suddenly crashed down on B and D Companies. It was estimated that over a hundred 88-mm. guns were pouring their shells with deadly accuracy into the tiny area of the two farms. Enemy forming up withered away under the fire of the battalion's mortars. Two hours later, he again attacked in great strength. Captain Hadow's voice came over the air—"There are more Germans than I have ever seen in my life about fifty yards away."

Surrounded on three sides in his O.P. on the railway, he directed the fire of the guns on to the enemy, who finally broke in disorder, leaving many dead. Tanks approaching the position were engaged and knocked out by the gunners and infantry. A strange quietness fell as the night closed in.

It was now clear to Major-General Thomas that throughout the day the enemy, in accordance with his usual practice, had been probing for a soft spot against which to launch a major assault. In the evening he learnt from Corps Headquarters that 3 Panzer Division and possibly other armoured forces had been ferried across the river. This confirmed his impression that the enemy's decisive stroke was imminent on the morrow. He therefore asked for all the medium bombers available to be directed next morning on to the enemy's obvious assembly areas facing the Division's right flank. The R.A.F. responded magnificently. Two sorties in very great strength were delivered early in the day and undoubtedly smashed all hopes the Germans ever had of putting in a full-scale attack against our bridgehead on the island. Whether they were caught forming up is not known, but the bombing was very heavy indeed.

At 3.28 a.m. the enemy returned to the attack on 5 Wiltshire's front in still greater strength.   Despite the intense fire of the artillery, they advanced as if drugged, flashing hand torches to see the way.   D Company's two forward platoons had to fall back, but the reserve platoon and the company headquarters held on, fighting a hand-to-hand battle with grenades inside the wrecked buildings. All the officers having fallen, C.S.M. Jones took command and held on.   The enemy still surged forward in the darkness, only to be held up by B Company, who fought with such determination that they eventually fell back, hotly pursued by a section of the carrier platoon. When daylight came Lieut.-Colonel Roberts having reorganized his battalion, was able to report that the enemy had had enough and that his position was re-established.   The heavy shelling, however, continued.

The survivors of B and D Companies were now combined under command of Captain Rudd.   At 10 p.m. heavy shelling again descended on the ruins of the farm and at midnight the enemy attacked once more, and this time succeeded in capturing the level crossing.
Captain Rudd, however, was still unbeaten.   At 1.35 p.m., supported by tanks from the right flank, he and his men followed up the heavy barrage directed by Captain Hadow in the forefront of the battle and finally regained the level crossing.   Seventy-five of the enemy surrendered.   For the rest of the day Captain Rudd and his men, battered by unceasing artillery and mortar fire, held grimly on.   A bold counter-attack by Major Robbins and C Company of 4 Wiltshire resulted in the surrender of an officer and thirty-two of the enemy.   Phosphorus smoke fired by the mortars of this battalion further shattered his morale. In this defensive battle it is impossible to say which was the more admirable, the dogged fighting spirit of the infantry or the courage and skill of the gunners superbly directed by Captain Hadow. 94 Field Regiment sustained a great loss in this battle when their commanding officer, Lieut.-Colonel T. I. Bishell, was hit by a shell fragment at brigade headquarters and mortally wounded.

Further on the left, 5 Dorset had beaten off an attack by men of 116 Panzer Division on 1st October.   For the next few days fighting of a lively character continued in the neighbourhood of the railway embankment.

During this battle a party of the enemy of the S.S. Hermann Goering Division succeeded in infiltrating into the factory buildings on the front of 7 Royal Hampshire.   Here kilns gave them complete protection from artillery bombardment.   The ground around these buildings was completely flat and under close observation from the far side of the river.   The operations therefore undertaken by the battalion to dislodge them proved long and costly.   Attack by Typhoons merely resulted in severe casualties to our own troops. The battalion attacked again on 3rd and 4th October.   Both British

and German fought with equal obstinacy and bitterness.   Captain
Anaka, the Canadian second in command of D Company, attacked
a machine-gun single handed and was mortally wounded.   Private
Barlow, a sniper, went in with a Bren gun and killed at least four
of the enemy before he too fell to a grenade.

By the evening of 4th October it had become evident that the 4th–6th
enemy's offensive had spent its force.   Progress by 8 and 12 Corps ^{Oct.}
now released 101 U.S. Airborne Division from its commitments on
the axis between Eindhoven and Grave.   This hard-fighting division,
later to distinguish itself so signally in the Ardennes, accordingly
came forward to relieve 43 Division.   On the 5th and 6th October,
the Division's share of the island, or at least what remained of it,
passed into United States hands and brigades withdrew south of the
Waal.   The high quality of these United States troops and their
obviously outstanding officers ensured an easy handover, although
5 Dorset had considerable difficulty in extricating themselves from
their exposed positions around Driel.   In view of the critical
situation here, the battalion left its anti-tank guns and mortars in
support of the Americans, who found themselves immediately faced
with fresh reinforcements of the enemy.   A bitter battle supported
by the Divisional artillery and the supporting arms of the 5 Dorsets
raged throughout the 6th.

Colonel Sink, a Texan, the commander of 506 R.C.T., on taking 5th
over the west flank of the position deployed his battalions mainly to ^{Oct.}
the west, holding the river line with a thin screen.   Supported by
tanks of the Scots Greys the Americans advanced on Orpeusden and
killed over 200 Germans at small cost to themselves.   These operations during the late afternoon revealed a strong enemy build-up to
the west; 5 D.C.L.I., who had been in Divisional reserve, were therefore placed at Colonel Sink's disposal in the evening.   The battalion
moved to Andelst railway-station ready to support the Americans
should the need arise on the 6th.

Early in the morning the anticipated enemy thrust developed 6th
around Orpeusden, where close-quarter fighting eventually resulted ^{Oct.}
in the Americans being pushed back to the eastern outskirts of the
village.   Here every movement stood revealed to the enemy on the
north bank of the Neder Rijn.   Colonel Sink therefore decided to
commit the D.C.L.I. to an assault on the town in conjunction with
1 Battalion, 506 Parachute Regiment, on their right.

The situation became more critical every minute as the morning
wore on.   The battalion led by D Company advanced, making use
of the cover of an evil-smelling ditch along the line of the road leading
into Orpeusden from the south-east.   Captain Spencer, the company
commander, in spite of the heavy fire made his way through to an
American major who, with about 150 men, was holding on with grim
determination.   Together they agreed on a plan of attack.   No

F.O.O. was available.   D Company advanced and had soon disposed of six enemy machine-gun crews holding a ditch.   On attempting a further advance they struck further bitter resistance.   The Americans met similar fierce opposition.   All counter-attacks, however, withered away in the face of British and American fire.   The courage of an American soldier in the inferno which had now developed deserves to be recorded.   He had been badly wounded in the foot, but was indignant when the D.C.L.I. proposed to improvise a stretcher to get him back.   He insisted that he was still capable of crawling and made it clear with transatlantic vigour that in his opinion the bearers would be better employed in holding the position against the Krauts.   The latter, incidentally, were most correct in obeying the rules of war and forbore from firing on our stretcher-bearers.

Major Hingston of B Company, which had followed D Company, eventually succeeded in joining Captain Spencer and the American major at a mill which was choked with British and U.S. wounded. Together they agreed, despite the heavy losses, to make another attempt to capture the burning village.   Dead Americans lay everywhere and the smell of burnt flesh fouled the air.   Major Hingston then began to collect his company for the attack.   That it was ever assembled was largely due to the courage of Private Basset (afterwards C.S.M.), the company runner.   This last attack went in at 4 p.m.   The village was entered and violent fighting ensued. Finally, the Americans having run out of ammunition, it was decided to withdraw to the start line.   Many men owe their lives to the courage of Lieutenant Birchenall, the battalion's pioneer officer, who with all the jeeps available brought back the wounded from the shambles at the mill.

At night Colonel Sink, who with Lieut.-Colonel Taylor had directed the battle from the forefront, brought in a fresh battalion and the D.C.L.I. withdrew.   Seated at the dining-room table of a house overlooking the battle, with heavy shells bursting all around, his imperturbable demeanour throughout had impressed all who saw him.

On this day soldiers of both nations vied with each other in their display of outstanding courage.   The Germans also fought bravely and well.   Colonel Sink later in an official report to Major-General Maxwell Taylor said of the D.C.L.I., "These troops attacked on schedule with vigour and determination in the face of withering enemy fire.   The courage and ability shown by these troops was an inspiration to the 1 Battalion Parachute Infantry.   The gallantry of the British officers and men was outstanding and instilled in the men of 506 Parachute Infantry the highest regard for the fighting ability of the British infantry."

The story of this "soldiers' battle" in which British and American

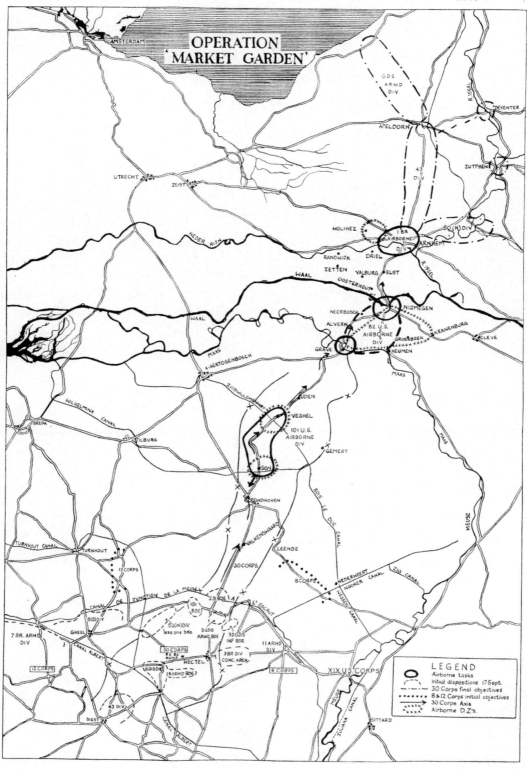

OPERATION
'MARKET GARDEN'

LEGEND
Airborne tasks
Initial dispositions 17 Sept.
30 Corps final objectives
8 & 12 Corps initial objectives
30 Corps Axis
Airborne D.Z's.

19. Men of the Wiltshire Regiment in Nijmegen, 24th September, 1944

20. Queueing up for books at the mobile library in Mook, 7th November, 1944

21. All that was left of Bauchem, 19th November, 1944

infantry fought side by side provides a fitting climax to the Division's operations on the island. Events at Arnhem, publicized in the press and on the screen, have undoubtedly tended to deflect attention from the solid achievement of 30 Corps. To the public, as with the ancient Greeks, the manner in which soldiers bear themselves in adversity has a greater appeal than mere military success. The military history of the Greeks is, however, not an infallible guide in the conduct of armies. The operations at Arnhem failed because 1 Airborne Division encountered greater forces than had been expected. In particular, the presence of 2 S.S. Panzer Division had an enormous effect on the battle. The enemy fought with great skill and determination. In fact, his quick recovery compels admiration. The weather too was against us and prevented the R.A.F. from ensuring the arrival of the airborne reinforcements which might have turned the scale.

30 Corps had, in fact, gained a brilliant and ultimately decisive victory. It had advanced sixty miles into enemy territory, crossed the rivers Maas and Waal in strength, and held its gains against repeated counter-attacks. General Dempsey could now, in conjunction with the First Canadian Army, clear his western flank and open up the badly needed port of Antwerp. In addition, he was in a position to drive the enemy from his east flank and thus rest his long front along the secure water obstacle provided by the Maas.

Which of the five British and United States divisions that fought under Lieut.-General Horrocks—Guards Armoured, 43rd, 50th, 82nd, and 101 U.S. Airborne, achieved most is of little moment. Each could be satisfied that it had fought to the limit of its capacity and hold its head high in this goodly company.

11

CHAPTER VIII

EAST OF NIJMEGEN

7th October to 10th November

(See Sketch Map 11)

THE situation which confronted Field-Marshal Montgomery at the end of the Arnhem battle must now be briefly considered. His plan to cross the Rhine and strike at the Ruhr obviously could not go forward until he had opened up the great port of Antwerp and shortened his communications, which still stretched all the way back to Normandy. The enemy, also, was still established in strength west of the Maas, particularly around Venlo, in country which in every way favoured protracted defence. In addition, no advance across the Rhine could be considered until the area between this river and the Maas had been cleared. He therefore planned to attack in a south-easterly direction from Nijmegen about 10th October, using 30 Corps. In this operation it was intended that 43 Division should play a major part.

By the beginning of October, however, the Germans had recovered from the shock of the Arnhem attack and succeeded in assembling strong forces to cover the Scheldt estuary. In addition, resistance to the advance of 8 and 12 Corps on the flanks of the axis to Nijmegen was proving obstinate. These considerations, apart from the necessity of retaining our grip on the island, left the Field-Marshal with inadequate forces for the time being to launch a major attack between the Maas and the Rhine. Had he done so at this time, he would have run a grave risk of being hemmed in between these two rivers. He therefore decided to postpone this operation. 12 Corps accordingly took over responsibility for the island and Second Army west flank during 7th/8th October; 12 and 8 Corps were also given the task of clearing the flanks up to the line of the Maas. These operations, in fact, in face of the revival of the enemy's morale and the flat, water-logged country, were to prove protracted, costly and difficult, and to occupy the greater part of October.

30 Corps thus found itself temporarily allotted the static role of defending the flank between the Waal and the Maas east of Nijmegen. Lieut.-General Horrocks, however, was ordered to plan the eventual resumption of the offensive on this front. This operation was given the title of "Veritable" and eventually put into execution in February, although not in its original form. Planning, down to brigadiers, went on in 43 Division throughout October and a model was even

7th/8th Oct.

constructed and kept under guard in a barn near Molenhoek. So far as the Division was concerned, it visualized an initial attack by 130 and 129 Brigades and exploitation on the evening of the first day by 214 Brigade in two columns with armour, Kangaroos, Flails and other assault engineer equipment to a depth of 10,000 yards during the hours of darkness through the heart of the Siegfried Line. This, had it ever been carried out, would undoubtedly have proved an operation not lacking in dramatic incident.

Immediately south-east of Nijmegen stretches a deep belt of sandy wooded hills from the crest of which the German frontier, the Reichswald Forest and the bright-green, onion-shaped church-tower of Kranenburg can be clearly seen. Along the northern edge, the main road into Germany divides the area into two parts. To the north lies the featureless reclaimed marshland of the valley of the Waal. South of this road, the country is more undulating and wooded. Another main road, following the banks of the Maas, runs roughly south from Nijmegen. The main railway-line from Holland to the Ruhr emerges from the woods at the once prosperous holiday village of Groesbeek to cross the frontier just east of Kranenburg. Between this frontier station and the Maas, within the dense forest of the Reichswald, lay the formidable defences of the northern extension of the Siegfried Line.

It was in this area between Groesbeek and the Reichswald that the 82 Airborne Division had successfully landed at the start of the Arnhem operations. Their brightly coloured parachutes—which, incidentally, provided excellent scarves—and the wrecks of their gliders still littered the well cultivated fields. In view of the threat to the Siegfried defences, fighting had been fierce, especially on the night of 30th September.

The Americans, however, despite their light equipment, had proved themselves more than a match for the strong German forces launched against them. A report received from them laconically sums up the fighting. It read, "In a three-battalion attack only one company of one battalion crossed the start line. Enemy called for truce to bury dead—refused. 82 U.S. Airborne Division offered to lend bulldozer for the job."

On taking over the front, Lieut.-General Horrocks decided to hold 8th it with this American division between Groesbeek and the Waal and Oct. 43 Division on their right down to the Maas south of Mook. 129 Brigade accordingly relieved 9 Infantry Brigade in reserve around Molenhoek on the banks of the Maas during the 8th. Their task included responsibility for the defence of the pontoon bridge at Mook, which had been constructed in anticipation of future operations in an easterly direction. The Divisional engineers at the same time took charge of the maintenance of this bridge. In view of recent experience at Nijmegen detailed arrangements were also made for its protection by A.A. guns and searchlights. On the following day 214 Brigade moved into the wooded area south-east of Mook, taking over from 185 Brigade of 3 Division. Finally, on the 10th, 130 Brigade relieved 505 R.C.T. of 82 U.S. Airborne Division in the defences east of Groesbeek. The Divisional artillery deployed in the wooded sandhills immediately east of the Maas. Divisional head-quarters was established amongst the orchards near Hattert. Here it was to remain in the open for the next month in circumstances of no great comfort. In fact, the spartan conditions in which the headquarters lived, as the weather deteriorated, impressed visitors from the forward areas of the Division.

For the next month, as the days shortened and the nights grew colder, brigades were interchanged approximately every seven days so that each gained equal experience of the front. The front edge of the Divisional position lay in full view of the dominating heights of the Reichswald. Movement therefore in the forward areas by day brought down swift enemy retaliation and all reliefs had to be carried out by night. The supply of hot food to troops in isolated posts proved a difficult problem. South-east of Mook the defences lay for the most part in woods. Here contact with the enemy was very close and mortar bombs bursting in the trees added to the tension. East of Groesbeek the country was more open, slits being sited amongst the villas and gardens. Uncharted American minefields added to the hazards of the area. Knapheide, De Horst and Nijerf were eerie villages, especially at night, as the enemy, harassed by our fire, constantly changed his dispositions.

Further back, the wooded sandhills gave ample cover from view, although the vast enemy ammunition dump south-west of Groesbeek was not a site which appealed to the unduly imaginative. Here in the midst of thousands of rounds of all types of shells and bombs, laid out in neat rows under the trees, stood a fully loaded ammunition train. Brigadier Essame's plans to start up this train and despatch it with time fuses on board in the direction of Kranenburg were well advanced when the enemy forestalled him. About noon, four shells burst high over the train, which immediately exploded with what must have been one of the biggest bangs of the war. Whole trucks ceased to exist and steel girders 7 feet long landed a mile away. The fact that it destroyed the only shelter in the neighbourhood was most annoying, especially as bad weather had finally set in. Further back, however, the sandhills gave excellent cover to the gunners, whose well protected gun positions undoubtedly reduced the casualty rate. Some of their dugouts were reminiscent of the Great War, many having stoves installed. When the batteries went forward, the stoves went with them. The ridge also provided excellent O.Ps. from which F.O.Os. had the added pleasure of being able for the first time to shoot into Germany.

Although temporarily allotted a static role, the Division missed no opportunity to make the enemy's life as uncomfortable as possible. As the supply position improved, consistent and heavy harassing fire programmes, carried out not only by the Gunners and 8 Middlesex but also by the 3-inch and 2-inch mortars of battalions ensured no opportunity was missed of reducing his numbers and morale. The German recovery had been remarkable. Every available man, no matter how young or how old or how unfit according to Allied standards, was pressed into service. Prisoners were even taken by the Division from a "Stomach" battalion, the members of which all suffered from gastric complaints and therefore had to be fed on a special scale of rations. There was also an "Eye" battalion, and an "Ear" battalion composed of deaf men. At the time these efforts on the part of the Germans were treated with derision. They do, however, show a will to resist which now compels at least respect. In similar circumstances in future other nations might be forced to adopt like expedients. There is, indeed, something to be said for employing low-category men on dangerous duties in war to ensure that an unduly high proportion of them is not left to carry on the race in peace. Perhaps the advent of atomic weapons may make expedients on these lines desirable and economical in fighting manpower. The Division's constant and unrelenting fire, in any case, had a marked effect on the enemy's morale. Prisoners complained that all their meals arrived cold and that the five shells delivered by the Divisional artillery for every German shell fired into our lines made life unbearable. South of Cuijk and St. Agatha the open flank protected by the Maas gave ample scope for medium machine-guns and 4·2-inch mortars of 8 Middlesex to harass the rear of the German positions around Middelaar. From here also snipers from all battalions found many a welcome target and kept the enemy below ground and immobile during daylight.

The planning in progress for the attack on the Reichswald defences brought with it a demand for detailed information. Probably the first British patrol to enter Germany was that of Lieutenant P. I. Thorpe of 5 Dorset, who was ordered to investigate a building believed to be a headquarters. When within 150 yards of the objective, some horses bolted and very nearly betrayed the patrol. It returned successfully, having obtained the information required. Sergeant Deane and Private Lyons of 5 D.C.L.I. penetrated 3,000 yards into the Reichswald and spent the whole of the next day studying the enemy's defences. Coming out during the course of the next night, they suddenly found the track through the forest was blocked by a German sentry. They picked up two empty boxes and, pretending to be a German ration-party, coolly walked past him and regained our lines. Corporal G. Butcher and Lance-Corporal Spittle of 4 Wiltshire also penetrated deep into the enemy lines.

Lieutenant Alliban and Corporal McQuillan of 4 Somerset Light Infantry spent eighteen hours behind the enemy lines in vile weather. Lieutenant Priani of this battalion led a particularly daring patrol which crossed the Maas from St. Agatha and returned with much valuable information. Lieutenants B. A. Tarrant, M. Stapylton Cotton and Sergeant Mackrell of 5 Wiltshire and Sergeant White and Private Palumbo of 5 D.C.L.I. all distinguished themselves as leaders of fighting patrols. These were but a few of the many patrols carried out by all infantry units. Patrolling, both for information and with purely offensive intent, continued both by day and night. Many actions must inevitably go unrecorded. Lance-Corporal Vigg of 4 Dorset sallied out alone and killed two Germans. To sum up, the Division thoroughly dominated the forward area and did its utmost to make life unbearable for the enemy. Houses found to be occupied by Germans were promptly set alight by mortar smoke bombs. At no time was there any doubt as to our mastery of no-man's-land. Harried by our patrols and be-devilled by our snipers, the enemy wisely kept well to ground.

In the liberated countries the order that no food should be taken from the inhabitants had been enforced—at least when too flagrantly violated. In any case, the speed of operations had offered little leisure for foraging. The troops now found themselves at last on the German border with time on their hands. Current orders gave no guidance with regard to the treatment of German livestock. The fighting of the past three weeks had caused such a disturbance amongst the animals on the farms that undoubtedly many must have got on the wrong side of the frontier. No known means enabled a German pig to be distinguished from a Dutch pig. Considerations of humanity obviously dictated that these animals should not be allowed to continue to run the risk of death or mutilation by shell-fire. Besides, rations, though good, were inclined to be monotonous. Many a joint of roast pork therefore gladdened the stomachs of the garrisons of the forward posts. Restriction of daylight movement by senior officers had its compensations. The amount of knowledge of the art of butchering now disclosed was surprising. Roast chicken and pheasant were also not unknown. The United States troops on the northern flank apparently had similar tastes, one soldier even going so far as to shoot four pigs with a revolver on our front in full view of the enemy. On being reminded that his action was somewhat irregular, he blandly offered one pig as a peace offering. Allied solidarity remained unshaken.

Leaflet shells fired by the Germans into our lines were greeted with derision. The propaganda, which sometimes included indecent pictures of alleged activities of U.S. troops in England, was clumsily worded. "Why get maimed or killed and make your family suffer when you could easily desert and stay safe as a prisoner of war?"—and "Why should English be killing Germans when both should be fighting Bolshevism?" were typical questions.

Our own efforts at psychological warfare, at least locally, were equally uninspired. An expert from the rear arrived with a loud-hailer in front of Groesbeek and under cover of a smoke-screen invited the Germans to desert. When the shower of shells which he evoked had subsided and the smoke had cleared, it was found that two of our men were missing, the enemy having taken the opportunity provided to stage a raid. The expert, happily still intact, departed promptly whence he came and never appeared again.

The Divisional staff one day received from 4 Wiltshire the unusual demand for a bitch on heat, which it was thought might lure a large German Alsatian war dog on their front from his allegiance. When the lady duly arrived, although her sex appeal was not in question, she proved to be a thin, shivering mongrel terrier with few attractions even as a pet. The Alsatian, like St. Anthony, refused to respond, but may have found more glamorous interests elsewhere, for he was not seen again.

To impress the reinforcements with the vast volume of fire at their command, 214 Brigade revived an expedient frequently practised in 1914–18—the "Mad Minute." At 7.14 p.m. on 21st October all was quiet. At 7.15 p.m. hell was let loose. Every rifle, Sten, Bren, mortar and pistol was fired as hard as it would go. As someone unkindly said, "Even the cooks fired their rifles." The artillery of all calibres fired rapid; Besas, machine-guns and tanks raked the back areas. On to trenches, gun areas and supply lines it went—into Germans and Germany. At 7.16 all suddenly stopped. The silence which followed was most dramatic until retaliation came. The idea might be of value in future, provided alternative positions are used and all traffic forward is suspended. It should at least impress on troops that provided every weapon is brought to bear, a well organized position should be impenetrable. It may also induce the enemy to reveal his defensive fire areas.

Whilst the Division faced the monotony inseparable from static defence, the Reconnaissance Regiment fought a different type of war. West of Nijmegen stretches a peninsula eighteen miles long and roughly five miles broad, lying between the Waal and the Maas. This area, which gained the name of the "Western Approaches," was entrusted to 8 Armoured Brigade with the Reconnaissance Regiment under their command. This armoured force accordingly deployed the regiment to give warning and held the tanks back for use in case of need. By day, the cars manned O.Ps. along the banks of the Waal with carrier and assault troops resting within call. By night, the carrier and assault troops took over two major strong-points at Wamel and Breumel and a chain of outposts from Leeuwen to Brevmel, while the cars went back into mobile reserve. 200 Dutch Resistance troops assisted with the defence along the river at night. The regiment's 6-pdrs. found many satisfactory targets beyond the river and a close friendship developed with Major Gosling's battery of the Essex Yeomanry, whose accurate and incessant shooting caused havoc beyond the Waal. Throughout the period contact was maintained with men of the Airborne Division in hiding around Tiel and their escape assisted. Lieut.-Colonel F. Lane Fox's departure early in the month was a sad loss to the Regiment. Throughout the worst of the Normandy battle his constant presence with the forward troops, his traditional high standards of honour and his indifference to personal danger had endeared him to all ranks.

The static role allotted to the Division, coming as it did at the end of a triumphal advance, inevitably brought with it an element of anti-climax. The weather got worse and worse. A winter campaign obviously had to be faced. Troops whose homes were around London received disquieting news of the damage done by V2's. The enemy obviously intended to continue the war. Both Lieut.-General Horrocks and Major-General Thomas had to face the fact that the risk now existed of a decline in morale. The Corps Commander's reaction was characteristic and effective. Day after day, sometimes even four times in twenty-four hours, he lectured to audiences of officers and N.C.Os. in the Village Hall at Hattert. Surely no Corps Commander ever delivered so many addresses with such enthusiasm and light-hearted humour. He never lost his freshness and never failed in his appeal. He told the full story of the Arnhem drive, of its failures and achievements. He made it clear that although the enemy had lost the war, he had still to be finished off, and that this could not be done until Antwerp was opened up. His audiences returned to their units re-inspired to fresh effort and confident of victory under his command. When the lessons of the war are finally assessed, Sir Brian Horrocks will take his place beside Rommel and Ney as a "soldiers' general." All had the same gift of direct appeal to the affection of the individual fighting man, and for them soldiers willingly hazarded their lives with light hearts and confidence in victory.

With the same end in view Major-General Thomas initiated a programme of vigorous training. He directed that every available daylight hour away from fighting should be devoted to military work. Reserve battalions trained in the line. The Reserve Brigade was allowed one clear day to bath and make up its deficiencies. The whole of the hours of daylight of the remainder of its time in reserve were devoted to training, and the sandhills resounded with the noise of bursting mortar bombs and the rattle of Brens. Work went on after dark. Newcomers learnt how to pick up mines and elementary first aid. "Back to battle drill" was the slogan. Attention was given to close-order drill, saluting and physical fitness. "We must get back to the alert, proud stride of the British soldier who realizes and shows he is a conqueror—knows it and knows he has proved it," he said in his training directive. "The motto of 43 Division has always been that nothing but the best will do. It still remains true, and it is only by sticking to it that we shall be able to maintain the impetus and standard of our battles—at least one of which has already been widely referred to as a classic victory."

To spread this gospel he reconstituted the Battle School. This opened in mid October in a large and comfortable house at Haute Heiuvel in the residential suburbs of Nijmegen. The Commandant, Major A. A. Grubb of 1 Worcestershire Regiment, was a battle-hardened company commander with a genius for training, modest and of great personal charm. His instructors were Major T. R. M. Ottowell, 4 Wiltshire, and Major K. Mead of 5 Dorset. These two also had fighting records which commanded universal respect, and ability and enthusiasm comparable to that of their Commandant. Three-and-a-half-day courses for platoon commanders and N.C.Os. at once started. Much of the Division's subsequent outstanding record in the field of minor tactics can be attributed to the teaching of the Commandant and his staff. The school remained in being until the end of the campaign, serving not only as a centre at which experience was digested and passed on, but also as a clinic at which new techniques were investigated and developed.

Probably no division in the B.L.A. from the point of view of the front-line soldier was ever better supplied than 43 Division. The unceasing drive which its commander imparted to its operations also made itself continuously felt towards the rear. In Lieut.-Colonel McCance and his two able assistants, Majors Barker and Donald Wilson, it possessed universal providers with drive and imagination, ever looking forward and ready to improvise, planning the needs of the soldier in the front line before all other considerations. Snipers suits appeared as if by magic in the forward posts. It was not long before every man had a second suit of battle-dress, into which he could change when coming back from the line. Somehow or other Lieut.-Colonel T. Leland, the C.R.A.S.C., found the means to carry this additional load.

The fighting on the "Island" had placed a heavy strain on the resources of R.E.M.E. Lieut.-Colonel J. M. Neilson had established his report centre at the roundabout by the road bridge in Nijmegen, one of the most dangerous places on the whole front. Here it had remained under almost incessant shell-fire. The combined advanced workshops established on the island itself had shared the dangers of the forward troops, and the recovery crews, often in circumstances of great danger, had succeeded in retrieving many vehicles. Lieutenant Brownlee, in particular, had never allowed heavy enemy fire to deflect him from his duty. On the night of the withdrawal from Arnhem he had remained to the last on the banks of the Neder Rijn recovering damaged Dukws. The halt east of Nijmegen now gave Lieut.-Colonel Neilson the opportunity to inspect and overhaul the Division's battle-scarred vehicles. This work went on continuously in the reserve positions throughout the month. Had it not been for the devotion to duty of the craftsmen at that time, the Division's vehicles could never have stood the strain of the winter campaign. Ultimately, a modern division depends for its success on the skill and unrelenting work of its craftsmen. Every member of R.E.M.E. in the Division can therefore claim that he played his part to the full in the Division's victories.

The share of the mobile bath and laundry unit in the maintenance of the Division's morale was important. Incidentally this unit, under the command of Captain E. H. Temme, the Channel swimmer, had fought its way through and lost some of its men and vehicles when the axis to Nijmegen was cut. To supplement their resources trucks were run into Nijmegen every day for baths and showers. Here woman attendants busied themselves in the bathrooms whilst the troops were at their ablutions, thus providing a touch of variety beyond the scope of the R.A.O.C.

The Divisional War Diary gives a poor indication of the unceasing activities of the administrative staff at this time. It mainly consists of the recording of issues of rum and the distribution of beer. Arrangements were made with a Belgian brewer for an ample supply of beer. Incidentally the Reconnaissance Regiment, according to the records, appears to have drunk twice as much as any other unit. It is too late now, however, to investigate this important question further. There survives also some sour correspondence concerning over-issues of rations on the "Island." The harder units fought the more they seemed to eat. This, of course, is what might be expected. The Division's thirst for tea, in particular, appears to have been remarkable. Further operations extinguished the correspondence and the "Q" staff, as before, continued to make certain that what the troops needed they got in full measure.

There now appeared in the reserve areas a bus which had been found abandoned at the foot of the Nijmegen railway bridge. After conversion by one of the Divisional workshops, this became the Wyvern Mobile Library, which was to go forward right up to the Elbe. Stocked with readable books provided by families and welfare organizations at home, it received a hearty welcome wherever it went and continued to be a familiar sight in the forward areas.

In order to give officers and men who had been fighting since D-Day a brief respite from the line, "Q" opened the Wyvern Country Club at the hotel in the market-square at Veghel, mid-way on the axis from Eindhoven to Nijmegen. The site was not altogether happily chosen, as Veghel had only very recently been the scene of severe fighting and the traffic of Second Army thundered through the streets by day and night. However, the Club gave 150 guests at a time a welcome break from routine and the Divisional catering adviser in his role of host succeeded in producing many amenities under most adverse conditions. All his efforts, however, to remove the all-pervading smell of dung and stale cigars proved unavailing.

The Officers' Club in Nijmegen was a phenomenal success until excessive enemy shelling caused it to be closed down.

Leave to Brussels for both officers and troops now started. Here the arrangements made by 21 Army Group were on a lavish and imaginative scale. No less than seventeen good hotels had been requisitioned and operated under the supervision of N.A.A.F.I. with conspicuous success. The shops were stocked with a fascinating display of goods and the entertainments available were of astonishing variety. The display of toys at "Bon Marché" attracted thousands of soldiers. The Germans had travelled free on the trams and the generous Belgians saw no reason why their liberators should not do the same. It was good to be a British soldier in Brussels in the autumn and the winter. You felt, and you were treated like, a conqueror. Many of the luxuries which were merely memories of the past in England could be obtained, although at a price. For forty-eight hours leave parties lived in another world; then they took the now familiar road back—Louvain, Bourg Leopold, Eindhoven, Veghel and the sinister St. Oedenrode, finishing the journey in the artificial daylight of the searchlights with star shells and bursts of red and gold marking the army front.

Not by any means the least attractive characteristic of the men of the Division was their capacity for making friends wherever they went. Language presented no problem. The Divisional mail from now onwards included an ever-increasing volume of letters addressed to France, Belgium and Holland. In fact, the route taken by the Division from Normandy onwards could be deduced from the outgoing mail. It became necessary to restrict correspondence to letters and plain postcards. Photographs of Nijmegen Bridge marked with a cross where a shell had fallen near the writer raised obvious security objections. Orders were therefore given that communications must be of a purely personal and family nature. The large number of incoming letters with Belgian, French and, later, Dutch postmarks were presumably of a similar character.

The British soldier has an insatiable curiosity with regard to the inner domestic life of other nations. No matter how strict the discipline and how severe the penalties, he delights in rummaging in the cupboards and drawers of an abandoned house. He will tell you that the French housewife never throws away even the smallest piece

of thread ; that she treasures her grandmother's corsets ; and that no
sock is ever so worn out as to justify throwing away.   The Dutch,
on the contrary, are not so mean.   Their weakness lies in hoarding
family photographs.   They seem to be addicted in peace to semi-
educational tours on bicycles and to being photographed beside
places of historic interest.   In fact, their albums gave an intimate
picture of their lives and ideals far more revealing than many novels.
A love of children is evident in every Dutch house.   The children
themselves in the reserve area seemed happy to stand and watch the
troops all day.

Amongst the sandhills near Mook stood a group of chalets until
recently inhabited by a colony of artists.   Art seems to play a greater
part in the life of the Dutch than amongst ourselves.   Original
works are common articles of commerce in the smallest towns.   In
consequence, the departed artists seemed to have had a very pleasant
life.   Their houses became a place of pilgrimage for soldiers in the
vicinity, especially as the artists seemed to have the same ideals as
their own as to the beauty of the female form—a good solid article
designed on functional lines to stand up to prolonged wear and tear.
There were plenty of pictures in the heavy draught and few in the
polo pony class.   One of the artists seemed to have been under the
impression that the war was no affair of his, for he had scribbled on
his easel in English: "We have suffered enough from your war.
Leave me at least these books which are the only joy remaining to me
in life."   He need not have worried.   The books were written for the
most part in German and devoted to the sufferings of medieval martyrs.

The parachutes which peppered the forward area were treasure
trove.   They consisted of real silk of a mottled green colour—good,
solid silk but for practical purposes suffering from too many seams.
However, practically every man provided himself with sufficient for
a scarf for his own use and the number of parcels sent home through
the field post office quadrupled.   They were usually marked
"Remnants" and the technique in most general use was to enclose
a letter to the effect that the sender had managed to pick up a few
things without coupons.   Reports from those with knowledge on
the subject indicated that most of the Dutch girls had underwear of
this expensive textile within a very short time.   Every girl with any
pretensions to good looks soon appeared wearing a virulent yellow
scarf made from the celanese triangles carried by the troops to
indicate their position to their own aircraft.

For the next four months the troops, when not in actual grips with
the enemy, were to live in closer contact with the Dutch than at any
time since the days of Marlborough.   Language, as ever, provided
no obstacle and it was no uncommon sight to see soldiers sitting
round the table with a Dutch family conducting with ease what was
apparently a conversation on the subject of film stars.   In this

respect they seemed to be more adaptable than their officers. Dutch impressions of the Division, were they available, would be most interesting. All that can be told is the soldiers' opinion of the Dutch. They were good people and they liked them. Above all things, they had a virtue which the soldiers held in the highest esteem. They were kind. When men were killed and buried by the roadside, Dutch women and children placed flowers on the graves. They even put a wreath on a notice-board marked "Foul Ground." When troops came out of the line, the Dutch women hurried to dry their greatcoats, to mend their clothes and do their washing. Most of the sweet ration went to the children. The Dutch woman's outlook seems to be almost entirely maternal. They certainly treated the troops of the Division as if they were their own sons.

The British habit of wearing boots in the house shocked the Dutch. The troops, on their part, were awed by the emphasis laid on spotless red tiles and houses in which cleanliness had been raised almost to a fetish. Only in Norfolk and Lincolnshire, thanks probably to the Dutch influence in the past, do these high standards prevail.

In contrast to the freedom of morals and manners of war-time England, the Dutch had retained strict ideas of female behaviour. A soldier who wished to take a girl for a walk was expected to take her younger brother as well. The resulting ill-assorted trios certainly ensured decorum, even if they lacked spontaneity. The Dutch themselves must be the last upholders of the ancient custom of "walking out" on Sunday afternoon. Dressed in their best black ceremonial suitings, their young men endeavoured to continue this routine. Very often a soldier would walk on one side of the girl and the Dutch swain on the other. It was all most correct. The Englishman is an undemonstrative starter in matters of this sort, but the Dutchman is even slower. No drama, therefore, shocked the sense of propriety of either nation. In spite of the disturbance of two wars and the impact of Hollywood, the British soldier still likes to be looked up to in preference to being treated as an equal.

The appalling lack of taste of the "best rooms" in many Dutch houses left the troops unmoved. To the artistically sensitive minority, some of these rooms were hideous beyond belief. It seemed incredible that any human being should be able to conceive anything quite so horrible as the antimacassars, the paintings and the furniture of some of the Dutch houses. Perhaps, however, in view of the large number of almost equally deplorable interiors in the small towns of the West Country itself, these comments are unkind.

Before the war the Dutch had thought it possible to be neutral against evil and that the practice of the homely virtues would bring its reward in this world. Disillusioned, they faced a winter of hunger and hardship with dignity and earned the gratitude of many a soldier for the warmth of their welcome and their practical help.

The Division's close contacts with the Dutch were fortunately not to be confined to this part of Holland.   On November 5th, just when a long stay east of Nijmegen appeared inevitable, orders for an extensive redeployment of the whole Army Group directed 30 Corps elsewhere.   Major-General Thomas departed on the 6th to meet the Corps Commander at headquarters of Ninth U.S. Army (code word "Conquer") in the south.   Next day his command post followed, and with it Major R. S. Williams-Thomas, the G.S.O.2 (Ops.). G.S.O.1's came and went.   Major Williams-Thomas stayed on to the end, to take the impact of a commander of inexhaustible energy, insatiable curiosity and highly critical brain, to answer the constant queries of three determined brigadiers, three high-power brigade majors and an extremely inquisitive Corps staff, to reduce decisions to the cold clarity of "typescript" and to clarify complex situations on the air.   Few men endured such strain for so long or with such good grace.

His little column of eight vehicles, including the great lumbering CVI and the G.O.C.'s caravan, took the road to Maastricht.

CHAPTER IX

THE GEILENKIRCHEN OFFENSIVE

18th to 23rd November

(See Sketch Map 12)

PREPARATION

IT must be admitted that the Germans had staged a remarkable recovery, comparable only to that of the French and British Armies at the Battle of the Marne in 1914. They now held a large armoured force in the shape of the Sixth Panzer Army in reserve, although it was not known exactly where it was. If this army could be brought to battle west of the Rhine, the possibility existed of ending the war before the end of the year. By early November the port of Antwerp was open and considerable U.S. forces had been brought forward. Determined to give the enemy no respite and to force a decision, General Eisenhower concentrated the First and Ninth U.S. Armies on a narrow front and directed them to attack in the general direction of Cologne. This decision involved a complete redeployment of 21 Army Group. The centre of gravity of Second Army was switched further south. 12 Corps was moved down to the right of 8 Corps and both these corps continued the operations to clear up the Venlo pocket. Relieved by 2 Canadian Corps east of Nijmegen, 30 Corps started its long move south on 10 November with a view to taking over the northern part of the Ninth U.S. Army sector north-east of Maastricht between Geilenkirchen and Maeseyck and participating in the offensive of the First and Ninth U.S. Armies.

North-east of Maastricht, the rivers Maas and Roer form a rough triangle the apex of which is Roermond. In the fighting in September the Americans had secured a bridgehead within this triangle and established themselves in the low-lying country on the German frontier. Flowing due north through Geilenkirchen to join the Roer at Heinsberg is the sluggish river Wurm. On the ridge to the east, the Americans faced the pillboxes of the Siegfried Line. In his thrust towards Cologne the Ninth U.S. Army Commander planned to cross the Roer at Linnich. The capture of the road centre at the little town of Geilenkirchen became therefore of vital importance. This task was accordingly given to 30 Corps as its share in the offensive.

At his planning conference on 7th November, Lieut.-General Horrocks revealed his intention of taking over the sector between the Wurm and the Maas with 43 Division on the right and Guards

Armoured Division on the left.   For the forthcoming battle 84 U.S. Infantry Division, at the moment holding the front north-west of Geilenkirchen, 113 U.S. Cavalry Group and four squadrons of 79 Armoured Division had been placed under his command.   Geilenkirchen lies in the valley of the Wurm.   To the north the plateau is 80 metres high ; to the east it rises to 120 metres.   The high ground north of the town would therefore be untenable until the plateau to the east had been secured.   General Horrocks accordingly proposed to encircle the town by first capturing the commanding ground to the east with 84 U.S. Division and then directing 43 Division on to the plateau to the north.   He then intended that 84 U.S. Division should attack from the south and seize the town.   The full weight of the Corps artillery and rocket-firing Typhoons of the R.A.F. were to support each phase of the attack.   Finally he explained that the battle could not be opened for at least another eight days and that ample time therefore existed for detailed planning and reconnaissance—a new experience for 43 Division.

10th
Nov.   Meanwhile the relief by 2 Canadian Division east of Nijmegen went smoothly and early on the 10th the long, cold drive south began. The column followed the now familiar road through Veghel and St. Oedenrode, with their grim memories, past the Philips factory at Eindhoven, across the sandy tracts at Valkenswaarde to Bourg Leopold into Belgium once more, then struck east into new country, finally to cross the Maas by the new pontoon bridge at Berg and into the mining district of Limburg where Holland juts into Germany. 129 Brigade and 13/18 Hussars were first to arrive and to experience the warm welcome of the Dutch mining population.   Divisional headquarters was already established, in buildings for the first time in the campaign, at Brunssum.   The brigade only stayed for one night in the comfortable houses, but long enough to make friendships.   Next day battalions made their way through the sparse woods which mark the German frontier to relieve 407 R.C.T. of 84 U.S. Division in their positions along the ridge which runs from Teveren to north of Gilrath and Birgden.   All three battalions, 4 Somerset Light Infantry on the right, 4 Wiltshire in the centre and 5 Wiltshire, took over the forward localities.   94 Field Regiment came into action in the straggling village of Niederbusch.   They were the first British gunners to put down their trails in Germany since Minden in 1759.]

The absence of marked differences in tactical outlook simplified the handover, which went forward with considerable cordiality and without a hitch.   One army marched out and the other marched in. It was almost as simple as that.   The smiling faces of the U.S. soldiers, who had only recently landed at Cherbourg, aroused considerable comment.   An almost uncanny quiet reigned over the sector.   The defences had been well chosen.   In particular the road

22. An A Squadron tank of 4/7 Royal Dragoon Guards loaded with men of 7th Somerset Light Infantry moving up to the concentration area for the attack on Neiderheide on morning of 18th November, 1944

23. 5 D.C.L.I. trudging into action near Neiderheide, Germany, 18th November, 1944

24. The C. in C. inspects the Dorsets in the Brunssum Area

25. Men of 7 Royal Hampshire Regiment advancing through minefields to the village of Putt, 21st January, 1945

from Gangelt to Gilrath, which straddled the position, was out of
enemy view and could be used by transport in daylight. There was
ample cover both in the houses and the woods for the concealment
of reserves. The village, however, seemed sinister and alien.
Although well-built they were meanly planned. Even the *Gast-
hauses* seemed funereal. The churches with their bulbous spires
lacked dignity. They were dark and forbidding within. Surprising
to relate, the cowed inhabitants were still in occupation. Within a
few hours it was brought home to them that a change in management
to their disadvantage had taken place. Battle-hardened soldiers,
completely ignoring their existence, removed the doors from their
houses to provide head-cover for their slits. Whatever blankets or
eiderdowns were wanted were coolly removed. Next day the
Military Police appeared and ordered them to go. Bewildered
parties of men, women and children, pushing a few possessions on
wheelbarrows moved painfully back through the rain and sleet to the
Dutch border. At long last the Germans were being paid in their
own coin. For years they had brought misery such as this to the
other peoples of Europe. Now they realized for the first time what
it meant to be a refugee, homeless, drifting nowhere in the November
rain. They left behind them their flocks of geese, their crowded
pig-sties, their cellars full of large supplies of food, the pickled
cucumbers, the beans and the fruits which the German housewife
knows how to preserve so well. Their attics were stuffed with
clothes and footwear. Their rooms were so full of new furniture as
to be overcrowded. Rationing had scarcely touched them. They
were plump and healthy looking. Most houses held their share of
French wine and brandy. Many of the big stoves concealed a ham
or two. There were ample stores of coal and wood. All this was
legitimate booty. In addition, every house had its cellar, in which
men in reserve could be rested in comparative comfort. Evidently
if a winter campaign had to be fought, Germany had much to
commend it as a theatre of operations in preference to Belgium,
France and Holland.

Soon after nightfall on the same day, the remainder of the Division
had concentrated in the densely populated mining area south and
south-west of Brunnsum. Billeting presented no difficulty.
Companies were merely allotted streets and the troops billeted
themselves. The big collieries, the "Staatsmijn Hendrik" and the
"Staatsmijn Wilhelmina," were in full blast. Their excellent hot
shower-baths were at once made available. The Dutch miners and
their wives showed themselves to be warm-hearted and generous.
For the moment the troops made the most of their time in reserve.
The rapid deterioration in the weather made this break all the more
welcome.

Major-General G. I. Thomas was in high spirits at the "O" Group

12

12th   which assembled at 9 a.m. on 12th November in the school at Brunn-
Nov.   sum. He divided the coming battle into four phases. In the first,
timed to start at 7 a.m. on "Z-Day," 84 U.S. Division were to attack
and capture the high ground east of the Wurm at Prummern. In
Phase 2, starting at 12.30 p.m. on the same day, 214 Brigade was
given the task of breaking through north of Geilenkirchen and cutting
the road which leaves the town in a north-easterly direction. In
this phase 130 Brigade was to capture Bauchem. Phase 3, the capture of Geilenkirchen by a regiment of 84 U.S. Division from the
south-west, was to follow next morning. Finally in Phase 4, 130
Brigade was to strike due north and capture Waldenrath and Straeten.
No less than six regiments of field artillery, four regiments of
mediums and two heavy batteries were available to support the attack.
In addition, medium bombers were to isolate the battlefield by
bombing the main road junctions over the Roer, and Typhoons
controlled by a contact car were being made available. Finally a
very heavy harassing fire programme by 8 Middlesex, augmented by
13/18 Hussars, 110 L.A.A. Regiment and 333 A.T.K. Battery was
being arranged to neutralize the area of 214 Brigade objectives and
Bauchem. No less than two million rounds of Mark VIII Z ammunition had been demanded. This was to start two nights before
the attack and to go on continuously.

General Thomas directed his commanders to reconnoitre and plan
on these lines. He anticipated that the minefields laid by 84 U.S.
Division would cause a certain amount of difficulty. At the time,
little was known as to their exact location. Brigade commanders
were therefore ordered to decide where they would debouch and to
lift the mines. In this task the R.E. were to give all the help they
could. Altogether it was eventually found that no less than fourteen
hundred mines would have to be lifted to enable 214 Brigade to
break out.

14th   By the morning of 14th November, 204 Field Company had
Nov.   picked up a considerable number of these American mines and loaded
them on lorries. Major Evill, the Company Commander, decided
to dump them near the Custom House on the German border, where
129 Brigade Headquarters was established. The lorries arrived here
soon after noon and No. 1 Platoon started to unload them. During
the morning Brigadier Mole had made a tour of his line. On
returning he noticed this unusual activity going on close to his headquarters and walked over to find out why this particular site had been
chosen. As he approached seven hundred mines spontaneously
detonated. There was an appalling explosion which blew a crater
thirty feet across and five feet deep. No fewer than fourteen men of
No. 1 Platoon were instantaneously killed and Brigadier Mole and six
sappers seriously wounded. Brigadier Mole was taken back to
No. 3 F.D.S. in Brunnsum, where he died the same evening.

He was buried next day in the cemetery at Brunnsum in the presence of his Divisional commander, his fellow brigadiers and his commanding officers, who had been by his side in many a battle. The Rev. I. D. Neill, the Senior Chaplain, conducted the burial service. The wife of the Burgomaster of Brunnsum laid a wreath. The buglers of the 4 Somerset Light Infantry sounded "Last Post" and "Reveille." The guns of the 94 Field Regiment, which had so often blasted open the dead Brigadier's way to victory, fired a last salute, directed, as he would have wished, against targets in the enemy's lines. Thus in the rain and sleet of a November afternoon on the liberated soil of Holland passed a Commander whose cool judgment, courage and skill had turned the tide in many a crisis, a soldier who in his bearing in battle epitomized the great traditions of his native Ulster, and a man who had earned in the brutal stress of war the affection and respect of the whole Division.

Throughout the hours of day reconnaissance parties of 214 and 130 Brigades invaded the forward area. The rickety church tower at Gilrath provided an excellent view-point over the plateau to the north. A house on the south-eastern outskirts of the village gave an almost equally good view. Most of the first day's objectives could be seen from the brickworks at Gilrath and the church at Teveren. The building up of the fire plan brought with it a constant demand for information which could only be obtained by patrols. The battalions of 129 Brigade rose nobly to the occasion and the information they gained undoubtedly contributed to the success of the other two brigades when the battle opened.

Work by the sappers on the tracks across the waste land immediately south of the forward area went on at high pressure. They were named Savile Row, Bond Street and Wyvern Road. The traffic plan for the battle was worked out in great detail.

Little has been said of the work of the Divisional and brigade staffs in the highly mobile battles of the summer and autumn. Good staff work is seldom noticed, whereas bad staff work becomes immediately apparent. In fact the work of the staffs had been arduous and incessant to an intense degree. Commanders occasionally got a respite; staffs never. The brigade majors of 214 and 130 Brigades, Majors W. J. Chalmers and C. G. Reinhold, now came into their own. Much of the success of the forthcoming battle must be attributed to the skill with which they handled the vast amount of detail involved in the planning. Large-scale maps and air photographs in vast quantities poured into the planning rooms which the brigadiers had opened at Rumpen and Merkelbeek. The move-up and deployment of 214 Brigade presented a problem of particular delicacy. The slightest error in timing would have resulted in disaster. The fire plan was no less complex. In Lieut.-Colonel Pethick 214 Brigade were more than fortunate to possess a

gunner of outstanding quality. In him and in Lieut.-Colonel
Concannon, Brigadier Boylan, the C.R.A. on whom rested most of
the responsibility of handling a formidable number of guns, had
regimental commanders on whom he could thoroughly rely. The
working out of the "Pepperpot," which was to go on continuously for
84 hours, also called for a major effort on the part of Lieut.-Colonel
Crawford and his company commanders. Planning by battalions was
almost equally elaborate. "Cloth" models produced by intelligence
sections enabled commanding officers to ensure that every man knew
the part he had to play and that all the possibilities of the coming
battle were thoroughly explored.

Thousands of rounds of artillery ammunition had to be dumped, as
few of the R.A.S.C. lorries could be brought right up to the guns,
and thus each gun detachment had to carry its three hundred rounds
and cartridges by hand in the darkness.

16th   The passing over of large numbers of heavy bombers about mid-
Nov. day on the 16th first revealed the fact that the offensive of the Ninth
and First U.S. Armies was under way. All concluded, rightly, that
Z-Day for the Division would be the 18th. At 6 p.m. the machine-
guns of 8 Middlesex opened up on to Tripsrath, Neiderheide and
Bauchem. The "Pepperpot"—an innovation which owed much to
Major-General Thomas's inventive mind—had started.

NEIDERHEIDE, HOCHEIDE, BAUCHEM AND TRIPSRATH

18th   The morning of 18th November dawned fine and frosty. Soon
Nov. after daylight the rumble of artillery fire and the vicious crack of
Typhoons announced that the battle had begun east of the Wurm.
Here a gap had to be cut in the minefield which covered the German
position. By 7.35 a.m. 334 Regiment had forced its way through
and, supported by the tanks of the Sherwood Rangers, begun to fight
its way forward towards the concrete defences around Prummern.
Many of the tanks, however, bogged down in the spongy ground.

Soon after eight o'clock the long column of 214 Brigade and 5
Dorset, the troops riding on the tanks of the 4/7 Dragoon Guards
and the 13/18 Hussars, emerged from Brunnsum on the road to
Shinveld and Gangelt. Crossing the German border, the troops debussed on the road to Gilrath and deployed in their assembly areas
amongst the birch trees on the sandy soil south of Niederbusch.
Here in bright sunshine they found to their surprise a hot meal and
rum awaiting them. Not a single shell or a mortar disturbed the
assembly. Indeed, no battle in the campaign ever opened in so
peaceful a setting. Representatives of the Press, with green labels
on their shoulders and cameras in their hands, moved amongst the
companies. Only the constant rumble of the artillery on the right
gave a hint of the grim work ahead. Major-General Thomas's

tactical headquarters unobtrusively opened near that of 214 Brigade amongst the assembled troops. About eleven o'clock the three leading companies of 7 Somerset Light Infantry began to move forward to their forming-up area in the two huge sand-quarries near the Gilrath brickworks. Still the enemy remained unaware of the coming assault. Time went on. Officers glanced at their watches. An occasional laugh relieved the tension. At noon the news flashed round that the final attack of 334 Regiment had gone in.

At last, at 12.17 p.m., the guns opened.

For the next twelve minutes the whole weight of the 250 guns of the artillery descended on the little village of Bauchem and the long smoke screen on the right flank began to form. Then the guns lifted to be replaced by the heavy mortar company of 8 Middlesex, the 3-inch mortar platoons of 4 Somerset Light Infantry and 4 Wiltshire, twenty tanks of the 13/18 Hussars, 110 L.A.A. Regiment and 333 A.T.K. Battery. For three hours the bombardment of this tiny village continued, effectively securing the right flank of the attack. Over 10,000 4·2-inch and 3,000 3-inch mortar bombs, thickened with 75-mm. shells from the tanks, incendiary and solid shot and 17-pdr. shells, were put down in this time. It is doubtful, indeed, whether any locality in the whole campaign received a more intense bombardment. 214 Brigade could thus thrust forward free from anxiety with regard to its open right flank and the enemy in Geilenkirchen.

On the stroke of 12.30, D and B Companies of 7 Somerset Light Infantry moved across their start line, the road from Gilrath to Bauchem, and advanced over the open fields on to their objective, the straggling village of Neiderheide, followed ten minutes later by C Company, whose task was to mop up the close country on the left flank. Crashes and spurts of smoke showed where the gunners were hammering the German positions. Streams of tracer from machine-guns and Bofors poured ahead. Deafening explosions from the heavies lifting the roofs of Geilenkirchen mingled with the unending blast of the mortar bombardment of Bauchem. Steadily the riflemen moved forward. There was some delay whilst D Company ejected the enemy with phosphorus grenades on the edge of the village. Such trenches as were forward of the woods were knee deep in water, and the Germans surrendered after some firing from the hip. C Company in the wooded area were similarly delayed. Here the prompt action and courage of Lance-Corporal S. Shepperd and his Bren group enabled the advance to be continued. By 3 p.m. Lieut.-Colonel H. A. Borradaile was able to report that all objectives had been gained and mopped up. About twenty casualties had been suffered and a hundred and twenty prisoners taken. They belonged to 183 Division, a second-class formation.

The battalion was now firmly on its objective. The tanks of A

Squadron 4/7 Dragoon Guards, however, soon struck trouble, not from the enemy, but from the soft ground. Tank after tank came to a standstill. Before the fighting transport of the battalion was half-way across the fields between Gilrath and Neiderheide, most of the vehicles were hopelessly bogged, buried above the axles. Heavy concentrations of enemy shells now descended both on the vehicles and Neiderheide.

Meanwhile 1 Worcestershire had threaded their way through the battered village of Gilrath and formed up in a depression in front of it. Lieut.-Colonel R. E. Osborne Smith, a rifle slung over his shoulder, moved amongst the troops. He had a word and a smile for everyone. Indeed, at no time in the campaign did his normal composure or quiet courtesy to all ranks ever desert him. At 2 p.m. he gave the order to start. B Company on the right and C Company on the left, keeping direction by compass and previously chosen landmarks, advanced on their objective—the little village of Rischden and the wood nearby. There was only slight opposition at first and the mines and wire gave little trouble. The section of 204 Field Company were soon busy marking and lifting the mines to enable the tanks of B Squadron 4/7 Dragoon Guards to get through to support A and D Companies in their attack on the final objective— Tripsrath. The enemy in the wood, pale and shaking from the effects of the ferocious bombardment, surrendered to C Company with relief. This company now moved forward to close up behind B Company, who had reached Rischden a thousand yards ahead.

South-west of Rischden stood a small square copse which the carrier platoon had been ordered to seize when this village had been taken. They now moved up towards it. Immediately two S.P. guns in the woods to the north opened up and shot them to ribbons. They had the range to a yard and in twenty minutes thirty-one men of the carrier platoon had fallen. B and C Companies grimly dug in. At this moment a shell splinter severely wounded Lieut.-Colonel Osborne Smith in the leg and he had to be evacuated.

Captain W. L. Leadbeater, the Adjutant, rose to the occasion. Hatless and regardless of personal risk, he ran around the forward positions and eventually succeeded in locating Major J. D. Ricketts, commanding B Company, who now took command. Major Ricketts' courage and decisive action at this crisis saved the day. The tanks which were to have supported the final advance on Tripsrath were hopelessly bogged near the start line. The guns had switched to support the attacks of the D.C.L.I. and 5 Dorset. The final objective lay 1,000 yards ahead. He brought forward A and D Companies, who had now been shelled continuously in their forming up area for three hours, and formed them up in front of Rischden. The final attack went in at 5.15 p.m. supported by a bombardment of mediums. Unfortunately the shells fell 600 yards short amongst D Company.

Nevertheless the two companies, followed by C Company, doggedly advanced across the main road. Ahead, 200 yards away, stood the church at Tripsrath. As the night closed in the three companies forced their way into the village.

Meanwhile in the soft ground around Neiderheide a serious situation had developed. Everywhere anti-tank guns, carriers and tanks stood immobile in the mud, powerless to move. A dense mass of transport piled up in Gilrath. 5 D.C.L.I., who had been given the task of capturing Hocheide and then swinging south to cut the road running north-east from Geilenkirchen and were due to cross their start line at Neiderheide at 3 p.m., literally had to force their way through the appalling congestion. Lieut.-Colonel Taylor using a megaphone battered his way through the confusion. Heavy shells crashed amongst the advancing troops. D Company, however, under Major Lonsdale, dressed in his best battle-dress and carrying a cane, accompanied by a troop of C Squadron of 4/7 Dragoon Guards, struck east through the smoke for his objective on time. B Company and the rest of the battalion successfully struggled through.

At this crisis Lieut.-Colonel Venour of 5 Dorset showed equal resource. He was due to cross his start line for the capture of Bauchem at 3.30 p.m. On entering Gilrath he found the congestion so great that the tanks of 13/18 Hussars which were supporting him could not get through. With remarkable promptitude he found another route and punctually crossed his start line as he had planned. The prompt and effective initiative of these two commanding officers undoubtedly averted a serious breakdown in this elaborately planned battle.

Every man of 5 Dorset knew exactly what he had to do and where he had to go. Morale was high. Moving with precision over the fifteen hundred yards of open fields ahead, D (Major G. R. Hartwell) and B (Captain P. Aspinall) Companies soon reached a line of trenches about 300 yards from the village. There was little spirited resistance. C Company (Major G. R. Packe) and A Company (Major H. C. Allen) now passed through and cleared the village. Finally D and A Companies turned the trenches and concrete emplacements south of what remained of Bauchem from the rear. When darkness fell, the removal of mines by the pioneers on the road from Gilrath had started and the anti-tank guns, ammunition and maintenance vehicles had joined. Patrols pushed into Geilenkirchen. It had been a most successful attack. A hundred and eighty-two prisoners had been taken at the cost of only four casualties. The savage bombardment had completely shattered their morale. In view of the immense weight of explosive which had rained on Bauchem, however, the proportion of dead was surprisingly small. More shells designed to burst in the ground rather than to secure blast on the surface would probably have caused the sides of the slits to cave in and buried the occupants. However, the whole success of the battle turned on the neutralization of Bauchem. This had been most effectively ensured by the artillery, the tanks and 8 Middlesex.

In the meantime all had gone well with the attack of the 5 D.C.L.I. Major Lonsdale with D Company, in spite of the fact that his tanks had stuck in the mud, drove the enemy out of Hocheide and consolidated. B Company followed south and east of the village and seized the high ground overlooking the small hamlet of Bruggerhof. Finally, it fell to A Company under Major Holland to put the finishing touch to the day's operations by cutting the road running north-east from Geilenkirchen. As night closed in, this company, with No. 7 Platoon under Lieutenant Olding in the lead, worked its way down in the rain and, unobserved by the enemy, took up a compact position commanding the road, thus sealing in the enemy in the town. They now reaped their reward. First to arrive were a platoon of the enemy marching in threes and led by their N.C.O. carrying a wireless set on his back heading for Geilenkirchen. A burst of L.M.G., Sten and rifle fire caught them unawares. Seven were killed, five surrendered and the rest escaped in the darkness. They came from 104 Panzer Grenadier Regiment and were good troops. No. 9 Platoon now mined the road with 75 grenades and covered them with twigs and leaves. Lieut.-Colonel Taylor later added a 6-pdr. gun and a medium machine-gun to the trap.

The next arrival from the enemy's rear came about 10 p.m. Down the road came a cart loaded with ammunition. To the intense amusement of the spectators, up went the cart and driver whilst the horse trotted on alone into the town. Half an hour later another cart appeared from Geilenkirchen. This time it was empty. Seeing the ammunition lying on the road, the driver, no doubt a conscientious man, started to load it on his own cart. He met exactly the same fate and once again the horse trotted away alone. The next visitors were a patrol of eight—unfortunately three survived to get away in the darkness. At 3 a.m. bigger game arrived in the shape of a Tiger tank coming from Geilenkirchen. It hit the mines and stopped. Then the crew jumped out and started to clear the mines. A burst of L.M.G. fire dispersed them, but the tank drove on.

Thus by nightfall all the Division's objectives had been taken. Geilenkirchen had been encircled, and on the right, 84 U.S. Division had fought and won a hard battle. On the whole, careful planning and overwhelming fire had been too much for 183 Volks Grenadier Division. 15 Panzer Grenadier Division and 21 S.S. Panzer Grenadier, however, were known to be in the neighbourhood and counter-attack seemed likely. The only disquieting feature of the day's operations had been the bad going for the tanks and other tracked vehicles. It cannot be claimed, however, that forethought had entirely ensured success. Had not commanders of the calibre of Major Ricketts, Lieut.-Colonel Taylor and Lieut.-Colonel Venour been on the spot to give the forward drive a fresh impetus at the critical moment, the results might have been far less decisive.

On the morrow, Major-General Thomas proposed to launch 130 Brigade northwards on Straeten and Waldenrath. Before he could do this, however, it was essential that 84 U.S. Division should complete the capture of Geilenkirchen and press on to the high ground above Wurm and Beek, which dominated his right flank.

TRIPSRATH AND DORSET AND HOVEN WOODS

In face of the expected counter-attack by high-grade enemy troops, the situation on the Divisional front was not without anxiety. *19th Nov.* Everywhere tanks, carriers and anti-tank guns had floundered in the liquid mud of the fields. No hot food could be got through during the night to the forward troops. In particular the three companies of the Worcesters in Tripsrath without their anti-tank guns faced a grim prospect as the day dawned on the 19th, wet and overcast. The ever-faithful B Squadron of 4/7 Dragoon Guards, however, succeeded two hours before dawn in getting five tanks into the village. When the light came an enemy S.P. gun appeared and knocked out three of the tanks. A fourth was bazookaed by a man whom the Worcesters shot—too late! At the same time a heavy attack came in against A Company. This was beaten off, leaving no fewer than forty dead in front of the forward platoon. They belonged to 104 Panzer Grenadier Regiment of 15 Panzer Grenadier Division. Some of these troops, however, infiltrated into the school at the northern end of the village. The need for the opening of the road through Geilenkirchen became every minute more and more urgent.

84 U.S. Division's attack started at daybreak. The town was strongly held and the Americans had to fight every inch of their way through. By the middle of the morning it had become apparent that the hope of resuming the advance with 130 Brigade against Straeten and Waldenrath during the day would have to be abandoned. A further enemy counter-attack from the woods to the west of Tripsrath against the reserve C Company of the Worcesters in Rischden at 11 a.m. brought home forcibly the fact that this battalion was faced by an enemy prepared to fight to the limit and stood in a dangerously exposed position. This attack was supported by two Tiger tanks and two S.P. guns. The enemy emerged from what was soon to be named "Dorset Wood" and, apparently unaware of our presence in Tripsrath, advanced on Rischden. C Company, occupying the southern part of Tripsrath, although they had no anti-tank guns took a heavy toll of the infantry. Fortunately the battalion's anti-tank guns and some tanks had reached Rischden. These opened up. Three of the enemy armoured vehicles went up

in flames, and the screams of their trapped crews could be heard above the noise of the firing.   One tank only limped back into the wood.   The surviving infantry bolted.

Tripsrath, obviously, could not be considered secure until control had been gained of the northern exits of the wood to the west (Dorset Wood) and the observation to the north from the spur north-east of the village had been taken.   In the middle of the morning Major-General Thomas therefore decided to make these his objectives for the day.   In any case, possession of these areas would be essential before 130 Brigade's attack on Straeten and Waldenrath could be launched.   He therefore relieved 5 Dorset in Bauchem with a company of 4 Somerset Light Infantry and ordered 130 Brigade to clear the woods between Tripsrath and Hatterath and 214 Brigade to advance with the 7 Somerset Light Infantry, clear the long wood which stretches from Hocheide to Hoven and seize the spur to the north-east of the Worcesters' position.

At 1.45 p.m., therefore, 5 Dorset, with a squadron of 13/18 Hussars in support, set off on their new task.   Crossing the open ground under cover of smoke from their own mortars, the battalion entered the woods.   For a time all went well with the advance of A and C Companies, who were in the lead.   On reaching a wide clearing, however, very heavy mortar and machine-gun fire held them up and pinned them to the ground throughout the hours of daylight. Major G. R. Hartwell with D Company, moving round the left flank, endeavoured to reach a fringe of wood from which to support the further move forward by A and C Companies.   Night closed before this objective could be gained, and the battalion reorganized for the resumption of the battle at daybreak.   Most of the vehicles had by now become bogged, but the maintenance column got through.

On the right flank the attack by the 7 Somerset Light Infantry had to be launched at equally short notice.   Leaving his carrier platoon and anti-tank guns to hold Neiderheide, for Geilenkirchen was still in enemy hands.   Lieut.-Colonel H. A. Borradaile, with A and C Companies leading, entered the southern end of Hoven wood at 3.30 p.m. This stretches from just north of Hocheide to the little hamlet of Hoven. It is about one and three-quarter miles long and on an average about six hundred yards broad.   About eight hundred yards south of Hoven is a narrow neck.   The support of four field regiments firing block concentrations with a lift of three hundred yards between each, enabled the battalion to fight its way through the dripping trees and soggy ground of the wood, and by 4.30 p.m. the neck of the wood had been gained at the cost of nineteen casualties.   Forty prisoners were taken.   The battalion's real difficulties now began.   There was only one muddy sloping path by which even tracked vehicles could reach the forward companies and this led outside the wood in full view of the enemy.   In addition it was very slippery and bordered by deep

ditches.   During the night vehicle after vehicle became hopelessly
bogged.   Enemy mortar bombs descended continuously on the
stranded vehicles and amongst the trees.   The shelling became worse
and worse.   It was only with the utmost difficulty that food was got
through to the forward companies.   After this experience, Major-
General Thomas decided that in future all attacking troops should
carry a 24-hour ration landing pack in their mess-tins.   This
measure saved many an anxious moment during later battles.

By the early afternoon Geilenkirchen had passed finally into the
hands of 333 R.C.T. of 84 U.S. Division.   Part of the garrison, however, preferred to fight their way out rather than surrender to A
Company of the D.C.L.I., who now awaited their prey near Bruggerhof.   Enemy in considerable numbers now closed with Nos. 9
and 8 Platoons and tried to penetrate the woods.   Three S.P. guns
emerged from the town.   Fortunately the 18 set was working well
and the full weight of the Divisional artillery quickly came down on
the company front.   The 3-inch mortars opened up.   No. 8
Platoon under Lieutenant Williams got to close quarters with the
enemy.   No. 9 Platoon disposed of the S.P. guns and their crews.
Major Holland shot the German officer in command with his revolver.
Corporal Lynch did great execution with his Bren.   Altogether the
battle lasted forty-five minutes.   The Americans at last appeared
and moved on down the valley on the enemy's heels.   Twenty-one
enemy dead and nine wounded were counted around the platoon's
positions.   There must have been many more, however, who were
never found.   Altogether it had been a most satisfactory company
battle at the price of only one killed and four wounded.   The arrival
of the C.Q.M.S. with the first hot food and rum they had had for
thirty-six hours raised the company's morale to an even higher pitch.

It is not easy to describe the sordid horror of the woods on the 20th
flanks of Tripsrath.   Within them it was at all times difficult to Nov.
know exactly where you were.   The men of 15 Panzer Grenadier
Regiment were at home amongst the trees and crept stealthily forward to snipe from the rear.   Mortar bombs and shells in ever-
increasing numbers exploded in the air the moment they touched the
upper branches.   Slits were no sooner dug than they filled with
water, and all the time the incessant rain dripped off the falling leaves.
The trees themselves seemed to magnify the noise of the incessant
fire and to bring an added menace to the sodden troops.   Every
thicket seemed to conceal an enemy.   In Dorset Wood many of the
carriers were stuck on the muddy tracks from Gilrath.

It will be recollected that nightfall on the nineteenth had brought
A and C Companies of the 5 Dorset, now sadly depleted in numbers,
to a standstill at close grips with the enemy.   D Company similarly
had been brought to a halt on the left flank.   The troops were now
entering their third day of battle.   The night was pitch black.

Nevertheless, preparations went forward to resume the attack at dawn.

With the shells of the whole Divisional artillery falling ahead, Major Hartwell with D Company came in from the left flank and, fighting every inch of the way, wiped out the enemy who had held up the advance of A and C Companies. The company then swung left and fought its way yard by yard through the woods to the northern-most edge. B Company under Captain P. Aspinall struggled successfully forward on their left. Soon after ten o'clock they had reached their objectives. Lieut.-Colonel Venour now moved A and C Companies, amalgamated under Major Allen, against the north-east arm of the wood overlooking Tripsrath. Bitter close-quarter fighting ensued and the enemy were overcome.

Before the eyes of 5 Dorset now lay the open country stretching towards Straeten and Waldenrath. Counter-attacks withered away in face of the prompt and accurate fire of the gunners. Vicious fire from enemy S.P. guns raked the troops as they dug in. The gunner officer, Captain Gilders, with B Company was killed. The battalion hung grimly on to its gains. They had fought many hard battles, but few harder than this or at a higher price. Altogether an entire battalion of first-class German troops had been destroyed. Brigadier B. A. Coad therefore decided to relieve them that night by 4 Dorset. It was fitting that the fruits of victory gained at so high a price should remain in the hands of another battalion of the regiment, amongst whose battle honours the name of Dorset Wood will always stand high. The battalion was to remain in this unspeakable discomfort and under very heavy shell-fire for a further seven days. Through a sea of mud, carrying parties somehow or other got food to the forward troops in their water-logged slits. In the many gun duels, Major P. Steele Perkins of 112 Field Regiment invariably had the last word. Recovery under incessant fire went forward under the eye of Lieut.-Colonel Neilson under conditions which less stout-hearted craftsmen than those of the Division's R.E.M.E. would have considered hopeless.

The whole front now felt the weight of the guns in the Siegfried Line. Shells of heavy calibre now raked Dorset and Hoven Woods. The Worcesters in Tripsrath grimly endured increasing bombardment. Although the road through the little suburb of An Den Linden at Geilenkirchen had now been opened by the sappers, movement by vehicles on the tracks in the fields reached a standstill. Even with extra pieces of track plate fitted to their tracks, the tanks could not get forward. Around Hocheide the muddy fields were churned to the consistency of porridge.

On the immediate right beyond the Wurm, the Americans con-
20th tinued their obstinate struggle amongst the concrete defences and the
Nov. mud. Fighting in Prummern proved obstinate and bloody. It was

evident, therefore, that the attack by 130 Brigade against Straeten
and Waldenrath would have to be abandoned.

The 84 U.S. Division continued its attack towards Beek and Wurm
on 21st November. At 11 a.m. one battalion of 405 Regiment
captured the high ground some 1,500 yards south of Beek. This
accomplished, 334 Regiment on the right and 333 Regiment on the
left began a frontal attack an hour later. In the pill-boxes along the
ridge east of the Wurm the enemy fought with the utmost ferocity
and by the end of the day little progress had been made. It was
therefore decided to continue the attack on the 22nd and that 43
Division should assist by capturing the high ground south-west of
Hoven and the village of Kraudorf. Contact with the U.S. troops
was to be made in Wurm. This task was entrusted to the commander of 214 Brigade who, with two of his battalions committed to
Tripsrath and Hoven Wood, had no option other than to give it to
5 D.C.L.I. 21st
Nov.

Brigadier Essame did not under-estimate the formidable task given
to this battalion. Provided 84 Division succeeded on the right flank.
the attack would deprive the enemy of observation over the bottleneck of Geilenkirchen and enable the road communications down the
Wurm valley to be used for maintenance on the right flank. Above
all, it would if successful release the forward troops from the squalor
and continued uncertainty of Hoven Wood. Doubt existed as to
whether tanks and anti-tank guns could reach Hoven and Kraudorf
over the fields. To the last moment no clear picture could be formed
of the enemy defences in the wood. However, the risks were taken. 22nd
Nov.

Lieut.-Colonel Taylor planned that C Company should attack first
and secure the wood south of Hoven. B Company was then to pass
through and capture the village. D Company was given Kraudorf
as its objective. As A Company was still committed to the Bruggerhof defences, D Company of 7 Somerset Light Infantry was
placed under command of Lieut.-Colonel Taylor as a reserve.

The attack opened at noon. Unfortunately the artillery bombardment and fire support from 7 Somerset Light Infantry had completely
missed the enemy sited in the woods just beyond the neck. A storm of
machine-gun and mortar fire descended on C Company and Lieut.-
Colonel Taylor's command post by the start line at the neck of the wood.
The reserve platoon was completely destroyed in a few seconds.
However, the left-hand platoon under Lieutenant Gay fought their
way amongst the enemy posts. Major Kitchen, who arrived at this
moment to take command, decided to fight the battle out. B Company under Major Gason therefore moved round the left flank and
joined in the battle. Casualties piled up thick and fast. Slowly,
however, the companies began to get the upper hand. Lieutenant
Birchenall of the pioneer platoon joined in with a Bren he had taken
from a casualty.

This check apparently in no way damped Lieut.-Colonel Taylor's determination to get forward. He now directed D Company to make a slight right hook outside the wood under cover of smoke and make for Hoven. This company under Captain Spencer, behind an excellent barrage, swept forward along the eastern edge killing the enemy as they advanced. Soon they reached the outskirts of Hoven. A pincer movement by the two leading platoons penetrated the houses, where fighting went on until nightfall. Lieutenant Savory's platoon met particularly fierce resistance. Forty prisoners were taken.

Brigadier Essame, who had come forward during the afternoon to Lieut.-Colonel Taylor's command post, now decided that the chances of taking Kraudorf that day had gone. He therefore ordered that Hoven should be consolidated. The brigadier also promised to release A Company from the defence of Bruggerhof. Unfortunately D Company of 7 Somerset Light Infantry, which had been ordered to follow D Company of the D.C.L.I., had become involved in the fighting on the rest of the battalion's front, although this was not realized until after dark. Despite the large number of wounded struggling to extricate themselves from the tangle of the woods, the high spirits of all ranks left a vivid impression even on the brigadier. Lieut.-Colonel Taylor, Captain Willcocks, his Intelligence Officer, and Major Brewis, his Gunner, might well have been at a rugger match at Twickenham rather than fighting a sanguinary battle at close grips with 15 Panzer Grenadier Division in a filthy German wood on a damp November afternoon.

Night descended and with it began a frightful struggle to evacuate the wounded, to get up food and ammunition and to move A Company, reinforced with a platoon of 7 Somerset Light Infantry, in support of D Company. The slightest move brought a burst of Spandau fire. The cries of the wounded added to the general misery. Major Lonsdale came up from A Echelon and took command of D Company. The pitiful remnants of C Company were reorganized. A circle of defensive fire around Hoven was arranged. The prisoners were got out. These included a truculent doctor. When asked why his people continued the hopeless struggle, he defiantly replied, "I am fighting for my country the same as you!" Soaked to the skin and sleepless, the D.C.L.I. faced their sixth day of battle.

The brigadier was sufficiently of his Commander's mind never to contemplate the abandonment of Hoven. If he had a dangerous salient to his line, so had the enemy. The shells during the day had come down on the wrong spot. This was no reason why they should not be put in the right place on the morrow. In spite of the truly appalling conditions in the wood, he knew the D.C.L.I. would fight on. So long as the U.S. troops on his right flank continued the struggle, he refused to quit. Major-General Thomas therefore placed 4 Wiltshire, at the moment resting in billets in the Brunnsum area, under his command so that he could impart a fresh impetus to the battle on the morrow. The brigadier could not expect to be able to launch them into the attack until several hours after daylight. The D.C.L.I. would therefore have to stand counter-attack at dawn alone.

Lieut.-General Horrocks now took a step completely in accordance with his character. He knew that he was faced with fresh enemy troops of high quality and that a heavy counterstroke was probable in the morning. He realized the precarious position of the D.C.L.I. to the full. Late that night in drenching rain he came forward to the brigadier, approved his decision, and, not without personal risk, went over at once to the Americans to ensure that they continued the battle at daybreak.

In fact, D Company shared the village of Hoven with the Germans. Just before dawn a battle broke out in the company headquarter building itself. It was beaten off, but a grenade smashed the wireless set and thus cut off contact with the guns. As the light grew stronger, large numbers of German infantry advanced down the hedgerows, to wither away in the face of heavy Bren and rifle fire. They soon returned again, this time supported by four S.P. guns. The battle raged for two and a half hours. Captain Spencer, the second in command, leaning over the window-sill of an upper room in the company headquarters, engaged a tank in the street with a Piat, only to be severely wounded by its gun. The buildings now burst into flames. The company headquarters became choked with British and German wounded. Eventually only Major Lonsdale and about fifteen men remained to carry on the fight. Ammunition had run out and they were forced to use German weapons. Rather than surrender, Major Lonsdale decided to cut his way out taking with him such of the wounded as could still walk. Aided by the smoke of the burning buildings, the party fought their way through.

Meanwhile, A Company under Major Kitchen had become involved in the battle. At dawn they caught the first enemy attack by surprise and beat them back with heavy loss. The enemy returned to the attack on the left flank, this time supported by two S.P. guns. It seemed as if the company would be cut off. Sergeant William's platoon therefore promptly counter-attacked and drove the enemy back for fifty yards, temporarily stabilizing the battle. Both Majors Kitchen and Holland were wounded and had to withdraw.

With Hoven gone, there was little point in maintaining A Company and the posts supporting it in their position. Orders were therefore given for its withdrawal to the neck of the wood.

The D.C.L.I., without tanks and anti-tank guns, had fought one of the fiercest battles of the campaign to the bitter end. The prisoners taken, except for a few stragglers, were all wounded. The enemy, who belonged to 10 S.S. Panzer Division apparently reinforced by two companies of 21 S.S. Panzer Division specially brought over from east of the Wurm, treated them with kindness, expressed their admiration for the battalion's fight and commented ruefully on their own heavy losses.

Reconnaissance by 4 Wiltshire Regiment for the recapture of Hoven went forward during the morning. About midday, however, the decision was reached that in view of the waterlogged state of the ground, both on the Divisional and U.S. fronts, the offensive would have to be temporarily abandoned. On the right, 84 U.S. Division had fought itself to a standstill. Neither tanks nor anti-tank guns could be got forward. The administrative situation had become desperate. In any case, the main objective of the offensive, the capture of Geilenkirchen, had been achieved.

Once again the Division had fought magnificently and raised its reputation for tactical skill, stubborn courage and eagerness to get to close grips with the enemy to an even higher level.

GROESBEEK

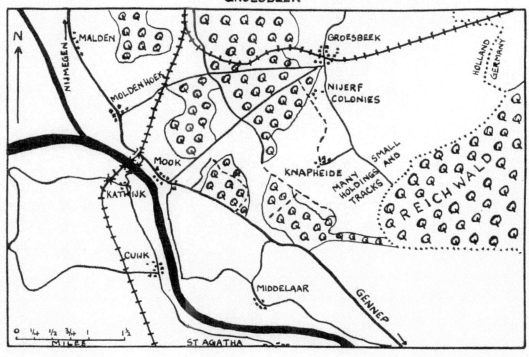

30 CORPS OPERATION CLIPPER
DISPOSITIONS and INTENTIONS 18 NOV 44

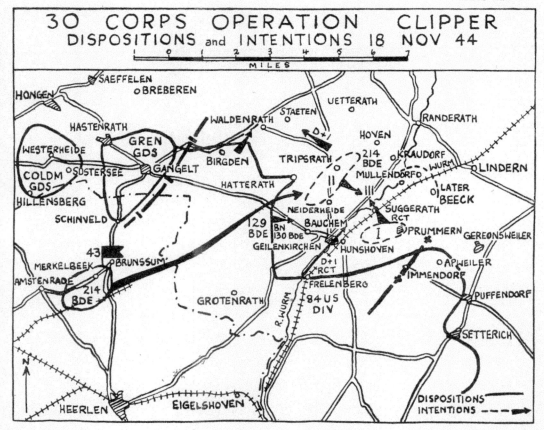

CHAPTER X

EARLY WINTER

(See Sketch Map 13)

THE DEFENCE OF THE GEILENKIRCHEN SECTOR

THE Division now reverted to the glamourless task of holding its gains. Before, however, completely static defence could be adopted a pocket of the enemy still remaining in a few houses at the extreme north-western tip of Tripsrath had to be eliminated. During the battle 1 Worcestershire had endured bombardment in the village on a scale comparable to that of the First World War. This gradually died down. Lieut.-Colonel N. C. E. Kenrick, commanding 5 Wiltshire, who took over the village on the 23rd, very soon decided that the enemy who remained must be removed. At first it was not thought that they were in any great strength and a fighting patrol of platoon strength was given the task of evicting them. After reconnaissance during the night it advanced to the attack at dawn on the 25th. By 9.30 they had driven the enemy back into a large barn at the end of the village and taken six prisoners. It now became clear, however, that the enemy had been considerably reinforced and under heavy shell-fire the patrol had to be withdrawn, leaving the men pinned down in the house immediately adjoining the barn with literally nothing but a wall between them and the Germans. Nine managed to get clear later when darkness fell. An attack in much stronger force therefore had to be planned for the next day. {25th Nov.}

At 3.45 p.m. on the 26th C Company under Major E. R. B. Field advanced to the attack. Ahead, very heavy fire crashed down on the enemy positions and on the enemy guns behind. Medium guns, 25-pdrs., 4·2-inch mortars and the 3-inch mortars of both 4 and 5 Wiltshire were all engaged. Two troops of tanks of the 13/18 Hussars moved up on the left flank and fired point-blank into the buildings. Lance-Corporal Hoptroff with a Piat and Private Kendall with a Bren knocked out two machine-guns before they had a chance of holding up the attack. The two leading platoons, brilliantly led by Lieutenant D. R. Over and Sergeant A. I. Hall and closely followed by the reserve platoon under Corporal Barnett, caught the enemy before they could emerge from their cellars. Two officers and fifty-three men of the 104 Panzer Grenadier Regiment surrendered. Many more were killed. On interrogation the prisoners revealed the fact that the Germans, on account of the Yellow Dragoon {26th Nov.}

flash and the ferocity of the infantry, had now decided that they were faced by a British "S.S." division.   At least so long as the Division remained in the line, they henceforward made no further attempt to challenge our possession of Tripsrath.

For the next fortnight, brigades in succession continued to hold the front from Bruggerhof to Birgden.   Winter set in rapidly.   On the right, 43 Reconnaissance Regiment with one squadron forward maintained a squadron continuously in position.   Clashes with the enemy were frequent and shell and mortar fire at times intense.   In Hoven and Dorset Woods the appalling conditions continued.   Slits had to be continually baled out.   The brushwood tracks became submerged in mud.   The problem of supplying the troops with food would have been insuperable had not Major-General Thomas secured a number of Weasels.   These vehicles, originally designed for use in Norway, with their wide, lightly built tracks and high metal sides, were able to slide over the mud.   Thanks to them the troops in the stench and wet of the woods were kept alive.   R.E.M.E. spared no effort to keep the Weasels in running order and succeeded despite their heavy casualty rate.   Movement of anti-tank guns was out of the question.   Battalions on relief therefore left them in position.   Base-plates of mortars sank in the mud.

In the villages conditions were physically less arduous.   Cellars provided shelter and the Germans had left ample supplies of fuel.   The long, straggling village of Birgden, however, beyond the crest of the ridge north of the Gangelt road, had an uncanny atmosphere of its own.   Within the shattered buildings, the garrison shared the place with the enemy.   At night the wind blew through the broken windows and eerie figures moved in the shadows.   Patrols stumbled over the fallen tiles.   Most German villages are sinister and Birgden had a terror peculiarly its own.   Men disappeared and were never heard of again.   There were several unpleasant incidents of a mysterious character.   Eventually it transpired that the Germans had a N.C.Os. Training School at Heinsberg and were using Birgden as a practice ground.

To relieve the strain on the infantry, Lieut.-General Horrocks took a novel step—the formation of a "Services" battalion.   This consisted of a headquarters formed from Corps H.Q. and four companies made up of Corps and Divisional R.A.S.C. and of R.E.M.E. 30 Corps.   Gunners later manned the anti-tank guns.   This improvised battalion held the battalion sector at Hatterath for some time.   Their high morale was most stimulating and all were proud of the chance which had come their way to give the infantry a rest.   The manner in which they triumphed over the hundred and one administrative difficulties which inevitably arose gained the respect of all who came in contact with them.   The infantry particularly appreciated the additional rest they gained as a result of this expedient. It is doubtful, however, whether the risk taken of losing valuable technicians was ever justified. Had the enemy attacked in strength in this sector at this time, as he might well have done, for the Corps position, dependent on the precarious bridges over the Maas, provided a tempting bait, the services of these technical soldiers would have been lost at the time they were needed most.

12 K.R.R.C. also, the motor battalion of 8 Armoured Brigade, helped to man the forward defences. This was a task for which they were not designed. In particular, their low rifle strength made their task at Birgden peculiarly difficult. However, they overcame all their troubles. Here again a risk was taken which, had not the enemy remained inactive, might well have impaired the battle-fitness of 8 Armoured Brigade.

The weather got still worse. The large numbers of sheepskin coats captured at Elst now came in evidence. Major-General Thomas appeared in a long leather overcoat of somewhat Edwardian cut. The first snow fell on 9th December. Troops coming back to rest in the mining villages around Brunnsum therefore made the most of the almost overwhelming hospitality of the Dutch. The women dried and mended their clothes. The troops sat round the table with the family. Brunnsum itself was not immune from long-range shell-fire and Divisional headquarters came in for some unpleasant attention. At night there were air-raid alarms. On the whole, however, units enjoyed life and made many friends.

It must be recorded, however, that not all the Dutch population were unquestionably loyal. Nazism had infected certain minor elements of the population before and during the occupation. Curfew, therefore, had to be strictly enforced and a heavy strain fell on Captain R. S. Hallmark and the Field Security Section. So severe did this become that he had to protest against the spate of fantastic requests which now poured in. These ranged from demands for coupons for coal and food and transport of beer to permits to enable the black market at Maastricht to be visited. He was even asked to pay an undertaker's bill and to allow a German girl pregnant by a Dutch miner to enter Holland to be married.

Field-Marshal Montgomery came to Divisional headquarters on 24th November and stayed to lunch. To the astonishment of the staff he was carrying an umbrella. The last Commander-in-Chief to appear with this essentially civilian article had been the Duke of Cambridge in 1870. Someone may have pointed this out, for the umbrella never appeared again. It is difficult in any case to imagine two field-marshals who had less in common.

He appeared again on the morning of 30th November, this time to present medals. After inspecting a guard of honour provided by the Reconnaissance Regiment, he entered the Trebeck Theatre at Rumpen, where the Life Guards Band had been playing for the past

hour to the assembled brigadiers, lieut.-colonels and as many troops
as the building could hold.   As each officer and man advanced to the
platform to be decorated a sergeant took a photograph.   The investiture over, the Field-Marshal proceeded to review the progress
of the war.   Looking back, he described the campaign as one which
would live in history.   He said that the Prime Minister had told him
in May that if we reached the Seine by Christmas he would be
satisfied.   We had not only crossed the Seine, but all of France,
passed through Belgium and across Holland and now fought the
Hun on German soil.   ''We have had five Christmasses at war,'' he
said, ''a sixth lies ahead, but that will be our last at war with Germany.''

He then outlined the leave scheme due to start in the New Year,
which would enable 3,000 men a day to go home for seven complete
days.

Finally, he paid a tribute to the achievements of the Division and
8 Armoured Brigade.   ''Go back,'' he said, ''go back and tell them
that I said they have done most awfully well.''   This was indeed
praise from the man whom all regarded as the greatest leader of their
time.   The investiture over, the Field-Marshal left to tell the 5
Dorset how greatly he admired their heroic fighting in the recent
battle.

Major-General Thomas's investiture of 5 D.C.L.I., some days
later, had a more sombre setting.   Standing on the outskirts of
Grotenrath overlooking the squalor of the battlefield, he decorated
Lieut.-Colonel Taylor and the surviving officers and men who had
gained their honours in the Arnhem fighting.   Overhead the sky
hung black and forbidding; it began to snow.   The flashes of the
guns lit up the gathering darkness.   The scene indeed epitomized
the stark reality of winter war.   Visibly moved, the General pinned
the ribbons on the breasts of his soldiers who had fought so bravely
and so well.

''SHEARS''

5th
Dec.
It is convenient at this point to review the situation as it confronted 21 Army Group at the beginning of December.   On the
right of the line in the Geilenkirchen sector stood 43 Division, with
the remainder of 30 Corps extending the front to the Maas at
Maeseyck.   From here to the north the rest of Second Army found
security within the broad bend of this river for almost fifty miles as
far as Cuijk in the familiar territory south of Nijmegen.   First
Canadian Army held the remainder of the front.

Since Arnhem the enemy had fought with determination and skill,
making full use of the most defensible country over which we were
ever forced to fight.   The weather had steadily deteriorated and only
limited use could be made of our overwhelming air superiority.

Although his losses had been severe, he now had a chance to re-organize his mauled formations under cover of the Maas. There was no doubt that temporarily he had recovered his breath and was sparing no effort which might enable him to recover the initiative or at least forestall any quick break-through. The Supreme Commander therefore, despite the rapidly deteriorating weather, decided to continue the battle so as to draw into it the enemy's formations which would otherwise be rested and re-equipped in readiness for the defence of the Ruhr and Greater Germany.

The German striking force, that is the Sixth Panzer Army, had been withdrawn from the line and was known to be covering the arc of Cologne. It was therefore decided that this formidable force should be made to fight during the winter so that it would be worn out when improving weather conditions permitted a full-scale general advance into Germany.

Field-Marshal Montgomery's plans for the destruction of the enemy west of the Rhine had been made in the autumn. The first phase, that is the advance to the line of the Maas and the Roer, was still incomplete, as the triangle between the two rivers south of Maeseyck still remained to be cleared. He therefore ordered Second Army to resume the offensive towards the Roer. Once again 30 Corps was to be the spearhead.

This operation was named "Shears." Although it never actually took place, it loomed large on the horizon of the commanders and staffs of 43 Division during the first two weeks of December and provided an interesting comparison with "Operation Blackcock," actually executed by 12 Corps in January with the same objectives, but in greatly different circumstances.

Lieut.-General Horrocks had at his disposal Guards Armoured, 7 Armoured, 43 and 52 (L.) Divisions. With them, he proposed to attack and destroy the enemy west of the Roer on the Corps front. His plan, which he gave out to the divisional commanders at a Corps conference on 2nd December, gave 43 Division the task of breaching the enemy defences astride the main road from Geilenkirchen to Heinsberg in sufficient depth and width to enable 52 (L.) Division to get out and advance on Heinsberg and the line of the Roer to the north. Having opened the way for 52 (L.) Division Major-General Thomas was then to attack due west from the area immediately north of Tripsrath and capture from the rear the villages of Schierwalden-rath and Langbroich so that Guards Armoured Division could break out at Birgden. This division was then to capture from the rear the enemy defences to the west along the line of the stream from Lang-broich to Havert and, this task completed, to strike north-west towards Echt so as to cut off the enemy on 7 Armoured Division's front. Finally, it was expected to capture Linne at the apex of the triangle south of Roermond. To round off the battle 7 Armoured

Division on the left flank was expected in the final stages to advance north-east roughly parallel with the Maas.

It will be seen that the plan was not lacking in complexity. Of course, in view of the high quality of the divisions engaged and the Corps commander's proved capacity to triumph over mere tactical difficulties, it would have been successful had it ever been put into operation. Few plans, however, during the campaign can have envisaged so many different attacks in such widely divergent directions.

If Major-General Thomas had any doubts as to the soundness of the plan, he certainly effectively concealed them at his "O" Group held in the school at Brunnsum on the following day. He was in the highest spirits. Of necessity, the task set to the Division involved most careful timing and planning in detail. On D-Day between 11.30 a.m. and 2.15, when 52 (L.) Division was due to emerge on the main road at Tripsrath, each of the three brigades had to fight a separate battle: 129 Brigade to capture Utterath and then move east to take Randerath; 214 Brigade to clear Hoven Wood, Kraudorf and Nirm, and the main road, and 130 Brigade to break out into Straeten. During the evening and night 129 Brigade was expected to roll up the east flank on the Roer and 130 Brigade to attack west and open the way for Guards Armoured Division by first light next morning. It will thus be seen that whilst one brigade was attacking to the east, another would be attacking west, and the third engaged in a wide variety of tasks.

Planning started. Reconnaissances were carried out. Ammunition was dumped. The complexities became worse and worse. By 7th December the stage had been reached at which the original planning notes were ordered to be destroyed. (One copy, however, survived.) A traffic problem on the Heinsberg Road of monumental proportions obviously had to be solved. By 10th December 84 U.S. Division had been brought into the party and the battle postponed to the 14th. On the 11th it was put back to the 16th. The weather still further deteriorated. Finally, to the regret of no one, it was finally abandoned on the 12th.

12th Dec.

Field-Marshal Montgomery had in fact decided to give priority to the attack south-east from Nijmegen, which 30 Corps had planned in October, known as "Veritable." 12 Corps therefore took over the Geilenkirchen front on 13th December and Lieut.-General Horrocks and his headquarters, in the greatest secrecy, with formation signs on all vehicles blacked out and the famous Corps flash removed, moved back into Holland to replan the assault on the Reichswald. "Shears," an unloved and dubious infant which was never born, passed into an oblivion from which it is perhaps somewhat tactless to disinter it.

13th Dec.

The Division, gradually relieved of its responsibilities in the line by 52 (L.) Division, now withdrew to the area north-east of Maastricht as a preliminary to the long move north. Major-General Thomas turned his mind to training. At a conference held in the hideous castle of Amstenrade, he outlined an arduous programme of three weeks' training for the battle in the north, with 34 Tank Brigade and elements of 79 Armoured Division. In particular, he proposed to practise co-operation with crocodiles and kangaroos and the assault on pill-boxes. No aspect of training likely to add still further to the Division's battle efficiency and the instruction of its reinforcements was left unexplored.

As he spoke, however, a situation had begun to develop to the south which was to change the whole character of the campaign. Von Rundstedt had that very morning thrown the full weight of the Fifth and Sixth Panzer Armies and the Seventh Army against the extended U.S. VIII Corps in the Ardennes.

THE ARDENNES OFFENSIVE

By 17th December there was little doubt as to the scale of the 18th German offensive and fifteen divisions had been identified. Dis-Dec. quieting news from the American front reached the Division in its billets north-east of Maastricht. The Luftwaffe had emerged with the new ME262, which had proved itself faster than any Allied fighter. There were rumours of airborne landings. Nevertheless advanced parties departed for the Tilburg area on the morning of the 18th. During the day it became increasingly clear that Von Rundstedt intended to drive through Malmedy to Liége, cross the Maas and advance on Antwerp to cut off 21 Army Group from the U.S. Armies and to force the river in the south at Dinant and Namur so as to secure his southern flank. In fact, he had attacked with his entire striking force, the Sixth and Fifth Panzer Armies and the Seventh Army. The main blow had fallen on the U.S. VIII Corps and overwhelmed its widely extended divisions.

The Division's move to the north started before daylight on the 19th 19th. A new moon and a clear sky made driving easy. At the Berg Dec. bridge signs of anxiety on the part of the sentries and police became apparent. As the long column moved on through Lanklaer and Asch, ugly rumours were passed by stray American soldiers and depressed-looking civilians to the troops in their lorries.

For the purpose of controlling the movement to the north, Second Army had set up an elaborate organization with special communications for controlling formations whilst on the road. About 8 a.m., therefore, it was possible to divert brigade groups to the south with surprising ease. By 11.30 a.m. Divisional headquarters had opened at Herck la Ville, half-way between Diest and Hasselt; 130 Brigade had concentrated at Hasselt; 214 Brigade had halted around Bilsen, and 129 Brigade had been diverted to Neerglabeek, south of Bree.

It thus stood ready to strike due south should the enemy cross the
Maas between Liége and Namur, as seemed distinctly probable.   He
had in fact made a breach approximately 20 miles broad and 25 miles
deep in the defences of the First U.S. Army and showed signs of
preparing to swing north-west towards the Maas and Liége.

The effect on the Belgians in the little Flemish towns of the sudden
irruption of the Division in their midst was electric.   Once again at
the critical moment, British troops had come to their rescue.   They
were back on their age-old battle-ground.   After all, the Widow
Wadman, failing to locate Uncle Toby's wound on his person, at least
knew he received it in the north-west bastion at Namur.   Their spirits
rose.   Their Belgian enthusiasm and hospitality knew no bounds and
their trust was most moving.   "I have never seen troops so good as
yours," said one Burgomaster.   "Aussi jeunes, aussi gais, aussi
debonnaires. I have lived through two wars and seen many armies, but
I have never seen such good soldiers as these.   All will now be well."

At this very moment General Eisenhower at Verdun had initiated
the drive from the south which, in conjunction with the operations
in the north was eventually to bring the enemy to a standstill.   North
of the breach, the First and Ninth U.S. Armies had no mobile
reserve.   Field-Marshal Montgomery, however, had the whole of
30 Corps out of the line.   All normal communications between
General Bradley's Headquarters at Luxembourg and the headquarters of the Ninth and First U.S. Armies in the north had been
severed.   Clearly, only one solution was applicable—to place all
troops in the north under the Field-Marshal.

20th   This decision reached the Division in its concentration area be-
Dec.   tween Hasselt and Liége soon after daybreak on the 20th.   It was
passed from mouth to mouth in a form not apparently recorded in
any official account.   The story ran that General Eisenhower at his
headquarters in Versailles, had raised the telephone and said to the
Field-Marshal, "Say, will you take over the north while I settle this
mess in the South?"   This may or may not be true.   What is
certain is that the knowledge that the Field-Marshal was once more
in charge removed any anxiety with regard to the situation so far as
43 Division was concerned.   Major-General Thomas's reaction at
the briefing of liaison officers on this morning also is worthy of
record.   He opened the conference with the remark: "The Boche
has had the impertinence to attack"; and went on to state that the
chance of annihilating the enemy in the open had at last come.

The Field-Marshal himself appeared in the middle of the morning
in the market-square of Bilsen, where H.Q. 214 Brigade was established in the medieval Hôtel de Ville.   Here he was met by General
Sir Miles Dempsey, the Army Commander.   Both retired to the
brigadier's caravan for half an hour.   General Dempsey, possibly
the least publicized commander of the war, then departed.   It is

strange that one who not only looked like a great army commander but actually was and behaved like one, should be so little known. Like Germanicus, the whole world would have judged him capable of commanding had he never commanded. The briefing finished, the Field-Marshal accepted a cup of tea. He then gathered the troops nearby around the brigade intelligence officers' map at the tail of a truck and showed them how he proposed to use 30 Corps to bring the enemy to a standstill and destroy him should he cross the Maas. Since August, when he had ceased to command all the armies in North-west Europe, he had seemed to have lost some of his fire. On this morning, however, he was his old dynamic, supremely self-confident self. At last the chance had come to bring the war to a speedy and decisive conclusion. He had indeed every reason to feel confident. With a striking force of three infantry divisions, one armoured division and three armoured brigades, later to be joined by a fourth to fall on the enemy should he cross the Maas, he alone of the Army Group Commanders had at last a chance of striking an immediately effective and decisive blow.

Lieut.-General Horrocks, recalled from his planning at Boxtel in the north, accordingly decided to place a strong reconnaissance screen of the 43 Reconnaissance Regiment and the Household Cavalry along the Maas from Huy to Visé and ordered 53 Division to take up a defensive position on the River Dyle so as to block any advance towards Brussels. Guards Armoured Division and 43 Division on their left flank stood ready to pounce on the enemy should he succeed in forcing the river. In an Order of the Day he said, "This German attack is the best thing that could have possibly happened, because it gives us the chance to defeat the Germans on our ground without having first to penetrate the Siegfried Line complete with minefields, anti-tank ditches, etc. In fact, this last desperate effort of the Germans may shorten the war by several months. 30 Corps is in mobile reserve, well positioned after some rapid regrouping to deal with any enemy penetration north of the Maas. I want all ranks to realize that we are now starting one of the decisive battles of the war. If everyone plays his part and goes all out, the Germans will take a knock from which they will never recover. Christmas 1944 may go down to history as the turning-point in the final stage of the war; we may not be able to have our usual dinner, but we will hold our Christmas festivities afterwards when the Boche has been properly defeated."

From the night of the 20th, the Reconnaissance Regiment, with 112 Field Regiment, two troops of 333 Anti-tank Regiment and two companies of 7 Royal Hampshire under command, had covered the Maas by a series of O.Ps., holding possible crossing places with small detachments. All three squadrons were in line. Each eventually had a company of infantry under command—one for the defence of

21st Dec.

the bridge at Huy, one on the railway bridge on the western outskirts of Liége and one at Visé. The front was so wide that the guns of 112 Field Regiment had later to be supplemented by those of 121 Medium Regiment and a battery of 94 Field Regiment. Misunderstandings with the Americans with regard to Liége had to be cleared up—indeed, international rivalry as to who should have the honour of defending it became somewhat acute. The matter was amicably settled. The United States retained Liége—and its flying bombs!

To meet the new situation, 129 Brigade moved forward to Weert on the 20th and Tongres on the 21st. Divisional headquarters opened at Wellen. On the 23rd, 130 Brigade advanced to Waremme north of Huy. The Royal Engineers reconnoitred all the bridges between Huy and Visé to ensure that preparations for demolition were complete—detonators, however, were not put in. Orders were sent out to ensure that the ferries were tied up at night to the north bank and prepared for sinking should the enemy reach the river. Meanwhile, the troops remained at one hour's notice to move. This state of readiness in fact meant that all vehicles had to be packed ready to move, with the men at close call. As the days wore on, it proved increasingly irritating. As news filtered through from east of the Maas, officers were continually occupied in reconnaissance to meet possible new situations. The enemy was reported to have a force of "Brandenburgers" using captured Shermans. Further airborne landings were anticipated. So far as the Division was concerned, however, none of these bugbears appeared. Operations never went beyond the planning and rehearsal stage.

23rd
Dec. On the 23rd the sky cleared and the aircraft of Bomber Command in great force passed overhead. This impressive display of our air might more than any other factor convinced the Division that the German offensive was doomed to failure. In fact, by this date the situation showed growing Allied stability along the northern shoulders of the bulge. To the south, General Patton's hastily organized thrust to relieve 101 U.S. Airborne Division in Bastogne had got under way; 43 Division had seen this American division fight on the "Island" and they had heard of General Patton. No doubts existed therefore in the minds of the troops as to the certainty of a successful conclusion at Bastogne. So far as 30 Corps was concerned a battle on the Maas itself rather than behind it seemed the most likely possibility. Lieut.-General Horrocks therefore now prepared to defend it with Guards Armoured Division on the right and 43 Division on the left, and to push reconnaissance to the south and east of the far bank, backed by 29 Armoured Brigade. These revealed that the German armour had reached Ciney, 15 miles south-west of Namur and Rochefort, 12 miles east of the Maas. In fact this represented the high-water mark of the offensive. The tide from 25th December onwards was to flow the other way.

Although the Division was never actually committed to this decisive battle, the reaction of the troops to what seemed at first a very serious threat throws a curious light on the mentality of the British soldier. They undoubtedly felt that whilst in war battles may come at any time, Christmas still comes but once a year. All units had made extensive preparations for the feast. Not only had N.A.A.F.I. excelled itself, but regimental associations had seen to it that their troops should lack nothing on this day. Local livestock of a seasonable character was also to play its part. As the 25th approached the tension grew. Von Rundstedt and his Panzer armies the other side of the river took a back seat. Relief was intense when a signal message on the 23rd announced that "Christmas will be celebrated on the 25th December." The majority of the Division were therefore able to prepare for the great day. Cafés and halls were requisitioned and the quartermasters and the cooks took charge.

The Field-Marshal's personal Christmas message read out to all troops of the Division must be recorded.

"The forces of the British Empire in Western Europe spend Christmas 1944 in the field. But what a change has come over the scene since last Christmas! The supreme Battle of Normandy carried with it the liberation of France and Belgium. Last Christmas we were in England, expectant and full of hope; this Christmas we are fighting in Germany. The conquest of Germany remains.

"It would have needed a brave man to say on D-Day, 6th June, that in three months we would be in Brussels and Antwerp, having liberated nearly the whole of France and Belgium; and in six months we would be fighting in Germany, having driven the enemy back across his own frontiers.

"But this is what has happened.

"And we must not fail to give praise and honour where it is due: 'This was the Lord's doing and it is marvellous in our eyes.'

"At Christmas time, whether in our homes or fighting in the field, we like to sing the carols we learnt as children; and in truth this is indeed a link between us and our families and friends in the home country: since they are singing the same verses. The old words express exactly what we all feel today: 'Glory to God in the highest, and on earth peace, good will toward men.'

"That is what we are fighting for, that is what we all desire: on earth peace, good will toward men.

"And so today we sing the Christmas hymns full of hope and steadfast in our belief that we shall soon achieve our heart's desire.

"Therefore with faith in God and with enthusiasm for our cause and for the day of battle, let us continue the contest with stout hearts and with determination to conquer.

"And at this time, I send to each one of you my best wishes and my Christmas greetings.

"Wherever you may be, fighting in the front line, or working on the lines of communication or in the ports, I wish all of you good luck and a happy 1945. We are all one great team; together, you and I, we have achieved much; and together we will see the thing through to the end.

"Good luck to you all!"

When the Field-Marshal is dead—but not before, for he is an opponent in argument as formidable, biting and ruthless as the late Bernard Shaw—aspirants for cheap literary notoriety will probably single out his extreme Protestant piety as a target for facetious comment. It must therefore be made clear that every word of this message carried conviction straight to the heart of every front-line soldier of the Division and of the Army which carried British military prestige to its zenith on the Continent.

Fortunately, although ready for action, the majority of the Division succeeded in celebrating the day in accordance with tradition. The Christmas Number of the "Wyvern," produced by Major H. H. Evans of the Education Branch, duly appeared in light-hearted vein. Few editors of news-sheets can ever have worked under greater stress than Major Evans and his staff. Failure to deliver the daily issue brought instant complaint. Frequently they had not only to keep up with the clock but also the Administrative Area, which often had to move just at the moment the paper was due to go to press. Throughout the campaign it did much to dispel the hundred and one rumours which inevitably circulate during operations and to keep the troops informed of the progress of the war.

Thus Christmas Day, after all, so far as the Division was concerned, provided a pleasant interlude in a grim period of winter war. Extension of notice to move to three hours made discreet celebration possible. As events turned out, it was not to play an active part in the Ardennes battle. Had the Germans reached the Maas, there can be no doubt that all the advantages of morale, skill and armament would have been with 30 Corps and that even fewer of the Fifth and Sixth Panzer Armies would have limped back into Germany.

26th Dec. On the 26th orders were issued for extensive regrouping of the Second Army, designed to enable 30 Corps to intervene in the Ardennes. The operations which followed are part of the history of Major-General Thomas, who now assumed command of 30 Corps to enable Lieut.-General Horrocks to take a brief rest before the coming battle in the north, but not of the Division. As a temporary measure, it was now placed under 12 Corps and started its move back to the Maastricht area before dawn on the 27th.

CHAPTER XI

THE ROER TRIANGLE

January 1945

(See Sketch Map 14)

THE difference in atmosphere between 30 and 12 Corps immediately 27th
Dec. impressed the whole Division. Its task as the Corps reserve was to be prepared to counter-attack should the enemy take the offensive in the direction of the Maastricht bridges—as, indeed, he might well have done. It is now known that Von Rundstedt had actually contemplated an attack by four infantry, two Panzer and one Panzer Grenadier Divisions due south from the area of Gangelt and Sittard to start on 23rd December. In this operation it was apparently proposed to isolate Geilenkirchen and drive due south along the east bank of the Maas towards Liége. It is idle to speculate what the result would have been had this project been put into force. It would, however, certainly have caused both the British Second and the Ninth U.S. Armies considerable embarrassment in view of their dependence on the bridges at Maastricht, Borgharen and Berg.

Whilst the troops were quartered in quite comfortable billets 27th
Dec.–
10th
Jan. around Meersen, north-east of Maastricht, Brigadier S. B. Rawlins, C.C.R.A. 30 Corps and temporarily in command of the Division, ensured that no possible task which might confront it in its reserve role should go unstudied. The actual front was held with 52 (L.) Division on the right and 7 Armoured Division on the left. Defensive positions were reconnoitred in the Brunnsum area and a "layback" sited between the Corps boundary at Nuth and Elsloo on the Maas. Counter-attack plans were worked out in detail. In addition one brigade was expected to be ready to go to the aid of Ninth U.S. Army as far away as Eynatten, south-east of Aachen. These contingencies demanded considerable travel over the icy roads. Every possibility must have been envisaged and, what is more, committed to typescript. In fact, the records of these hypothetical operations planned during the first ten days of January are of formidable proportions but barren of interest. It is indeed astonishing what a volume of paper a staff can produce when faced with a situation in which the enemy is assumed to have the initiative and allowed to commit their misgivings to paper.

Except on 1st January, when 110 L.A.A. Regiment started the New Year well by shooting down six aircraft, including one ME262 (a jet) out of approximately fifty which attacked the Administrative Area, the weather was vile. Alternate frosts, snowfalls and thaws made driving most dangerous. Tracked vehicles, particularly tanks, were paralysed. On ice a tank is almost uncontrollable because the metal track provides no friction sideways, and so whenever it gets on a camber it slides until it hits the first piece of resistance, be it pavement, house or car. It was grotesque to see these great elephants with spinning tracks fail to climb even the little slopes of the camber of the road, slide away into the gutter and then stop. 6 Guards Tank Brigade, under the command of the Division, were reduced for several days to practical impotence.

Despite the snow and sleet and the digging of defensive positions in the back gardens of the startled burghers around Brunnsum some training was carried out. One unit at least managed to inoculate its reinforcements for the coming battles. The procedure adopted is intriguing. The reinforcements dug slits, which they then occupied. The mortar platoon then fired sixty 3-inch mortar bombs within seventy-five yards of them. After this treatment it was considered that "they would meet enemy fire with the maximum equanimity which is possible in any human being." Another unit held a tactical exercise without troops in a snowstorm. Life in the Division was hard at times, but it was never dull.

The troops social contacts around Brunnsum continued to flourish. They engaged in snowball fights with the children and saw the New Year in with the parents. A good deal of food and practically all the sweet ration undoubtedly reached the hungry Dutch. Indeed, when the war ended, some men even came back and married the girls.

11th Jan. On the 11th the Division moved back to the line in relief of 52 (L.) Division; 214 Brigade took over the right brigade sector astride the Heinsberg road and 129 Brigade came in on their left in the sector from Hatterath to Hastenrath north of Gangelt. On the following day 130 Brigade moved into immediate reserve along the road from Gangelt to Geilenkirchen. All were once more on familiar ground. The anti-tank guns handed over in early December were still in position. The front, however, was now quiet in the extreme. The main problem to be faced was how to keep alive in the bitter frost, which on several nights reached 20 degrees below zero (Centigrade). Automatics froze and had to be treated with low-test oil. Water cans solidified and melted snow had to be used for washing. Self-heating soups were provided. Boots and socks were removed twice daily and feet massaged. All the men were extremely well-clothed. Every rifleman had a sniper suit and there were ample supplies of sweaters, scarves, gloves and warm underclothing. In consequence they remained surprisingly well. 214 Brigade actually remained in the front line without relief for sixteen days. There were practically no sick. Constant patrolling in white suits kept their minds occupied and their bodies exercised. A bus service to the baths at Brunnsum for a hundred men a day from each unit provided a welcome break from the boredom of the line.

The slightest sign of activity, offensive or otherwise, on the part of the enemy brought swift retribution. In fact, he generally showed little inclination to reveal himself—an attitude which in the circumstances can be well understood. An American gunner officer, with apparently an unlimited call on guns of tremendous calibre, became an exceedingly popular visitor around Tripsrath. He was always ready to engage any target suggested to him and provided endless entertainment. Many will remember care-free hours spent in his company deleting the more prominent German architectural features from the winter landscape. When the Americans co-operate, they do so in a big way.

"BLACKCOCK"

The counter-offensive in the Ardennes had merely imposed a delay on the project of continuing the attack throughout the winter, so that when spring came the enemy should be battle weary. By the first week in January the initiative had been recaptured and it was accordingly decided that "Shears," the operation planned by 30 Corps in December to destroy the enemy in Roer triangle, should be remounted by 12 Corps in the latter half of the month. So long as the enemy remained east of the Roer, there was always the possibility that he might put in a quick attack through Sittard, and in any case the ground up to the Roer would provide a firm base from which to stage the proposed advance to the Rhine by the American armies.

The battlefield lay in full view of the high ground east of the Roer, and since November the enemy had spared no effort to strengthen his position. Three main lines of defence had been constructed. The front line comprised a continuous length of trenches and weapon pits, with trip wires and mines in front. A reserve line ran parallel with it 1,000 yards behind. The second main defences began in the Siegfried Line at Utterath and passed through Waldfeucht to link up with the Juliana Canal at Echt. The third main line was incomplete and extended only from the Siegfried Line at Dremmen to Haaren. The area east of Heinsberg, being the Siegfried Line, had been made extremely strong. It was a mass of pillboxes and trenches. West of this area the defences were less formidable. Two divisions, 183 and 176, were disposed on this front. The former, facing Tripsrath, covered approximately 12,000 yards of front. 176 Division, however, was responsible for more than twice this distance. The enemy had in fact laid out his resources to meet attack primarily from our right flank, as planned in "Shears." It was known that he had about 90 field guns, 36 medium and 187.5-mm. guns. No tactical reserve of infantry or armour existed, nor was any likely to appear in view of the toll taken in the withdrawal in the Ardennes.

Events were to prove the wisdom of Lieut.-General Ritchie's decision to take advantage of the advanced positions on the left for the initial assault. The success of the operations clearly depended on the ability of the armour, especially the flails, crocodiles and kangaroos, of 79 Armoured Division to negotiate the ground. Frosty conditions, in fact, were essential. The weather, however, had so far displayed alternating conditions of frost and thaw. In addition, the bitter cold was likely to impose a severe strain on the endurance of the hardiest troops. In the evolution of his plan "Blackcock" Lieut.-General Ritchie therefore designed the operation in stages which could be advanced or postponed according to the vagaries of the weather. In any case, dependence on an air plan was out of the question.

The tasks given to the three divisions involved, 7 Armoured, 43 and 52 (L.), were given code names as shown in sketch map 14. Each task started from the north and west and was followed by an advance from the south. In this way, the villages on the front were to be captured and cleared by a series of turning movements which struck at the rear of the enemy troops. It will be seen that 7 Armoured Division on the left was allotted "Angel," "Dolphin" and "Globe"; 52 (L.) Division in the centre "Crown," "Bear," "Eagle" and "Fleece"; whilst to 43 Division on the right fell "Hart," "Jug" and "Kettle." The origin of these inspiring names is obscure. The whole operation was planned to take ten days. A formidable plan of artillery support was arranged for each phase involving no less than five to eight field regiments, three to six medium regiments and a varying number of heavy and super-heavy regiments. In fact, 183 and 176 Divisions were to be blasted off the face of the earth bit by bit at intervals dictated partly by the weather and partly by the time necessary to concentrate the armour and artillery for each phase.

Planning within 43 Division, assisted by excellent air photographs, started on 11th January. The execution of the Division's tasks depended on successful progress by 52 (L.) and 7 Armoured Divisions. It was not expected therefore that it could intervene until the third or fourth day. In brief, 130 Brigade was made responsible for "Hart" and later the second part of "Jug"; 129 Brigade for the first part of "Jug"; and 214 Brigade for "Kettle." The Divisional artillery in the area of the Gangelt road was to support all the attacks in conjunction with all the other guns of the corps. Elaborate "Pepperpot" plans were worked out by 8 Middlesex.

Extreme cold and slashing rain postponed the start of the battle. However, an exceptionally heavy bombardment on the left of the

26. Bren carriers of 8 Middlesex Regiment in Operation " Blackcock," 21st January, 1945

27. Flooded streets on the Division's only axis—Kranenburg, 13th February, 1945

division at dawn on the 16th disclosed the fact that the offensive was at last under way. In spite of the appalling weather 7 Armoured had advanced 8,000 yards in the direction of Montfort by the 18th and 52 (L.) Division on the same day had completed the occupation of the enemy front line between Breberen and Havert on the immediate left of 43 Division. Further advances were contemplated for the 20th for both of these divisions. The situation was at last ripe for 43 Division to intervene. So far in the operations, mines and the bad going had given more trouble than the enemy's troops, whose resistance, although active at times, could not be described as obstinate.

THE ADVANCE TO THE ROER
20th–25th January

The corps main effort on 20th January took the form of an attack due north from the Breberen area by the 52 (L.) Division on to Bocket and Waldfeucht. 4 Somerset Light Infantry, the left forward battalion of 129 Brigade, were quick to take advantage of the fluid situation which had developed on their front and in intermittent snow and sleet attacked and captured Schummer Quartier without resistance. At 1.30 p.m. a reconnaissance patrol under Lieutenant Dodd reported that Langbroich was unoccupied apart from three civilians, one male and two female. It had been intended that 130 Brigade should capture this village on the following day. Major J. L. Brind, who was commanding in the absence of Lieut.-Colonel Lipscomb on leave, saved them the trouble by advancing and taking over the village. On the left flank 52 (L.) Division's attack went well and 5 Wiltshire moved forward to relieve them of responsibility for Breberen soon after midday.

130 Brigade launched 4 Dorset against Schier Waldenrath at first light on the 21st. The bombardment and "pepperpot" were on an impressive scale. The battalion moved forward in kangaroos of 1 Canadian A.P.C. Regiment; the flails flogged the minefields and the tanks of 4 Coldstream Guards poured a continuous stream of fire into the houses. Opposition was light—most of the enemy were dead or had escaped, for only twelve prisoners were taken. Booby-traps and mines were the main problems to be overcome. By the early afternoon the operation had been completed and the kangaroos withdrawn to ferry forward 7 Royal Hampshire on the morrow. 5 Dorset moved forward in relief of 4 Somerset Light Infantry at Langbroich. The stage was thus set for the attack next day on Putt and Waldenrath.

Major Rooke's attack with the 7 Royal Hampshire was a triumph of planning and skilful handling. Supported by an impressive artillery bombardment and a terrifying "pepperpot" provided by thirty Churchills of 3 Tank Scots Guards in a row blasting with

20th Jan.

21st Jan.

22nd Jan.

14

their 75's, the battalion thrust forward in the kangaroos. The enemy in Putt could not face the flames of the supporting crocodiles and the village was soon in our hands. Soon after midday the battalion had fought its way into Waldenrath and taken over 200 prisoners at a cost of only 30 casualties. Thus satisfactorily, 130 Brigade completed Phase "Hart." It was now 129 Brigade's turn to continue the offensive by embarking on Phase "Jug."

23rd Jan. By early next morning the armoured column of 4 Wiltshire had formed up in Birgden ready for the attack on Straeten. With its kangaroos, crocodiles, flails and the supporting tanks of No. 2 Squadron, Grenadier Guards it made an impressive array. The troops, all clothed in snow-suits, white-painted gas capes or sheets taken from the houses in Birgden, were in great heart. The bombardment started with an appalling crash in which rockets, Bofors, medium machine-guns and mortars all played their part. The column moved forward. Unlocated mines at the exit from Waldenrath caused a long delay and a rain of heavy shells descended on the waiting column. Eventually these were removed and the advance resumed. On approaching Straeten the companies debussed, and, supported by a stream of Besa fire and belching flame from the crocodiles, fell upon the enemy in their slits before they had time to put their heads up. Soon all companies were on their objectives and mopping up began. Over 400 of the enemy surrendered. Careful planning and skilful execution thus once more brought their reward.

Meanwhile 4 Somerset Light Infantry had moved up to Waldenrath, ready to attack Scheifendahl, 2,000 yards ahead. Only sufficient kangaroos to mount one company had arrived by the time the attack was due to begin. B Company therefore took them, whilst D Company had to advance on their right on foot when the barrage opened. Unfortunately seven of the eleven kangaroos were blown up on mines during the advance. However, the assault on the village, when once under way, met with complete success. With Scheifendahl in his possession by 3 p.m., Major Brind decided to push on to Erpen and an hour later resumed the attack with A Company in kangaroos. The 1,500 yards of open country ahead were soon crossed and Erpen captured. The operation had been an outstanding success; 150 prisoners, four infantry guns, two mortars and two 88-mm. guns were taken. By nightfall, the village had been completely cleared and a determined counter-attack beaten off.

23rd–24th Jan. To the north 52 (L.) Division had also had a successful day and cleared Aphoven. During the night it pushed ahead and captured Heinsberg.

24th Jan. 129 Brigade resumed the advance the following afternoon. On the left, C Company of 4 Somerset Light Infantry seized Schleiden without difficulty. On their right, 5 Wiltshire after a heavy preliminary bombardment moved forward over the snow-covered fields on to Utterath. The formidable column, in its hundred armoured vehicles, surged forward. The sight of this mass of tanks, kangaroos, crocodiles and carriers proved too much for the enemy, and within a few minutes the village had fallen without a blow. There was only one British casualty. Prisoners continued to come in throughout the night. Little doubt now remained that, as far as 183 and 176 Divisions were concerned, the battle was over.

"Blackcock" thus ended in an atmosphere of anti-climax. Icy conditions and mines alone delayed the armoured column of 5 Dorset in its advance on Schalhausen. 4 Dorset followed and took Grebben. By last light, 7 Royal Hampshire had occupied Dremmen and pushed on to Porseln. 214 Brigade, which had occupied a ring-side seat throughout the battle, prodded its way through the minefields unopposed to Nirm, Kraudorf and Randerath, arresting a few depressed stragglers *en route*. Contact was made with 102 U.S. Division, who had had a similar easy passage on their right. 25th Jan.

The night, otherwise quiet, was enlivened by an element of comedy. The air photographs issued on a lavish scale before the attack, revealed what was apparently a huge crater on the Heinsberg road. Much Sapper effort had therefore been put into the construction of a very large Bailey bridge on sledges and named, with no great subtlety, "Sydney" after the famous bridge in Australia. The unfortunate sapper in charge of this unwieldy contraption duly arrived and drove up and down the road all night, at no small risk to himself from mines. To his astonishment, no crater could be found. Seldom in the history of the campaign can a spot of dust on a camera lens have caused so much inconvenience to the branch of the Army least celebrated for its sense of humour.

On the extreme left of the corps front 7 Armoured Division finally brought the operations to an end by occupying Posterholt on the 26th. 130 Brigade established company groups in Randerath, Dremmen and Schalhausen and based its defences primarily on the reverse slopes to the west, as the villages in the Roer valley were in full enemy view and the smoke haze which had so far been maintained by 112 Pioneer Company could not be continued indefinitely. The remainder of the Division moved back to the Brunnsum area, to be followed on the 29th by 130 Brigade. 26th–27th Jan.

Regarded as a mopping-up operation on the grand scale "Blackcock" was a great success. As the enemy had no reserves and displayed fighting spirit only on isolated occasions, it cannot, at least so far as 43 Division was concerned, be regarded as a great victory. Indeed, an operation in which the enemy allows himself to be reduced piecemeal and almost at leisure can hardly be described as a battle. If any unit deserves to be singled out for special distinction, it is 1 Canadian Armoured Personnel Carrier Regiment, who day after day, with little time for rest or maintenance, conveyed the infantry 29th Jan.

through minefields and over ice and snow towards their objectives. These stout-hearted Canadians gained the admiration of everyone who came in contact with them.

Despite the damnable weather, the Division's morale remained high. Sick rates were surprisingly low. The reinforcements found their feet in the Divisional team. Above all, the experience gained in co-operation with the assault engineers, crocodiles and kangaroos of 79 Armoured Division was to prove invaluable in the bitter fighting which lay only a week or two ahead.

28th
Dec.
The imposition of wireless silence on the morning of the 28th did not prevent the news of Major-General Thomas's return from his successful command of 30 Corps in the Ardennes from almost instantly reaching all ranks of the Division. It brought with it a perceptible feeling of increased confidence and relief. Until his iron grip was removed, few had realized how much they depended on his judgment and strong will. Although personalities play a greater part in war than in almost any other human activity, it is not easy in a man's lifetime to tell the whole truth. A history of the 43 Division without an appreciation of Major-General Thomas's character would be tame and dull—in fact, it would never rise above the level of a paraphrased war diary or a series of congested slabs of military journalese. Personalities in a man's lifetime are apt to be misinterpreted. Fortunately, Xenophon, 2,300 years ago, described the character of his commander, Clearcus the Spartan. The similarity between this ancient Greek soldier and the Commander of the 43 Division is sufficiently striking to justify quotation. This is what Xenophon says of Clearcus:

"This seems to me to be the record of a man who was devoted to war. He could have lived in peace without incurring any reproaches or any harm, but he chose to make war. He could have lived a life of ease, but he preferred a hard life with warfare. He could have had money and security, but he chose to make the money he had less by engaging in war.

"All this shows how devoted he was to war. As for his great qualities as a soldier, they appear in the facts that he was fond of adventure, ready to lead an attack on the enemy by day or night, and that when he was in an awkward position, he kept his head, as everyone agrees who was with him anywhere. It was said that he had all the qualities of leadership which a man of his sort could have. He had an outstanding ability for planning means by which an army could get supplies, and seeing that they appeared; and he was well able to impress on those who were with him that Clearcus was a man to be obeyed. He achieved this result by his toughness. He had a forbidding appearance and a harsh voice. His punishments were severe ones and were sometimes inflicted in anger. . . . With him punishment was a matter of principle, for he thought

HITLER'S LAST THROW

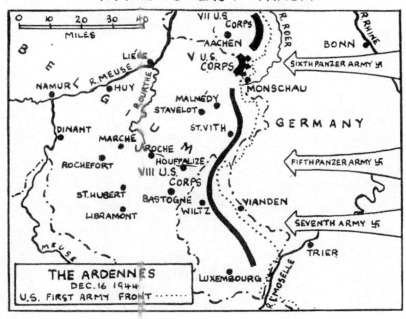

OPERATION BLACKCOCK

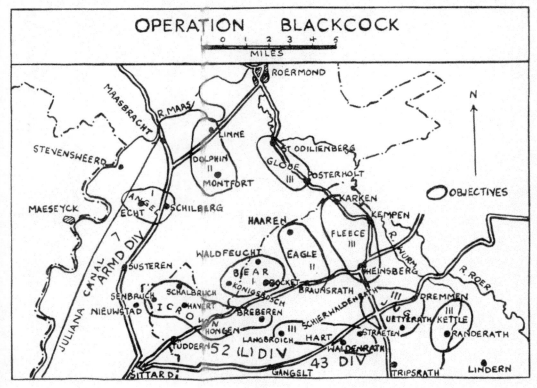

that an army without discipline was good for nothing; indeed, it is reputed that he said that a soldier ought to be more frightened of his commander than of the enemy if he was going to turn out one who could keep a good guard, or abstain from doing harm to his own side, or go into battle without second thoughts. So it happened that in difficult positions the soldiers would give him complete confidence and wished for no one better. On these occasions they said his forbidding look seemed positively cheerful and his toughness appeared as confidence in the face of the enemy, so that it was no longer toughness to them, but something to make them feel safe. . . . Once they began to win victories with him, one could see how important were the factors which made his men into good soldiers. As a commander, then, this was what he was like; but he was said not to be very fond of serving under anybody else's command. At the time of his death, he was about fifty years old."

It is pleasant to reflect that whilst Clearcus had his head cut off by Tissaphernes, his re-incarnation has reached the Army Council.*

* Those interested in this classical digression will find in the character of Proxenus the Boetian a further striking parallel with several British commanders in 1940-42. Ignorance of Greek need be no obstacle—pages 90 to 92 of Xenophon's *The Persian Expedition* (Penguin Books) give all the facts in simple English, and if quoted can be guaranteed to give an air of profound reflection and scholarship to even the most platitudinous lectures.

CHAPTER XII

THE REICHSWALD

8th February to 8th March

(See Sketch Maps 15, 16 and 17)

"VERITABLE"

ALTHOUGH the enemy's offensive in the Ardennes had imposed delay, the broad pattern of Allied strategy remained unchanged. General Eisenhower envisaged the operations designed to lead to Germany's collapse as falling into three phases : first the destruction of the enemy forces west of the Rhine and closing with the river ; second the forcing of the crossings of the Rhine ; and finally the advance into the heart of Reich. The time had now arrived to launch the first phase, for on the eastern front the Russians had started an immense attack on 12th January and before the end of the month had crossed the German frontier.

The Allied plan visualized a series of blows along the entire length of the front. The campaign was to begin in the north. Here Field-Marshal Montgomery, with the Ninth U.S. Army under his command in addition to the British and Canadian forces, decided to develop two formidable thrusts which would converge on the Rhine opposite Wesel. From the Nijmegen salient, the First Canadian Army was to launch Operation "Veritable" between the Maas and the Rhine south-eastwards through the Reichswald Forest and the northern tip of the Siegfried Line. From the Roer, the Ninth U.S. Army, with twelve divisions, was to stage operation "Grenade," thrusting north-east with the object of linking up with First Canadian Army's advance on a line from Geldern to Wesel. The Field-Marshal insisted that once the battle started it was to be continued by day and night until the Germans were pushed back east of the Rhine. The Ninth U.S. Army's advance was scheduled to begin two days after the opening of "Veritable" after the capture of the Roer dams by First U.S. Army. In fact, owing to the opening of the sluices and the raising of the level of Roer by 4 feet, it had to be delayed for a fortnight, thus forcing First Canadian Army to meet the full impact of most of the available German reserves.

The build up for "Veritable" was enormous, and indeed, for a time in February, General Crerar was to control thirteen divisions, nine of which were from the United Kingdom. The weight of artillery was particularly impressive. More than a thousand guns, one-third of which were mediums, heavies or super heavies, were to bring down a volume of fire equal to, if not greater than, that supporting any British army during the war. Air support was also planned on a maximum scale. The Second Tactical Air Force, with a potential strength of 1,000 fighters and fighter bombers, was to provide close support. Bomber Command also was to employ up to 1,000 heavy bombers in the immediate battle area and further assistance was expected from the U.S.A.A.F. A feature of this overwhelming offensive in the air was to be the complete destruction of the three German towns vital to the enemy's defences, Cleve, Goch and Emmerich.

General Crerar, in brief, planned the battle in three phases. In the first phase, 30 Corps under Lieut.-General Sir Brian Horrocks was given the task of clearing the Reichswald and making good the line from Gennep via Asperden to Cleve. In the second phase, General Simonds, 2 Canadian Corps, was to come in on the left and advance abreast with 30 Corps to a line from Weeze to Emmerich. Finally, a general advance was to take place to the line from Geldern to Xanten.

As 30 Corps' advance had to take place between the Maas and the Rhine, there was no room for manœuvre and no scope for cleverness. The way had literally to be blasted open through three defensive systems, the centre of which was the Siegfried Line. North of the road from Kranenburg to Cleve the area had been flooded. The only other good road was that from Mook via Gennep to Hekkens, which unfortunately was completely dominated from the south edge of the Reichswald and it could not be used until the forest had been cleared. The key to the situation therefore was the Materborn gap, a narrow neck of high ground between the Reichswald and the town of Cleve. This feature dominated Cleve. Once through the gap, a certain amount of elbow-room would be available. General Horrocks hoped to break through the Materborn Gap before it could be closed by the German reserves, to flood the plain east of the Reichswald with troops, and then, if his luck held, seize the bridge over the Rhine at Wesel. Had the thaw not set in he might have succeeded.

The initial assault was to be carried out by five divisions in the order from right to left, 51 (H.), 53 (W.), 15 (3), 2 Canadian, 3 Canadian. Guards Armoured and 43 Division constituted his reserve. To enumerate the tasks of all the assaulting divisions would be tedious and of little interest. That of 15 (S.) Division must however be grasped. They were ordered to capture Kranenburg, breach the Siegfried defences north of the Reichswald, capture the high ground at Nutterden, and then seize the key to the whole situation, the Materborn feature. Finally they were to clear and hold Cleve.

When the Materborn feature had been captured, it was intended that 43 Division should pass through on the second day of the battle, capture Goch and then exploit in a south-easterly direction by seizing in succession Weeze, Kervelaer and Geldern. Guards Armoured Division were to follow and exploit generally in the direction of Wesel on the left flank.

1st–3rd Feb. The assembly of this vast force for the coming battle presented a most intricate problem. The impression had to be given to the enemy that an attack was intended over the River Maas from the S'Hertogenbosch area and, at the same time, all formations had to link up with their armour, especially the unit of 79 Armoured Division. 43 Division's move to the Herenthals area east of Antwerp was complete by February 3rd when Major-General Thomas at an "O" Group first revealed the task which lay ahead. As the operations of the Division would be dependent on the progress of the remainder of 30 Corps, it was impossible for him at this stage to produce a final plan. He did, however, visualize an advance on a two-brigade front after passing the Materborn, with 129 Brigade Group on the left and TAC.H.Q., 214 and 130 Brigade Groups on the right. Brigade commanders withdrew to consider, with the aid of air photographs of Goch, Weeze, Kervelaer and Geldern and a vast number of maps, the many possibilities which the development of the battle might offer.

Meanwhile the troops made the most of the hospitality of the Belgians and watched the continual procession of V weapons passing overhead *en route* to Antwerp.

7th Feb. On the 7th the Division moved to a tightly packed concentration area between Eindhoven and Helmond. Tactical Headquarters, including H.Q. 8 Armoured Brigade, had already preceded them to Nijmegen during the night and the Divisional artillery had gone into action in the familiar area of Mook ready to support 51 Division on the following day.

By the evening the immense concentration of troops was complete. Despite the bad-weather forecast, which must inevitably restrict the programme for close air support, General Crerar decided that his intentions to attack could be concealed no longer and ordered the battle to begin the following morning.

8th Feb. At 5 a.m. therefore, whilst it was still dark, the greatest artillery barrage in British history opened up on the German positions. It literally deafened everyone in the neighbourhood of the guns for several hours. The night was lit by flashes of every colour and the tracer of the Bofers guns weaved patterns in the sky. It was light enough to read a book. Into this inferno the tanks of the armoured brigades, the 8 Middlesex and three other machine-gun battalions poured an unceasing stream of fire. Dawn came with low cloud heralding several days' continuous rain. It was impossible to see more than eight hundred yards ahead in the swirling eddies of smoke which drifted over the battlefield. At 7.40 a.m. the bombardment

ceased for ten minutes and a smoke screen was laid down. This
lured the enemy to put down defensive fire and enabled the Survey
Regiment to locate the batteries which were still active.

At half-past ten, the four assaulting divisions attacked. Numbed
by the bombardment, the enemy had in many cases lost the will to
fight. The barrage moved slowly eastwards as the troops and tanks
moved forward. In spite of mines and the appalling mud, by midnight all the day's objectives had been taken. Many of the tanks,
however, had sunk in the wet ground. 15 (S.) Division took
Kranenburg without their support. Most of the flails and crocodiles
bogged down. In the Reichswald Forest, along appalling tracks,
the 53 Welsh Division fought its way forward. On the right flank
51 Highland Division struck strong opposition. At the other end of
the line, 2 Canadian Division took Wyler and Zifflich.

Meanwhile, 129 and 214 Brigades and the Reconnaissance Regiment had moved up from Eindhoven and Helmond to the southern
outskirts of Nijmegen, where in the Colonial Barracks and the suburb
of Driehuizen they spent a night under most congested conditions.

During the afternoon the units of 8 Armoured Brigade and the
companies of 8 Middlesex, their task in the "Pepperpot" completed,
joined their brigades. 130 Brigade arrived on the morrow with
Main and Rear Divisional Headquarters.

9th
Feb.

Although 15 Scottish Division had taken all its objectives on the
8th, the tracks in its sector had completely collapsed by the end of
the day and the only way forward became the main road from
Kranenburg to Cleve. Pushing ahead throughout the night in the
face of mines, road blocks and trenches, 44 Brigade under Brigadier
Cumming-Bruce somehow or other maintained the advance. The
Frasselt ditch was carried at dawn. The brigade passed on towards
Nutterden and stormed the great bunkers of the Siegfried Line at
Hingstberg and Wolfsberg. It was now noon.

At this stage Major-General C. M. Barber, the commander of
15th (S.) Division, had intended to push through his other two
brigades to capture the "Materborn feature." Through no fault of
his or of his troops, the attack was already eleven hours behind
schedule. Indeed, 44 Brigade, superbly led, had already surmounted
difficulties which would have defeated less determined troops.
There was no hope, whatever, in face of the practically complete
collapse of the tracks in rear, of deploying the two reserve brigades
before nightfall. Major-General Barber therefore ordered Brigadier
Cumming-Bruce to seize the Materborn.

The "Materborn feature" in fact consists of two hills about a mile
west of Cleve and the village of Materborn. The lower and more
westerly of these features runs roughly north and south through
Esperance. Against this Esperance feature Brigadier Cumming-
Bruce sent the Royal Scots. The higher and more easterly feature

runs north and south through Bresserberg. Against it the brigadier sent the K.O.S.B. in kangaroos. At the same time the Gordons advanced from Nutterden towards Donsbreuggen. Soon after 3 p.m. the enemy had been overcome on both these features just in time to forestall elements of 7 Parachute Division, the first of the German reinforcing divisions, which had been sent to occupy it. 15 Scottish Division, even though they did not completely dominate the Materborn Gap, had gained a decisive success. Major-General Barber accordingly ordered up his Reconnaissance Regiment from Nijmegen to probe eastward and find a route through Cleve for 43 Division.

In the distant future, students of this history (if any) will infer that not the least attractive characteristic of the Corps Commander, Lieut.-General Sir Brian Horrocks, was his optimism. The 15 (S.) Division had just—but only just—gained the crest of Materborn. Their tanks, flails, crocodiles, carriers, and wheeled vehicles of all sorts lay inert in the mud all over the battlefield. Only one usable road led to Cleve, and this was jammed, nose to tail, with the transport not only of 15 (S.) Division but also of quite a representative proportion of First Canadian Army. The floods north of this surviving axis were rapidly rising. It was raining and the weather forecast was bad. Nevertheless as night closed in, he ordered 43 Division to advance as originally planned, through the Materborn Gap to Goch, Weeze, Kervelaer and beyond.

The spirit which animated this dramatic decision is beyond criticism. The need to debouch into the open country south of Cleve before the enemy could intervene effectively with his reserves was urgent and justified the obvious risks. In fact, however, his decision was to produce in the next forty-eight hours a situation unrivalled in its exasperating complexity throughout the campaign.

It should not be thought by posterity that what may be considered an error of judgment on his part affected his prestige with his commanders and troops in any way. He himself almost invariably displayed extreme generosity and understanding towards mere tactical error. What he could never forgive was reluctance to close with the enemy. Those under him felt the same.

CLEVE

10th–12th February

(See Sketch Map 15)

9th Feb. Night had closed in when 4 Wiltshire Regiment, the leading battalion of 129 Brigade Group, passed the traffic post on the eastern outskirts of Nijmegen and took the road to Kranenburg and Cleve. For the first time since Normandy most of the wheeled vehicles had been left behind and the troops were riding "quick lift" on the tanks of the Sherwood Rangers and the other tracked vehicles. It was bitterly cold, with spasms of icy rain. An air raid on Nijmegen enlivened the departure of the long column. To the north an occasional gun flash lit up the great expanse of water north of the road. Spasmodic shelling from long-range guns caused splashes in the surrounding bog. Now and then a few German aircraft bombed the road by the light of flares. Here and there, a few searchlights cast a vague, intermittent light over the desolation. At last, about midnight, the ruins of Kranenburg were reached. Here the roads were awash. The floods were obviously rising fast. The Germans had, in fact, blown the Rhine dykes. Lieut.-Colonel J. E. L. Corbyn, the commanding officer of 4 Wiltshire, after passing Kranenburg found the headquarters of a brigade of 15 (S.) Division and obtained the first definite information of the situation ahead. He was told that their forward troops were two miles short of Cleve and that the defences were thought to be disorganized by the heavy raid on the night of the 7th. As far as he could ascertain, the main road into Cleve was definitely blocked, but 15 Scottish Reconnaissance Regiment had actually found a way through by a secondary road branching off east of Nutterden through a gap in the woods. He therefore decided to take this route, and with a troop of 15 Scottish Reconnaissance Regiment and one of his own platoons personally led the head of the column forward into the darkness ahead. After passing Nutterden, the head of the column eventually reached the woods. A Spandau suddenly came to life. The leading troops were off their vehicles in a flash. Lieut.-Colonel Corbyn found that the road ahead was blocked by a fallen tree. A fierce battle now developed in the darkness. C Company closed with the enemy and, supported by the tanks, overwhelmed him in a confused but successful battle. The road block was carried and D Company moved forward on foot. The column pushed on in the darkness, the tanks firing into every house. Progress was slow owing to the gigantic craters. However, just as dawn was breaking at 5.20 a.m. the head of the battalion had reached the park on the south-eastern outskirts of Cleve, near the point where the roads from Goch and Bedburg join. Behind it, the battalion stood strung out amongst the chaotic confusion of the ruins of the south-eastern suburbs of the town.

Lieut.-Colonel Kenrick, the acting brigade commander, now decided to order 4 Wiltshire to halt where they were in a position of all-round defence and to advance due south with the remainder of his brigade, 4 Somerset Light Infantry on the left and 5 Wiltshire on their right.

It is almost impossible to describe the sanguinary and confused fighting which now broke out amongst the huge bomb-craters and ruins of Cleve. In fact, the main German defences were sited on the slopes above Materborn and the arrival of 129 Brigade in Cleve itself had taken them completely by surprise. The fighting raged all day. Tigers and Panthers fought a dozen isolated battles in the streets. Brigade Headquarters itself became involved in the fighting, in which the G.S.O.3, Captain McGowan, was killed. Three of the company commanders of 5 Wiltshire, returning from an "O" Group, became casualties. The fighting around the cemetery on the Materborn road reached unexampled ferocity. Shelling and mortaring became intense. Throughout the day 4 Somerset Light Infantry fought one of their bitterest and most prolonged actions of the war. It is impossible to say which was the more admirable, the courage and tenacity of the many small groups in their isolated battles or the imperturbable skill of their commanding officers, Lieut.-Colonels Lipscomb and Corbyn and Major Hyde, who eventually brought the situation under control despite all the efforts of fresh German troops of the highest quality who had now intervened.

When the dawn broke, wet and cold, it is hard to decide which of the three major-generals, British and German, in the neighbourhood of Cleve faced the more frustrating situation. Major-General Fiebig, the commander of the German 84 Division, which had so far borne the brunt of the battle, found himself personally involved in the fighting with 129 Brigade which had superimposed itself around his headquarters in Cleve. He was apparently endeavouring to deploy west of Cleve and Materborn what was left of his own division and 6 Para. Division, supported by tanks and S.P. guns of 116 Panzer Division. These fresh troops had only just arrived and found themselves faced by a situation as vague and confusing as that confronting 129 Brigade. Both sides had reacted with equal violence.

Major-General Thomas with his Tactical Headquarters, following the tail of 129 Brigade, had reached Nutterden. Behind him, nose to tail, 214 Brigade Group stood strung out along the road leading back to Kranenburg. 130 Brigade Group was still in Nijmegen. On his right, 53 (W.) Division were vaguely reported to be in the northern tip of the Reichswald Forest around the Stoppelberg, gravely handicapped by the complete collapse of the communications behind them. Vague and alarming reports of fighting in Cleve enabled no clear picture of the situation in the town itself to be formed for many hours.

It had been agreed with Major-General Barber that whatever part of 43 Division was left on the main road would pull into the side with its head at Nutterden from 8 a.m. to 10 a.m. to enable 227 Brigade of 15 Scottish Division to move up and finish the capture of the Materborn feature to the north, and to proceed with its original task of clearing Cleve. Accordingly when eight o'clock arrived, 214 Brigade Group duly did its best to pull off the road, using every possible side lane. 227 Brigade of 15 (S.) Division now arrived from the south, led by the Argylls. 214 Brigade however, with all the goodwill in the world, found it a physical impossibility properly to clear the road. A traffic jam of huge and bewildering proportions rapidly developed and it was not until after endless delays that the Scottish column eventually reached the main road. The reconnaissance group of the Scots Guards did eventually get through the jam and push on to the Cleverburg, where it was held up. Finally the Argylls decided to go through on foot and reached the Materborn at nightfall. The Gordons slowly pushed through on their north flank towards Donsbruggen. The frightful traffic congestion around Nutterden, which lasted all day, thus practically completely frustrated all Major-General Barber's attempts to carry out the task he had been ordered to perform.

The position of Major-General Thomas with his Tactical Headquarters in the heart of the traffic jam at Nutterden was unenviable. All communications with 129 Brigade had broken down. The enemy started to shell the main road. General Thomas had hoped to start the day with 214 Brigade on the right of 129 Brigade on the road from Materborn to Cleve. Instead, this brigade was almost hopelessly entangled in the tight mass of transport stretching back to Kranenburg. During the night, 15 (S.) Reconnaissance Regiment had found a just usable track leading south-east from Nutterden through the forest to Cloister and Materborn, but had reported organized defences, which they were unable to penetrate, near Cloister. In all the air photographs, which had been closely studied, this had appeared as a very white, straight road. Some months before, when the operation was originally planned, the Dutch Resistance had reported this to be a concrete road made for tanks and part of the Siegfried Defences. Major-General Thomas had therefore arranged with Major-General Ross of 53 (W.) Division to get control of it for him. Major-General Ross had evidently kept his word. Brigadier Essame and Lieut.-Colonel Barker were therefore sent off to reconnoitre it. They found, as 15 (S.) Reconnaissance Regiment had already reported, that the trail consisted not of concrete but of white sand. Returning to his brigade with this information, Brigadier Essame proposed to advance by this route with 5 D.C.L.I. leading as soon as the traffic jam could be unravelled. Meanwhile, however, Major-General Thomas had also personally reconnoitred the track with Lieut.-Colonel Kinnersley and, hoping to find a fluid situation beyond the wood, decided to lead with the Reconnaissance Regiment. Unfortunately the latter were at the tail of 214 Brigade's column. This was, as events turned out, an unfortunate decision. Their difficulties in forcing their way forward with the transport and tanks of 214 and 227 Brigade occupying every reasonably dry stretch of road or track can be imagined. Eventually, however, they reached Nutterden. B Squadron was then directed down the track through the forest towards Materborn. The track itself was scarcely practicable for their unwieldy vehicles and on approaching Saalhof, east of Cloister, they struck strong opposition.   As a result, through no fault of their own, they jammed the track and hindered the advance of 5 D.C.L.I., the leading battalion of 214 Brigade, which eventually disentangled itself from the chaos on the main road and followed them.   It was now early afternoon.   The leading company of the D.C.L.I., on reaching the fields and farms in the open country to the east of the forest, found the Reconnaissance Regiment held up at Saalhof.   A quick fire-plan was made and the village carried in the fading light.   Fighting went on from house to house.   Lieut.-Colonel Taylor now attempted to press through Cloister to Materborn in the dark.   The opposition, however, proved too strong and he eventually decided to resume the advance at dawn.   The rest of 214 Brigade curled up in rear along the track, clear at last of the traffic chaos on the main road and thankful that they still had three days' rations with them.

Within Cleve, fighting continued throughout the night and it was not until a late hour that a clear picture of the situation there emerged. Back at Kranenburg the road was now three feet deep in water and only three-ton lorries could get through.   130 Brigade therefore had to remain at Nijmegen.   It was, however, at last possible to bring some sort of order to the operations for the following day.   Somewhat divergent views were at last reconciled and it was finally agreed that 15 (S.) Division should take over Cleve on the 11th from 129 Brigade to enable the latter to concentrate for an advance on Bedburg. Brigadier Essame, with 214 Brigade, was ordered, not without emphasis, to continue his advance on Materborn village and Hau on the main road from Goch.

It had been a day of nightmare traffic congestion which made coherent troop movement almost impossible.   In fact it had been proved—it is hoped for all time—that two divisions cannot operate satisfactorily on one axis—especially when the axis itself leads through a bog and is itself in places under water.   In the circumstances it is not surprising that throughout the day the contacts of many of the commanders involved had been of a character which cannot justly be described as being noteworthy for their cordiality.

11th   In Cleve sporadic and confused fighting continued throughout
Feb.   the night.   At dawn a determined counter-attack against 5 Wiltshire left the battalion unshaken, and when it failed, yielded no less than a hundred and eighty para. troops, who were trapped by Lieutenant A. Fussey and No. 7 Platoon and surrendered.   As the day wore on, 15 Scottish Division advanced into the town and relieved 129 Brigade of responsibility for its defence.   The brigade drew back to reorganize for the resumption of the advance and get what sleep it could in the ruins.

During the night B Company of 5 D.C.L.I., under Major Hutchins, moving by devious routes had penetrated in rear of the enemy's lines in the direction of Hau and returned in the early hours to the battalion at Saalhof bringing back with it fifteen prisoners and considerable, though confusing, information.

Two miles south-east of Cleve stood a large sanatorium named Bedburg. Between this large block of buildings and its surrounding gardens and the easternmost edge of the Reichswald Forest there is a ridge of high ground about the village of Hau which traverses both the main road and railway running due south from Cleve to Goch. With a view to seizing this ridge and thus severing the enemy's communications with Goch, Brigadier Essame launched 214 Brigade to the attack early on the afternoon of the 11th.

The battle opened at 2 p.m. with a set-piece attack on Materborn village by the D.C.L.I. supported by the 4/7 Dragoon Guards. All went well. Two German tanks were knocked out and the enemy, blasted out of his senses by the fire of the Divisional artillery, put up comparatively little resistance. The majority bolted, leaving behind much of their equipment.

Hot on their heels, and long before Materborn village had been cleared, came Lieut.-Colonel Ivor Reeves with 7 Somerset Light Infantry. Pockets of enemy still holding out in the houses and villas delayed deployment on the start line by half an hour. However, C Company under Major Durie pressed on and soon had advanced a thousand yards.

Four hundred yards ahead lay the junction of four roads—one from Materborn, one going north to Cleve, the Goch road, and one going due east—later to be known as "Tiger Corner." At the cross-roads stood a burning S.P. gun. Other S.P. guns and many Spandaus now opened up on Major Durie's company. One of our tanks was hit, but the rest of the squadron now saturated the enemy infantry with their fire. A brilliant attack fought inch by inch amongst the houses by No. 13 Platoon under Lieutenant E. Lawson finally left the vital cross-roads in our hands. The light was fading fast and heavy sleet had begun to fall.

Lieut.-Colonel Ivor Reeves now arrived. There were still another thousand yards to go. Ahead, the road to Hau, bare of cover, ran straight into the darkness. Spandaus seemed to answer every move. The troops were almost dropping with cold and fatigue. However, Lieut.-Colonel Reeves decided to press on without his tanks. In fact, this was a sound decision, as the tanks could have done little in the dark. B Squadron of 4/7 Dragoon Guards therefore pulled back a few hundred yards, whilst the battalion, still led by Major Durie, fought its way slowly down the road, dealing with each house in turn. By midnight his men had almost reached the limit of fatigue. He therefore took a bold decision—to advance straight down the road to his objective and leave the companies following to mop up. By 2 a.m. he had reached the bend of the road at Hau. On his right stood the eastern fringes of the Reichswald ; in front, on his left, stood Forst Cleve. The road and railway ran side by side through this gap. He had reached his objective. Fighting now continued all night at close quarters with the Germans. Meanwhile, A Company under Major Roberts had swung right into the village of Hau, where hand-to-hand fighting went on all night around the farmhouses and in the streets. The rest of the battalion now came up and by 5.30 a.m., after thirteen hours of close-quarter fighting in the dark was firm upon its objective. Seventy prisoners had been taken and many more of the enemy killed.

Lieut.-Colonel Hope-Thomson with 1 Worcestershire had followed in the wake of 7 Somerset Light Infantry throughout the night and reached "Tiger Corner." When dawn broke, D Company advanced on the houses at Kukkuk, five hundred yards ahead on the road to Bedburg, and in spite of heavy Spandau fire overwhelmed the Germans in the houses. The battalion had now a secure base from which to launch their final attack. An extensive artillery plan had been prepared for this phase—however, it was now learnt that this could not be put down for another three hours. Lieut.-Colonel Hope-Thomson therefore decided to advance without artillery support to his final objective on the ridge covering the cross-roads and facing Bedburg. Here the battalion consolidated.

During the morning 7 Somerset Light Infantry gained contact with 53 (Welsh) Division advancing through the Reichswald Forest. B Squadron of 43 Reconnaissance Regiment pushed through and reconnoitred Nieder dam, a thousand yards ahead. Here the squadron had struck fierce opposition and withdrew after losing three armoured cars.

The enemy's reaction to this startling success was swift and vicious. Three counter-attacks were launched against 7 Somerset Light Infantry, only to wither away in the fire of the infantry, the tanks and the guns. 1 Worcestershire were subjected to incessant and heavy shell-fire. During the morning a mobile column of 46 Brigade succeeded in breaking out to the east in their rear and fought its way into Qualberg and Hasselt on the Calcar road.

129 Brigade was now once more on the move. Led by 4 Somerset Light Infantry, the brigade took the road to Bedburg. The route ran through woods and half a mile from the start was found to be cratered and mined. Major Cooke Hurle, commanding the vanguard (D Company), found a diversion along a track and, overcoming opposition at the Schloss and Freudenberg, pressed on until held up by a strongly entrenched enemy infantry in the side of the railway embankment. A determined attack secured fifty prisoners. Many dead lay at the side of the road. Lieut.-Colonel Lipscomb

28. Schloss Moyland—Divisional Headquarters at end of February, 1945

29. In the ruins of Cleve, 12th February, 1945

30. Xanten on capture by 129 Brigade on 8th March, 1945

now deployed the remainder of his battalion and by nightfall the whole of Bedburg was in his grip. The remainder of the brigade curled up for the night in the rain along the road from Cleve.

Thus in the short space of thirty hours the situation had been completely transformed. Before the final advance on Goch could begin the vital high ground south-east of Bedburg had still to be taken. This was to involve prolonged and bitter fighting. Nevertheless, the Division, sleepless and frozen stiff, had at least shaken itself free of the congestion and confusion of the Materborn Gap and the ruins of Cleve.

In the capture of Cleve there is an element of paradox. If the Division had been held back as military prudence dictated and 15 (S.) Division thus been permitted to attack the town on orthodox lines on the morning of February 10th in accordance with the original plan, it is quite conceivable that the cost might have been high, for 6 Para. Division would by then have been properly deployed to meet them. As events turned out, 129 Brigade's irruption into the town in the dead of night produced a situation completely beyond the capacity of Major-General Fiebig and his colleague, the commander of 6 Para. Division, to control. They are entitled to some professional sympathy. A night attack on a defended city by a division in column of route on another division's only axis through a bog cannot rightly be regarded as a normal operation of war, even if the advanced guard is fortunate enough to be led by a commander of the calibre of Lieut.-Colonel Corbyn, whose bold action at the road block outside Cleve has a parallel in that of Ludendorff at Liège in 1914.

What always will rankle in the minds of those who fought at Cleve is the oafish stupidity of the attack by Bomber Command, which, with its deep cratering, completely blocked the roads within the town. Air-Marshal Sir Arthur Harris in his *Bomber Offensive* has seen fit to observe that the army at Caen was slow to take advantage of his hammer-blow. With seven months' more experience at his disposal, he repeated the error at Cleve. Those who advised him as to the type of bombing to be adopted carry a heavy responsibility. They should have known that after the capture of the Materborn, 43 Division would need reasonably clear roads to exploit the situation to the south. Instead, if Cleve had not been bombed at all, the Division would at least have fulfilled its commander's intention and reached the road from Materborn to Cleve on a two-brigade front by dawn. As it was, the vast destruction and huge craters paralysed all movement during the critical hours before daylight. What does stand out, however, as an example for all time is the magnificent leadership of the battalion commanders, who, faced with the unforeseen, overwhelmed some of the best troops of the German army in the chaos of Cleve.

15

THE ADVANCE TO THE GOCH ESCARPMENT
13th to 17th February
(*See Sketch Map* 17)

Although the advance of 214 Brigade to Hau and 129 Brigade to Bedburg had eased the situation in Cleve and enabled the Divisional artillery to deploy complete around Materborn, the position of Major-General Thomas on the night of the 12th was by no means enviable. The only axis between Beek and Nutterden was four feet deep in water. 129 Field Ambulance was handling the casualties of all three British divisions. Somehow or other, supplies were being got through in Dukws. 130 Brigade, from Nijmegen, had temporarily been placed at the disposal of 53 Division as a reserve and moved into the Reichswald Forest during the afternoon. The appearance of 116 Panzer Division and 15 Panzer Grenadier Division on the front showed that no easy passage lay ahead. He himself had caught a chill and was confined to his caravan in the squalor of the ruins of Nutterden, where the water was rapidly rising. Unable to tolerate these conditions any longer, he moved his tactical headquarters by way of the track through the forest to the Cloister at Materborn. What he endured on the journey, he alone knows. In the courtyard of the Cloister he remained, with a high temperature, for the next few days surrounded by guns firing day and night. In spite of pressure from the Corps Commander, he persisted in his refusal to be evacuated and employed Brigadier Essame, whose brigade was temporarily static, to keep himself in touch with the operations.

Both he and Major-General Barber had, in fact, closed with the enemy's next defensive position barring the way to Calcar and Goch. It ran from the woods around Moyland across a low feature known as the Eselsberg, a mile south-east of Bedburg, to Forst Cleve, completely blocking the way to the south. The battle which now started was to involve not only all three brigades of the Division but 15 (S.) Division as well in some of the fiercest and most costly fighting they ever experienced. 116 Panzer and 15 Panzer Grenadier Divisions were prepared to sell their lives at a hard price. The postponement of the U.S. offensive from the Roer front had enabled the enemy to concentrate no fewer than nine divisions against First Canadian Army and to revive the hope that a chance still existed of wresting victory from defeat at the eleventh hour. It is not surprising therefore that the first three days of the battle should have been characterized by desperate in-fighting and short advances as the Division gradually broke the enemy's will to continue the struggle.

The 13th was to prove a particularly bitter day for 129 Brigade. Its temporary commander, Lieut.-Colonel N. C. E. Kenrick, opened the battle by directing 5 Wiltshire against the ridge immediately south-east of Bedburg, which he required as a start-line for his thrust of 1,000 yards by 4 Wiltshire on to Trippenberg and the cross-roads immediately to the south. Intense shell-fire caught and greeted the 5 Wiltshire as they deployed and caused many casualities. However, they pressed grimly on and gained the ridge. In the afternoon 4 Wiltshire resumed the attack with heavy artillery support. The tanks sank in the soft ground. Nevertheless the battalion fought its way forward yard by yard and had reached the houses and farms of Trippenberg by nightfall. A violent counter-attack at dawn supported by tanks penetrated the position. Nevertheless the battalion held on, and, although one company was overrun, thanks particularly to the courage of Captain Townsend the enemy were brought to a halt. Shelling reached fantastic proportions.

This vicious counterstroke delayed the start of 5 Wiltshire until 11 a.m. Concentrated fire from machine-guns, mortars and S.P. guns soon pinned A and D Companies to the ground. C Company on the right became immediately engaged in stiff hand-to-hand fighting with men of 15 Panzer Grenadiers. Major Hyde, the commanding officer, himself wounded, ordered the battalion to dig in where they were. All senior officers, with the exception of Major Dottridge, were now casualties. The shell-fire continued with un-abated violence. During the afternoon Major J. L. Brind arrived to take over command.

Despite the heavy losses the battalion had sustained and the extreme fatigue of the men, he decided to continue the attack by night without artillery support so as to secure a start-line for 130 Brigade on the morrow. Fighting their way forward in the dark, the battalion at last reached the cross-roads four hundred yards east of Forst Cleve in the face of violent machine-gun fire. Altogether the battalion lost 200 men. They and 4 Wiltshire had however gained a firm foothold on the vital high ground south-east of Bedburg and held it in the face of fanatical counter-attacks.

During the day 15 (S.) Division had been involved in equally bitter and inconclusive fighting in Moyland woods on their immediate left.

It was now the turn of 130 Brigade to continue the battle. The leading battalion commander, Lieut.-Colonel W. G. Roberts, of 4 Dorset, faced at first light a situation of unparalleled complexity. 5 Wiltshire had done all, indeed, almost more than all that was humanly possible and were now exhausted. Shell, mortar and Spandau fire and the inevitable confusion following close fighting in the dark made reconnaissance a task of the utmost difficulty. However, by 10.30 a.m. a new plan was evolved and the attack resumed. Almost immediately 4 Dorset found themselves involved in fighting of the utmost ferocity with a fresh German battalion, the Battle Group Hutze, who resisted to the last. In the face of withering fire, C Company on the right under Major Gill and A Company on the left under Major Symonds closed with the enemy. The

15th Feb

picture survives of the tall figure of Major Symonds blowing his whistle and bowling his steel helmet in the direction of the enemy. A group of farm buildings only fell to A company after three assaults. Both company commanders were wounded. C Company eventually gained its objective under the brilliant leadership of Captain Kirkwood. There were few prisoners. Shell and mortar fire reached a crescendo. However, fighting forward almost inch by inch, the battalion had gained sufficient ground by 3.30 p.m. for 7 Royal Hampshire, under Major Rooke, Lieut.-Colonel D. E. B. Talbot having temporarily taken over command of the brigade, to pass through. The battle continued with unabated fury. Heavy machine-gun fire from the north-east end of Forst Cleve poured into the flank of the battalion. Nevertheless, the battalion struggled on at close grips with Van der Heydte's paratroops in the gathering darkness. The fighting continued throughout the night. Over 60 prisoners were taken and many of the enemy killed.

All day on the Division's left flank in Moyland woods the 15 (S.) Division had struck equally ferocious opposition. There was no sign of a break in the German morale. Indeed, it seemed as if a deadlock had been reached. For the 16th the outlook on both Divisional fronts seemed black indeed.

In a prolonged battle such as this between troops of equally high morale and armament, there comes a crisis when those directly engaged reach the limit of endurance. The commander who can time his final stroke with his reserve for this critical moment wins the victory. This has been common knowledge since the days of Caesar. The ability to sense this decisive moment distinguishes the outstanding commander from the competent mediocrity. During the 15th, Major-General Thomas divined that this stage would be reached about noon on the morrow. This was his plan. Despite pressure to become involved in Forst Cleve, which he judged to be an objective suited rather to Typhoons and the Canadian "mattrass" than to infantry—the former would at least have no difficulty in recognizing the target—he decided that 214 Brigade, augmented by 4 Somerset Light Infantry, should attack about midday on the 16th from a start-line joining approximately the hamlets of Blacknik and Berkhovel, about 800 yards south-east of the north-east corner of Forst Cleve and still in enemy hands. He gave Brigadier Essame as a first objective the eastern end of the village of Pfalzdorf and a minor feature in the flat country still further to the east. A third battalion in kangaroos was then to be thrust forward to capture the villages of Imigshof, Bergmanshoff and Schroenshof, thus cutting the road from Goch to Calcar. Finally, a fourth battalion was to pass through by night and seize the escarpment immediately north of Goch. As a final task, the brigade were to extend their grip on the escarpment to the south-east.

Timely briefing on the afternoon of the 15th enabled a fire-plan to be evolved by the C.R.A., Brigadier K. F. Mackay Lewis and Lieut.-Colonel F. B. Wyldbore-Smith which for brilliance in planning and execution constitutes probably the Divisional artillery's greatest achievement during the war.

The success of the whole operation turned on the ability of 130 Brigade to secure a start-line on which 214 Brigade could deploy on a two-battalion front in time to complete the first two stages of the operation before night closed in.   The operations of 5 Dorset during the night of the 15th/16th and the following morning therefore form an integral part of the battle, which was to carry the Division to the outskirts of Goch, to restore fluidity to the operations and to enable First Canadian Army to deploy for a further advance on a front of two corps.

It had been intended that 5 Dorset should pass through 4 Dorset and 7 Royal Hampshire on the afternoon of the 15th to secure the start-line from Blacknik to Berkhovel required for 214 Brigade. Night arrived with both leading battalions still at close grips with the enemy. 5 Dorset were therefore ordered to carry out the operation under cover of darkness.   The battalion faced a most difficult undertaking.   Not only were the enemy unlocated, but the positions reached by the other two battalions were only vaguely known. However, just before midnight D Company, under Major G. R. Hartwell, succeeded in reaching Berkhovel, which they found to be held by the enemy.   C Company attempted to work round the left flank.   In fact, the battalion's arrival had coincided with an enemy counter-attack on the 7 Royal Hampshire.   Lieut.-Colonel Venour therefore decided to withdraw his battalion and put in a fresh attack in the morning with tanks. 15th–
16th
Feb.

The attack went in at 9.30 a.m.   C Company skirted the village of Berkhovel and, working their way across country, reached their objective.   A Company, under Major H. C. Allen, fought their way down the main road about Blacknik, and suffering severe casualties, were ultimately brought to a standstill.   D Company now thrust forward and fighting all the way gained a slight rise on the right of the road.   Close-range fire from S.P. guns made the position of A and C Companies almost intolerable.   Exhausted though they were, 130 Brigade had scored a decisive success in the nick of time, for the head of 214 Brigade column was now drawing near along the road from Bedburg. 16th
Feb.

As 1 Worcestershires and 7 Somerset Light Infantry, moving down the Bedburg road, emerged on the open fields only just captured by 5 Dorset and started to deploy, the enemy opened up on them with every gun he had, and with deadly accuracy.   In the confusion inseparable from arrival in a position in which all the enemy had not yet been entirely subdued, the two commanding officers, Lieut.-

Colonels Hope-Thomson and Ivor Reeves, rose to the occasion. Lieut.-Colonel Ivor Reeves struck off from the main road to the right and reached his start-line with A and D Companies just before our guns were due to open. A Company's tanks were with them; D Company's had not yet arrived. Lieut.-Colonel Ivor Reeves nevertheless gave the order to advance and the two companies thrust forward on time, close to the bursting shells of the Divisional artillery. It was 3.20 p.m. On the Worcester's front, Lieut.-Colonel Hope-Thomson, finding that 5 Dorset had not entirely gained possession of his proposed start-line, with the assistance of Major Hartwell of 5 Dorset, had to modify his arrangements for deployment in a hurricane of bursting shells. Finally, at 3.45 p.m., his battalion's attack got under way.

Only a gunner will fully realize the complications involved in this last-minute change in the fire-plan and the difficulties of supporting two battalions attacking side by side and progressing at varying rates. That Lieut.-Colonel Wyldbore-Smith, of 179 Field Regiment, solved the problem and continued to solve it throughout the remainder of the hours of daylight constitutes a brilliant achievement in gunnery. The infantry responded to this magnificent support. The tanks of 4/7 Dragoon Guards were right forward and, mingled with the men on foot, poured a stream of fire into the enemy positions. On the extreme right A Company of 7 Somerset Light Infantry fought their way ahead. Every German who resisted was shot dead. Major Roberts and his men ruthlessly and relentlessly pressed on. Each forward section had its own tank, which first with 75-mm. cannon and then with its Besa guns set the houses on fire. Prisoners began to stream back. By 5 p.m. the company had advanced 2,500 yards and secured three lateral roads. D Company's attack led across country. Captain Graham, the company commander, although wounded in the hand, soon found his company caught in intense fire from a group of farms on his left. His tanks had still not arrived. The company therefore attacked and carried the farms without their support. The prisoners were despatched to the rear without escort.

Two Shermans now approached from the rear and with one on each side of him, Captain Graham continued to advance. Two platoons quickly followed, but he maintained his lead and reached the final objective ahead of them. There was little opposition here —fortunately, for the company had taken severe punishment, Lieutenant Larret's platoon being reduced to nine men. Under the eyes of their commanding officer, the company dug in. By nightfall the battalion had taken 413 prisoners and advanced nearly 3,000 yards.

Once started, 1 Worcestershire attack went equally well. The intermediate objective was quickly seized and prisoners started to move back. D Company, pushing on to their final objective, suddenly came under heavy Spandau fire from a group of farm buildings. Lieutenant Pullen at once dashed forward with his platoon and carried the position at the bayonet point. The rest of the company were quick to respond and reached the final objective. Three officers and 120 men surrendered. At 5.45 p.m. Lieut.-Colonel Hope-Thomson reported that he had completed his task.

All the afternoon, 5 D.C.L.I., mounted in their kangaroos, and B Squadron 4/7 Dragoon Guards had waited on the outskirts of Bedburg. Brigadier Essame now gave the order to advance. In the fast-fading light, the dense mass of armour surged due south down the road from Bedburg and, reaching the open country about Blacknik, deployed into five columns and headed due south for the villages of Imigshof, Bergmanshoff and Schroenshof, 6,000 yards ahead. This overwhelming stroke was too much for the enemy. In the dark and confusion he went to ground. By 8 p.m. Lieut.-Colonel Taylor and his armoured column had cut the road from Goch to Calcar and laagered on the objective. Contact between the obstinate defenders of Moyland and Goch had been irreparably severed.

The day's battle was not yet over. 214 Brigade had still another card to play. The operation now to be described is high military art. It should be attempted only by those prepared to take risks and then only by troops of the highest quality led by experienced commanders. A night attack over country which has never been seen in daylight, and starting from ground only just captured, involves a step into an unknown bristling with incalculable hazards.

Lieut.-Colonel Lipscomb, commanding 4 Somerset Light Infantry and his intelligence officer arrived in the midst of the leading companies of 7 Somerset Light Infantry east of Pfalzdorf just as the light was fading. The battle here was by no means at an end. Ignoring the shell-fire and the mopping-up going on around them, they put down tapes to mark out the areas on which the battalion, now on its way forward, could form up for a night advance to the escarpment. Very fortunately a series of parallel tracks, which Lieut.-Colonel Lipscomb had studied on the map, led to the companies' objectives.

Half an hour after midnight the battalion, ready despite the uncertainties inseparable from a start-line on an objective only just subdued, began its advance to the escarpment in silence. The enemy were taken completely by surprise. A Company, under Major Beckhurst, struck the stiffest opposition. When just short of their objective they were challenged by a German voice and a Spandau opened up. This was silenced, but others at once burst into life. A Wasp failed to function. The company therefore withdrew a little and called for artillery support. Our shells landed square on the target; the company crept forward and finally, the moment the fire ceased, charged the enemy, shouting as they did so.

Despite a wire fence they were soon in their midst.   The German company commander and 68 men surrendered—he spoke good English and observed that in his six years of war he had never known the British to attack by night.   Before dawn the battalion stood firm on a front of 1,000 yards on the escarpment overlooking Goch, having taken 250 prisoners.

17th Feb.   The Division's advance had in the short space of 24 hours created a deep salient stretching from Moyland Wood, where the enemy continued to resist with the utmost obstinacy, to a depth of nearly 8,000 yards.   Lieut.-General Horrocks at once ordered 53 Division to close up with the escarpment west of the railway from Cleve to Goch.   This the Division did with remarkable promptitude.   Around Moyland, however, several days were to elapse and much life to be expended before the enemy was finally overwhelmed by the Canadians.   Major-General Thomas, on his part, was quick to exploit his success.   130 Brigade, given the task of clearing Forst Cleve, entrusted it to 4 Dorset and a company of 7 Royal Hampshire. In view of the frightful bombardment by the Canadian "mattrass" and the Typhoons to which this wood had been subjected, it is not surprising that but few of the enemy were found inside.   214 Brigade were ordered to continue the advance to the escarpment to the south-east as far as the bend in the Niers River and the woods immediately west of Bucholt.

Accordingly the brigade resumed the attack with 7 Somerset Light Infantry on the right and 1 Worcestershire on the left.   After a quick "O" Group 7 Somerset advanced on a three-company front at 11 a.m.   On the right, A Company, brilliantly supported by 4/7 Dragoon Guards, fought their way through a maze of houses and trenches and wire which grew thicker every yard they advanced.   In the centre, B Company dealt with farms and strong-points, and in spite of tough resistance had reached the escarpment by 2.30 p.m. On the left, a hamlet near Imigshof only fell to C Company after every building had been set alight.   Here the enemy resisted with the greatest tenacity, but eventually surrendered.   There were over 200 of them.   Resistance around a tower now produced a situation of the utmost difficulty.   However, Major Durie, with the co-operation of the Worcestershires on his left, eventually succeeded in capturing it, along with five 75-mm. anti-tank guns.   The trenches around were in good order and manned with machine-guns complete with ammunition.   Under the eyes of their C.O., the battalion dug in along the escarpment as the light faded.

On the Somerset's left, 1 Worcestershire fought an equally grim battle throughout the afternoon.   The enemy fought to the limit, contesting every inch of the ground with every weapon he had, especially Nebelwerfers.   Nevertheless by nightfall the battalion had advanced 1,500 yards.   On this flank the enemy was clearly determined to resist to the last. The shell-fire around Imigshof and Bergmanshoff, where the D.C.L.I. were deployed, reached fantastic proportions. Indeed, at no time in the campaign were the enemy's guns handled with greater effect. However, thanks to the skill and hand-fighting qualities displayed again and again in many company and platoon battles throughout the long afternoon, the two battalions were able to report by nightfall that they now looked down on the chimneys of Goch on a front of 4,000 yards. At the same time Brigadier Essame had been able to move over 4 Somerset Light Infantry to guard his sensitive left flank north of Imigshof. The total of prisoners taken had passed the thousand mark. The enemy's abandoned equipment littered the battlefield.

The Divisional artillery now opened up on the town and shelled it ruthlessly without a pause. Immediately below the escarpment stretched an anti-tank ditch twenty feet deep with sloping sides. 260 and 204 Field Companies of the Divisional engineers now arrived, and covered by 7 Somerset Light Infantry had constructed no fewer than seven crossings over it by the next morning. Patrols of this battalion, notably those led by Sergeant Haskell and Lance-Sergeant Evans, penetrated beyond the second anti-tank ditch a thousand yards ahead,which encircled the centre of the town. By the early afternoon 44 Brigade of 15 (S.) Division with all its flails, crocodiles, Avres, bulldozers and bridgelayers, stood ready deployed for the final assault on Goch. On the west, 51 Division were within striking distance; 53 Division had closed with 43 Division's right flank. Goch, the pivot of the Siegfried Line, was doomed. 18th Feb.

Lieut.-General Horrocks has seen fit to describe the break-out on the 16th by 214 Brigade as the highlight of the operations in the Reichswald and the turning-point of the battle. Until this moment, it had seemed to reproduce on all divisional fronts the frustrating and interminable complexities of siege warfare.

It is now known that after the loss of Cleve, the enemy decided to fight on the line running from Hasselt on the Calcar road, through the Eselsberg to the north-west corner of Forst Cleve. He had three divisions available, 84 on the right, reinforced by numerous battle groups, and 15 Panzer Grenadier Division on the left, each supported by tanks and S.Ps. of 116 Panzer Division, the commander of which co-ordinated the defence and seems to have run the battle. As our pressure increased, he flung in units of 7 Para. and 180 Divisions to fill the gaps. The main weight of 43 Division's attack fell on the front of 15 Panzer Grenadier Division. Nevertheless, on the 17th he could still produce three fresh battalions to hold the escarpment after 4 Somerset Light Infantry had secured the first foothold. The final effort of 7 Somerset Light Infantry and 1 Worcestershire therefore constitutes no mean achievement, coming as it did at the end of seven days of almost continuous action.

Seen in true perspective, the operation began on the 12th, when 214 and 129 Brigades closed with the enemy's position. There followed in the mud of the Eselsberg, midway between Moyland Wood and Forst Cleve, a continuous battle of attrition obstinately sustained first by 129 Brigade and then by 130 Brigade and characterized by the bitter fighting and small advances inevitable when equally determined troops of high quality get to grips. At the crucial moment on the 16th, Major-General Thomas threw in his reserve in such strength and with such violence as to swamp the enemy just as night closed in. The advance of 4 Somerset Light Infantry during the hours of darkness, followed next day by the thrust to the south-east, finally completed his defeat.

The breakout by 214 Brigade was well planned, magnificently supported and superbly timed. All this, however, would have been of no avail had the four battalions not been led by commanders of outstanding fighting quality whom their officers and men would follow anywhere, and supported by tanks prepared to go forward, whatever the risk, side by side with the leading infantry. Five regiments above all others therefore share the honour of turning the tide in the Reichswald—the 4/7 Dragoon Guards, the Royal Artillery, the Somerset Light Infantry, the D.C.L.I. and the Worcestershire. The capture of the Goch escarpment is not the least of the achievements in their long and honourable histories.

In ten days' desperate fighting the Division, with open flanks, had advanced 10,000 yards down the Siegfried Line, rolled up the German defences from the north and taken 2,400 prisoners. Until the breakout of 214 Brigade, the Corps Commander had faced the prospect of stalemate in the mud. Now at last the gleam of victory shone through the clouds.

UNDER 2 CANADIAN CORPS

18th Feb.   Before he could mount his attack on the next main German defensive position barring the way to Wesel, General Crerar had still finally to subdue Goch and gain all the high ground along the road from Goch to Calcar. This covered the approach to the ridge between Calcar and Udem, an essential feature of the formidable Hochwald defences. Although the assault on Goch by 15 Scottish Division started at 3 p.m. on the 18th, it was not until the 21st that operations by this division, 51 (H.) Division, and 53 (W.) Division, finally extinguished resistance in the town. On the other flank 2 and 3 Canadian Divisions had intervened in Moyland Wood and to the south at the same time as 43 Division was thrusting towards the escarpment. 3 Canadian Division at Moyland encountered some of the most savage opposition in their considerable experience. Shelling reached an intensity unequalled since Normandy. To the south on the Calcar road, 4 Canadian Infantry Brigade of 2 Canadian

Division on the 19th February fought one of its bloodiest battles. Although they reached their objectives, their losses were severe. The enemy, reinforced by units of Panzer Lehr Division, counter-attacked again and again with the utmost savagery. The battle continued with unabated ferocity throughout the 20th and 21st, when the Canadians finally flung the enemy out of Moyland Wood and brought the fighting to a decisive conclusion.

On the 20th these operations on their immediate flank drew 214 Brigade, still in position on the escarpment and to the north, into their orbit. Five hundred yards south of the Calcar road, facing 4 Somerset Light Infantry, stood the village of Halvenboom. Here a gap existed between 5 D.C.L.I. and the 4 Canadian Infantry Brigade. The village stood at the bottom of a long, gentle slope. On being ordered to seize it, Lieut.-Colonel Lipscomb gave the task to C and D Companies. C Company at 11 a.m. advanced in kangaroos, which found the muddy approaches hard going. A tornado of shell and mortar fire caught the company as they approached. In a few minutes they had lost a large number of men, including their Company Commander, Major Mallalieu. Major David Richards, commanding B Squadron 4/7 Dragoon Guards, which was supporting the attack, at once took charge and organized the defence of the village. D Company was thus able to pass through and finish the operation. The loss of Major Mallalieu was one of the greatest the battalion had ever sustained. He had been in the forefront of the battle ever since Normandy, and his inspiring presence and matchless courage had time and time again carried his men forward through many a dark hour. The battalion rejoined its normal brigade on the following day in Cleve. Seldom in the course of the campaign had a brief respite from battle been more gallantly and effectively earned.

General Crerar had already started to regroup for his next bound forward. 130 Brigade were the first to be affected. North of Cleve between Emmerich and Milligen stretched a waste of water like an inland sea, dotted here and there with farmsteads and little islands of high ground as far as the Rhine. This watery area had been captured by 3 Canadian Division, whose unique experience of amphibious war both in Normandy and on the Scheldt had gained them the title of the "Water Rats." The high ground on the north bank completely commanded this watery wilderness and had to be kept permanently screened by a Pioneer smoke detachment in Nijmegen. All communications were by buffaloes and amphibious weasels. On the 20th, Brigadier Coad started to take over from 8 Canadian Brigade what must have been the most fantastic defensive position he has ever held either in Europe or Korea. It was five miles long. Contact patrols between the isolated companies had to travel by boat.

On the afternoon of the 20th, the 5 Dorset set sail in buffaloes from the landing stage on the canal in the heart of Cleve to take over the centre sector around Griethausen.   This included a factory on the very bank of the river.   4 Dorset followed *en voyage* for the area north of Kellen.   7 Royal Hampshire had already left early in the morning in T.C.Vs. for the embarkation point at Beek near Nijmegen. Two companies embarked that afternoon for Milligen, to be followed by the rest of the battalion the following day.   Brigade headquarters remained in the northern end of Cleve.   Here the brigade was to remain until 11th March, each battalion occupying the Milligen sector, where contact with the enemy was close, for five days. Shelling, especially north of Cleve, was at times severe and movement by day not without its hazards.   Our gunners were engaged elsewhere and little ammunition could be spared for retaliation. However, battalions made good use of their mortars, and 110 L.A.A. Regiment in a ground role ensured that the enemy did not go unpunished.   The brigade for the first time found itself involved in military government.   The civil population, marooned in isolated farms, were got under control and eventually evacuated to Bedburg. The operation was not without humour.   The civilians had to cross the main axis with their cows.   A march table had therefore to be made out for these animals, thus raising a unique problem of staff duties.   On the whole both the Germans and the cows were equally docile and bewildered.

21st Feb.   On the 21st the Division joined 2 Canadian Corps under Lieut.-General C. G. Simonds.   The progress of operations now permitted first 129 Brigade and then 214 Brigade to be moved back for three days' rest in Cleve.   Once it had been a gracious summer resort of well-laid-out villas and thriving local industries centred around its ancient cathedral and the castle of Schwanenburg, immortalized in Wagner's *Lohengrin*.   During the Renaissance its sons had made no mean contribution to the revival of the arts.   Now it lay in utter ruin comparable only to Caen.   Several thousand bodies lay buried beneath the débris.   The bomb craters were packed so tightly together that they overlapped.   Not a house was undamaged and piles of smashed furniture, clothing, books were spilled in hopeless confusion into the gardens.   The streets were crammed with armour and guns.   There were huge dumps of petrol and ammunition everywhere.   In spite of the congestion and occasional shelling from heavy guns beyond the Rhine, it was none the less a haven of rest to the troops.   There still survived sufficient ground-floor rooms and cellars to satisfy their overwhelming need for sleep in shelter from the rain.   For the first time there came a first brief hint of spring in 23rd Feb. the air.   There was good news from the south.   On the 23rd the floods on the Roer had subsided sufficiently for the Ninth U.S. Army to launch Operation "Grenade."   Ever since the start of "Veritable" the enemy had been moving troops from the American front to the Reichswald. This made the American's task somewhat easier, and within two days both Düren and Jülich had fallen. The enemy was thus at last, as had always been intended, caught between the powerful pincers of two converging armies. For the moment, however, the American attack in no way lessened the stubborn resistance on the First Canadian Army front.

General Crerar's plan for the final phase of the drive to the Rhine, known as "Blockbuster," was designed on blitz lines and took the form of a deliberate assault across the plateau between Calcar and Udem against the strong enemy defences of the Hochwald. When a gap sufficiently large had been created, he intended to pass through 4 Canadian and 11 British Armoured Divisions to Xanten and the Wesel crossings. The operation was to be continuous, movement light being used by night. All but a few of the guns of 30 Corps, 2 Canadian Corps and First Canadian Army and the whole air effort of 21 Army Group were to support the first phase—the capture of the high ground south of Calcar. When this and the southern end of the Hochwald forest had been gained, Lieut.-General Simonds proposed to use the railway to Xanten, which passes between this forest and the smaller Balberger Wald, as his main axis of advance.

In this operation, due to start on 26th February, 43 Division was not allotted a leading part, its task being merely to protect the left flank and to take over ground won by the Canadian divisions. Nevertheless, Major-General Thomas was particularly anxious that the troops should understand its design and be kept up to date with its progress. In the event, the enemy was to fight with the courage of despair, and twelve days of protracted and costly operations lay ahead before he was finally driven across the Rhine.

THE ADVANCE TO XANTEN
26th February to 9th March
(See Sketch Maps 16 and 17)

In order to release 6 Canadian Brigade for the coming attack, 129 Brigade returned to the line south of Moyland on the 24th. The position included the Schloss and its aged Baroness and her retainers, who had taken refuge in the vast cellars. This old moated castle had been a favourite hunting retreat of Frederick the Great. The Baron, who had once been attached to the Embassy in London, was not available, but pictures of him in copies of the *Sketch* and *Tatler* strewn amongst the confusion lent an incongruous note. The Baroness herself, seated proudly in an armchair, left no one in doubt of her strong disapproval of both the British and Canadian armies. Indeed, the presence of hordes of troops with roaring petrol cookers in the canopied state bedrooms must have been most inconvenient.

In view, however, of the sanguinary fighting which had only just ended around her stately home, it is remarkable that she was still alive. Later, on 1st March, Divisional Headquarters were to become her guests and to endure, in the vast rooms and cellars, low temperatures which left no doubt in the minds of the staff as to the hardiness of the German aristocracy.

26th Feb. Supported by a very heavy artillery bombardment, the attack by 2 and 3 Canadian Divisions on the high ground running due south from Calcar to Udem went in early on the 26th. Resistance proved bitter and obstinate. The soft ground soon slowed down the tanks. Close infantry fighting went on all day, and the fanatical paratroopers had literally to be burnt out of their positions with wasps. On the extreme southern flank around Keppeln fighting reached the greatest intensity. 4 Canadian Armoured Division's armoured brigade, projected into the battle against the ridge north-east of Udem, lost many tanks. 129 Brigade, moving forward on the afternoon of the 26th to take over the high ground overlooking Calcar which 6 Canadian Brigade had captured, found many burnt-out wasps and the wrack of a battle fought to the bitter end by both sides. The sodden, featureless fields presented a scene of ruin comparable only to Ypres in the First World War. The battle **27th Feb.** continued on the 27th, and by the evening the whole of the ridge from Calcar to Udem was in Canadian hands and 4 Canadian Armoured Division had reached the ill-omened gap between the Hochwald and the Balberger Wald.

These operations caused the enemy to evacuate Calcar, which 5 Wiltshire entered without opposition on the afternoon of the 27th. All the bridges, however, had been destroyed. At the same time 214 Brigade came forward and took over the ground gained by 6 Canadian Brigade midway between Calcar and Udem. Winter had **28th Feb.** returned and sleet was falling. On the 28th on the Canadian front facing to Hochwald and the gap, a deadlock was reached and casualties on both sides were extremely heavy. The German commander, General Schlemm, had in fact committed 116 Panzer Division and brought up reserves of experienced paratroops to block the road from Calcar to Xanten north of the Hochwald, and placed an assault battalion, supported by many tanks and guns, in the gap. By the night of the 28th February it was apparent that further hard fighting lay ahead.

The tasks entrusted to the infantry of the Division had so far been of an unspectacular character. The Reconnaissance Regiment, however, now came into its own. Between the Calcar–Xanten road and the Rhine stretched a flat expanse of low-lying country, interspersed with minor roads linking up a number of substantially built villages. This strip of alluvial plain is about fourteen miles long and varies in width from about six miles to three miles at its narrowest point at the tip of the Hochwald and Marienbaum and Vynen.   This was to be the hunting ground of the regiment for the next ten days in their task of protecting and clearing the east flank of the corps.

On the morning of the 26th, the regiment, with its headquarters at Kellen two miles north-east of Cleve, was holding the line of the Kalflach, a water barrier which runs roughly from Calcar northwards to Emmerich, opposite which it flows into the Rhine.   On the previous night a patrol under Lieutenant Wood had penetrated the village of Crieth on the banks of the river.   Major-General Thomas, when he briefed Lieut.-Colonel C. H. Kinnersley, thought that the regiment in its advance would be faced by a screen of paratroopers. These he ordered the regiment to drive back and at the same time to protect the left flank of the Division from opposite Emmerich to the south-east as it advanced to Xanten.   It followed, therefore, that as the advance progressed the regiment's responsibilities would increase.

As a first step, 204 Field Company bridged the Kalflach opposite   26th Huisberden.   At 6.30 p.m. the assault troop of A Squadron passed   Feb. over and occupied Wissel without opposition.   B Squadron's assault troop followed under Lieutenant Shute and soon after midnight reached a mill south of the town.   Lieutenant Wood pushed on towards Grieth and, after surprising a party of Germans and taking some prisoners, entered the place during the morning to find that the enemy had departed.

Lieut.-Colonel Kinnersley therefore decided to strike due south to   27th Calcar and Honnepel.   By 0500 hours it was found that the latter   Feb. village was held by enemy of about platoon strength.   B Squadron's assault troop dealt with these, and by early afternoon both these places had been reached.

It now became clear to Lieut.-Colonel Kinnersley that he was faced   28th by enemy rearguards armed with machine-guns and that they were   Feb. likely to crater the roads as they withdrew.   In the event this appreciation proved sound.   In view of the open nature of the country, he therefore decided to continue the advance for the most part by night, the carrier sections and assault troops working forward on foot with cars following close behind in support, locating the craters and then covering the sappers whilst they filled them.   This system of moving the cars in support of foot patrols proved of the greatest efficacy and enabled them to make much longer bounds than normal unsupported infantry patrols.   A series of most successful operations followed, made possible by the intrepid and untiring work of 204 Field Company under command of Major Moore.   Hochend and Hanselaer were now taken and crater-filling continued.   Apeldorn, however, was obviously firmly held. Major Blood commanding C Squadron therefore decided to carry it by assault and succeeded in reaching the outskirts by nightfall.   By daylight A   1st Squadron, which had come up in relief, was in contact all along the   March front and had found all the routes forward blocked by craters, mines and blown bridges; heavy mortar and machine-gun fire descended intermittently.   C Squadron now took over the front from Kehrum to Apeldorn whilst A Squadron prolonged the line to the Rhine. Vigorous patrolling forward continued towards Vynen, Marienbaum and Mormter, which developed into a number of extremely lively troop battles with artillery support.   By the evening of the 3/4th March complete information had been gained of the situation in Marienbaum, Vynen and Wardt.

By this time the bitter fighting in the Hochwald by the Canadians was nearing its end, although it was not until the 4th that opposition was finally extinguished.   Major-General Thomas therefore ordered 214 Brigade to advance on the 3rd and capture Kehrum and Marien-baum.

3rd
March 7 Somerset Light Infantry accordingly descended from the plateau, entered the straggling red-brick village of Kehrum, and pushing through it in the direction of Marienbaum reached the trench system of the Hochwald defences.   Here concertina wire, trenches and dug-outs barred the way to a depth which varied from a quarter to three-quarters of a mile.   Only on the main road was any attempt made to defend it.   D Company, however, soon dealt with this. 5 D.C.L.I. now followed and in the fading light clashed with a strong enemy position in a square wood just beyond a formidable anti-tank ditch.   It was therefore decided that 204 Field Company should bridge this gap during the night and that the advance should be resumed in the morning.   The attack went in soon after daylight under a barrage on a two-company front.   The enemy put up little resistance and fifteen prisoners and an anti-tank gun were captured. The battalion then deployed on a three-company front and swept through the large, stoutly built village.   The sappers quickly got to work building two Bailey bridges and moving with their bulldozers the fallen trees which straddled the road.   Vynen, a mile to the east, fell to 1 Worcestershire with equal ease, although the shelling from the far bank of the Rhine was at times intense.   At night a patrol under Lieutenant Stride penetrated as far as Wardt, about 2,000 yards south-east, and found it strongly held.   Unfortunately Lieut-enant Stride was killed.   B and C Companies, however, succeeded in capturing this village on the following day.

4th
March

5th
March 5 D.C.L.I. resumed the advance in the early morning mist.   The road to Xanten ran straight as an arrow.   All went well until deter-mined opposition was met about a mile and a half west of the town. The battalion dug in.   Meanwhile 11 Troop of the Reconnaissance Regiment under Lieutenant Groves had passed through and found themselves held up by a crater.   An anti-tank gun opened up, and after a lively engagement the patrol withdrew within the infantry position.   The mist now lifted to reveal the great Roman arch and the church of Xanten just ahead. A vicious and accurate mortar bombardment now began and continued all day. There could be no doubt that the enemy had no intention whatever of abandoning Xanten until compelled to do so. It, and the high ground to the south, constituted part of the final perimeter of his remaining bridgehead at Wesel. This contained the remnants of four corps, whose nine emaciated divisions now occupied an area of fifteen square miles. Nothing short of a deliberate attack, with special assault equipment, was likely to subdue the opposition, strengthened as it was by an anti-tank ditch, minefields and dug in emplacements. It was therefore decided that 2 Canadian and 43 Divisions should deliver the final blow. The Canadians were given the task of seizing the western edge of the town and the high ground to the south. Xanten itself, the last enemy stronghold west of the Rhine, was allotted to the Division. This decision was finally reached on the 6th after a Canadian attack, executed with the utmost courage, in full view of the D.C.L.I., had proved abortive.

The honour of striking the final knock-out blow west of the Rhine thus fell to 129 Brigade.

The heavy enemy fire and the severe losses sustained by the Canadians convinced Brigadier J. O. E. Vandeleur that a deliberate and probably costly battle had still to be fought before the enemy could finally be driven across the Rhine. On the right, the long, straight road leading into the town provided the only possible approach, as the ground on either side was waterlogged. At right angles to it, a quarter of a mile from the town, stretched a deep anti-tank ditch, with two huge craters in it where it crossed the road. Xanten itself, the birthplace of Siegfried and an ancient Roman frontier station, lay in ruins. In front of Lüttingen open, low-lying fields, destitute of cover, stretched for nearly a mile. In addition, the two battalions of 16 Panzer Regiment holding the position had been ordered by the Fuhrer himself to fight to the last man and the last round. Ample meat for the crocodiles and wasps therefore lay ahead. Air photographs disclosed a network of trenches. Brigadier Vandeleur decided to attack on a two-battalion front just before dawn, so as to secure the crossings of the anti-tank ditch by daylight, and arranged an elaborate and heavy programme of artillery support. He gave Xanten to the 4 Somerset Light Infantry and Lüttingen to the 5 Wiltshire as their objectives. The anti-tank ditch presented an exasperating problem. No patrol could get near enough to measure its width. Air photographs estimated it at 90 feet. A Bailey bridge of this length was therefore constructed which, in fact, was 20 feet short. Fortunately, Major-General Thomas took no risks and managed to borrow from the Division's old friends, 34 Tank Brigade, a Jumbo as a second string. This, having crossed the communications of most of the Army Group, arrived just in time.

16

The attack started at 5 a.m. on the 8th. On the right B Company of 4 Somerset Light Infantry under Major Hutchinson advanced behind a tremendous barrage to seize the crossing over the anti-tank ditch. As they approached it, violent Spandau fire held them up. The fire of the crocodiles appeared ineffective and the barrage moved on. Undaunted, Major Hutchinson quickly made a new plan and decided to fight his way forward without artillery support. Section by section, the company fought its way ahead over the ditch. Corporal Grant single-handed destroyed an entire Spandau team with a grenade. Eventually the company gained the upper hand, thrust their way across, and the scissors bridge sent by 34 Tank Brigade having been put down, proceeded to destroy the remainder of the enemy with the help of the crocodiles. By 9.30 a.m. they were on their objective, having taken thirty-nine prisoners. Many enemy dead lay around. A and C Companies, followed by D Company and D Company of 4 Wiltshire, were now able to pass over and carry on the battle within the ruins of the town. By 4.30 p.m. they had extinguished all opposition and over a hundred sullen parachutists had been despatched to the rear. Contact was gained with the Canadians in the southern end of the town. Meanwhile R.A.S.C. lorries loaded with rubble rapidly filled the craters under fire.

5 Wiltshire, attacking on the left, encountered equally bitter resistance.

Here, A Company in the flat and sodden fields found itself held up by intense opposition from an isolated copse. Bitter and costly fighting followed. C Company reached the edge of the village of Lüttingen by first light, carried a line of slit-trenches and dashed in amongst the houses. The work of clearing, house by house, began. The enemy, however, infiltrated more troops into the village and by the time the company reached the centre, close-quarter fighting of a complex and costly character had developed. The company grimly held on. The arrival of D Company about midday restored the situation. Lieut.-Colonel Kenrick now made a fresh plan. By nightfall the village had been finally subdued. The enemy in the copse, however, fought to the end. No less than three attacks had to be staged before it at last fell to Captain Mottram, Lieutenant
Fisher and the survivors of B Company. Next morning an attack by the 4 Wiltshire north-east from Xanten eliminated the last traces of resistance around Lüttingen. So far as the Division was concerned, Operation "Veritable" was complete.

52 (L.) Division, 2 Canadian Corps, and 16 U.S. Corps now moved up to the river and by 10 p.m. on the 10th all organized resistance west of the Rhine was at an end. The Allied armies now stood along the west bank from Dusseldorf to Nijmegen. Far to the south on 7th March the First U.S. Army had seized the Luden-

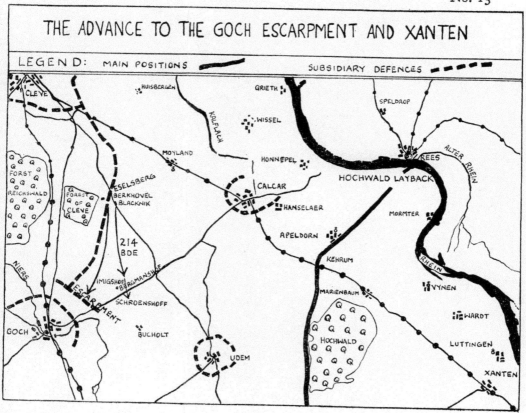

THE ADVANCE TO THE GOCH ESCARPMENT AND XANTEN

LEGEND: MAIN POSITIONS ━━━━ SUBSIDIARY DEFENCES ╍╍╍

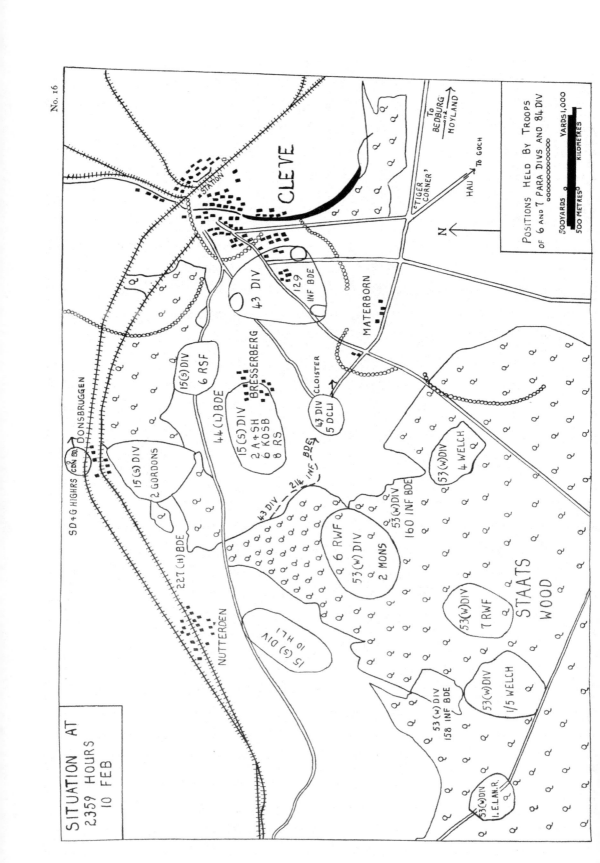

SITUATION AT
2359 HOURS
10 FEB

POSITIONS HELD BY TROOPS
OF 6 AND 7 PARA DIVS AND 84 DIV

500 YARDS 0   YARDS 1,000
500 METRES 0   KILOMETRES

N

CLEVE

To
BEDBURG
AND
MOYLAND
'TIGER
CORNER'
HAU   To GOCH

STATION

43 DIV
129
INF BDE

MATERBORN

43 DIV
5 DCLI
CLOISTER

44 (L) BDE
15 (S) DIV
2 A & SH
6 KOSB
8 RS
BRESSERBERG

15 (S) DIV
6 RSF

15 (S) DIV
2 GORDONS

DONSBRUGGEN
S D & G HIGHRS (CDN BD)

227 (H) BDE

NUTTERDEN

15 (S) DIV
10 HLI

43 DIV
2/4 INF BDE

53 (W) DIV
6 RWF
2 MONS

53 (W) DIV
4 WELCH
160 INF BDE

53 (W) DIV
7 RWF

STAATS
WOOD

53 (W) DIV
1/5 WELCH

53 (W) DIV
158 INF BDE

53 (W) DIV
1 E LAN R.

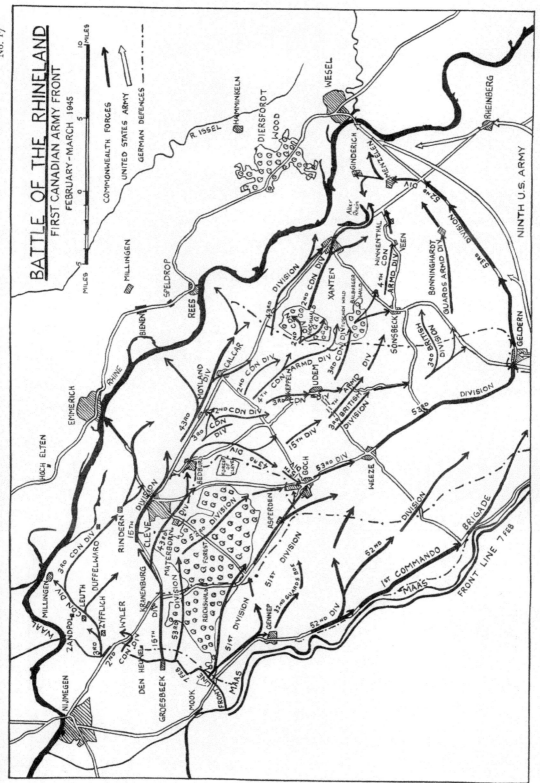

BATTLE OF THE RHINELAND
FIRST CANADIAN ARMY FRONT
FEBRUARY-MARCH 1945

COMMONWEALTH FORCES
UNITED STATES ARMY
GERMAN DEFENCES

MILES 5 0 5 10 MILES

dorff railway bridge at Remagan. The end of the war was at last in sight.

In deciding to fight in the Reichswald, Hitler finally sealed the doom of the German armies in the west. The First Parachute Army, admittedly, succeeded in withdrawing its battered divisions to the far bank of the Rhine. They were, however, so depleted as to be in no condition to deny the crossing. At one stage they had reached a strength of three infantry, four parachute, one panzer grenadier and two panzer divisions, supported by 700 mortars and 1,000 guns. They were well commanded and their troops fought generally with all the skill, experience and ferocity characteristic of the German army at its best. It is not surprising, therefore, that our casualties were heavy.

For the Division, the "Reichswald" was the greatest ordeal since Normandy. For a whole month in almost unspeakable conditions of danger and exposure the troops were almost continuously in action. At no time were commanders placed under greater strain or for so long. Nevertheless morale and fighting efficiency probably reached its highest level at this time. All arms, services and staffs played their part to the full, cheerfully and well. The Division faced the flower of the German army fighting for their country with fatalistic courage, as all men should fight, and beat them in the open field.

CHAPTER XIII

THE RHINE CROSSING

23rd to 29th March

OVERTURE TO THE LAST ACT

(See Sketch Map 18)

IT had now become evident to the whole world that the campaign was approaching its climax. From all fronts came convincing evidence of the enemy's inevitable collapse. Already to the south the U.S. armies had crossed the Rhine and were driving ahead. Before, however, the British and American armies in the north could proceed with the assault across the river, the scattered formations of First Canadian, Second British and Ninth U.S. Armies had to be concentrated and administrative preparations completed. Vast tonnages of ammunition and engineer stores had to be built up in the devastated area over which "Veritable" had been fought.

11th–12th March The re-grouping of Second Army released the Division from its responsibilities for holding the Rhine north of Xanten. These were handed over to 52 (L.) Division on 11th and 12th March and brigades moved back in T.C.Vs. to the east bank of the Maas around Gennep, Afferden and Well. Here 130 Brigade returned from the north. This sandy area had only recently been the German front line. It was intersected with an elaborate trench system and still strewn with mines. Scarcely a building remained standing and the majority of the troops had to find shelter in two-man bivouac tents. Fortunately the weather remained fine. The main embarrassment proved to be not rain but dust. Sparkling March days brought more than a hint of spring and some units even worked in shirt-sleeves. This was to be the Division's last rest during the campaign. It followed the usual routine of baths, kit inspections and reorganization. Shell-holes were filled in and football grounds made. 129 Brigade held a sports meeting. All civilians had been evacuated and the luxuries of eggs and fresh vegetables had temporarily to be forgone. Perhaps, however, this was no real drawback. The German housewife is a thrifty soul and her foresight, so far as the villages on the Rhine bank were concerned, had resulted in many cases of biliousness due to an over-rich diet. E.N.S.A. and cinema shows were made available on an unprecedented scale, one lady of the variety stage, wearing a jerkin decorated with almost all the formation signs of the Army Group, adding considerably to the traffic congestion, which, especially on the road from Afferden to Goch, reached staggering proportions both by day and night. The banks of the Maas within the Divisional area were piled high with enormous dumps of ammunition. The road from Goch to Bedburg constituted probably the largest accumulation of engineer equipment ever assembled in the history of the Army. Never in living memory can so many rations have been piled up in one spot as at Kevelaer.

In high spirits, the infantry went ahead with their training. Reinforcements were absorbed. On the Maas, each unit practised driving into buffaloes and loading on rafts. Overhead, formation after formation of Allied aircraft headed for the heart of the Reich.

For staffs, however, life proved by no means carefree. There came an urgent demand for staff tables. Conference with Lieut.-Colonel Urquhart, the G.S.O.1, succeeded conference as the terms of reference changed. Only those who have wrestled with the complexities of light scales, raft and buffalo loads can fully realize the exasperation involved. Many junior staff officers worked through the night only to be told at dawn that the basic assumptions on which their calculations had been based were no longer valid.

Divisional "O" Groups, it will have been gathered, were always **19th March** of a strictly formal character, slightly reminiscent of the darker side of school life. That held in the ruins of the Seminary at Siebengewald, near Goch, on the 19th in no way departed from what had by now become a tradition.

The operation about to be undertaken had been given the title of "Plunder." The British Second Army now consisted of 2 Canadian Corps, 8, 12 and 30 Corps. It was to make the crossing on a two-corps front from Wesel to Emmerich, with 12 Corps on the right and 30 Corps on the left. 30 Corps had under command Guards Armoured Division, 43 Division, 51 Highland Division, 3 British Division and 8 Armoured Brigade. "Varsity," the landing by XVIII U.S. Airborne Corps, was to be executed on 12 Corps front.

51 (H.) Division, which had been practising intensive amphibious operations on the Maas near Roermond, had the task of securing an initial bridgehead, sufficiently deep to permit bridges to be built on the corps front, and of capturing Rees and Haldern. For the assault, it had 9 Canadian Brigade under command. Immediately after, one brigade and divisional headquarters of 43 Division were to be passed across the river. The Division was then to take 9 Canadian Brigade under command and be responsible for the left flank. The remainder of the Division was then to cross, followed by the rest of 3 Canadian Division. When these moves had been completed, Lieut.-General Horrocks proposed to develop the advance on a three-divisional front, with 51 (H.) Division on the right, 43 Division in the centre, and 3 Canadian Division on the left.

In outline, Major-General Thomas had decided that 130 Brigade should cross first, followed by 129 and 214 Brigades. The actual move over the river involved handing over the Division to "Bank Control," staffed by the Royals. Not the least of the problems to be solved, therefore, was how to regain rapid control on reaching the far bank. To this end, he set up a Divisional landing organization under Lieut.-Colonel A. F. Johnson, R.A., 59 A.T.K. Regiment, and arranged, at this "O" Group, a rehearsal which actually took place on the 21st on the Maas. Similar arrangements, on a smaller scale, were made within brigades.

He made no attempt to minimize the opposition which still lay ahead. He said frankly that for the first three or four days stubborn fighting might be expected and that 116 PZ Division and 15 Panzer Grenadier Division, known to be fifteen miles north-east of Emmerich, would probably intervene. Events, in fact, justified this appreciation to the day.

Lieut.-General Horrocks "O" Group on the 21st, at the village hall at Pfalzdorf near Goch, struck a lighter note. All the senior officers in the corps collected in the bright sunshine outside—spirits already bright were raised to an even higher pitch when they went inside. Neither the Corps nor the Army Commander, General Dempsey, left anyone in doubt that the final phase of the war had at last come.

That night an enormous procession of buffaloes, armoured bull-dozers, R.A.F. winches to operate the rafts, armoured sledges, 6-ton matador lorries, R.A.S.C. three-tonners, Avres and 50-foot pontoon tractors set out without lights for its concentration area by the river 22nd bank. The Divisional artillery moved up opposite Rees the fol-March lowing night to join the seventeen field regiments, ten medium regiments, two heavy regiments and two super-heavy batteries supporting the crossing. On the left at Honnepel, 8 Middlesex 23rd arrived to take part in the "pepperpot." Throughout the daylight March all lay silent beneath their camouflage in the open fields below the bund of the Rhine. A dense smoke-screen, operated from Emmerich, covered the front.

Between five and six o'clock, 227 aircraft of Bomber Command passed over. From the right flank came the heavy continuous thud of their bombs falling on Wesel. Then at 6 p.m. the stupendous artillery bombardment opened up. An avalanche of metal and streams of tracer poured across the river and continued unabated for three hours. Then, in the darkness, the leading buffaloes of 30 Armoured Brigade, carrying infantry of 51 (H.) Division, slid into the water. The battle had begun.

ACROSS THE RHINE
25th to 29th March

24th Saturday, 24th March, dawned as a cloudless day. Just before March ten o'clock the great air armada of 18 Airborne Corps appeared, dead on time.   From all directions streams of aircraft converged on the army front opposite Wesel.   There were over four thousand Dakotas, Stirlings, Halifaxes, Lancasters, Fortresses, and Liberators, and the 1,200 fighters protecting them.   Less than an hour before they had been in England.   129 and 214 Brigades on the banks of the Maas cheered wildly.   130 Brigade, travelling in lorries through Kevelaer and Goch towards the Rhine Bank, looked up and realized that victory was now certain.   It was the task of these airborne troops to seize the bridges over the River Ijssel on 12 Corps front and link up with 15 Scottish Division and 1 Commando Brigade.   The operation was a complete success.   Three important bridges were captured intact and by six o'clock in the evening the Airborne Corps had linked up with 12 Corps on the right.

Despite the easy crossing during the night, 51 (H.) Division and later 9 Canadian Infantry Brigade on 30 Corps front found opposition stiffening as the day wore on.   51 Division soon became engaged in bitter fighting in the outskirts of Rees.   The bend of the Rhine between this town and Emmerich is dead flat.   It is, moreover, split into three corridors by three long lagoons, which are in fact old beds of the Rhine.   The country therefore offered great advantages to the enemy in that he could only be dislodged by frontal attack.   15 Panzer Grenadier Division exploited this situation to the full, despite the heavy weight of our artillery bombardment, described by themselves as fantastic.   By the evening of the 24th, however, 51 (D.) Division had reached the outskirts of Bienen, penetrated Speldrop and were in, though not yet masters of, Rees.   On 12 Corps front Wesel had been taken and all objectives for the day gained—the situation was extremely satisfactory.

The 25th proved to be a day of bitter fighting for the 9 Canadian Brigade and 51 Division.   Speldrop did not finally fall to the Canadians until heavy losses had been sustained by both sides. Houses had to be cleared at the point of the bayonet and single Germans made suicidal attempts to break up our attacks.   At Bienen, fighting developed at such close quarters that our artillery could not help.   51 (H.) Division continued steadily with the clearing of Rees.

Divisional tactical headquarters and 130 Brigade had moved into the marshalling area around Marienbaum on the 24th.   Here Bank Control, run by the Royals with all the courtesy and efficiency of a good travel agency, had laid out assembly areas, well signed and policed, between the bund of the Rhine and the well-known road from Cleve to Xanten.   Here they waited until the afternoon of the 25th, when in brilliant sunshine they were called forward, and without a sign of enemy interference crossed the river in buffaloes to land on the far side about a mile north of Rees.   At 4 p.m. Major-General Thomas took charge of the left sector of the corps front, 9 Canadian Brigade coming under his command.   The task given him was to

25th March

capture Millingen, a small town about a mile north-east of Bienen and the relatively high ground to the north-east. (It was, in fact, only sixteen metres above sea-level.)

The leading battalion of 130 Brigade, 5 Dorset, found itself committed to battle almost as soon as it landed. Androp on Millingen Meer, between Speldrop and Bienen, had been the scene of several hotly contested engagements with 51 Division. Before the advance on Millingen could go forward, this opposition had to be finally crushed. Lieut.-Colonel A. E. C. Bredin was therefore ordered to **26th March** capture the place that very night. In order to ensure full artillery support, he delayed his start until 1.30 a.m. C Company under Major R. W. Hewson then moved to a position in the featureless country between Speldrop and Androp and sent out patrols to either flank. B Company (Captain J. G. Riley) and D Company (Captain J. L. Betts) then advanced on the village and captured it in the face of only moderate resistance which was satisfactorily removed with grenades. This effective stroke, carried out without previous reconnaissance in daylight, combined with the final extinction of resistance in Bienen by the H.L.I. of Canada, enabled the advance on Millingen to be staged. In view of the startling progress on the corps right flank the resistance put up by 15 Panzer Grenadier Division and 7 Para. Division was particularly exasperating. Around Bienen the enemy was supported by considerable artillery and mortar fire and the Canadians' gains were hard won.

Major-General Thomas now directed 9 Canadian Brigade on to the railway due north of Bienen and the northern outskirts of Millingen and ordered Brigadier B. A. Coad to clear the remainder of the town. 4 Dorset, under Lieut.-Colonel W. G. Roberts, with one company of 7 Royal Hampshire and one Squadron of 13/18 Hussars under command, penetrated the town, after A Company, under Major Symonds, had seized the river bridge. Many of the enemy fought it out to a finish amongst the houses. However, by the afternoon the place was finally subdued. Brigadier Coad then moved 7 Royal Hampshire against the south-eastern suburbs. Here fighting continued throughout the night and by dawn over 200 prisoners had been taken.

27th March Meanwhile, the last traces of resistance having been finally extinguished in Rees, the assembly of the remainder of the Division around Esserden had rapidly progressed. 129 Brigade crossed in buffaloes in the early hours of the 26th. Soon after daylight a Class 9 and a Class 15 bridge were operating smoothly. 214 Brigade were thus able to cross dryshod and spared all the complications of embarkation during the night of 26th–27th. The congestion around Esserden on the morning of the 27th reached its climax. Battalions were concentrated in areas no larger than a football ground. They presented a target beyond a gunner's wildest dreams. When they rose from their slits *en masse* it seemed as if the Last Trump had sounded.   But no shells came over.   There could be no doubt that the final break was near.

The crossing of the Ijssel at Anholt three miles ahead now consti- 27th March tuted the Division's objective.   On their right 51 (H.) Division were moving on Isselburg.   On the left opposition on the Canadian front was decreasing.   About a mile and a half ahead, astride the main road from Millingen to Anholt, stretched a partially constructed *Autobahn* running along a low, sandy ridge covered with spruce woods on the far side.   This clearly constituted the enemy's next defensive position.   Major-General Thomas accordingly decided to clear the intervening ground up to the Autobahn with 129 Brigade, and then to assault with 214 Brigade.   4/7 Dragoon Guards and a squadron of kangaroos were placed under command of this brigade, which was ordered to exploit the attack as far as the village of Meghelen, about a mile beyond the Autobahn.   130 Brigade were ordered to continue clearing the line of the railway from Emmerich to Wesel in a south-easterly direction.   Before dawn, 129 Brigade had moved up to the burning ruins of Millingen and at 9 a.m. Brigadier Vandeleur, with the 4 Wiltshire on the right and the 5 Wiltshire on the left, resumed the advance.   4 Wiltshire met little opposition, but on arrival on their objective came under heavy small-arms fire from the Autobahn.   Shelling and mortaring increased as the morning wore on.   5 Wiltshire had little difficulty at first, but they also, on approaching the Autobahn, encountered rifle and machine-gun fire. A and D Companies slowly worked their way forward to within 200 yards.   It was now midday.   Only seven hours' daylight remained for 214 Brigade to complete their operation.   Traffic congestion in Millingen had become acute.   Brigadiers Vandeleur and Essame therefore arranged that 5 Wiltshire should be withdrawn for at least four hundred yards to ensure that 214 Brigade should begin its advance from a reasonably secure and clearly defined start-line.   To pass one brigade through another in circumstances such as these is an operation calculated to try the patience of even the most placid commanders, and incredibly exasperating not only to those who are already in contact with the enemy, but to those who have to carry on with the advance.   On this occasion the presence in the immediate neighbourhood of several parties of the enemy—who had been quite understandably overlooked—added to the uncertainties.   In the circumstances it is remarkable that Major G. G. Reinhold of 1 Worcestershire (late B.M. 130 Brigade) and Lieut.-Colonel Ivor Reeves of 7 Somerset Light Infantry were able to carry out their reconnaissances and launch their battalions to the attack on time at 2 p.m.   The 15 Panzer Grenadier Division were in fact strongly entrenched amongst the hedges, trees and houses along the Autobahn, and using with no small skill and determination their

Spandaus and S.P. guns. Very heavy shell-fire complicated the issue of orders and the deployment of both battalions.

Now began a most involved battle. The country was intersected by ditches and every hedge and house seemed to contain a Spandau. The tanks of 4/7 Dragoon Guards found the going bad and could give little practical help. Throughout the afternoon companies fought their way slowly forward. On the extreme right of the brigade front, A Company of 1 Worcestershire, under Major P. G. Hall, paid a heavy price, but gained their objective by 5 p.m. D Company on its left, under Major B. R. N. Elder, found themselves temporarily forced to ground and only completed their task after dark. It had been expected that 51 (H.) Division, on the Division's right flank, would attack simultaneously. In fact, their operation did not start until 5.30 p.m. The battalion's difficulties can therefore be well understood. Nevertheless by nightfall they were securely dug in on their objectives.

7 Somerset Light Infantry, on the left of the brigade front, found their task no easier. A Company under Major Roberts were held up from the start. About twenty men of B Company under Major K. J. Whitehead, however, succeeded in reaching the great concrete fly-over buttress of the Autobahn on the main road to Anholt. This was no mean feat, and earned for Corporal Comm the D.C.M., a decoration not lightly given. Fighting went on throughout the afternoon. Lieut.-Colonel Ivor Reeves, coming forward, was wounded and Major C. B. Brooke-Smith took over command. The wasps were brought up. Not until after dark were the enemy finally driven out of their strong positions and the battalion consolidated beyond the Autobahn. It had been a bitter battle. Nevertheless at no stage in the campaign did this battalion get to grips with the enemy with greater enthusiasm.

In spite of the confused situation around the Autobahn, the 5 D.C.L.I. in kangaroos and B Squadron 4/7 Dragoon Guards, who had waited nose-to-tail all the afternoon in Millingen, were ordered forward as the light faded to exploit as far as Meghelen, about a mile and a half ahead. In actual fact the situation was by no means ripe for exploitation. None the less the eruption of this mass of armour, accompanied by smoke and high-explosive distributed with apparent impartiality, drove both friend and foe to the ground. On reaching the Autobahn the leading tanks encountered bazookas. Lieut.-Colonel Taylor therefore decided to continue the advance through the night on foot. By dawn, fighting all the way, the battalion had reached the outskirts of Meghelen. Lieut.-Colonel Taylor now brought up his tanks and crocodiles and started to deal with the village. B Squadron of 4/7 Dragoon Guards opened up, and the crocodiles proceeded systematically to burn down the houses, starting at the south end and working north. For the majority of

28th
March

the defenders this was the last straw, and many surrendered. No sooner had the battalion established itself than the enemy opened up on the village with a very heavy and effective bombardment—by far the most intense since "Veritable." This final outburst could only mean one thing—he had had enough and was firing off his last rounds before falling back. However, the parachutists had fought well. Approximately four hundred had been killed in the twenty-four hours' operations and 150 taken prisoners. Any of the British commanders engaged in this battle would welcome them under his command or as Allies in another war. No one now bears them any grudge for stealing what has always been regarded as a British prerogative—never knowing when they were beaten.

The clearing of Meghelen occupied most of the morning. About noon B Squadron of the Reconnaissance Regiment managed to get through the burning village and to reconnoitre along the Anholt road. 5 Troop in the lead soon found itself held up in the woods about a mile from the town, and the leading Daimler was put out of action. Meanwhile 2 Troop of A Squadron succeeded in getting out a short distance to the north, but also was held up. Although 51 Division had penetrated to Isselburg on the right and seized a bridge intact, it was evident that on the Divisional front that the enemy still intended to defend the crossings of the Ijssel at Anholt. The main road led through dense forest right down to the river and road crossing opposite this little town. A direct advance would therefore have involved tedious wood clearing and an obvious direct assault. However, now that 214 Brigade held Meghelen this could be avoided. Major-General Thomas therefore ordered 130 Brigade to pass through this place, force a crossing at Landfort and build a Class 40 bridge.

Brigadier Coad began his advance at 5 p.m., with 4 Dorset on the right and 7 Royal Hampshire on the left. Landfort, a small village on the west bank of the river, fell to 4 Dorset by nightfall. 7 Royal Hampshire protecting their left flank came under heavy fire from beyond the river. On this battalion's left flank, there was considerable fighting for D Company's objective and crocodiles had to be brought forward to deal with the enemy holding a group of buildings which finally was captured by A Company at dusk. It was clear that an assault crossing by night in the face of opposition would have to be staged. This task fell to 5 Dorset. The night was 28th– exceptionally dark and at the last moment Lieut.-Colonel Bredin 29th had to change the site of the crossing. However, B Company March under Captain J. G. Riley embarked in assault boats and passed over. Having reorganized, he pushed on to clear a wood beyond the main road which was parallel with the river. B Company (Captain J. L. Betts) followed and moved out to the right flank. Both these companies now systematically proceeded to round up the enemy in

the woods and houses.   A Company then crossed and seized the high
ground between the other two companies.   The Pioneer Platoon
built a light bridge and by dawn all the battalion's anti-tank guns
were in position on the far bank.   When daylight came the enemy
shelled the bridgehead viciously.   Patrols, pushed forward into the
woods ahead, found the enemy still present in strength.   The
Divisional artillery most effectively sped them on their way.   By
8.30 a.m. the Divisional engineers had completed a Class 40 bridge.

Brigadier Coad now directed 4 Dorset on to Anholt.   The town
fell with little opposition.   7 Royal Hampshire at the same time
thrust forward two and a half miles and reached the Priesterbeek
west of Dinxperlo, thus saving much minor bridging later on.   In
this brisk advance, the battalion captured no less than 125 prisoners
of 17 Para. Regiment in a number of lively actions.   Later in the day
4 Wiltshire extended the bridgehead to the line of the Priesterbeek
on the right of 7 Royal Hampshire with little difficulty.   The
Divisional engineers without a moment's delay started to repair the
bridges.   A Squadron of the Reconnaissance Regiment, pushing out
early to the north-west over the Dutch frontier, advanced four miles
to the village of Wels and took 48 prisoners, a mixed party of Volks-
turm and parachutists.   A mile further on at Gendringen, 2 Troop
under Lieutenant L. Avery found the Germans still dug in.

There could be no doubt that the breakout was coming.   The
momentum of the assault had never been allowed to flag.   Everywhere the enemy had proved himself incapable of containing the
bridgehead across the Rhine.   On the army right flank resistance
had obviously collapsed.   The advance was rapidly developing on a
three-corps front with 8 Corps in the lead.   Further to the right, the
Ninth and First U.S. Armies had made spectacular thrusts forward.

No fewer than six British armoured brigades, representing a thousand tanks, now stood ready deployed for the pursuit, and nothing
could stop them.   Never before had such a mass of armour been placed
so surely and with such speed.

The complete destruction of the German armies in the west was
in sight.

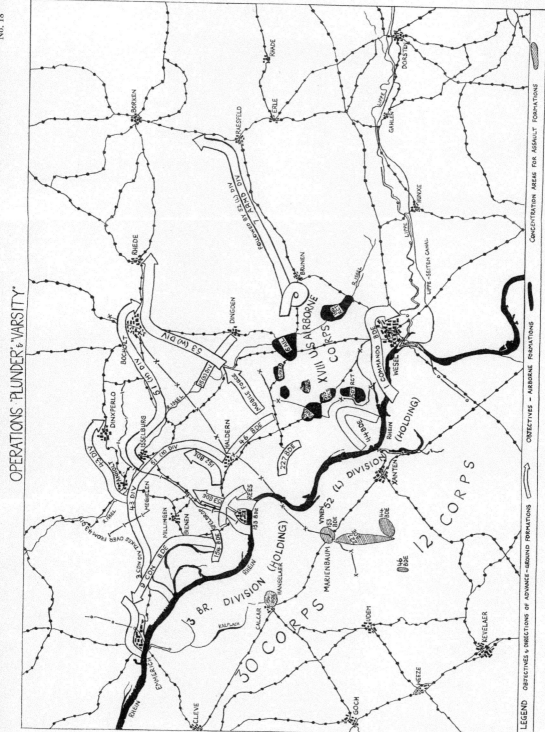

OPERATIONS "PLUNDER" & "VARSITY"

LEGEND   OBJECTIVES & DIRECTIONS OF ADVANCE - GROUND FORMATIONS   OBJECTIVES - AIRBORNE FORMATIONS   CONCENTRATION AREAS FOR ASSAULT FORMATIONS

CHAPTER XIV

THE PURSUIT

THE ADVANCE TO HENGELO
30th March to 3rd April
(See Sketch Maps 19 and 20)

IN his personal message to the troops before the crossing of the Rhine, the Field-Marshal had said: "Having crossed the Rhine, we will crack about in the plains of Northern Germany, chasing the enemy from pillar to post. The swifter and more energetic our action the sooner the war will be over, and that is what we all desire; to get on with the job and finish off the German war as soon as possible. Over the River Rhine, then, let us go. And good hunting to you all on the other side. May the 'Lord mighty in battle' give us the victory. . . ."

The Lord had indeed delivered the enemy into his hand. The directive for the breakthrough breathes the spirit of the more martial passages of the Old Testament, which have often afforded inspiration to British soldiers in the past from the time of Cromwell, and, it is to be hoped, will do so again. The books of Samuel, Kings and Judges, in the matter of the spirit in which battles should be conducted, are indubitably sound. "Every officer and man must have his personal weapon ready to hand; in the event of attack or treachery, we shoot to kill. . . . The operations will be conducted with speed and violence by the armoured columns; foremost commanders must always be quick to by-pass resistance with the leading troops and to push on deep into enemy rear areas; if a column is held up on one route, another one must push on. This is the time to take risks and go flat out for the River Elbe. If we reach the River Elbe quickly, we win the war."

30 Corps Operation, "Forrard On," inaugurated as far as the 29th Division was concerned at an "O" Group in a marquee on the sodden March fields not far from the Rhine bank on the evening of the 29th, reflected the immense drive now imparted from above to the operations. The corps, advancing as mobile protection for the left flank of Second Army, was to break out of the bridgehead. Guards Armoured Division were to push forward on the axis Groenlo–Enschede–Quakenbrück–Bremen, followed by 3 Division. 43 Division was given the task of protecting the left flank and opening "Club" route. This involved, in its first stage, an advance of twenty-five miles due north from Anholt through that part of Holland

which projects east of the Rhine to the Twente Canal at Lochem.   It was hoped to seize the crossings over this canal, move east on Hengelo and, re-entering Germany, cross the Vechte at Nordhorn and push on to the Dortmund–Ems Canal at Lingen.

For this advance Major-General Thomas organized the Division into five groups.   First came the "Armoured Thrust Group," with Brigadier E. Prior-Palmer of 8 Armoured Brigade, consisting of 4/7 Dragoon Guards less a squadron, 12 K.R.R.C., 4 Somerset Light Infantry in kangaroos of 1 Canadian A.P.C. Regiment, 147 Field Regiment and 260 Field Company.   Next, in order of march, came the "Follow-up Group" under Brigadier Vandeleur of 129 Brigade. 214 and 130 Brigades and the Divisional tail constituted the remaining groups.   To this already formidable force the Royals and 121 Medium Regiment had been added.   For practical purposes, therefore, the Division had all the potentialities of both an armoured and an infantry division.   The two battalion lifts of kangaroos raised high hopes of decisive and swift action should enemy resistance completely collapse.   The ample infantry reserve also held out a prospect of continuous operations, both by day and night, without placing an undue strain on the troops.   It was almost dark when Major-General Thomas finished his orders.   The situation offered boundless possibilities and uncertainties.   There was much to be done if the advance was to begin at daylight.

30th
March   The outlook from the point of view of the Germans was utterly and completely hopeless.   Unfortunately this obvious fact had not yet penetrated the minds of 6 Parachute Division, who throughout the 30th fought a stiff rearguard action and still retained their artillery.

The assembly of the Armoured Thrust Group at Anholt early next morning—it was Good Friday—produced a traffic jam of vast and fantastic proportions.   The narrow streets and the only two bridges added to the complications.   There was much waving and shouting before the trying process of "marrying up" even approached the semblance of order.   As the morning wore on the traffic, as far as the eye could reach, remained jammed solid and stationary.   Will-power, exhortation and force of personality exerted from the highest levels seemed equally powerless to get it on the move.

The right column, consisting of 4 Somerset Light Infantry and C Squadron 4/7 Dragoon Guards, had, in fact, struck opposition at the village of Sinderen five miles ahead.   A tank had been lost to a bazooka and 88's were concentrating on the road.   Until D Company had cleared the village with tank support the advance could not get under way.   This they did with all the speed which could be expected.   On the left, 12 K.R.R.C. with B Squadron of 4/7 Dragoon Guards, in spite of intermittent shell-fire from S.Ps., got forward for about eight miles to Silvolde, where they were heavily shelled.

The right column, having disposed of the enemy in Sinderen, now rolled forward with little difficulty until the outskirts of Varsseveld were reached about 7 p.m. Here accurate enemy S.P. fire opened up on the column, causing some casualties. Lieut.-Colonel Lipscomb therefore decided to assault the town by night without armoured support and thus gain surprise. A patrol under Lieutenant May accompanied by Sergeant Adriaanse, the Dutch interpreter, penetrated the town and after clashing with the enemy brought back information with regard to his dispositions which was of great value. 4 Somerset Light Infantry's attack went in at 1.15 a.m. It was a brilliant success. First A and B Companies cleared the southern edges. Then C Company passed through and took the northern end of the town. Darkness made the problem of dealing with the large numbers of prisoners particularly difficult. Finally D Company made for the Slingerbeek to the north-east and secured a small bridgehead. By dawn all resistance had been extinguished in the town. Both the bridges over the Slingerbeek, however, had unfortunately been blown. 5 Wiltshire therefore crossed to the far side to cover the construction of a bridge by 260 Field Company. By nightfall this was complete. 31st March

Despite the fatigue of both the tank crews and the infantry, Brigadier Prior-Palmer decided to face all the hazards of an advance by night. At 11 p.m. the vanguard, consisting of C Company under Major Watts of 4 Somerset Light Infantry, riding on the tanks of A Squadron 4/7 Dragoon Guards, forged ahead without lights into the darkness followed by the rest of the battalion. Two towed 88's tried to join the column. In the confusion one got away, but the other was captured after a brief fight. Just short of Ruurlo, ten miles ahead, Lieutenant P. J. A. Kirk of A Squadron spotted a moving light and dim figures ahead near a bridge. They were, in fact, a demolition party engaged in putting the finishing touches to a 500-lb. aerial bomb. Sergeant Hayman, the pioneer sergeant of 4 Somerset Light Infantry, at once appreciated that it was a race against time. He won the race. Under covering fire from the Bren gunner of his assault section, he at once cut the fuse connected to the bomb. He then searched the bridge, discovering five Tellermines connected by Cordtex fuse with the bomb on top. These he cut; and then, with the assistance of two volunteers, with the sangfroid characteristic of the pioneer sergeants throughout the Division, rolled the bomb clear.

The column now moved on to Ruurlo without further trouble, but found the place held. Major Watts deployed the vanguard. The chief opposition inside came from light anti-aircraft guns mounted at the street-corners. Whilst these were being dealt with both Lieut.-Colonels Lipscomb and Barker, with their own headquarters, halted a few hundred yards short of the town, suddenly found themselves personally involved in a battle. On the left of the road stood a large house marked with a Red Cross and surrounded by a moat. 1st April

It was still pitch dark.   Suddenly the tank in front of Lieut.-Colonel Lipscomb's carrier was hit by a Panzerfaust.   A violent exchange of fire now burst out.   However, both headquarters gave a good account of themselves.   Major Hutchinson brought his company forward and captured the house.   Altogether some sixty prisoners were taken, including the commandant and adjutant.

When daylight came the column was reorganized, and after a little trouble at Barchem, approached Lochem late in the morning.   It was held by the enemy.   By early afternoon B Company of the Somersets found themselves pinned to the ground by small-arms fire on a wide front.   It was therefore decided to assault the town, and A Company under Major Beckhurst moved forward.   A running fight amongst the houses now developed, supported by the tanks. Many Germans surrendered after a fight.   Their positions were well chosen and it was not till late in the day that the battle finally died down.   Both the infantry and the tank crews had been continuously in action for 72 hours and were now on the verge of exhaustion. However, when darkness fell the eastern half of the town had been taken.   4 Wiltshire were now brought forward and attacked at 11 p.m. in silence and without any preliminary bombardment.   By dawn the Germans had been driven out.   Whilst the fighting had continued, the Dutch inhabitants had remained behind locked doors. Now they emerged and gave the visitors an overwhelming welcome. Collaborators were rounded up and order rapidly restored.   Fire, however, still continued from the far bank of the Twente Canal and all the bridges were found to be destroyed.

Major Beckhurst relates an unusual incident in connection with the fighting here.   "During the height of the battle a captured German stretcher-bearer was brought to my H.Q.   All my own stretcher-bearers were fully occupied in dealing with casualties and this man at once volunteered to go and bring in two of our own wounded who were awaiting attention.   Single-handed he brought both of these men back, although he was under heavy fire from his own side all the time.   It was a very gallant performance and a curious sidelight on German mentality."   The truth is that the man did his duty according to his lights.   So did many of his comrades.   The eleventh hour was long past; the German Army was obviously doomed; nevertheless they blew up the bridges over the canal and brought the advance via the north bank temporarily to a standstill.

1st April   Meanwhile the opening of the bridge across the Slingerbeek at Varsseveld had enabled Major-General Thomas to direct 214 Brigade Group north-east against the crossings of the Twente Canal opposite Goor, ten miles east of Lochem.   Preceded by a squadron of the Royals and C Squadron of the Reconnaissance Regiment, and with 1 Worcestershire as advanced guard, the Brigade followed the column of 129 Brigade as far as Ruurlo soon after first light.   Here there was

31. Men of the Dorset Regiment boarding a Buffalo ready to cross the Rhine, 25th March, 1945

32. Infantry of 130 Brigade leaving T.C.Vs. for the attack on Cloppenburg, 13th April, 1945

33. The C. in C. at Divisional Headquarters at Brunssum on 25th November, 1944, with Major-General Thomas, Brigadier Boylan, Colonel Furnival, the late Lieut.-Colonel McCance, Lieut.-Colonel Trethowan, Lieut.-Colonel Grant Peterkin and Lieut. Spencer-Moore

considerable congestion, but at last a way was found through the
town.   Under the eyes of the Dutch in their Sunday best, for it was
Easter Sunday, the column at last got clear.   It is possible to have
too much of a good thing.   C Squadron, under Major Blood, of the
Reconnaissance Regiment and the squadron of the Royals both had
armoured cars.   Had there been fewer, progress would have been
more rapid.   When the leading car was bazookaed on entering
Dipenheim, two miles south of the canal at Goor, the time was
obviously ripe for the infantry to intervene.   This, however, with
the only way forward blocked by stationary armoured cars, was no
easy proposition.   However Major J. D. Ricketts, commanding the
vanguard, with B Company mounted on the tanks of the 13/18
Hussars, eventually forced his way through.   The leading tank was
knocked out.   Nevertheless the company dashed on.   Just at that
very moment, when they were within fifteen yards of the bridge, there
came a huge flash and a roar.   When the flying debris had settled,
what had once been a bridge was now a jagged gap.   Not without
annoyance and reflecting that it was All Fools' Day, the battalion
lined the south bank, opened up with their 3-inch mortars, and prepared for the assault crossing which they felt that the brigadier would
now inevitably consider necessary.

On the other flank, feeling their way forward to the north-west,
the remainder of the Reconnaissance Regiment found themselves
slowed down by demolitions.   However, on the axis of Guards
Armoured Division, where extensive obstructions had so far made
only a relatively slow advance possible, the front suddenly became
fluid.   By 11 a.m. a bridge over the Twente, one mile west of the
large town of Enschede, had been seized.   This was blown up after
four tanks had crossed.   However, 2 Household Cavalry Regiment
found another further west.

The town was quickly encircled, and by nightfall had been
captured, with many prisoners.   3 Division now followed on the
axis of the Guards, whom Lieut.-General Horrocks now directed to
drive on to the Dortmund–Ems Canal, and ordered the 43 Division
to secure the left flank at Hengelo.

Three miles west of Hengelo and north of the Twente Canal is the   *2nd
village of Delden.   Here there were two bridges and a lock gate,   April*
which seemed to afford the possibility of a crossing to the east of the
town.   Major-General Thomas therefore brought up the Sherwood
Rangers and the 12 K.R.R.C.   Brigadier Prior-Palmer was ordered
to hand over at Lochem to 129 Brigade and make with all speed for
the crossings at Delden.   The force got under way at 4 a.m. and,
headed by two troops of the Royals, had soon covered fifteen miles,
only to find soon after dawn that the bridges were down.   A crossing,
however, by the lock gate seemed a possibility.   B Company of 12
K.R.R.C. put in a bold attack, only to be met with heavy fire from

17

concealed Spandaus and mortars. After a most gallant attempt in which severe casualties were suffered, the company had to be withdrawn. Brigadier Coad, whose brigade was now moving forward through Ruurlo by a very complex route, had joined Brigadier Prior-Palmer at an early hour. After the failure of 12 K.R.R.C. to cross by *coup de main*, it had become evident to both that no alternative to a formal assault by 130 Brigade now remained. The necessary preparations were accordingly put in hand.

The Twente Canal ends at Enschede, which, incidentally, was now firmly held by 3 Division. To Major-General Thomas therefore, when he arrived on the scene, there seemed no point in incurring the casualties inevitable in a direct frontal assault across the Canal. A move round the flank by 130 Brigade through Enschede would inevitably be complicated and, in view of the congestion on the axis of Guards Armoured and 3 Division, demand pressure to secure a right of way. No one, however, was better qualified than he to overcome difficulties of this sort. A plan therefore was quickly evolved to assault Hengelo from the direction of Enschede. A squadron of the Royals, the Sherwood Rangers Yeomanry and 12 K.R.R.C. were placed under command of Brigadier Coad for the operation and the Reconnaissance Regiment ordered to take over the front along the Canal.

The flank march to Enschede, started at midnight in torrential rain was a remarkable achievement. The route was merely a cross-country track. The maps available were poor and little or nothing was known of the country ahead. Nevertheless, thanks partly to the help of guides from 3 Division in Enschede, the assault on Hengelo was under way by 9 a.m. Lieut.-Colonel Bredin launched 5 Dorset straight down the main road. C Company, in the lead, under Major R. W. Hewson, led the advance. A machine-gun post at the approaches to the town was quickly disposed of and mines removed. D Company under Major Hartwell moved round the right flank and seized a factory in the centre of the town. A Company under Major H. C. Allen moved across the open ground to the south and rapidly turned the canal defences. B Company (Major K. W. G. Roe) passed through and reached the site south-west of the town, where it was intended that 204 Field Company should construct a bridge. Meanwhile Lieut.-Colonel Talbot with 7 Royal Hampshire had made a wide sweep from the north-east and entered the north of the town. Large numbers of prisoners now gave themselves up. The Royals found themselves at one time in some difficulty, but the arrival of 4 Dorset soon convinced the enemy that further resistance was futile. Brigadier Coad, with Hengelo in his possession and the defences of the Twente Canal finally turned, now despatched 4 Dorset to the town of Borne, three miles ahead, which fell with little opposition. As a result, Lieut.-Colonel Roberts was able to cancel the fire plan and thus save the town from destruction. In gratitude, the in-

3rd
April

habitants have commemorated their liberation by naming one of their principal squares after the Dorset Regiment. Finally in the evening he moved out 12 K.R.R.C. towards Delden, where they had met such obstinate resistance on the previous day. Next morning they made contact with 4 Canadian Armoured Division, advancing from their bridgehead on the Twente Canal.

The Dutch are normally a phlegmatic people. Their enthusiastic welcome of their liberators at Hengelo, however, passed all bounds. The town, except for bombing around the railway station, had suffered little damage and the troops were soon in billets which seemed of surpassing luxury after the bad conditions under which they had lived so long. Orange flags appeared everywhere. The railway line, which had carried the V2 weapons into Holland, was cut. The people of the town after five and a half years under the Nazi yoke were at last free. The final stroke had been achieved by a complex manœuvre skilfully executed. Not for the first time sweat had saved blood.

Elsewhere on the corps front Guards Armoured Division had reached the Ems at Lingen. Further to the right the remainder of Second Army were at Osnabrück and Rheine, and faced only loose and unco-ordinated opposition. So far on 30 Corps front the enemy's fighting spirit showed no signs of giving way in the face of our greatly superior numbers and equipment. The para-troops, although composed of units drawn from many and various formations, still fought on. A brief pause necessitated by the need to build bridges at Lingen was now to give them a brief respite. Nevertheless their fate was irrevocably sealed.

ON TO HÄSELUNNE
7th to 9th April

The utter hopelessness of the German situation was now evident to all the world. By 1st April no fewer than 21 divisions under Field-Marshal Model had been surrounded in the Ruhr by the American armies and 21 Army Group. General Patton's thrust into southern Germany went forward dramatically and nothing could stop it. On the 5th, 8 Corps reached the Weser, to be followed by 12 Corps on the following day, when 7 Armoured Division captured Hoya, twenty miles south of Bremen. The line of forward troops of 21 Army Group thus ran irregularly from east to west to 30 Corps' temporarily static position in the Lingen bridgehead.

7th April

Until this phase of the campaign 30 Corps had been regarded by friend and foe alike as the spearhead of the Army. Now, instead of running free through the towns and villages of North Germany, it found itself still faced by stubborn rearguards, road blocks, mines and demolitions. Responsibility for the sufferings of the German

population, which the advance of 30 Corps necessitated, rests on the
shoulders of Lieut.-General Erdmann, who, it must be admitted,
conducted the withdrawal to Bremen with great professional skill.
He must have realized that the ruin of Germany was inevitable, and
that the surrender of all her armies could only be a matter of days.
Instead of conducting his operations in the setting of a foreign
country, so congenial to the Germans in the past, he now proceeded
to display all his skill, experience and powers of leadership in his own,
in the face of an opponent with complete command of the air and
equipped with a vast array of destructive mechanical equipment.
The manner in which, travelling in a captured jeep, he raked together
the remnants of many formations into battle groups which still fought
on, will always compel professional respect.   Whether his pre-
dominating motive was regard for his own reputation or for that of
the German army is not known.   He may even have fought on
because he liked fighting.   At the time his obstinacy seemed to be
the height of folly and callousness.   Perhaps however in the light of
history it may be considered that in the eclipse of the German armies,
he, like Ney in the retreat from Moscow, rescued something which
was worth saving.   He at least with certain others, when his time
comes, can go forward with his German conception of military
honour intact to make his report to the shade of Frederick the Great.

In any case, the chaos he had created at Lingen did not permit the
advance to be resumed until the 7th.   Both the Guards Armoured
Division and the Division had to pass over the newly constructed
bridges over the Ems and the Canal.   Frightful traffic congestion
rapidly developed and it was not until the late afternoon that the
advanced guard, consisting of 13/18 Hussars, 12 K.R.R.C. and 7
Somerset Light Infantry in kangaroos finally got on the move.
Darkness prevented the Reconnaissance Regiment from deploying.
However, in the late afternoon the column at last heaved forward and
swiftly advanced straight down the main road to Bremen for seven
miles.   Just short of the village of Bawinkel a very strong road block
of heavy felled trees, interlaced and covered by another built-up
block of timber, earth and rocks, brought it to a halt.   Many similar
blocks, often booby-trapped and mined, were to be met with on
succeeding days.   Only a petard could compete with them.   This
literally blasted them to bits.   The debris was then swept up by
"Sherdozers."   This obstacle having been removed, B Company of
the 7 Somerset Light Infantry pushed into the village.

8th   C Squadron of the Reconnaissance Regiment were off the mark
April   with the dawn.   In Bawinkel Major Bindon Blood almost immediately clashed with the enemy rearguard at a crater.   These
were quickly dealt with and the repair of the crater begun.   On
reaching the outskirts of the village a brisk battle now developed
amongst the buildings.   Major Blood and his squadron pushed on,

leaving the tanks and infantry to collect the remains, and drove on to reconnoitre the line of the Hase river, five miles ahead. North of the main road stretched a pine forest, traversed by vague tracks across the soft sand which were not marked on the map and were hard going. Nevertheless 9 Troop got through to the river at Buckelte, a village about two and a half miles north of the main road. The bridge here had been demolished a long time before—only the two ends survived. Further east, 10 Troop found that the bridge was blown and shot up Germans bathing on the far bank.

East of the main road, A Squadron had found hard going in the face of determined opposition all the way, but had got forward.

It was obvious to Major-General Thomas that the enemy's main defences would be sited astride the Bremen road. C Squadron's rapid advance to Buckelte and the news that the river there was, at the most, only lightly defended immediately prompted him to turn the enemy's flank at Häselunne from the north. This task he gave to 214 Brigade. Brigadier Essame therefore ordered 7 Somerset Light Infantry to cross at Buckelte. In order to distract the enemy's attention from this flank move, he instructed the D.C.L.I. to press ahead down the main road and create the impression that a frontal assault over the Hase was intended. In fact, the latter task was executed almost too well, as the D.C.L.I., as usual, were not slow to attract the attention of most of the enemy in the neighbourhood and soon got to close grips in the woods and minefields east of the river.

It was an afternoon of glorious spring sunshine. Buckelte proved to be a charming village. Daffodils, tulips, jonquils, and all the fruit-trees were in bloom. A dozen German troops sunbathing were quickly rounded up and the preparations for the crossing put in hand. To his great satisfaction, on arrival Brigadier Essame found that Lieut.-Colonel Brooke Smith had discarded the site for the crossing he had proposed and found another around a bend. This was a most fortunate decision, for the assault when it went in at 8 p.m. achieved complete surprise. The battalion rapidly crossed the river, formed up in a wood on the far bank and advanced to the assault of Hamm, opposite which it was intended to build a Class 9 bridge. There were some casualties and opposition proved strong immediately west of the village. A wide flanking movement to the north, however, by C and D Companies proved too much for the enemy, who surrendered. Soon after midnight Hamm had fallen and work on the bridge begun. Owing to the bad approaches, the work took longer than had been expected. However, by dawn it was ready and 1 Worcestershire, whom Lieut.-Colonel M. R. J. Hope-Thomson had brought up in the darkness, crossed over. Judged by text-book standards, the operation now executed was perfect. Ammunition had been coming forward for days and none had been expended. The town of Häselunne therefore sustained damage likely to keep the

9th April

local housing authorities busy for many years. To this the enemy added his quota when he withdrew. The two distilleries, however, were fortunately undamaged and yielded an astronomical quantity of low-grade gin, which the Corps Welfare Officer, Colonel Alabaster, was not slow to appropriate. Retailed by N.A.A.F.I., at a low, but not too low, a price, it was to form the basis of many a celebration for months to come. By noon Lieut.-Colonel Henniker, the C.R.E., had started his preparations for building a Class 40 bridge over the Hase in the town. 7 Somerset Light Infantry rapidly occupied the northern end.

During the night 5 D.C.L.I. had secured a footbridge south of the town. Thanks to the success of the flanking movement to the north, this was no longer necessary. The Brigadier therefore despatched them behind the Worcestershire on to the village of Eltern, where C Squadron of the Reconnaissance Regiment had been in contact for most of the day, a mile to the east on the Bremen road. This they occupied without difficulty as darkness fell.

Major-General Thomas had hoped to continue the advance at first light on the 10th on a two-brigade front, maintaining touch with 4 Canadian Armoured Division on his left and Guards Armoured Division on his right. In fact, the construction of the Class 40 bridge proved by no means easy. The sappers sustained several casualties from concealed mines and it was not till 10.30 a.m. on the 10th that the bridge was finally ready to take the tanks of 8 Armoured Brigade.

During these two days the brilliance with which Major Blood had handed C Squadron of the Reconnaissance Regiment, had made the task of the commanders responsible for this considerable bound forward comparatively easy and clear-cut. At no time were they better served by the Reconnaissance Regiment—and this is saying a great deal.

THE THRUST TO CLOPPENBURG
10th to 13th April

Despite the news from the south that the Allied advance was proceeding practically unopposed, the fact had to be faced so far as 30 Corps was concerned that further obstinate enemy rearguards were likely to continue the struggle for some time. The parachute divisions appeared to be functioning in five components, the G.O.C. and his staff, the provost, a supply echelon, flak batteries and the "stragglers." The procedure was apparently simple. Behind the line the provost, with unlimited authority, set up a string of posts on all roads leading out of the Corps rear boundary. The definition of "straggler" was the whim or suspicion of the N.C.O. on the spot. Men separated from their units, leave parties and even specialists

were formed up into battle groups at these posts and sent forward
into the line.   The supply echelon commandeered whatever ammunition, weapons and rations it could.   Lastly, the flak batteries
provided the artillery support as the field batteries were out of
ammunition.   The 88's, however, could help themselves in their
retreat from the many A.A. sites scattered to considerable depth
around Bremen.   This miracle of improvisation, in fact, worked
despite its obvious futility, as there could now be no hope of restoring
any of the regular divisions or recreating any form of rearward
organization.

Lieut.-General Horrocks therefore made it quite clear that the
advance must not be considered as a race between the Division and
Guards Armoured Division.   Already there had been unnecessary
loss of life on the part of small parties moving off the main axis of
advance and clashing with isolated parties of the enemy who had
been overlooked.   He therefore insisted that as divisions moved
forward, the areas behind the leading troops should be systematically
mopped up.

Before the Division could deploy on a two-brigade front the road-
junction at Herzlake, five miles east of Häselunne on the main route
to Cloppenburg, had to be cleared.   From here a reasonably good
road took off to the north-west to link up with a network of minor
roads connecting the villages in the close country which lay between
the line of advance of 4 Canadian Armoured Division and "Heart
Route," 43 Division's main axis.   This new and, it must be admitted,
rather vague route was now christened "Joker" and allotted to 129
Brigade.   130 Brigade was to continue the advance on the main axis.
B Squadron of the Reconnaissance Regiment was deployed early on
the 10th and Lieutenant James with 7 Troop soon found that the
bridge to the west of Herzlake was blown.   This obstacle held up the
advance of 129 Brigade from Häselunne and the main road soon
became a solid mass of vehicles.   Manœuvre, therefore, proved most
difficult for all concerned.   However, Lieutenant Roycroft with
7 Troop found a way round to the north and by last light had gained
contact with the enemy on 129 Brigade's new axis.

The leading battalion of the brigade, 5 Wiltshire, when eventually
clear of the bottleneck at the Häselunne bridge found its advance
everywhere obstructed by mines and road blocks.   All of these were
defended and had to be reduced in detail.   The advance therefore
inevitably was slow.   It continued throughout the night, and by
dawn the battalion had reached the outskirts of Holte, four miles
north of Herzlake.   It was not until the morning of the 11th that
traffic at last began to flow freely forward.

The tail of 129 Brigade held up Brigadier Coad and 130 Brigade,
who had left Lingen at first light, for some time.   When, however,
the road junction at Herzlake was at last clear, his advanced guard,

10th
April

11th
April

consisting of the Sherwood Rangers and 12 K.R.R.C., made a rapid bound forward of ten miles to the outskirts of Löningen, a considerable town.   Here they struck determined resistance, particularly in the wood to the south.   They were faced in fact by a composite battalion of the Grossdeutschland Brigade, mostly boys of from 16 to 18 years of age, but including a company of potential officers.   In the late afternoon, therefore, Brigadier Coad staged a deliberate attack by the 4 Dorset.   The potential officers fought with the utmost ferocity.   However, before midnight they had been overwhelmed.   Determined to allow the enemy no respite, Brigadier Coad now pushed through 7 Royal Hampshire with orders to capture the road-junction on the far side of the town.

In the darkness and confusion, Lieut.-Colonel Talbot pressed on for 3,000 yards, only to find at first light that the main road beyond the town was obstructed by an enormous crater.   This was rapidly filled, and by 10 a.m. the brigade column once more surged forward.

Meanwhile on the northern route, Brigadier Vandeleur with 129 Brigade had made a similar bound forward.   4 Wiltshire, despite road blocks, bazooka teams hidden in ditches and isolated parties in houses, forced their way forward.   The villages of Herssom and Vinner fell after a struggle.   Every house in which resistance was met was put to flame.   By dusk A Company had reached the outskirts of the village of Wactum, five miles due north of 130 Brigade in Löningen.   Here mines and an enormous road block caused a momentary check.   However, a hastily organized night attack by 3 a.m. removed all traces of resistance.   The battalion had covered twelve miles in the day, mostly on foot and fighting all the way.

12th
April
The crater on the main axis having been filled, Brigadier Coad pressed on with his advance in the mid-morning.   Six miles ahead at Lastrup, the advanced guard once more found itself held up.   Lieut.-Colonel A. E. C. Bredin with 5 Dorset therefore had to be committed to a deliberate attack on the town.   The leading companies, B under Major K. W. G. Roe and A under Major H. C. Allen, rapidly deployed and drove across the open fields to the outskirts of the town.   Here they dismounted and, under cover of smoke and artillery concentrations, advanced to the assault, supported by the Sherwood Rangers.   The enemy, however, had only stayed long enough to force the battalion to deploy.   He now broke off the action to repeat the process a few miles further on.   Hot on his heels, the battalion pressed ahead to this next rear-guard position, three miles further on.   Here A and C Companies once more put in a vigorous attack as night fell.   Searchlights close behind lit up the scene as the battalion consolidated amongst the burning farms.

13th
April
Brigadier Coad again thrust forward at first light.   The ten miles to Cloppenburg were soon passed.   Once more he found himself faced by determined opposition despite the dramatic speed with

which his advance was now proceeding. Cloppenburg is a considerable town and a vital road centre. It is not surprising therefore that 7 Royal Hampshire encountered fanatical resistance, especially in the northern half of the town. The battle raged in the streets from house to house. Soon many of the buildings were on fire. Enemy shells and mortar bombs rained down upon the battalion. Two S.P. guns firing down the streets at point blank range and bazookas fired at high angle compelled the battalion to fight every inch of the way forward. However, by the late afternoon a bridge on the far side had been captured. As night fell 5 D.C.L.I. pressed through the smoking town as the mopping-up went on. Fighting raged in the streets all night. The Grossdeutschland Group showed little disposition to surrender and fought on as if they were still in Normandy. 130 Brigade had advanced 27 miles in less than three days, fighting by day and by night all the way. In the circumstances an armoured division could have done no better—indeed, it is doubtful if it could have done so well. The enemy had been ruthlessly driven back without a pause. During this day, 129 Brigade had also got forward as far as Gronheim, eight miles north-west of Cloppenburg. Major-General Thomas had hoped with this turning movement to encircle a large number of the enemy. The roads, however, now petered out into very boggy country. Further advance on a two-brigade front was therefore no longer possible. Meanwhile between the two axes the Reconnaissance Regiment rapidly rounded up such of the enemy as had escaped from the clutches of the two forward brigades.

FORST CLOPPENBURG AND AHLHORN
14th to 16th April

An observer from another solar system, in a flying saucer or other inter-stellar conveyance, looking down at that time on the plains of northern Germany on the front of 30 Corps would have formed no high opinion of the sanity of the earth's inhabitants. He would have seen one tribe of men engaged in blowing holes in the roads of his own country and another tribe, equipped with a vast array of unlovely machines, filling them up again. The fact that one tribe was busy destroying its own property would have added to his bewilderment. The result, when viewed from the air a few weeks later, showed along the track of the Division a swath of burnt-out farms, blown bridges and wrecked villages. The troops had come a long way and were impatient to see their journey's end. The slightest opposition therefore paid a heavy price, for the phosphorus grenades and wasps of the infantry and the armoured bulldozers, petards, crocodiles and other mechanical contraptions of 79 Armoured Division were ready to hand and liberally used.

Ten miles to the east of Cloppenburg lay the enemy's last

remaining escape route from the debacle in the south to Oldenburg and Bremen. Against this, and in particular the cross-roads at the village of Ahlhorn, Major-General Thomas directed 214 Brigade late in the afternoon of the 13th. Brigadier Essame had therefore ordered 5 D.C.L.I. to leave, as far as possible, the fighting going on in Cloppenburg to 130 Brigade—a task they were pursuing with the utmost vigour and speed—and, advancing by way of the bridge in the northern suburbs, to push on throughout the night so as to secure the line of the railway, a mile to the east, by dawn. Lieut.-Colonel Taylor fulfilled his contract to the letter. In the eastern suburbs B Company under Major Holland, which led the advance, found itself checked as night fell. A quick plan to remove the opposition was made, and the company, supported by tanks of the Sherwood Rangers and a rifle platoon of 12 K.R.R.C., advanced to the attack. The enemy were using bazookas and there were some casualties to the tank crews. Every house was thoroughly searched. It was a cold, star-lit night. On their right 7 Royal Hampshire fought a similar battle. By 10 o'clock the company had gained a firm base from which Lieut.-Colonel Taylor now proceeded to develop his attack by passing C Company through to the railway. This three-thousand-yard advance, involving house-clearing all the way, occupied the rest of the night. The Grossdeutschland Group were in no mood to surrender either to the D.C.L.I. or 130 Brigade. The headlights of their lorries could be seen in the town. However, by dawn C Company had gained the railway and despatched many prisoners to the rear. Ahead, lay a kidney-shaped feature commanding the exits from Cloppenburg. Against this soon after dawn Lieut.-Colonel Taylor launched A and D Companies. Despite continued Spandau fire, the feature was successfully seized, a whole German company surrendering *en masse* to D Company.

14th April The 1 Worcestershire now took the lead, advancing down the main road. Major B. R. N. Elder, commanding D, the foremost company, found himself still faced with the now familiar problem of craters and road blocks, manned usually by small groups of riflemen. At these blocks he brought forward the petards and bulldozers with the column, blasted down the great timber baulks and earth barriers, cleared the debris, filled the holes and pushed on. An S.P. gun still shelled the column. On either side of the road stretched the dense forest of Cloppenburg, closely planted with pine and spruce, into which the enemy could escape at will. The brigadier therefore ordered the 7 Somerset Light Infantry, following behind the Worcesters, to clear the east flank to a depth of 2,000 yards.

By the afternoon the line of the River Lethe, 2,000 yards short of the Ahlhorn cross-roads, had been reached. Major Elder was not in the least surprised to find that the bridge had been blown. He therefore crossed and fanned out, forming a bridgehead about 500 yards

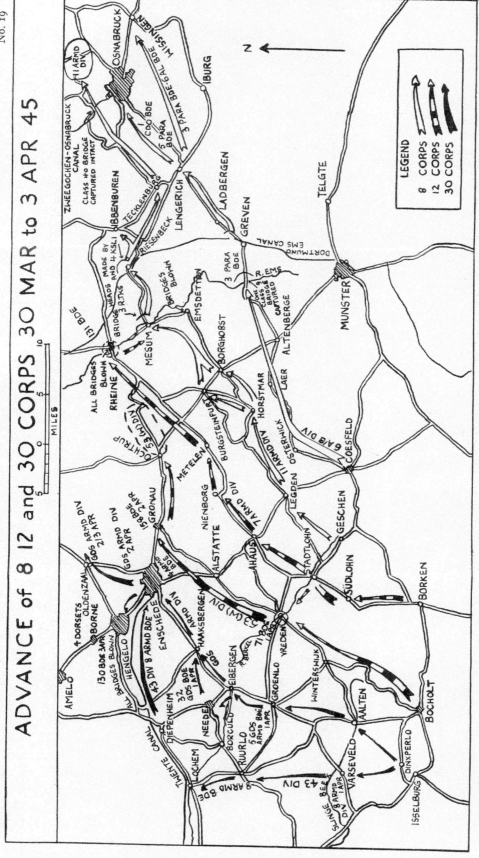

ADVANCE of 8 12 and 30 CORPS, 30 MAR to 3 APR 45

in depth.   17 Platoon's position was at the furthermost point of the perimeter and somewhat isolated.   Their wireless failed and for two hours they fought a lone battle against two tanks and a number of infantry.   Eventually the enemy was beaten off, leaving ten dead. In this action Major Elder was severely wounded.

Meanwhile, A Company had found a bridge over the Lethe four hundred yards to the south, and now established themselves on the right of D Company to cover the construction of the bridge on the main road.   204 Field Company started to work, but were so severely shelled that operations had temporarily to be suspended during the night.

The dawn of 15th April is memorable because it brought with it the enemy's last attack against the Division.   It might have been thought that after the mauling at Cloppenburg he would have had no further stomach for the fight.   This was far from the case.

15th April

At 5 a.m. his artillery fire switched from the bridging site to the forward platoons.   The main thrust, consisting of about 200 infantry and two tanks, came down a ride in the woods to the north-east and had some success.   The two forward platoons of A Company were overrun and Lieutenant Smith was killed.   D Company's right flank crumbled, but Lieutenant Crossingham's platoon stood firm and did much slaughter.   For two hours a fierce close-quarter battle raged in the woods, but eventually Major P. G. Hall, by a supreme effort, rallied his company and beat the enemy off.   The enemy fell back leaving a large number of dead and 60 prisoners.   In fact, a complete enemy battle group had been destroyed.   Later in the day, when the advance was resumed, old men and women emerged from the woods and neighbouring villages to carry away their dead, who lay in long rows in front of the Worcestershire's position.   Many were young boys; others were old men who had been hurriedly pressed into uniform.   It was a sombre scene, pathetic in its utter futility even to the battle-hardened troops of the Division.

The Brigadier now moved 7 Somerset Light Infantry through the woods north of the road to turn the flank of the enemy facing the Worcestershires.   The move was accomplished with little difficulty and a considerable number of prisoners were taken.   The Worcestershires then linked up.   At 5.30 p.m. all was ready for the final assault on Ahlhorn.   A and D Companies of 7 Somerset Light Infantry, supported by tanks of the 13/18 Hussars and covering their left flank with smoke, descended on the cross-roads.   Thirty-five prisoners, including two immaculate Luftwaffe officers, fell to A Company. D Company killed a number and took further prisoners.   Sergeant H. Carroll of 7 Platoon captured the telephone exchange.   On the switchboard were two sockets labelled "Bremen," one of which was plugged in.   He put in the other lead and said, summoning the greater part of his German vocabulary, "Wer da, bitte?" and received the answer, "Hier ist Bremen." If not yet in sight, the Division's goal drew near.

With the enemy's last escape route to the north thus finally cut at Ahlhorn, 30 Corps Headquarters called a halt to the Division's advance. The operations of Second Army were now entering a new and final phase.

THE BREMEN OPERATIONS

16th to 27th April

(See Sketch Map 20)

16th
April

The situation on the whole front was now changing from hour to hour with astonishing speed. In detail it was so complex that to follow it on the map at the time was by no means easy. In outline, however, the intentions of the Army Commander were clear-cut. In brief, the task now given to 8 Corps, on the right, was to force the Elbe from the area of Celle and Lüneburg, so familiar to the Division after the end of the fighting. 12 Corps, in the centre, were directed on Hamburg and 30 Corps ordered to capture Bremen.

It was clear to Lieut.-General Horrocks that in view of the large forces by which he was still opposed, Bremen would take time to capture. The larger part of the town lies north of the River Weser and can most easily be attacked from the east. 52 (L.) Division, at the moment under command of 12 Corps, was well placed to carry out this operation. It was therefore arranged that this division should come under his command after the crossing of the Weser had been secured at Verden, and that 43 Division should hold itself in readiness to intervene here. West of the river, he ordered 3 Division and 51 (H.) Division to continue their advance north-east in the general direction of Bremen and Delmenhorst. The city had thus to face a two-divisional assault on each bank of the Weser.

This decision temporarily elbowed the Division out of the lead. East of Ahlhorn, 51 Division's advance now cut across the front. 214 Brigade therefore confined its activities to rounding up stragglers in the woods.

The Division was now given the by no means onerous task of protecting the left flank of the corps. 129 Brigade was therefore moved to the area of Visbek and Varnhorn, south-east of Ahlhorn, in relief of 152 Brigade of 51 Division. The operations which followed

17th
April

on the succeeding days can only be described as mopping-up expeditions on a battalion scale. There was still some shelling and

18th
April

mines continued to cause casualties. On the 18th contact was lost with the enemy. The brigade therefore moved forward and on the 20th reached Dötlingen, midway between Wildeshausen and Delmenhorst, conforming with the move forward of 51 Division.

Operations at this stage were not without an element of anti-climax. On the 18th, even the Divisional axis from Häselunne to Cloppenburg had to be surrendered to 2 Canadian Corps. The departure of 130 Brigade, to operate under command of 52 (L.) Division on the west bank of the Weser on the 19th, was a further blow. On arrival after a long move, this brigade found itself given the unexciting task of providing fire support for the 52 (L.) Division, who were advancing on the other bank. Finally, on 22nd April, command of 129 Brigade passed to 51 (H.) Division. This was the proverbial last straw. Like an actor who has successfully played a leading part in a long drama and finds himself relegated to the back row when the curtain falls, the Division faced a damp climax unworthy of its achievements.

Before the war Bremen had had a population of half a million. Next to Hamburg, it is the largest port in Germany. Behind it stretched a long history going back to the Middle Ages, when the Hanseatic League, here and at Hamburg and Lübeck, had built up a vast trade in which our own ancestors had shared. The merchants of Bremen , in the past, played a conspicuous part in the development of the modern world, and their lovely old houses and public buildings in the Altstadt, east of the river, formed part of the heritage of Europe as well as Germany. The city had expanded into the Neustadt, west of the Weser. Here were sited the U-boat pens, the Focke Wulf aircraft factory, the Atlas works and many other large industrial undertakings. The Nord Deutscher Lloyd had operated from the huge docks. Into this city the remnants of the parachute army had now withdrawn and reinforced the already considerable garrison.

With the vast armament of his own corps behind him and the striking force of the R.A.F. at his command, Lieut.-General Horrocks was in no inordinate hurry to complete the capture of the city. With his resources, to have thrown away British and German civilian life unnecessarily at this stage of the campaign, merely to score a dramatic triumph, would have been out of character. On the 20th when the 3 and 51 Divisions approached the western outskirts, he fired four hundred shells containing leaflets into the city. They read: "The choice is yours. The British Army is lying outside Bremen, supported by the R.A.F., and is about to capture the city. There are two ways in which this can take place. Either by the employment of all the means at the disposal of the Army and R.A.F. or by the occupation of the town after unconditional surrender. The choice is yours as to which course is followed. Yours is the responsibility for the unnecessary bloodshed which will result if you choose the first way. Otherwise you must send an envoy under the protection of a white flag over to the British lines. You have 24 hours in which to decide." Contact was also gained with the German commander to the same effect by telephone.

19th
April

22nd
April

No German in the town, however, was morally big enough to face the inevitable. Responsibility for the sufferings of the civilians in Bremen and the utter ruin of the city during the next six days rests fairly and squarely on the shoulders of their leaders, whose callousness and stupidity were unequalled even in the history of Germany.

22nd April This prolonged and futile resistance brought the Division once more to the front. Major-General Thomas on 22nd April resumed command of 130th Brigade Group, now located north-east of Verden, and moved forward 214 Brigade Group to the west bank of the Weser near this town. At this time, the 52 (L.) Division, advancing from Verden by the Bremen road parallel to the Weser, had captured Achim and reached the village of Uphuysen, three miles from the city. On the right of 30 Corps, 12 Corps with 32 Guards Brigade had reached Rothenburg, twenty miles north-east of the crossing of the Weser at Verden.

In view of the considerable strength of the enemy forces withdrawing north into the Cuxhaven peninsula, it was still considered necessary to protect the corps' right flank. Major-General Thomas's instructions for the 23rd therefore were to assume responsibility for the security of 52 (L.) Division's right flank and to develop a thrust to cut the great Hamburg–Bremen Autobahn six miles north-east of Achim. He was then to be prepared to turn left-handed and advance on Bremen along the Autobahn.

23rd April The operations now started by 130 Brigade, although not comparable with those of Normandy and the Reichswald, were none the less strenuous. As resistance became more spasmodic, so the scope of both mounted and infantry movement became more ambitious. The brigade's axis of advance ran through sandy tracks and bogs which made the going bad for A Squadron of the Reconnaissance Regiment. 7 Royal Hampshire first cleared the woods north of Welle and secured the high ground beyond. 5 Dorset then passed through and, brushing aside sporadic opposition in the woods by last light had got forward about eight miles to the village of Ahausen. The majority of the hundred prisoners taken came from 480 Division, which still showed some disposition to fight. At night Lieut.-Colonel Roberts moved 4 Dorset on to the high ground to the north and at dawn **24th April** pushed forward a further two miles to Hellewege. A brisk engagement ensued here in which he was wounded. The enemy were, however, successfully chased off, abandoning a medium and some anti-tank guns.

214 Brigade and B and C Squadrons of the Reconnaissance Regiment, ordered to clear the area between 52 (L.) Division's axis through Achim and the Autobahn six miles to the north, found similar miscellaneous and unco-ordinated opposition. The country proved to be largely reclaimed marshland, which restricted vehicle movement to the tracks. There were a considerable number of

enemy in the area, fighting on lines which bordered on insanity. A party of sailors fought bravely but most ineffectively—they were facing the wrong direction. Mines had been scattered in accordance with no apparent plan. The prisoners taken came from every conceivable unit, including the civil police. 7 Somerset Light Infantry started the operations soon after midnight on the right, 5 D.C.L.I. joining in on their flank after dawn. Late in the afternoon both battalions reached the Autobahn after a series of isolated battles with bewildered parties of the enemy who had no instructions other than to fight to the last. A partial explanation of the enemy's eccentric dispositions is provided by the fact that the brigade's lines of advance practically coincided with the outer ring of A.A. sites around the city. These yielded amongst the prisoners half a dozen women in uniform, the German equivalent of the A.T.S. Literature striking a decidedly anti-feminist note, and originated apparently at G.H.Q., had fortunately been widely distributed throughout the brigade. "Your attitude towards women is wrong in Germany," said the pamphlets. "Do you know German women have been trained to seduce you? Is it worth a knife in the back? A weapon can be concealed by women on the chest between the breasts, on the abdomen, on the upper leg, under the buttocks, in a muff, in a handbag, in a hood or coat. . . . How can you search women? The answer to that one is difficult. It may be your life at stake. You may find a weapon by forcing them to pull their dress tight against their bodies here and there. If it is a small object you are hunting for, you must have another woman to do the searching and to do it thoroughly in a private room." In the light of this depressing admonition from the highest military level, it is almost pointless to record that the German A.T.S. were treated with the utmost correctness. Besides, they were very plain.

Whilst these interesting but not very productive operations were going on, another heavy bombing attack was delivered by Bomber Command on Bremen. 52 (L.) Division took immediate advantage and secured the southern edge of the town during the night. When daylight came, medium bomber attacks continued at thirty-minute intervals for five hours. 52 (L.) Division therefore made rapid progress throughout the day. By 4 p.m. two of its brigades had penetrated two miles into the town between the railway and the river. This move forward at last cleared 52 (L.) Division's axis and thus made any further development of a separate axis for 43 Division superfluous. 130 Brigade were therefore motored over to Oyten on the Autobahn two miles east of Bremen. At the same time, 129 Brigade had now been released by 51 Division and concentrated near Achim. A clear-cut task at last faced the Division—to clear Bremen east of the railway line which bisects the city. Operations on 214 Brigade front were therefore suspended and the

24th–
25th
April

25th
April

bridges they had secured, with some loss, beyond the Autobahn blown up.

25th
April

On arrival at Oyten, 130 Brigade found themselves faced by a task of no great difficulty. The bulk of the enemy had obviously withdrawn into Bremen. 5 Dorset crossed the Autobahn and seized the village of Sagehorn, over-running two hospitals full of German wounded and liberating a trainload of Allied prisoners-of-war. 7 Royal Hampshire pushed patrols into the residential suburb of Rockwinkel. The clearance of this large area provided the brigade's main task for the 26th. The enemy here had given up the struggle. Over 1,000 surrendered, abandoning about fifty anti-aircraft guns.

Meanwhile in Bremen itself events approached a dramatic climax. West of the Weser 3 Division had reached the outskirts of the city and was on the point of delivering its final assault. 52 (L.) Division, operating between the railway and the river, had got well forward during the 25th. The railway itself after passing the southern end of the Burgher Park—the Hyde Park of Bremen—throws off a branch line at Utbremer Vorst which bends backwards to run parallel with the main lines. The loop thus formed provided a clearly defined brigade task. It was known that the core of the defence was sited in the Burgher Park within this loop. When therefore Major-General Thomas ordered 129 Brigade to clear this area, he gave them the double honour of striking the *coup de grace* at the siege of Bremen and fighting the Division's last major action of the campaign.

Brigadier J. O. Vandeleur accordingly decided to advance on a two-battalion front as far as the Burgher Park and then with his reserve battalion, 4 Somerset Light Infantry, in kangaroos, to strike the final blow. In fact, events were to take the course he had anticipated.

In bright sunshine, 4 and 5 Wiltshire reached their start-lines in Rockwinkel in T.C.Vs. soon after dawn and dismounted without interference. On the right, the route of 4 Wiltshire led through the eastern fringe of the city. The method of advance selected involved, of necessity, a somewhat complicated system of leap-frogging companies and intermediate objectives. Lieut.-Colonel Corbyn had intended to start at 7.30 a.m. Whilst waiting for this hour, all seemed so quiet ahead that he set off in a dingo with Major T. Greenshields of 224 Battery. Twenty minutes later he returned to report that the first two objectives were clear. The two leading companies scrambled into the carriers and raced ahead with orders to go flat out to their sixth objective. A road block of steel rails at the bridge over the Autobahn brought them to a halt. It was defended only by two boys with a Spandau. These two heroes were given a kick in the pants and sent packing, and the local population got to work clearing the block. A few hundred yards away to the north stood a huge flak

34. View of Bremen, 26th April, 1945

The Last Waltz

D B Wilson · 45 ·

35. The 43rd Division and 8 Armoured Brigade take the floor for the last time,
Cuxhaven Peninsula, 1st May, 1945

battery surrounded by high blast walls. A Company promptly rounded up the garrison, 164 in number, without a blow.

The road block having been removed, B Company pressed on, to be momentarily checked by a 20-mm. gun firing down a side-street. A handy petard soon dealt with this.

C Company struck the next opposition—a heavily defended concentration camp whose guards decided to resist. The prompt initiative of Sergeants Stacey and Packer in closing with the enemy enabled the company to put in a quick attack with artillery support, which effectively settled their fate. Other road blocks were dealt with similar alacrity and by the afternoon the battalion had begun to close with its final objective—the Burgher Park.

A Company now started to enter the northern part of the Park. They were immediately greeted by very heavy fire from some German barracks, which for the moment compelled them to fall back into the surrounding houses with the loss of twelve men. B Company now came up and Lieutenant MacLean took a patrol forward to find out whether the bridges over the ornamental water within the Park would take tanks. Major P. J. Colverson of C Company now came forward to find out the situation, and unfortunately, driving past the barracks in his carrier, came under Spandau fire at point-blank range and was killed. The battalion had clearly struck serious resistance. By ill luck at this juncture, Lieut.-Colonel Corbyn, whilst watching our guns deal with the barracks, was wounded by one of our own shells falling short.

Meanwhile, 5 Wiltshire on the brigade's left flank had got forward with similar speed. After liberating a camp of slave workers the battalion had cleared the race-course without difficulty and approached a large barracks. C Company, in the lead, approached with caution. After covering all exits through the outer walls with Bren guns, Lieutenant Blackman with one section entered the main gate. A German soldier standing inside, at once put up his hands, to be followed by 97 more all anxious to surrender. A and B Companies continued their methodical advance through wreckage of fallen tram wires, bomb debris and the closely built-up houses of the town. C and D Companies once more resumed the lead.

Civilians now told the leading men of C Company that the Germans ahead were waiting to give themselves up. Whether they deliberately wished to lead the Company into a trap or not is unknown. The fact remains that as 13 Platoon, under Lieutenant Blackman, approached the cross-roads a few hundred yards from the Park, machine-gun fire burst out from both sides of the road. In a flash the Platoon had taken cover in the nearest houses and returned the fire. The tanks of the Sherwood Rangers were prompt to join in with murderous fire. The battle raged for nearly an hour, but at last the fire of the tanks destroyed most of the machine-gun positions.

18

Violent sniping in the maze of buildings continued, however, for a long time.

On the battalion's left flank D Company had moved forward along the railway line, keeping touch with 52 (L.) Division. No opposition was met until they reached the large open square which was their objective, almost level with the Park. They quickly dug in amongst the gardens of the houses. Hearing from troops of 52 (L.) Division that a large number of the enemy were holding out in an air-raid bunker in the Park, Captain Edwards went forward to see for himself. At the south-east corner of the Park five roads joined. This spot was obviously the core of the enemy defences, and was promptly christened Hyde Park Corner. At least one concrete bunker in the Park near here was known to be the headquarters of the Bremen defences. Captain Edwards was convinced that the battalion could deal with this problem without assistance. Brigadier Vandeleur, however, had kept the 4 Somerset Light Infantry in reserve all day to deliver the final blow. Preparations for deliberate assault were therefore put in hand at once, the C.R.A., Brigadier K. F. Mackay Lewis arranging on the spot artillery support from all guns within range, including mediums and heavies. Two troops of crocodiles were brought up.

At last light, 10 p.m., C Company under Major Watts advanced on Hyde Park Corner. The houses here were large and solid and their gardens surrounded by high walls. Some of the enemy were dug in along the edge of the Park. Others opened fire with Panzer-fausts and Spandaus from the cellars and upper storeys. The company, by the light of the crocodiles' belching fire, closed in, and within half an hour had compelled a large number of Wehrmacht and sailors to surrender.

Lieut.-Colonel Lipscomb now launched A and B Companies and the crocodiles northwards into the Burgher Park. The battle which ensued was almost appalling in its magnificence. When the enemy attempted to come out of the houses and fight in the open he was caught by the fire of the infantry and the Besas of the crocodiles. When he stayed inside the houses he was roasted alive. Burning houses cast a lurid light over the flame-throwers as they slowly waddled up the streets and over the infantry as they dashed from house to house. The roar of the flames mingled with the crack and rattle of small-arms fire. This was a battle after the brigadier's own heart, and it was only with difficulty that he was persuaded to refrain from personally fighting with the leading section.

Having thus decisively disposed of the enemy, the Somersets continued their advance along the verge of the Park. The road was littered with branches of trees, smashed buses and civilian cars destroyed by the bombardment. Major Beckhurst with A Company now came up with Major B. G. P. Pope of 4 Wiltshire, who was reconnoitring in the area. The latter pointed out an enormous concrete bunker some thirty feet high in the Park. It had only one entrance. The two majors accompanied by a section entered. Inside they found a rabbit warren of staircases and small rooms, all in the utmost disorder. About thirty officers were seated at little wooden tables piled with empty champagne bottles. The passages were crowded with ordinary soldiers. There was also a hospital bay with fourteen patients and an engine room still working to generate electric light and pump in fresh air. The Somersets had captured the headquarters of Major-General Sieber, the static commander of the Bremen garrison, who turned out to be a very stuffy, aged military gentleman. He and his staff were promptly whisked away to the Divisional cage. All of them were of the type associated in all armies with sedentary duties. By midnight all resistance in the neighbourhood of this bunker had come to an end.

When day broke 4 Wiltshire resumed their attack on the northern end of the Park. B Company on the right crossed the canal unopposed in the canoes of the Bremen Canoe Club. D Company, however, came under fire from a small barrack and were on the point of assaulting it when a party of the enemy emerged and surrendered. Major Pope entered and found that it was the Gun Operations Room of the Bremen Anti-Aircraft Defences. Inside was Lieut.-General Fritz Becker, the Defence Commander of Bremen. He provided a pleasant contrast to Major-General Sieber—tall, academic-looking and inclined to be sociable. He knew little of the situation, for he had been compelled to direct the battle over civil telephone lines, which our bombing had for the most part destroyed. With him was a vice-admiral and a large staff, all equally bewildered.

The Nazi Headquarters was also found during the morning. Unfortunately the Somersets arrived too late, as the Gauleiter and his wife had just committed suicide in an upstairs room. They had both shot themselves and an empty bottle of brandy stood on the table between them.

The leading battalion of 214 Brigade, 1 Worcestershire, had closed up to the Burgher Park during the night, and during the morning advanced unopposed into the northern suburbs of the town, C Company pushing its forward elements towards the river Hamme, a tributary of the Weser. A large road block beneath a railway bridge offended Lieut.-Colonel A. A. Grubb, the Commandant of the Divisional Battle School, who was temporarily commanding the battalion. Without delay he summoned a petard and staged a demonstration, presumably for the benefit of the company and the civilian spectators. Unfortunately the resulting explosion was not entirely in the direction expected, and Lieut.-Colonel Grubb retired with a nasty wound in the arm, literally in the words of Shakespeare "hoist with his own petard." 5 D.C.L.I. took possession of the local

27th April

jail, reputed to contain 1,000 dangerous criminals, without difficulty. All day prisoners streamed into the Divisional cage, and by nightfall 2,771, including 99 officers and 831 hospital cases, had been taken during this forty-eight hours.

In the rain which now began to fall, Bremen presented a scene of sordid horror almost beyond description. Great piles of rubble blocked the streets, the twisted lamp standards silhouetted grotesquely against the sky, the stench of buildings still burning offended the nostrils and the open sewers stank to heaven. The people were broken-spirited and listless. Many of them were literally green in colour, for the ventilation in the big air-raid bunkers had broken down and the sanitary arrangements inside had collapsed. They were docile, bewildered and hopeless. The fighting had released thousands of slave labourers from Eastern Europe and Russian prisoners, who broke loose and fell without restraint on the large stores of liquor in the town. Their behaviour, especially that of the Russians, can only be described as abominable. Brutal treatment by the Germans had reduced them below the level of beasts, but it is doubtful whether they ever had far to fall. Some even drank themselves to death on the commercial spirit in the docks. Fighting, rape and open murder broke out, and our troops had to intervene. None had any idea of sanitary discipline, and their huts and surroundings had reached a stage of human degradation and filth beyond the conception of any Western European. No one in the Division regretted the order to hand over the charnel-house, which had once been a great civilized city, to 52 (L.) Division, and to move out into the clean air of the Cuxhaven peninsula on the morning of the 28th.

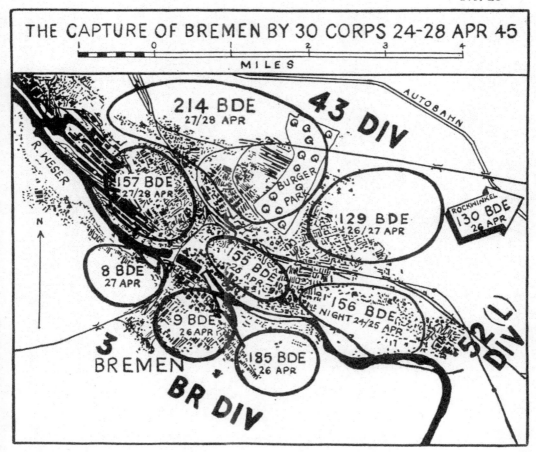

THE CAPTURE OF BREMEN BY 30 CORPS 24-28 APR 45

MILES

43 DIV

AUTOBAHN

214 BDE
27/28 APR

157 BDE
27/28 APR

BURGER
PARK

129 BDE
26/27 APR

ROCKWINKEL
130 BDE
26 APR

R. WESER

N

8 BDE
27 APR

155 BDE
26 APR

156 BDE
NIGHT 24/25 APR

52 (L) DIV

9 BDE
26 APR

185 BDE
26 APR

3
BREMEN

BR DIV

CHAPTER XV

THE CUXHAVEN PENINSULA

29th April to 5th May

(See Sketch Map 21)

LIEUT.-GENERAL HORROCK'S final drive between the Weser and the Elbe took the form of an advance due north on a three-divisional front, Guards Armoured Division on the right, 51 (H.) Division in the centre and 43 Division on the left.   In the middle of the peninsula stands the town of Bremervörde, which is linked to the north-east end of Bremen by the Hamme Canal.   Immediately to the east of this canal stretches a broad belt of peat bogs and low-lying, reclaimed land, into which considerable numbers of the enemy were known to have withdrawn.   To 43 Division therefore fell the dual responsibility of clearing this area and, at the same time, advancing on the crossing over the Hamme at Kuhstedt, the most direct route to Bremerhaven at the mouth of the Weser.

Throughout the 28th the Divisional engineers had worked on the reconstruction of the bridges over the Wumme and Ottersbrug, which had been captured intact and blown up only four days before to protect the rear of the Division during the assault on Bremen. They were ready by dawn on the 29th, when the Division, headed by A and C Squadrons of the Reconnaissance Regiment, immediately followed by 130 Brigade, once more took the road.   By 6.15 a.m. A Squadron had cleared Quelkhorn, taken some prisoners, and, removing a road-block, pushed on two miles to Bucholz.   Here the vanguard of 130 Brigade, that is 5 Dorset with a squadron of Sherwood Rangers under command, had to intervene.   It was a vile, cold day and the rain came down in a steady downpour on the long Divisional column.   As the day wore on the drenched crews of the tanks looked only slightly more miserable than the infantry under the doubtful canvas hoods of their T.C.Vs.   Tank commanders brightened the scene a little, sheltering under gaily coloured umbrellas, which swayed dripping above their turrets.   Sodden mascots flapped limply against the bonnets of the trucks.

Bucholz was soon dealt with and the head of the column pressed forward.   A mile or so short of Tarmstedt, five miles further on, B Company of 5 Dorset were greeted by heavy shell and Nebelwerfer fire.   They had, in fact, caught up with the rear-guard of 15 Panzer Grenadier Division, still fighting to the bitter end.   D Company went forward on foot to some farm buildings, then C Company in kangaroos dashed forward, dismounted at the outskirts of Tarmstedt and started to clear the south-west corner. Determined fighting broke out amongst the rubble, in which Captain P. I. Thorpe was killed. This was a sad blow, as he had fought right through the campaign. D Company moved up and began to search the eastern . part of the village. A Company followed in kangaroos. A sea mine buried in the road, the first of many to be encountered during the succeeding days, blew up a kangaroo. Fighting went on all night and the wasps had to be brought up to drive the enemy into the open. It was not until the early hours, when A Company beat off a determined counter-attack, that the village could be reported clear.

Meanwhile A Squadron of the Reconnaissance Regiment had made some progress in the face of infantry and Nebelwerfer fire in the marshy country west of Quelkhorn. Here in the late afternoon, Major-General Thomas ordered 214 Brigade to intervene and clear the country up to the line of the Bremen–Tarmstedt road. The brigade therefore branched off to the west on a two-battalion front, 5 D.C.L.I. directed on to the crossing of the Worpe stream at Grasburg and 7 Somerset Light Infantry on to Truppermoor. Resistance took the form of isolated groups of infantry with Spandaus and intense bursts of Nebelwerfer fire. The brigade were, in fact, chasing a Nebelwerfer school engaged in firing their remaining stock of ammunition, and the assistance of 179 Field Regiment in dealing with them

30th April proved invaluable. By dawn 7 Somerset Light Infantry, who had advanced 7,000 yards during the night, found themselves halted by two large craters. Tanks could not leave the roads because of the ten-foot-deep ditches. Those which attempted to do so sank deep into the surrounding bog. 5 D.C.L.I. were more fortunate and soon after first light had secured a crossing at Grasburg without great difficulty. The bridge, however, had been blown. 204 Field Company constructed a bridge over which 1 Worcestershire crossed

1st May at first light on 1st May and started to clear the country to the north, taking a considerable number of prisoners, who had little stomach for further fighting. 7 Somerset Light Infantry crossed by the same bridge and with little difficulty reached the Artists' Colony on a wooded hill at Worpswede. The Brigade had in fact come to the end of a cul-de-sac, which, all resistance having been eliminated, they were not sorry to hand over to 52 (L.) Division on the following day. The Brigade withdrew into reserve around the newly liberated merchant-navy prisoners-of-war camp at Westertimke. The scene here was vividly reminiscent of the London Docks. Thousands of the Empire's seamen, English, Scottish, Welsh, Lascars, West Indians and Chinese roamed the countryside in high spirits and unchecked. The Germans had never even shaken their morale. An elaborate system of barter with the local farmers had flourished. There were over twenty concealed wireless sets. Captain Nottman, the senior British officer, had been throughout the real fountain of authority in the camp. The Germans' attempts to seduce the Lascars from their allegiance had been an ignominious failure. The whole spirit of the Royal Merchant Navy breathed in a very dark West Indian fireman, who, wearing a bowler hat and smoking a cigar, cycled around in a somewhat intoxicated condition. On meeting an officer he raised his bowler hat and promptly fell off the bicycle. Not in the least disconcerted, he solemnly replaced his bowler, and with the remark "We British always win" continued on his carefree and erratic way.

Meanwhile on the Division's right, Guards Armoured Division had reached Bremervörde and despatched a brigade group north-east to Stade on the Elbe. 51 (H.) Division followed. 130 Brigade resumed the advance at first light, with 4 Dorset leading. In spite of continual obstruction by mines and Nebelwerfer fire Hepstedt was taken and 7 Royal Hampshire passed through to capture Breddorf.

Heavily cratered roads and mines slowed down the progress to 1st Rhade, which when reached by 5 Dorset was found to be empty. May North of this place the road forward was merely a causeway through a peat bog and here and there were over a dozen craters in a space of about a mile. Some of these were as much as 90 feet wide and impossible to sidestep. All of these had to be bridged under heavy fire from enemy S.P. guns by the sappers, covered by 5 Dorset. Meanwhile, a patrol under Lieutenant M. M. Montfort worked its way forward towards the high ground at Glinstedt. This they found to be held in strength by the enemy. The bridging of the craters was not complete until the afternoon of the 3rd May. By 3rd dusk 4 Dorset had carried Glinstedt in the face of opposition and May Brigadier Coad had despatched 7 Royal Hampshire to the village of Augustendorf to the north.

7 Royal Hampshire patrols now crossed the canal, and returned 4th with the Burgomaster of Gnarrenburg. This official stated that the May German troops were leaving and expressed his desire to surrender. The battalion promptly seized the village. The bridge, however, had been destroyed. Brigadier Coad quickly extended this bridgehead, the 5 Dorset by means of a precarious footbridge thrusting forward unopposed to Kuhstedt, which they reached during the afternoon. By 6 p.m. 553 Field Company had completed a Class 40 bridge. The stage was set for the final advance on Bremerhaven.

No inkling of the negotiations for surrender, which had started on the 3rd, had reached the troops in the Division and the 8 Armoured Brigade. It is true they had heard from the B.B.C. of the fall of Hamburg and the capitulation of two German armies in Italy. Hamburg and Italy, however, were a long way off. The remnants of the enemy on their immediate front had still to be finally brought to their knees. The end could not be far off; however, it seemed still some way ahead. They had been ordered to capture Bremer-haven, if necessary by storm. Only therefore when they reached it and looked out over the North Sea could the war end.

Admittedly, since the morning of the 3rd the Divisional staff had sensed a strange relaxation in the usually intense pressure from Head-quarters 30 Corps. Not a hint of this, however, had reached the brigades and battalions. Indeed, they had been fighting for so long that the urgent atmosphere of continuous battle had become part of their being.

Major-General Thomas had been up with 130 Brigade in their bridgehead over the Hamme Canal during the afternoon. Well satisfied with their progress, he set out on his way back in the evening with the intention, as was his wont, of calling at the headquarters of the other two brigades and briefing their commanders for the final advance on Bremerhaven on the morrow. Of the events taking place at that very moment, in the large marquee at Headquarters 21 Army Group on Lüneburg Heide, he knew nothing.

About 8 p.m. he drew up in his ark at the long, low barrack hut on edge of the merchant-navy prisoner-of-war camp at Westertimke, where 214 Brigade had set up their headquarters. He climbed up the steps of the brigadier's caravan, seated himself in the chair at the desk, propped up his large map board in front of him and pushing back his cap, with the motoring goggles covering the faded red band, on to the back of his head, started without unnecessary preliminaries to explain to Brigadier Essame, with all his habitual incisiveness and clarity, his plan for the capture of Bremerhaven on the morrow.

The progress of Guards Armoured and 51 Division was first reviewed. Having described 130 Brigade's outstandingly rapid development of the bridgehead over the Hamme during the day, he declared his intention of passing 129 and 214 Brigade through on the morrow to capture Bremerhaven. As usual, the Reconnaissance Regiment were to start crossing the bridge at first light. They were first to patrol north and establish contact with the 51 Division; second, to patrol south and establish an observation screen—here followed a string of map references which the Brigadier proceeded to mark on his map; third, to reconnoitre out on the axis Kuhstedt–Beverstedt–Bremerhaven.

At this point there was a knock on the door, which burst open, shaking the whole caravan, to disclose the tall figure of Major W. J. Chalmers, the Brigade Major. Both commanders looked up with cold astonishment. Only an event of world-shaking moment could justify an interruption when the general was giving out his orders. It was 8.40 p.m.

"Sir," said the Brigade Major, standing with some difficulty at attention in the low doorway of the caravan. "The B.B.C. have just

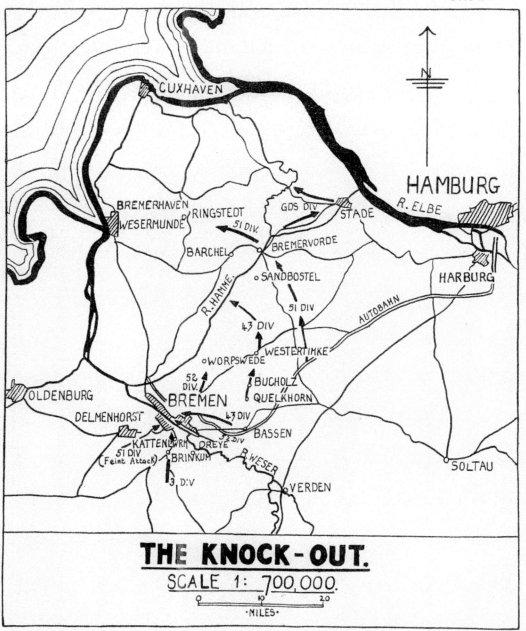

THE KNOCK-OUT.

SCALE 1: 700,000.

announced the unconditional surrender of the German Forces opposing Field-Marshal Montgomery in N.W. Europe."

"I take my orders from the Corps Commander, not the B.B.C.," answered Major-General Thomas, not without asperity. The Brigade Major promptly withdrew and closed the door behind him. The briefing continued.

129 Brigade group were to advance on the axis Kuhstedt–Beverstedt–Heerstedt–Bremerhaven. In the event of opposition from the south-west, a battalion group was to be moved to the south-west. 214 Brigade were to follow in rear of 129 Brigade and to be prepared to deploy on an axis to the north, so that the Division could converge on Bremerhaven on a two-brigade front. With a magnifying-glass the approaches to the port on the eastern flank across the marshes and watercourses of the Gieste stream were examined. The operations ahead apparently offered many interesting possibilities. With the clarity and enthusiasm of long habit, the general dilated at length on the manner in which he expected the brigadier to develop the battle on the morrow—a battle, incidentally, in which the brigadier could no longer believe. Outside, apart from the low hum of the brigade's signal section charging its batteries, all was quiet. Still the briefing went on.

At last, just as the brigadier was marking the traffic posts for the morrow on his own talc, there came a further knock on the door. It was the Brigade Major once more—this time armed with documentary evidence in the shape of a signal message in his hand.

"A personal message to you, sir, from the Corps Commander, timed 2115 hrs."

"Read it."

"Germans surrendered unconditionally at 1820 hrs. Hostilities on all Second Army Front will cease at 0800 hours tomorrow 5th May 45 No repeat No advance beyond present front line without further orders from me."

Without comment the general pulled the canvas cover over his talc, rose and climbed down from the caravan. With the brigadier by his side he walked over in silence to his ark, waiting twenty yards away. Just as he was about to climb in, he turned to the brigadier and said, "The troops have done us damn well." He then entered the steel door of the ark, slammed it to, and standing upright, acknowledged the brigadier's salute. The ark shot off at speed down the road. It was nearly dark.

From the direction of Ostertimke a few Verey lights went up. To the south, tracer fired by 110 L.A.A. Regiment momentarily lit up the overcast sky. 130 Brigade in the bridgehead beyond the Hamme Canal fired a few mortar flares. Now that the end had come there was no wild rejoicing.

For nearly six years all in the Division and the 8 Armoured Brigade had dedicated their lives to one end, the destruction of the German armies. Now this had been accomplished and they could, each and all, think of themselves as individuals again. The mind flashed back to the horror and filth of the Reichswald, the long and dangerous road to Nijmegen and the Island, the fighting in the summer sunshine on the banks of the Seine, and finally to the grim slopes of Hill 112 near Caen. There could be no mad jubilation now that their duty was at last accomplished.

The Division and its commander had done what they had set out to do. In nearly twelve months of continuous battle, from Normandy to North Germany, they had displayed time and time again a ruthless and brilliant efficiency which had stricken with terror and overwhelmed the finest troops of the German Army. From start to finish they had remained true to the articles of military faith in which they so profoundly believed.

Wessex, the very heart of England and the home of soldiers for over a thousand years, once more had reason to be proud of her sons.

POSTSCRIPT

A few days later the following letter arrived from Lieut.-General Horrocks :

"Now that hostilities have finally finished I feel I must write and thank you, and your Division, for the splendid part which you have played in the final defeat of the German Army.

"When I look back on the past ten months and think of the many difficult battles that have been fought by 30 Corps, I always find that the Wyvern has played a prominent part in them all. The capture of Mont Pincon, the crossing of the Seine, the fighting around Nijmegen, the battles at Geilenkirchen, Operation 'Veritable' and the final advance into Germany ; it is a formidable list. I doubt whether any other division has had so much hard fighting during the campaign and has been so uniformly successful.

"Of all your triumphs the greatest, I am certain, was the famous advance from Cleve to the escarpment north of Goch. This was a bitterly contested action and it was the turning-point in Operation 'Veritable'."

This, from the commander who had led his Corps personally always in the forefront of the battle, from Alamein to the heart of Germany, still remains so far as the Division is concerned the final verdict on their part in the campaign.

The 12,482 casualties of the Division, in comparison with those of others and particularly of the enemy who crossed its path, must, in spite of the severity of its many battles, be considered as comparatively light. Time and time again big risks were taken that, by virtue of their inspired audacity and nice calculation, brought their reward at comparatively low cost. That this was primarily due to the skill with which it was trained and led by its commanders, from lance-corporal to major-general, has been the theme of this book. Above all, the vibrant will and military intellect of one man dominated its operations from start to finish.

Today, another fine generation fills the ranks of the Division. They too will remember how their forebears fought their way gloriously across a continent, and if called upon themselves go forward with the light of battle in their eyes and the will ruthlessly to destroy the Queen's enemies. Once more the hordes of the barbarian without threaten the civilization of the West. Of the future, this alone is certain. As in the days of the later Roman Empire, so will it be tomorrow : the last word is invariably with the Legions.

APPENDIX A

43RD (WESSEX) DIVISION ORDER OF BATTLE
6th June 1944 to 5th May 1945

H.Q.   43 (Wessex) Infantry
                                  Division
H.Q.   129 Infantry Brigade
       4 Somerset Light Infantry
       4 Wiltshire
       5 Wiltshire
H.Q.   130 Infantry Brigade
       7 Royal Hampshire
       4 Dorsets
       5 Dorsets
H.Q.   214 Infantry Brigade
       7 Somerset Light Infantry
       1 Worcestershire
       5 Duke of Cornwall's Light
          Infantry

RECONNAISSANCE
      43   Reconnaissance   Regiment
        (The   Gloucestershire
        Regiment).

MACHINE GUN BATTALION
    8 Middlesex

R.A.
    94 Field Regiment
    112 Field Regiment
    179 Field Regiment
    59 Anti-Tank Regiment
    110 L.A.A. Regiment

R.E.
    204 Field Company
    260 Field Company
    553 Field Company
    207 Field Park Company

SIGNALS
    43 Wessex Divisional Signals

R.A.S.C.
    504 Company
    505 Company
    54 Company
    506 Company

R.A.M.C.
    129 Field Ambulance
    130 Field Ambulance
    213 Field Ambulance
    14 Field Dressing Station
    15 Field Dressing Station
    38 Field Hygiene Section

R.A.O.C.
    43 Ordnance Field Park
    306 Mobile Laundry and Bath
        Unit

R.E.M.E.
    129 Infantry Brigade Workshop
    130 Infantry Brigade Workshop
    214 Infantry Brigade Workshop

PROVOST
    43 Wessex Division Provost
    Company R.C.M.P.

FIELD SECURITY
    57 Field Security Section

POSTAL UNIT

APPENDIX B

LIST OF COMMANDERS, SENIOR STAFF OFFICERS AND HEADS OF SERVICES

6th June 1944 to 5th May 1945

(Rank held in 1951 shown in brackets)

COMMANDER, 43 WESSEX DIVISION
Major-General G. Ivor Thomas
(General Sir G. Ivor Thomas, Quartermaster-General to the Forces)

G.S.Os., 43 WESSEX DIVISION
Lieut.-Colonel D. Meynell (Colonel)
Lieut.-Colonel J. A. Grant-Peterkin
Lieut.-Colonel R. W. Urquhart (Brigadier)

A.A. AND Q.M.Gs., 43 WESSEX DIVISION
Lieut.-Colonel J. B. McCance (Brigadier, deceased)
Lieut.-Colonel D. A. B. Clarke

COMMANDERS

R.A.C.
43 Reconnaissance Regt. (The Gloucestershire Regiment)
Lieut.-Colonel F. Lane Fox
Lieut.-Colonel C. H. Kinnersley

ROYAL ARTILLERY
C.R.A.
Brigadier G. W. E. Heath (Major-General)
Brigadier E. T. A. C. Boylan
Brigadier K. F. Mackay Lewis (Major-General)
B.M.
Major G. S. Heathcote
Major P. G. E. Davies
Major H. G. Loosely

94 *Field Regiment*
Lieut.-Colonel T. I. Bishell (killed)
Lieut.-Colonel M. P. Concannon

112 *Field Regiment*
Lieut.-Colonel G. E. G. Gadsden

179 *Field Regiment*
Lieut.-Colonel G. L. Pethick (wounded)
Lieut.-Colonel W. D. Blacker (killed)
Lieut.-Colonel Sir John E. Backhouse (killed)
Lieut.-Colonel F. B. Wyldbore-Smith

59 *A.T. Regiment*
   Lieut.-Colonel H. S. Barker (killed)
   Lieut.-Colonel A. F. Johnson
110 *L.A.A. Regiment*
   Lieut.-Colonel O. W. R. Dent (killed)
   Lieut.-Colonel F. S. Cowan

ROYAL ENGINEERS
  Lieut.-Colonel H. E. Pike (Brigadier)
  Lieut.-Colonel T. H. Evill
  Lieut.-Colonel M. C. A. Henniker (Brigadier)

ROYAL SIGNALS
  Lieut.-Colonel M. Trethowan
    No. 1 Coy.   Major R. H. Harrison
    No. 2 Coy.   Major J. H. Collins
    No. 3 Coy.   Major Vincent (Royal Australian Army)
    H.Q. Coy.   Captain R. Walker

H.Q. 129 INF. BDE
  COMMANDERS
   Brigadier G. H. L. Mole (killed)
   Brigadier J. O. E. Vandeleur
  B.M.
   Major R. G. Levett
   Major B. G. D. Garside
  D.A.A. AND Q.M.G.   Major O. S. Masefield
    4 *Somerset Light Infantry*
     Lieut.-Colonel W. S. C. Curtis
     Lieut.-Colonel C. G. Lipscomb (Brigadier)
    4 *Wiltshire*
     Lieut.-Colonel E. L. Luce
     Lieut.-Colonel J. E. L. Corbyn
    5 *Wiltshire*
     Lieut.-Colonel N. C. E. Kenrick (Colonel)
     Lieut.-Colonel J. H. C. Pearson (killed)
     Lieut.-Colonel W. G. Roberts
     Lieut.-Colonel J. L. Brind

H.Q. 130 INF. BDE
  COMMANDERS
   Brigadier N. D. Leslie
   Brigadier B. B. Walton
   Brigadier B. A. Coad (Major-General)
  B.M.
   Major G. G. Reinhold
   Major A. N. Buchanan
  D.A.A. AND Q.M.G.   Major D. G. Pascall
    7 *Royal Hampshire*
     Lieut.-Colonel D. W. G. Ray (killed)
     Lieut.-Colonel J. R. C. Mallock (killed)
     Lieut.-Colonel D. E. B. Talbot (Colonel)

4 *Dorsets*
Lieut.-Colonel H. E. Cowie
Lieut.-Colonel G. Tilley
Lieut.-Colonel W. G. Roberts
5 *Dorsets*
Lieut.-Colonel B. A. Coad (Major-General)
Lieut.-Colonel W. A. Venour
Lieut.-Colonel A. E. C. Bredin

H.Q. 214 INF. BDE
COMMANDER: Brigadier H. Essame (Major-General)
B.M.
Major J. E. L. Corbyn (Lieut.-Colonel)
Major W. J. Chalmers

D.A.A. AND Q.M.G.   Major J. L. Denison
7 *Somerset Light Infantry*
Lieut.-Colonel R. G. P. Besley (wounded)
Lieut.-Colonel G. C. P. Lance (killed)
Lieut.-Colonel E. J. Bruford (killed)
Lieut.-Colonel J. W. Nichol
Lieut.-Colonel H. A. Borradaile
Major T. B. Elliott (wounded)
Lieut.-Colonel I. L. Reeves (wounded)
Lieut.-Colonel C. Brooke Smith
1 *Worcestershire*
Lieut.-Colonel A. R. Harrison
Lieut.-Colonel R. E. Osborne-Smith (wounded)
Lieut.-Colonel A. W. N. L. Vickers
Lieut.-Colonel M. R. J. Hope-Thomson
5 *Duke of Cornwall's Light Infantry*
Lieut.-Colonel J. W. Atherton (killed)
Lieut.-Colonel R. W. James (killed)
Lieut.-Colonel G. Taylor (Brigadier)

MACHINE GUN BATTALION
8 *Middlesex*   Lieut.-Colonel M. Crawford (Colonel)

8 ARMOURED BRIGADE
COMMANDER: Brigadier G. E. Prior-Palmer (Major-General)
B.M.   Major R. Dayer Smith

D.A.A. AND Q.M.G.   Major W. Spanton
4/7 *Royal Dragoon Guards*
Lieut.-Colonel R. G. G. Byron
Lieut.-Colonel G. K. Barker
13/18 *Royal Hussars*
Lieut.-Colonel R. T. G. Harrap (killed)
Lieut.-Colonel V. A. B. Dunkerley
Lieut.-Colonel The Earl of Feversham
The Nottingham Yeomanry (Sherwood Rangers)
Lieut.-Colonel J. Anderson
Lieut.-Colonel S. Christopherson

12/60 *K.R.R.C.*
Lieut.-Colonel R. G. R. Oxley
Lieut.-Colonel the Hon. M. Edwards

147 *Field Regiment (Essex Yeomanry)*
Lieut.-Colonel R. A. Phayre (Brigadier)
Lieut.-Colonel H. R. L. Hodges (Colonel)

SERVICES

CHAPLAIN *Senior Chaplain* The Rev. I. D. Neill

R.A.S.C.
Lieut.-Colonel F. J. Leland (killed)
Lieut.-Colonel E. H. Reeder (Colonel)

MEDICAL
Colonel K. A. M. Tomory (Major-General)
Colonel L. T. Furnivall

A.D.M.S.
129 *Field Ambulance*
Lieut.-Colonel A. D. Bourne
Lieut.-Colonel W. Stewart

130 *Field Ambulance*
Lieut.-Colonel F. L. Ker
Lieut.-Colonel R. A. Smart

213 *Field Ambulance*
Lieut.-Colonel E. A. L. Murphy
Lieut.-Colonel J. Clay

14 *F.D.S.* Major Clark

15 *F.D.S.*
Major J. A. Manifold
Major N. L. Crawford

38 *Field Hygiene Section* Major Hobson

R.A.O.C.
C.R.A.O.C. Lieut.-Colonel V. A. Lines
43 O.F.P. Major R. L. Streather
306 MOBILE LAUNDRY AND BATH UNIT Captain E. H. Temme

R.E.M.E.
C.R.E.M.E. Lieut.-Colonel J. M. Neilson
129 INF. BDE WORKSHOP Major N. W. Knowles
130 INF. BDE WORKSHOP Major Bailey
214 INF. BDE WORKSHOP Major S. Yeol

A.P.M.
Major M. Ingram
Provost Company—Captain Winwood
57 F.S. Section—Captain R. S. Hallmark

EDUCATION Captain H. H. Evans. R.A.E.C. (Lieut.-Colonel)

POSTAL Lieutenant R. G. Wildgoose

54 FIELD CASH OFFICER Captain S. F. E. Leibe (Major)

19

APPENDIX C

NORMAL GROUPING FOR MOBILE OPERATIONS

129 INF. BDE GP
Bde H.Q.
Three Bns
AMG Coy One Hy Mortar Pl.
94 Fd Regt
235 A.-Tk Bty
260 Fd Coy
129 Fd Amb.
One SP Tp 360 L.A.A. Bty

130 INF. BDE GP
Bde H.Q.
Three bns
B Coy One Hy Mortar Pl.
112 Fd Regt
233 A.-Tk Bty
553 Fd Coy
130 Fd Amb.
One SP Tp 362 L.A.A. Bty

214 INF. BDE GP
Bde H.Q.
Three Bns
AMG Coy One Hy Mortar Pl.
179 Fd Regt
333 A.-Tk Bty
204 Fd Coy
213 Fd Amb.
One SP Tp 361 L.A.A. Bty

DIV. TPS
Div. H.Q. incl.
  H.Q. R.A.
  H.Q. R.E.
  H.Q. R.A.S.C.
  H.Q. R.E.M.E.
  57 FS Sec.
  Postal Unit (less personnel att.
    R.A.S.C. Coy)
H.Q. 8 Mx.
43 Recce Regt
H.Q. 59 A.-Tk Regt
  236 A.-Tk Bty

H.Q. 110 L.A.A. Regt
  360 L.A.A. Bty (less one
    SP Tp)
  361 L.A.A. Bty (less one
    SP Tp)
  362 L.A.A. Bty (less one
    SP Tp)
207 Fd Pk Coy
Div. Sigs (less 2, 3 and 4 coys)
  504 Coy R.A.S.C. (Inf. Bde)
  505 Coy R.A.S.C. (Inf. Bde)
  54 Coy R.A.S.C. (Inf. Bde)
  506 Coy R.A.S.C. (Inf. Div.
  14 FDS   [Tps)
  15 FDS
38 Fd Hyg. Sec.
129 Inf. Bde Wksp R.E.M.E.
130 Inf. Bde Wksp R.E.M.E.
214 Inf. Bde Wksp R.E.M.E.
Pro. Coy
43 Inf. Div. Ord Fd Pk

GROUPING OF ADM. UNITS AND
  B ECHS.
The following will normally be
located, under Div. control, in the
Div. Adm. Area:
  Comd. Adm. Gp
  129 Inf. Bde Gp B Ech.
  130 Inf. Bde Gp B Ech.
  214 Inf. Bde Gp B Ech.
  Div. Tps B Ech.
  207 Fd Pk Coy
  504 Coy R.A.S.C. (Inf. Bde) (129)
  505 Coy R.A.S.C. (Inf. Bde) (130)
  54 Coy R.A.S.C. (Inf. Bde) (214)
  506 Coy R.A.S.C. (Inf. Div. Tps)
  38 Fd Hyg. Sec.
  129 Inf. Bde Wksp R.E.M.E.
  130 Inf. Bde Wksp R.E.M.E.
  214 Inf. Bde Wksp R.E.M.E.
  All LADs except LADs of Inf.
    Bdes and Div. Sigs
  43 Inf. Div. Ord. Fd Pk

APPENDIX D

CASUALTIES
24th June 1944 to 5th May 1945

	Officers	Other Ranks
Killed	131	1,456
Wounded	481	7,811
Missing	86	2,517
Missing rejoined	9	800

Total all ranks—12,482

APPENDIX E

THE DIVISION'S MEMORIALS

THE idea of a Memorial fund was first conceived after the end of hostilities in North-west Europe, whilst most units in the Division were still intact and it was still possible to canvas the views of all the officers and men in the Division as to the form any Memorial should take.

The unanimity was quite astonishing. Although every type of memorial was considered, such as building houses, and endowing wards in hospitals, there was no doubt that the vast majority of the Division were in favour of preserving as much of the beauty of Wessex and the West Country as funds would allow, and the final scheme endorsed by all was as follows:

1. To make a permanent Memorial on Hill 112 near CAEN, where the Division first went into action and where more casualties were suffered than in any other battle.

2. To acquire and present to the National Trust tracts of country in Wessex and the West Country which it was thought should be preserved for the nation and to erect upon this land, when acquired, replicas of the proposed Memorial on Hill 112.

3. To prepare, as far as possible, a complete Roll of all those officers and men who were killed whilst serving with the Division in the North-west European Campaign.

The first of these objects was, with the aid of the Divisional engineers, rapidly accomplished, but red tape intervened and it was some time before the Memorial was properly recognized. Eventually the Imperial War Graves Commission accepted full responsibility for it and its future maintenance after a capital sum had been provided out of the Trust for its endowment.

Much more difficulty was experienced in attaining the second object, but a start was made when, owing to the generosity of the Duchy of Cornwall through their Agent, Lieut.-Colonel W. G. Roberts, D.S.O., a nine-hundred-and-ninety-nine year lease of Castle Hill at Mere was obtained and vested in the Parish Council of Mere, and a Memorial erected thereon which was unveiled by General Sir Ivor Thomas, K.C.B., K.B.E., D.S.O., M.C., on the 21st May, 1949.

The Trustees of the Memorial fund were continually seeking other suitable sites and eventually acquired Wynyard's Gap near Crewkerne in Somerset and, at the moment, a similar Memorial is being erected there, which will, it is hoped, be unveiled during the course of 1952.

Then, fortunately, Sir Richard Onslow, an old member of the Division (he served in the Duke of Cornwall's Light Infantry), came forward with the suggestion that he should present Rough Tor to the National Trust as a part of the Memorial and particularly in memory of those of all ranks of the Duke of Cornwall's Light Infantry who died whilst serving in the Division.

There were various complications in connection with this, but they have now all been surmounted and Rough Tor has been vested in the National Trust. The Memorial to be erected here is still under consideration, as there is evidence that at one time there was an old Saxon chapel on Rough Tor and it is possible that any Memorial erected will take into consideration the previous existence of this old chapel.

The Memorial Roll was, after a great deal of difficulty, compiled with the aid of the various officers in charge of records and with the greatest assistance from individual units who formed part of the Division. The Roll was prepared in book form and is a very fine example of the bookbinders art.

At a ceremony held at Salisbury Cathedral on the same day as the unveiling of the Memorial at Mere, General Sir Ivor Thomas, K.C.B., K.B.E., D.S.O., M.C., deposited the Roll in the safe keeping of the cathedral authorities at Salisbury, where it lies in the War Memorial Chapel for all to see.

From time to time when ex-members of the Division met, the subject of a history of the Division has been discussed and the Trustees of the Memorial fund were eventually approached to discover whether any of the funds could be used for financing the publication of such a history. After consideration, the Trustees felt that it was a proper use to make of a portion of the funds and the present history is the result. The Trustees feel that all those members of the Division who subscribed to the Memorial fund will welcome the authorization given by the Trustees.

A sum in excess of £16,000 was raised and even after all present commitments have been met, there is likely to be a considerable balance. Its extent cannot yet be estimated, but in due course the Trustees will, after the fullest enquiry, decide what service or allied charities should be the recipients of any surplus.

It is impossible now to keep in touch with all those who subscribed to the original fund, but the contributor of this appendix will always be happy to supply any information which he has on the subject and eventually a final balance sheet will be prepared and sent to anybody who registers his name and address.

APPENDIX F

LIST OF CANADIAN OFFICERS ATTACHED TO INFANTRY
UNITS OF 43 WESSEX DIVISION

		Joined	*S.O.S.*
4 *Wiltshire Regiment*			
CDN/164	Lieutenant J. T. Irwin	24/4/44	
198	Lieutenant W. I. Smith	24/4/44	15/8/45
360	Lieutenant J. H. Rutherford	Serving 31/5/44	
5 *Wiltshire Regiment*			
333	Lieutenant J. R. Caincross ⎫		
27	Lieutenant R. Ludford ⎬ Joined during		
47	Lieutenant A. J. Willick ⎭ May 1944		
330	Lieutenant E. O. Baker		1/8/45
371	Lieutenant D. C. Cuddy	10/7/44	
493	Captain G. Robichaud	2/7/44	
305	Lieutenant R. Massey	2/7/44	10/4/45
652	Lieutenant H. C. Roper	7/9/44	
275	Captain W. B. Motham	12/2/45	
224	Lieutenant O'Halloran	18/3/45	
240	Lieutenant J. J. Dempster	18/3/45	
5 *Duke of Cornwall's Light Infantry*			
10	Lieutenant Arthur	10/4/44	
298	Captain J. H. J. Gauthier ⎫	2/12/44	
290	Lieutenant B. D. J. Comolli ⎬ Joined during		
300	Lieutenant E. Hardy ⎭ June 1944		
279	Lieutenant M. C. P. Rush		
4 *Somerset Light Infantry*			
195	Lieutenant O. W. Shuttleworth ⎫		
50	Lieutenant G. V. Wright ⎬ Joined during 17/7/45		
119	Captain J. S. Townshend ⎭ May 1944		
170	Lieutenant E. F. Larret		
211	Lieutenant R. J. G. Deziel	Aug. 1944	
229	Captain D. C. Thompson	29/12/44	
7 *Somerset Light Infantry*			
CDN/170	Lieutenant E. F. Larret	25/4/44	15/11/45
506	Lieutenant H. M. Jones	28/5/44	K.I.A. 8/7/44
247	Lieutenant P. Mercier	28/5/44	
328	Lieutenant W. Tharp	9/6/44	
562	Captain M. O. Lamb	25/11/44	11/12/44
275	Captain W. B. Mottram	22/10/44	12/2/45
114	Lieutenant W. A. Colbert	9/12/44	
663	Captain D. G. Wilson	21/3/45	
119	Captain J. Townshend	–/6/44	13/7/44

	Joined	*S.O.S.*

1 *Worcestershire Regiment*

	Joined	*S.O.S.*
163 Lieutenant W. G. Hunt	24/4/44	6/11/44
109 Lieutenant J. M. Bennett	12/4/44	
422 Lieutenant A. Brygider	10/6/44	
338 Lieutenant P. H. Fiset	} Joined during	} Appear only in
548 Lieutenant J. F. O. Davies	} Aug.	} Aug./44 return

7 *Royal Hampshire Regiment*

123 Lieutenant H. J. Anaka	24/4/44	
212 Lieutenant M. I. Dougherty	24/4/44	
414 Lieutenant G. F. Heald	24/4/44	
54 Captain F. A. N. Chesham	13/4/44	
475 Lieutenant H. A. Taylor	25/10/44	

4 *Dorset Regiment*

60 Lieutenant E. G. Andrews	12/4/44	K.I.A. 8/8/44
65 Lieutenant W. A. Bennett	12/4/44	
126 Captain R. A. With	25/4/44	
286 Lieutenant E. C. Ambery	} Joined during	
396 Lieutenant R. C. Fee	} May 1944	
412 Lieutenant R. M. Goddard		
302 Captain T. B. King	Aug 1944	
631 Lieutenant C. B. Jeffries	1/10/44	

5 *Dorset Regiment*

CDN/ 70 Lieutenant R. B. Cambridge		
155 Lieutenant W. A. Hill	} Joined during	
157 Lieutenant W. J. Hiscocks	} May 1944	
295 Lieutenant M. Flynn		
590 Captain D. K. Brown	9/8/44	
672 Lieutenant H. Matthews	6/9/44	14/2/45
629 Lieutenant W. J. Hudson	1/12/44	

INDEX

Lightning Source UK Ltd.
Milton Keynes UK
UKHW051233281021
392990UK00005B/352